WORLD BANK ANNUAL CONFERENCE ON DEVELOPMENT ECONOMICS 1990

- **THE TRANSITION FROM ADJUSTMENT TO GROWTH**
  Rudiger W. Dornbusch
  Max Corden
- **SUSTAINABLE DEVELOPMENT AND THE ENVIRONMENT**
  Karl-Goran Maler & Partha Dasgupta
  Peter Nijkamp
- **POPULATION CHANGE AND ECONOMIC DEVELOPMENT**
  John C. Caldwell
  Ronald D. Lee
  Kenneth M. Chomitz & Nancy Birdsall
- **PUBLIC PROJECT APPRAISAL**
  I.M.D. Little & James A. Mirrlees
  Jock R. Anderson & John C. Quiggin
  Ravi Kanbur
- **ROUND TABLE DISCUSSION**

April 26 and 27, 1990
Washington, D.C.

Proceedings of the World Bank Annual Conference on Development Economics 1989

Supplement to The World Bank Economic Review
and The World Bank Research Observer

Introduction *Stanley Fischer and Dennis de Tray*	1
Keynote Address: Development Policy Research: The Task Ahead *Manmohan Singh*	11
Developing Countries and the Uruguay Round of Trade Negotiations *Marcelo de Paiva Abreu* 　Comment, *Andrzej Olechowski*　47 　Comment, *Gary P. Sampson*　49 　Floor Discussion　55	21
Saving in Developing Countries: Theory and Review *Angus Deaton* 　Comment, *Fumio Hayashi*　97 　Comment, *Steven B. Webb*　101 　Floor Discussion　105	61
Social Sector Pricing Policy Revisited: A Survey of Some Recent Controversies *Emmanuel Jimenez* 　Comment, *Benno J. Ndulu*　139 　Comment, *Nicholas Stern*　143 　Floor Discussion　149	109

The Role of Institutions in Development 153
Brian Van Arkadie

Comment, *John Nellis* 177

Comment, *Pranab Bardhan* 181

Floor Discussion 187

The Noncompetitive Theory of International Trade and Trade Policy 193
Elhanan Helpman

Comment, *T. N. Srinivasan* 217

Comment, *Nancy Barry* 223

Floor Discussion 227

The Policy Response of Agriculture 231
Hans Binswanger

Comment, *Avishay Braverman* 259

Comment, *Alberto Valdés* 263

Floor Discussion 269

Roundtable Discussion 273

Introduction

Stanley Fischer and Dennis de Tray

The papers in this volume were presented at the first annual World Bank Conference on Development Economics, held April 27–28, 1989, in Washington, D.C. The conference series brings researchers from the Bank's member countries together with Bank staff to stimulate interaction and exchange of ideas and information. Participants at the 1989 conference came from a range of research, academic, and policymaking institutions in both developing and developed countries. The ultimate object of the series is, by enhancing the knowledge base, to improve both member country and Bank policymaking.

Outside researchers and Bank researchers have much to offer each other. Academics and other outside researchers can and do bring different and new ways of thinking to the Bank. That is especially important for an institution as large, as busy, and as involved in policy in so many countries, as the Bank. The temptation for Bank researchers is to look inward, to talk to each other, and to assume that shared habits of thought are the right ones. Although academics too share certain modes of thought, the differences between the two groups are potentially productive. In addition, the best academics are probably closer to the cutting edge of research; they are also more free to think speculatively and to develop new theories and fresh insights.

One of the purposes of the conference series is to expose Bank economists to recent developments in economics whose policy implications may not yet be clear but which are beginning to affect thinking outside the Bank and which may one day become the conventional wisdom. One example in this volume is the paper on recent developments in strategic trade theory by Elhanan Helpman. The topic is extremely important, the Bank has well-known policy views in this area, and the new theories seem to have the potential for reversing those views. The paper generated a very lively discussion, during which both Helpman and the discussants agreed that the knowledge needed for a country to benefit from the possibilities implied in the new theories is probably too detailed to make such policies empirically useful. But it is far better to reach that conclusion on the basis of an informed discussion of the theory and its empirical requirements than on a priori grounds.

The Bank for its part brings to the outside research community an extremely rich and varied research agenda and an unparalleled wealth of practical knowledge about developing countries. The Bank's research agenda springs mainly from its operational experience and is therefore down to earth. Part of the research agenda comes from an attempt to anticipate future problems, but even here the Bank tends to be practical, asking for the operational implications of each paper and research project. Of course, one can go too far in that regard, for not every useful piece of research has an immediate payoff; the right question is whether a particular piece of research will eventually have real-world implications, rather than whether it has immediate operational relevance. Nonetheless, this challenge to produce research that is operationally relevant imposes an extremely useful discipline on researchers in and out of the Bank.

Development problems are far too difficult for any one institution to believe that it has the final answers to them. The Bank's approach to development is pragmatic and open-minded. In making policy decisions, and in thinking about development strategies, the Bank has to search for better ways of helping our member countries, to entertain new ideas, to question old ones, and to listen, talk, and learn from critics. Being open-minded, however, does not mean being softheaded. After thinking and talking, the Bank and its member countries have to act, one way or the other, in light of the relevant analytical and policy-related arguments. And because decisions have to be made, the Bank cannot agree with everyone on every topic. Nonetheless, the Bank has to keep on reexamining the way it does business and be prepared to change if necessary. This conference series is one way for the Bank to listen to and ask for help from outside researchers in dealing with the difficult development issues that our member countries face. To help in this process, we have described the Bank's current research program in an addendum to this introduction. (Requests for additional information on the World Bank's research program should be directed to the Research Administrator's Office, World Bank, Washington, D.C. 20433, U.S.A.)

This first World Bank Annual Conference on Development Economics did not focus on a single subject or theme. Instead, each author was asked to review and assess the policy implications of one of six distinct subjects. This decision to explore a set of issues rather than a single theme reflects a desire to stress policy issues and to communicate findings to a broad spectrum of development practitioners rather than a group of research specialists in a narrow field. Future conferences are expected to continue this broad coverage.

The conference began with a keynote address by Manmohan Singh, secretary general of the South Commission. Singh identified some of the major areas of challenge for researchers dealing with development: the role of the state, the management of the public sector, and reform of the international trading regime. Though he did not discuss them in detail in his address, he also cited food security and human resource development as deserving priority attention. Singh sees the critical question for the modernization of the state as not so much its size as the overall quality and effectiveness of its impact. He felt that better management of the public sector and its careful delineation would be critical for private sector development as well as for the prospects for reform in the socialist economies: both issues he felt would need location-specific answers. For the trading system, Singh asked whether developed country markets would still be available if developing countries which have pursued inward-looking development strategies were to switch to export-orientation based on labor-intensive manufactured goods. Singh concluded by calling for an international mechanism to impartially evaluate the development performance of developing countries undergoing structural reform.

Marcelo Abreu of the Catholic University of Rio de Janeiro presented the first paper, "Developing Countries and the Uruguay Round of Trade Negotiations." With the Uruguay Round well under way, Abreu asks what negotiating stances developing countries should be taking. On what issues should they stand firm and where should they be willing to make concessions? What stands should the various subcoalitions—agricultural exporters, food importers, garment manufacturers—take? This is a complex and important set of negotiations, one in which the stakes for the developing countries are greater than ever before. Abreu's paper highlights the importance of restoring GATT discipline to the trade in goods, even while GATT is pushing ahead with the extension of GATT-like rules to services and intellectual property rights. He also sees a considerable need to focus on the issue of unilateral liberalization, under conditionality or otherwise, and its effect on developing countries' negotiating positions at the GATT.

Angus Deaton of Princeton University presented the second paper, "Saving in Developing Countries: Theory and Evidence." Deaton's assigned task was to survey the literature on determinants of saving to assess its policy implications and the existing theoretical and empirical gaps. He attacked this issue by developing a new framework for analyzing saving in developing countries. Deaton's approach emphasizes that motives for saving in developing countries are likely to differ from motives in developed countries. Households in developed countries save in large part to accumulate wealth; in contrast household saving in developing countries, especially in rural areas, in large part is a means of guarding against declines of consumption from an already precarious consumption base. As Deaton points out, this precautionary view of saving has very different implications for public policy seeking to influence saving than do conventional accumulation-based models of saving behavior. Deaton also cites the tremendous need for better data, and his ongoing research for the Côte d'Ivoire using this precautionary saving model.

Bank staff member Emanuel Jimenez explored a controversial current policy issue in the third paper, "Social Sector Pricing Policy Revisited: A Survey of Some Recent Controversies." Declining fiscal budgets and increasing demands for health and education services have forced governments and donors to look for alternatives to general revenue financing of publicly provided goods and services. The pricing of public sector goods and services is an area that generates strongly held positions both for and against, especially when social services such as health and education are on the line. Jimenez clarifies the debate by drawing the distinction between ideological differences and disputes over empirical relationships. He points out that, even setting ideological differences aside, considerably more empirical evidence is needed to demonstrate that the poor can be protected from the negative consequences of pricing health and education services if the momentum of social sector price reform is to be maintained. Jimenez believes that selective user charges can yield some improvements in equity as well as in efficiency, besides achieving fiscal gains. His paper, however, argues for systematic evaluations of actual attempts at social sector price reform.

Brian Van Arkadie of the University of Dar es Salaam took on one of the more difficult assignments of the conference: to assess the policy implications of the literature on the role that institutions have played in promoting—or slowing—development. He chose to define the term "institution" broadly to encompass both the "rules of the game"—laws and regulations—and formal government organizations. Van Arkadie does not believe that it would be appropriate to come up with a "check-list of 'good' and 'bad' institutions," and in any case, the literature is long on generalizations and short on empirical evidence. His paper throws light on the factors to be considered in appraising institutional performance, and on how institutions can be changed to enhance their performance. Van Arkadie suggests that it is best to seek answers to specific and relevant questions about the role of institutions, and not attempt to draw up a grand theory about it.

Elhanan Helpman of Tel Aviv University was asked to focus on the policy lessons of the recent and rapidly growing literature on strategic trade theory. Strategic trade theory appears to have radical implications for trade policy. Whereas conventional trade theory and its proponents generally support unrestricted trade regimes, Helpman shows that in many circumstances the new theory argues for selective interventions. In the final accounting, however, both Helpman and the audience agreed that the information requirements of the new theory made it extremely difficult to implement in real-world policy settings. In the absence of much improved information on the way economies work and on their strategic behavior, conventional wisdom—minimal intervention and uniform tariffs—seems likely to continue to be the order of the day.

In the conference's final paper Hans Binswanger, a staff member of the World Bank, looked at the implications for policy of available theoretical and empirical evidence on agricultural supply response. Many recent adjustment programs have had as one of their cornerstones the rebuilding of the country's agricultural sector. Binswanger shows that the effectiveness of such policies depends on much more than "getting prices right." He demonstrates that in the aggregate, short-run agricultural supply responses are inherently inelastic, though the long-run responses to agricultural policy changes can be great. Without technological change or considerable infrastructural investment, price changes alone may have much less effect on overall agricultural output than hoped for. Binswanger concludes that in formulating adjustment programs, attention to agricultural growth cannot be delayed until adjustment is completed, precisely because of the long response lags involved.

The final session of the conference brought together six acknowledged development experts in a panel discussion to review the current state of development policy research in their own areas of expertise. Each drew the audience's attention to the existing gaps in our understanding of development processes, and outlined problems and concerns relating to developing countries that should shape new directions for basic, applied, and policy research in the future.

The organization of an international conference is even more demanding than that of a national conference, and the organization of a new type of conference more demanding yet. We owe special thanks to the World Bank staff who were responsible for so efficiently organizing the conference and overseeing the comings and goings of its participants: Shekhar Shah, the Bank's deputy research administrator, provided overall guidance and management for the conference and this volume; Andrea Hodson organized the conference logistics. We would also like to thank the editorial staff who put together these proceedings, especially Philippa Shepherd and Pat McNees, and the secretarial staff who provided able support, especially Manny Jandu.

ADDENDUM: THE WORLD BANK'S RESEARCH PROGRAM

Because the World Bank engages its members in a comprehensive dialog over the entire range of economic policies, it has to undertake research and maintain expertise on a broad front.

Divisional and Departmental Research

Current research activities are best described by reviewing the divisions and departments that make up the research wing of the World Bank's Policy, Research, and External Affairs complex. The names of these units provide a useful summary of the range of research interests within the Bank. We start with Bank units which deal primarily with macroeconomic and related issues.

- Macroeconomic Adjustment and Growth Division. About 25 percent of the Bank's current lending supports adjustment programs being undertaken by member countries. Although member country and Bank experience in this area is growing, there is much still to be learned. Two problems receiving particular attention now are the issue of the appropriate sequencing of adjustment policies—especially the interactions between external and internal adjustments, and ways of minimizing the negative social consequences of adjustment.

- Public Economics Division. The research and policy development program of the Public Economics Division covers five broad and interrelated areas: taxation, sector pricing, public expenditures, intergovernmental fiscal arrangements, macro-fiscal linkages. It supports and strengthens the Bank's operational and technical assistance capabilities in various areas of fiscal reform, particularly in the context of adjustment programs.

- Trade Policy and International Trade divisions. The importance of trade to development is such that two divisions serve the Bank's needs in this area, one dealing with domestic trade policies on both the import and export sides, and the other dealing with the international trade environment. The Uruguay Round of trade negotiations and continuing trade reforms in member countries ensure lively programs in each area.

• Financial Policy and Systems Division. The question of how to expand and restructure ailing financial systems is receiving increasing emphasis in World Bank lending and policy advice. *World Development Report 1989* dramatized the serious plight of the financial systems in many developing countries, as well as the critical role these systems play in the development process. The Bank's research efforts in this area are growing rapidly and will likely continue to grow.

• Public Sector Management and Private Sector Development Division. Worldwide experience in the last few decades emphasizes the need to increase efficiency in public sector activities. Bank and other research is focusing on ways to increase the efficiency of the public sector while preserving services, especially to the poor. Privatization is one, but certainly not the only, avenue. Although there is general agreement on the objectives in this area, there is considerable debate about the institutional changes needed to get from here to there, and research on these issues is proceeding apace.

Promoting private sector activities in general is also an area of significant emphasis at the Bank. In many countries with active adjustment programs, the private sector, especially small-scale enterprises, is at the forefront of efforts to rebuild economies and to improve economic growth. What can the Bank do to encourage private development? How can countries move from highly controlled, public-sector-dominated economies to more responsive, diversified economies in which the private sector plays a leading role? The following units address these issues.

• Debt and International Finance Division. It will come as no surprise to learn that the Bank is concerned with the policy and economic implications of international debt, both official and commercial. Debt is also an area in which it is relatively straightforward to see the link between academic research and the policy debate, for academic research has been highly instrumental in shaping the debate. Bank-sponsored research has contributed, and will continue to contribute, to this debate on several fronts, including debt measurement issues. We are also concerned to look at the forms of capital flows that may emerge in the wake of the debt crisis, and the policy measures that need to be taken to facilitate such new flows. The Bank has principal responsibility among other international agencies for the compilation and dissemination of data on the external debt of developing countries and for improvements in the quality of the data.

• International Commodity Markets Division. The Bank's commodity markets division is responsible for forecasts of the prices of commodities produced by Bank-funded projects. It thus makes price projections for all major commodities and many others over long forecasting horizons. The projections are used to evaluate proposed projects and are thus immediately operationally relevant. The division maintains an active research program to improve its understanding of the operation of particular commodity markets, and it also examines commodity production and trade policies and commodity risk management and finance for individual countries.

- International Economic Analysis and Prospects Division. Evaluation of Bank and member country projects and policies also requires analysis and projections of the development of the international economy. This division combines the use of global models with topical research to predict short-run developments and long-run trends, and to examine alternative scenarios for the international economy. Besides acting as secretariat to the Bank's Planning Assumptions Committee, which proves assumptions for all key global aggregates, the division also takes a leading role in the preparation of relevant parts of the Bank's *Annual Report* and *World Development Report*.

The research divisions just described focus on country and international issues. Much of the Bank's research work also focuses on sectoral issues. We turn now to describe units that work in the sectoral areas.

- Agriculture and Rural Development Department. The issues here have been at the core of Bank research efforts for several decades. In addition, experience, not all of it favorable, with some aspects of agricultural sector lending and with rural development projects has raised renewed interest in such issues as project evaluation under uncertainty, the role of property rights, credit markets, agricultural trade liberalization, and rural infrastructure in promoting agricultural development.

- Environment Department. Academics have more and more realized that environmental concerns are critical and are likely to become more important as the years pass. These concerns are not new to the Bank, but they pose many important positive and normative research issues, at both the microeconomic and macroeconomic level. The environment and environmental economic issues have been singled out as a priority for Bank research during the next few years.

- Infrastructure and Urban Development Department. Current infrastructure concerns relate to transport, water supply, and sanitation. In transport, research focuses on pricing, regulatory, and financing issues, private sector participation, infrastructure management and maintenance, enterprise reform, and the role of freight logistics management in improving trade performance. Sectoral concerns on water supply and sanitation relate to institutional development and privatization, financing, service provision and costs, and usage and disposal patterns as they affect the environment and the possibilities of recycling.

Urban development is growing in importance as the developing world's populations move to urban areas, putting increasing pressure on the urban infrastructure. Research focuses on urban policies for macroeconomic adjustment and growth, with four priorities: urban infrastructure investment and its effects on productivity and growth; land and housing markets and their impact on private saving and investment; municipal finance and links to financial markets; and housing finance. New research initiatives also relate to the urban environment, waste management, and private sector participation.

• Industry and Energy Department. The Bank's work on industrial issues has changed as emphasis has shifted toward policy-based lending and away from production in the public sector. The challenge for research is to find policies that will enable the industrial sectors of developing economies to grow and cope with international competition, rather than to search for winners and losers to prescribe to individual member countries.

Energy issues have also changed with the times. Today, the main areas being researched are underpricing of energy, energy sector inefficiencies and suboptimal performance, inadequate resources for expansion programs, and weak financial condition of electric utilities. Energy staff are seeking corrective measures involving private sector participation, regulation, and greater autonomy for utilities. Considerable effort is also being directed at minimizing the adverse environmental impacts of providing an adequate energy supply.

• Population and Human Resources Department. Human resources hold the key to economic growth and development. The Bank's research directions in the area of human resources are best summarized by the titles of the divisions that make up the Population and Human Resources Department: Education and Employment; Women in Development; Population, Health, and Nutrition; and Welfare and Human Resources. The Bank allocates substantial resources to these cross-cutting themes, and research and policy work in these areas focus on issues of quality of service provision, cost-effectiveness, user demand, and how to implement and sustain policy change.

The Central Research Program

Bank staff manage all, and carry out most of, the socioeconomic research sponsored by the institution. To supplement its own divisional resources, the Bank maintains a centrally administered Research Support Budget (RSB) that provides resources to Bank units to undertake specific research projects. RSB funds are used mainly to support research collaborations with outside researchers, and this process is one of the main avenues through which non-Bank researchers become involved in Bank research.

There are two basic requirements for projects financed through the RSB. The first is that the project must have ultimately discernible real-world implications for developing countries. The second is that the project be rooted within the Bank, specifically that it be sponsored by a Bank unit, which will administer it and take responsibility for its successful completion. These requirements are designed to ensure that Bank-sponsored research projects are both relevant to the Bank's concerns and well managed.

This insistence on operational relevance distinguishes the Bank from other sources of research and research funding. Ultimately, the Bank tries to ensure that research undertaken with its resources has at least a reasonable chance of improving the development prospects of its member countries through either improved policy formulation or better project design.

The Research Support Budget sets priorities for developing research in areas likely to be important in coming years. The present list of priorities is the environment, socialist economy reform, and private sector development. The development of research capacity in developing member countries is also receiving special attention. The Research Administrator's office takes an active role in seeking to develop the research program in these priority areas. The priorities are reviewed and updated as research programs develop.

This brief overview of the Bank's research structure underscores the Bank's broad commitment to and need for policy-oriented research. (Of course, Bank project design also draws heavily on traditional scientific and engineering research, and the Bank supports such research quite heavily through mechanisms such as the Consultative Group on International Agricultural Research. Given the nature of this conference, we have restricted our review of Bank research activities largely to economics.) The breadth of the Bank's research interests and concerns reflects the nature of development economics: although often seen as a subdiscipline of economics akin to labor economics or international trade, in fact it embodies all economic subdisciplines, distinguishing itself by applying these subdisciplines to a particular set out countries. Because development economics is not a separate discipline, experts in virtually any of the traditional economic and other social science subdisciplines can contribute to "development" research if they direct their expertise to the specific circumstances—the institutional and social character—of developing countries.

KEYNOTE ADDRESS

Development Policy Research: The Task Ahead

Manmohan Singh

I. Overview

The postwar period of development is a history of triumph—not of failure. The increase in life expectancy, the fall in infant mortality, the rate of growth, the achievements in any number of developing countries—nobody at the end of the Second World War would have expected so much. A billion people are still hungry, but it would now be two billion without the achievements that have been made [Rosenstein-Rodan 1984].

Postwar progress on the development front until the closing years of the 1970s did much to shake the world's faith in the Marshallian dictum "*Natura non facit saltum*" (nature does not make leaps). The relation between the world of ideas and the world of action is by no means unambiguous, but it is fair to assert that the pioneers of development economics did a lot to sustain faith in the possibilities of economic progress in the developing countries.

World War II to the 1980s: An Era of Optimism

The basic thrust of development economics has been activist—that development can be managed. The analysis of strategic factors in development, of development strategies, and of investment criteria has thus sharpened the focus for policy intervention as well as yielding valuable insights into the growth process.

The earlier postwar works singled out capital accumulation and the allied process of saving as central to the management of development. The strategic role of investment is still unquestioned. But later works, in bringing out the vital role of technical progress, entrepreneurship, and human resource development, have enlarged our understanding of growth as the product of a more complex process.

The later literature has also sought to correct an earlier tendency to assign rather a passive role to the rural sector. Rising agricultural productivity is now regarded as crucial in the successful management of development.

Manmohan Singh is secretary general of the South Commission, Geneva. The views expressed are the personal views of the author and should not be attributed to the South Commission.

© 1990 The International Bank for Reconstruction and Development / THE WORLD BANK.

At the international level, analysis of the relation between the periphery and the center, and of how gains from participation are distributed in the international division of labor, spurred reformulation of the theory of international economic policy, particularly of protection. It also stimulated the search for new international arrangements for more equitable management of North-South relations. The establishment of several international institutions—the United Nations Development Programme, the International Development Association, the three regional development banks, and the United Nations Conference on Trade and Development—owes much to the inspiration of the pioneer work in development economics.

The optimistic spirit of mainstream development economics—expressed in the view of some of our pioneers that self-sustained growth could take off within a single generation—provided the psychological underpinning for substantial mobilization of latent national energies, and for international support for the development cause during the first three postwar decades.

The 1980s: A Change in Climate

The events of the 1980s have assailed that optimism. The economies of East Asia and Southeast Asia have continued to grow rapidly, and the slower-moving countries of South Asia have also managed to improve their performance. But most countries in Africa and Latin America have retrogressed sharply. The result is a profound disillusionment, and skepticism about prevailing development strategies, policies, and programs.

The crisis of development challenges the entire development community to come up with strategies to put the affected countries back on the path of sustained growth. Development research must assist this effort.

The search will not be easy. Several obstacles stand in the way, which have to be surmounted or neutralized to revive growth impulses and then to sustain their momentum.

First among these obstacles is a world trading environment far less expansionary than in the golden years from 1945 to 1973, when annual export volume growth at a steady 6 to 7 percent provided a climate hospitable to the expansion of manufactured exports from developing countries. It is highly questionable whether the emerging international environment will be as friendly.

Second, the 1980s have seen a sharp deterioration in the export of capital from developed to developing countries. For several developing countries, the net transfer of resources from industrial nations is now negative. The burden of external debt is now a recognized obstacle to the revival of growth in most countries of Africa and Latin America. Yet no viable solutions have emerged from the voluminous discussions of this subject in recent years. The economic chaos and uncertainty created by the debt overhang strongly encourage capital flight at the same time as they deter the infusion of fresh capital from abroad. The climate is not conducive to large-scale private international flows, except to East and Southeast Asia. With the possible exception of Japan, no industrial country seems inclined to step up official flows—either bilateral or multilateral—to the developing world.

A third difficulty that developing countries have to face is the negative fallout from accelerated technical progress in developed countries—such as reduced use of raw materials per unit of final product. In addition, technological advances in areas such as microelectronics, computer numerically controlled machines, and computer-aided designs threaten the traditional division of products into labor-intensive and capital-intensive categories. As a result, cheap labor may cease to be the dominant determinant of comparative advantage, to the detriment even of developing countries making traditionally labor-intensive products, such as textiles.

With a few exceptions, the technological distance between the developing and the developed countries is widening. Neoclassical international trade theory, by postulating identical production functions for different products in various countries, assumes this problem away. That this assumption is unrealistic becomes obvious when we consider that technical knowledge is often private property, that new advances in science and technology are increasingly being privatized, and that developed countries are now making concerted attempts to coerce developing countries into conforming their domestic legislation on the protection of intellectual property to the interests of technology exporters. We must face up squarely to the consequences of unequal international access to technical knowledge. On the domestic front too the present situation has its shortcomings. First is the serious pressure on resources from population growth rates, currently 2 to 3 percent or more.

Sustained development over a period of about twenty-five years was earlier expected to alter attitudes toward childbearing fundamentally and thus bring a reduction in birth rates that would offset the welcome reduction in death rates attendant on the process of development. This change in attitude has not materialized in most countries outside East Asia. Fertility rates *are* declining, but far too slowly.

While many developing countries are faced with a net outflow of capital, their domestic requirements for capital per unit of output may well rise. Often, the capital stock is technologically obsolescent. And past neglect both of proper maintenance and of timely replacement squeezes resources still more. The increased demand for social overhead capital associated with urbanization has a similar impact. Furthermore, capital requirements have often been kept low by neglecting environmental protection in the process of resource use. In several developing countries, land and water degradation now seriously threatens the sustainability of growth—but if compensatory measures are adopted, the cost of output is bound to increase. Investment and savings associated with a given growth rate will therefore need to be much higher than in the past.

Finally, the inducement to save is itself under pressure because the influential, upper-income groups in developing countries cannot resist the temptation to adopt the life styles and consumption patterns of the societies of the post-industrial age. These demands will, no doubt, siphon resources from essential investments, while undermining the cohesion and unity in developing societies. The widening social gap between the ruling minority and the great mass of people can erode the moral authority of these elites to command willing acceptance of restraint on the growth of consumption. As a result, inflationary pressures may become endemic, reinforcing in turn the demand for authoritarian political structures, which inevitably bring further alienation and instability.

The Task Ahead

The task of reviving and sustaining development in the developing world in the decade that lies ahead is formidable. It will demand highly innovative measures to counteract the negative influences now at work. An improvement in the external economic environment would help, but cannot be counted on. Developing countries must think in terms of an efficient policy framework that will sustain the pace of development even if the international economic environment fails to improve. The need for structural reform to promote greater mobilization and more efficient use of domestic resources is inescapable.

In what follows, I deal with two issues of reform prominent in current debate: the role of the state and the reform of the trade regime. (Food security and development of human resources are no less important but are not discussed here for want of time.) The discussion leads into consideration of a third bone of contention—concerned, again, with reform, but this time reform of the assistance mechanism itself, rather than the countries assisted: the question of how (and how much) to impose conditions on development loans.

My analysis is not intended to be exhaustive. Its objective is limited. I accept the necessity of reform, but I argue that no single development model can be applied universally. The agenda must be tailored to the specific requirements of each country. I also argue that some of the now fashionable reform packages, with strong ideological overtones, distract attention from the fundamental task of modernizing the state for the successful management of development. In the final section, I discuss the case for an independent, objective international mechanism for laying down performance norms and assessing the performance of countries that are receiving external assistance.

II. THE ROLE OF THE STATE

In the postwar years, most developing-country governments have been activist in their management of development. Mainstream development economics has on the whole supported this activism on the grounds of pervasive market imperfections, externalities, and discontinuities and deficiencies in the private sector's risk-taking and entrepreneurial ability. As a result, the state's role has expanded, both in the regulation of private activity and in the actual operation of strategically important enterprises.

In the 1980s, the setbacks to development have eroded confidence in past development strategies and brought this state activism under fire. Even more influential has been the reassertion of a strong pro–private sector ideology in the major developed countries, which has inevitably spilled over to the international financial institutions. The developing world is now being called upon to accept a development and structural adjustment model in which the state's role is drastically reduced. A voluminous literature now argues that excessive state interference in developing countries has distorted the price structure, promoted inefficient resource use, and given rise to undesirable rents for influential pressure groups. The tendency now is to blame the development setback of the 1980s entirely on the cumulative process of excessive state dominance of development. This view is clearly one-sided, for it ignores the traumatic impact—particularly in Latin America and Africa[1]—of international events beyond the control of developing countries (such as the virtual cessation of international bank lending, the steep rise in real rates of interest, and the collapse of international commodity prices). Also overlooked is the highly interventionist role of the state in the most successful economies of East Asia (on this point, see Anglade and Fortin 1987).

Even so, any objective observer must concede that developing countries often operate an overextended state apparatus, forgetting that administrative capabilities are one of the scarcest factors of production. The result is that scarce administrative resources are spread too thinly to achieve the basic development objectives. Furthermore, the assumption implicit in much of Anglo-Saxon economics that the state is a platonic guardian of the public interest does not hold good all the time. In this regard, political economists would do well to pay more systematic attention to the influence of organized pressure groups on government decisionmaking in developing countries. The role of the state in the economic life of the developing countries thus needs to be reappraised, but the appraisal must be marked, not by strong ideological overtones, but by pragmatic consideration of feasible alternatives.

My own guess is that a good case can be made for substantial deregulation in many developing countries. Judging by the Indian experience, for instance, such regulatory measures as industrial licensing and import controls could be loosened with much social and economic advantage. However, there are no universal rules to determine the proper mix of regulation, promotion, and reliance on market forces. The agenda has to be country-specific—an area offering much scope for fruitful research.

---

1. Professor Albert Fishlow (1987) has shown that the relative severity of the external shock has been an important reason why Latin American economies have performed less well in the post-1980 period than East Asian economies.

Modernization of State Apparatus

In practice, the issue is not so much the size of government as its quality and effectiveness. Most developing countries lack an alternative to a strong, purposeful government providing a strategic sense of direction for the development process.

An example is food policy, recent discussions of which have been dominated by a concern to get prices right. Certainly, remunerative farm prices are a linchpin of a workable agricultural strategy. Farmers do respond to price incentives. But the aggregate supply function of farm produce as a whole (as opposed to that of any single crop) is likely to be greatly influenced by the state of available agricultural technology, credit, and marketing arrangements, and by the management of water resources. The efficient performance of all these activities calls for collective action and often large investments by the public sector. The modernization of the state is therefore crucial to the management of development.

The state's capacity for autonomous action should then be enhanced in strategic areas that cannot be left to the care of market forces—a vision not inconsistent with shedding regulatory functions that may have outlived their usefulness. But there are several other critical considerations. A firm commitment to the rule of law and respect for human rights is one. The improvement of selection, training, and skill formation in public services is another. The maximum possible decentralization and use of appropriate consultative devices to involve local communities at the grass-roots level is yet another important dimension. A reform of the tax system designed to provide for a built-in elasticity and buoyancy in the tax structure is a high priority, as is the establishment of cost-effective delivery systems to provide basic social services, such as health and education. The final issue is the provision of institutional safeguards to ensure that the state performs its essential functions efficiently and equitably, and to curb the manipulative power of organized vested interests. In this context, the role of democracy and what has come to be known as "glasnost" in the Soviet Union is critical.

Deregulation is often advocated as a means of depoliticizing economic processes. But in real life, politics cannot be wished away in the management of development. So, we should try to get the politics right. Deregulation, when accompanied by competition, can help reduce the grip of organized vested interests on the machinery of the state. But competition, as Adam Smith recognized long ago, cannot be regarded as a natural outcome and requires a political framework for its enforcement and effectiveness. A reform package has to be much more comprehensive than simple deregulation.

In the final analysis, only a multidisciplinary and multidimensional approach can devise credibile, coherent, and legitimate reform. There is no alternative to political reforms designed to promote participatory and people-centered approaches to development. People want to be consulted, involved, and taken into confidence. Modernizing of the state means reforming institutions to make all this possible. For by now, it is fairly obvious that reform by stealth is not going to work.

Management of the Public Sector

Even the most conservative advocates of the private sector have recognized that the long gestation period for social overhead capital projects, the large investments required, and the state of capital markets in developing countries make these projects less than enticing to the private sector. For this reason, public sector involvement in expanding social overhead capital has not provoked much resistance.

Many developing countries, however, take the more expansive view of including in the public sector's purview a number of industries considered to be of strategic importance. State intervention has sometimes been justified on grounds similar to those applicable to social overhead capital, such as barriers to entry and lack of private initiative (Levy 1988). Another argument is that, because profits constitute the most important source of accumulation in a dynamic economy and are an important determinant of income distribution, their socialization and the prevention of their wasteful consumption by private capitalists could at once accelerate accumulation and help reduce inequalities of income and wealth. And another justification for state involvement is that public enterprises can set the pace for strengthening technological capabilities and accelerating technical progress.[2]

The surge of pro–private sector ideological fervor since the late 1970s has rekindled the old antagonism toward the public sector of developing countries. With public enterprises increasingly viewed as an inefficient drag on the economy, privatization now figures prominently in the programs of structural reform sponsored by the World Bank and the International Monetary Fund.

Anti–public sector sentiment cannot, however, be dismissed as purely an expression of ideological bias. There have been visible gaps in the performance of the public sector. Results of public sector operation in India, for example, have fallen far short of original expectations. The enterprises have been effective in bringing some balance to the regional distribution of industry—an important consideration in managing a polity as diverse as India—and have been pioneers in introducing new technology. But, perhaps because of the monopolistic environment in which they often operate, they have not kept abreast of technological developments. The biggest disappointment has been their failure to generate adequate surpluses to finance sustained expansion of investment. Both operational deficiencies and restrictions on their freedom to vary prices have contributed to this outcome.

---

2. All these arguments played an important role in the expansion of the public sector in India during the First and the Second Five-Year Plans (see Singh 1986).

But if further expansion of the public sector is not the answer, neither is wholesale privatization of existing public enterprises. Even in countries where the private sector is quite well developed, such as India, private sector management even of unsophisticated industries, such as textiles, has been far from encouraging. The privatization experience of developed capitalist countries has little relevance for developing countries with limited entrepreneurial and risk-taking capabilities. Moreover, economic policies do not operate in a political vacuum. Often, proposals for large-scale privatization do not enjoy wide public support. Thus, in practice, there is often no alternative but to get on with the task of improving the efficiency of public enterprises.

How best to manage the public sector is a key issue of contemporary development policy. Can new ground rules be devised for giving autonomy to public enterprises, so that they can function without day-to-day government interference in their operation? Is it realistic to expect government, as owner, to pass an ordinance of self-denial, of noninterference in the day-to-day operations of public enterprises? Will managers—whose appointment and removal are in the hand of government—exercise their powers or play safe by consulting frequently with government authorities even on day-to-day matters? And, since many public enterprises function in a noncompetitive environment, how can effective pricing policies be evolved which neither reward inefficiency nor provide undeserved monopoly rents? The answers to these profoundly important questions are again likely to be location-specific. Here, then, is another area for fruitful multidisciplinary research.

The outcome of efforts to improve the working of the public sector depends a great deal on the character of the government. Under a regime that regards the state as the private property of rulers, the development potential of the public sector cannot be realized. With a rotten state structure, public enterprises cannot be pacesetters of development. But then a rotten state structure is also unlikely to provide a hospitable climate for the functioning of private enterprise by the rules set down in orthodox textbooks. It should not be difficult to make a realistic assessment of the limitations of the "crony capitalism" which flourishes in a number of developing countries. Nor should we perhaps overlook the potential for reform of defective state structures as an inescapable part of the process of growing up.

In the final analysis, the quality of a polity is a major determinant of the pace of development. And the quality of a polity cannot be divorced from the quality of the state. Privatization is no panacea for all the ills of the public sector. It must not distract attention from the essential nation-building task of modernizing state structures. There are no shortcuts to prosperity and progress.

III. Reform of the Trade Regime

Citing the success of the East Asian countries' export-oriented development strategies, international financial institutions have been pushing the developing countries toward more export-oriented policies for managing their external payments. Intense pressure has been brought to bear on developing countries to devalue and liberalize their import regime so as to enhance the relative profitability of exports.

A dynamic export sector is clearly important for the efficient management of the economy, since import needs inevitably rise at least as fast as national income in the process of development. Thus, there is certainly a strong case for protection levels to be rationalized in line with perceived long-term comparative advantage and, over time, to be reduced to provide the stimulus of foreign competition in domestic markets. And the anti-export bias implicit in the incentives of tariff and exchange rate systems needs to be removed.

Industrialization based on the export of labor-intensive products has contributed to the growth of output and employment in the labor surplus economies of East Asia. And such countries as India have missed valuable opportunities by underestimating the growth potential of labor-intensive industrial products and by investing too little in export efforts. In many African countries, however, domestic supply conditions—including the level of development of human resources—do not favor export-led industrialization based on labor-intensive products. They have to rely on the export of products intensive in natural resources—often produced with the help of transnational corporations—which cannot generate the same dynamic effects on income and employment as labor-intensive industrial products.

So, what scope is there for growth of exports of labor-intensive manufactures from developing to developed countries? Once demand conditions improve, supply bottlenecks can be overcome. But will markets still be available if all the countries that have pursued inward-looking development strategies switch over to export-oriented strategies based on labor-intensive manufactures? This is a critical empirical question: a reliable answer to it can have a material influence on future development strategies. The beginnings of an answer may be indicated by the priority accorded to developing countries' interests in the Uruguay Round of multilateral trade negotiations.

IV. Development Assistance and Conditionality

In the 1980s both international financial institutions and bilateral donors have massively increased the conditionality attached to their development assistance. In principle, one cannot object to performance norms and conditionality designed to ensure that this assistance is used to promote genuine development. Such an assurance can only strengthen the hands of those in the developed countries who believe in a concerted global attack on world poverty. But the developing countries also need an assurance that any monitoring and policy stipulations are based on objective analysis and are in no way colored by ideological preference and prejudice. The international credit mechanism is in the final analysis a highly political mechanism. Creditors—particularly those who act as lenders of last resort—are in a strong bargaining position and are often able to impose their views on borrowers. Only an impartial international evaluation of development performance can inspire the confidence and respect of both donors and recipients. The rationale for such a mechanism is well set out in the essay from which I quoted at the outset:

> Today we have competence, finance and no democracy in the international banks—and democracy and no finance in the United Nations. The 1954 ECLA report proclaimed the need for a separation of programming and financing. An independent body—not responsible to either creditors or debtors—should evaluate the programmes, and resources should be allocated according to that verdict. The World Bank has a good staff . . . but the developing countries have no confidence in the vote of its board because creditor countries have the overwhelming majority; the developed countries, on the other hand, have no confidence in the United Nations. It is part of national sovereignty for each nation to limit its own rights. There will be no satisfactory solution to this problem without some sort of arbitration. Only an International Development Council—an International Court of Economic Justice—can solve the problem. The Committee of IX of the Alliance for Progress was an attempt to apply such an International arbitration. It failed because of sabotage on both sides, but all great ideas first fail. All progress is first proclaimed to be impossible, but is then realized [Rosenstein-Rodan 1984].

The experience of the 1980s suggests that this may well be an idea whose time has come. At all events, it should figure prominently on the agenda for development policy research.

References

Anglade, Christian, and Carlos Fortin. 1987. "The Role of the State in Latin America's Strategic Options." *CEPAL Review* 31 (April): 219–44.

Fishlow, Albert. 1987. "Some Reflections on Comparative Latin American Economic Performance and Policy." *World Institute for Development Economics Research Working Papers* 22 (1): 42.

Levy, Brian. 1988. "The State-Owned Enterprise as an Entrepreneurial Substitute in Developing Countries: The Case of Nitrogen Fertilizer." *World Development* 16: 10.

Rosenstein-Rodan, Paul N. 1984. "Natura Facit Saltum: Analysis of the Disequilibrium Growth Process." In Gerald M. Meier and Dudley Seers, eds., *Pioneers in Development*. New York: Oxford University Press.

Singh, Manmohan. 1986. "The Quest for Equity in Development." R. R. Kale Memorial Lecture, Gokhale Institute of Politics and Economics. Pune, India.

Developing Countries and the Uruguay Round of Trade Negotiations

Marcelo de Paiva Abreu

This paper, which summarizes recent developments in the Uruguay Round of multilateral trade negotiations, addresses the key questions developing countries must consider in their negotiating: What are the trade and welfare costs and benefits of protection for developing countries? How will developing countries be affected by, and what might they concede in connection with, tariffs and tariff escalation, the protection of textiles and apparel, such market access issues as antidumping and countervailing duties, and such "gray area" measures as voluntary export restraints? What concessions should they want—and be willing to make? What do they stand to gain or lose from the so-called new themes of the Uruguay Round: trade-related investment measures, intellectual property, and services? What do net importers of food products stand to lose or gain from reduced agricultural protection? How will dismantling the Multifibre Arrangement affect developing countries? How will overall trade liberalization affect them? And should trade issues be negotiated in isolation from such factors as the debt crisis and conditions imposed by international agencies?

The aim of this paper is to assess the effect of protectionist policies, in both industrial and developing countries, on the interests and influence of developing countries in the current Uruguay Round of multilateral trade negotiations under the General Agreement on Tariffs and Trade (GATT).

I. Overview

The GATT rests on three pillars. Two of them—the most favored nation principle (MFN), which automatically extends bilateral concessions to all GATT participants, and the prohibition of nontariff trade restrictions—are well in line with theoretical requirements. But the third—the principle of reciprocal concessions (in effect the "balancing" of reductions in import tax revenues)—has no adequate rationale in trade theory. Indeed, this principle encourages negotiating tactics that in some respects impede liberalization.

Marcelo de Paiva Abreu is a professor of economics at Catholic University, Rio de Janeiro. He wishes to thank officials of GATT and of the Brazilian Government for their cooperation. The paper does not necessarily reflect the views of these officials.

© 1990 The International Bank for Reconstruction and Development / THE WORLD BANK.

The first pillar—the MFN clause—has been eroded by the organization of free trade or preferential trade zones. The second—the "tariffs only" principle—was shaken right from the start by article XI:2(c) of the original rules, which allowed imposition of quantitative restrictions on imports of agricultural products (see Abreu and Fritsch 1987, pp. 24–29). This explicit breach of GATT principles reflected the Geneva negotiators' need to reconcile their drive for free trade with the widespread commitment of industrial country governments (notably the United States) to price support programs, export subsidies, and import restrictions for temperate zone products.

The original GATT rules did not do the same for manufactures. Controls were only permitted under circumstances either of exceptional balance of payments difficulties or of "disruptive" import growth—the so-called injury clause imposed by the U.S. Congress as a condition for approval to negotiate the postwar trade treaties (see Gardner 1969, p. 159). Thus, once balance of payments conditions stabilized in Europe in the late 1950s, it was through the "injury" argument that most restrictive practices against manufacturing imports crept in. A landmark in the process was the U.S.-sponsored Long Term Agreement in cotton textiles in the early 1960s, a quantitative trade restrictive agreement that totally contradicted GATT principles. This was the beginning of a long history of textile and clothing protection which culminated in a series of Multifibre Arrangements (MFAs). More recently, such inherently illegal quantitative restrictions negotiated outside the GATT have been generalized and thinly disguised as "voluntary export restraints" (VERs).

The third pillar of the GATT—the principle of reciprocity—has remained in place, and it remains a problem. Although successive multilateral trade negotiations (MTNs) achieved impressive results in reforming tariffs until the mid-1960s, it became increasingly clear that in practice the operation of the liberal and formally equitable rules of the GATT was distributing the benefits of trade liberalization unevenly. The traditional approach has been to measure the value of tariff concessions as equivalent to import volumes in a given year multiplied by the tariff rate changes granted on those products. This practice implied that in the "reciprocal bargaining" process established at MTNs, the substantive concessions favored industrial nations or trading blocs (which exchanged bilateral concessions that were generalized through the MFN clause), and excluded products of export interest to developing countries because they were not interesting as a basis for exchanging concessions between developing countries (see UNCTAD 1968, p. 94; GATT 1979, pp. 120–22). GATT came thus to be seen as a rich men's club from which developing countries derived little advantage.

Although such deficiencies, identified by the Haberler Report (GATT 1958, pp. 8–12) were formally on the GATT agenda by the late 1950s, no practical changes were immediately forthcoming. The only noticeable change was the rather formal recognition, inserted under a new Part IV in 1965, of the possibility of special treatment for developing countries. The developing countries' growing disillusionment gradually undermined the GATT's position as a forum for the discussion of North-South trade relations, finding expression at the first U.N. Conference on Trade and Development (UNCTAD) in 1964 in demands that industrial countries extend a Generalized System of Preferences (GSP) to all developing countries. Beginning in 1971, all industrial countries introduced GSP schemes by 1976.

Developing countries, which had been marginal participants in the Kennedy Round (1964–67) were more active in the Tokyo Round (1973–79). The Tokyo Round brought tariff reductions, codes on nontariff barriers, and the "framework agreement." The framework agreement, on which the developing countries were especially active, provided through its "enabling clause" a standing legal basis for GSP to breach the most favored nation principle. The agreement also made it easier for developing countries to adopt trade measures to foster particular industries. In return, developing countries agreed to a "graduation" principle which related the capacity to make concessions to level of development (see Winham 1986, pp. 141–46, 274–80).

The codes negotiated in the Tokyo Round to counter rising nontariff protection ended up by undermining the MFN clause because the principle of MFN conditionality was raised to try to limit MFN treatment to signatories of specific codes. The rights of nonsignatories to MFN were explicitly recognized by the GATT in 1979, but the trade policies of some contracting parties did not seem to reflect this decision (see Hudec 1987, pp. 81 ff., and Winham 1986, pp. 355–60).

For many years the trade policy interests of the group of developing countries could be reasonably described as convergent. But as the economic structure of many of these countries has grown more heterogeneous, so has their trade structure. Many developing countries are still basically producers of commodities, but quite a few are not. Their agenda for trade negotiation therefore differs. Even between primary producers, differing commodity export structure—for instance, between temperate and tropical agricultural commodities—can mean conflicting aims for trade policy. Discriminating preferential treatment results in divisive tensions between developing countries with a similar export structure. This paper tries to take these differences into account.

II. GATT Negotiations in the 1980s

The balance of priorities reflected in the 1982 GATT Ministerial Declaration—the forerunner of the Uruguay Round of MTNs—had shifted quite drastically by the launching of a new round in 1986. A backlog of unresolved issues—nontariff barriers, agricultural subsidies, and other problems relating to trade in goods—had originally headed the agenda. By 1986 these had yielded the limelight to the "new themes"—a set of issues selected by the United States in a strategic move to adapt the rules governing direct investment and intellectual property rights to a changing environment affecting the growth opportunities and the competitive edge of U.S. firms.

New Themes: TRIPs, TRIMs, and Trade in Services

The new themes were a somewhat heterogeneous bunch of issues, some of which had been only marginally treated by the GATT in the past, covering trade-related aspects of intellectual property rights (TRIPs), trade-related investment measures (TRIMs), and trade in services (for more detailed discussion, see Abreu and Fritsch 1988). ("High technology" goods, initially included, were dropped from the list of "new themes," as it turned out to be difficult to show how they differed from other goods from the point of view of GATT rules.) With the support of Japan, and more equivocal backing from the other industrial countries, the United States pressed for the inclusion of the new themes in the agenda for the next MTNs. Some developing countries resisted all three; most opposed inclusion of trade in services.

TRIPs—regulated mainly by international conventions under the jurisdiction of such agencies as the World Intellectual Property Organization (WIPO) and UNESCO—had traditionally been of little interest to GATT. Dissatisfied with the enforcement of the rules and with their allegedly increasing infringement, especially in semi-industrialized countries, the industrial countries included TRIPs in the 1982 Ministerial Declaration with a view to bringing them under the aegis of GATT rules and enforcement capabilities. This early initiative met with strong developing-country resistance in a clash of views that has continued and is unlikely to be soon resolved.

TRIMs. GATT discussions on TRIMs centered on the legality of national regulations that require foreign firms to export a given amount of their output, or to purchase a given amount of their inputs or equipment from domestic suppliers. A GATT panel established in 1984 concluded that the export performance regulations are not inconsistent with GATT rules, but that the import content obligations were inconsistent with Article III:4. Developing countries have reserved their position.

Trade in services. In the 1982 ministerial session, the United States pressed hard for discussion of enlarging GATT to cover trade in services to be included in the work program. Opposition from many developing and even some industrial countries, on grounds of insufficient information, deferred discussion of the issue until the 1984 session, to give time for national studies and stimulate the exchange of information.

Placing trade in services within the GATT framework was initially the most divisive of the new themes. Developing countries felt that the unresolved traditional issues that originally headed the agenda in the 1982 Ministerial Declaration should not have been displaced by the debate on services. And they feared that the issue was likely to strengthen the hand of the industrial countries in the new round of negotiations. Developing-country misgivings were shared by some members of the European Community (EC), whose support for putting services into the GATT framework was less than wholehearted because of the complex legal and technical problems involved, and because the theme covers a large number of sector-specific issues that encroach on the territory of other international organizations.

The Negotiations: 1986–1989

When the ministers arrived in Punta del Este in September 1986, they had before them two formal agenda proposals. One, tabled by Colombia and Switzerland—with overwhelming support from developed countries and substantial support from developing countries—included all the new themes in a single track. The other, tabled by the G-10 coalition—a group of developing countries formed by Argentina, Brazil, Cuba, the Arab Republic of Egypt, India, Nicaragua, Nigeria, Peru, Tanzania, and Yugoslavia—included none of them.

The Colombian-Swiss proposal had in fact foundered before Punta del Este, when the EC withdrew its support to the wording on agriculture. The eventual compromise reached at Punta del Este in the Uruguay Round Declaration (GATT 1986) distinguished trade in services from the other subjects formally encompassed in the negotiations, including the other new themes. With GATT Secretariat support, the ministers established a special Group on Negotiations on Services to carry out negotiations in this area and make recommendations to the Trade Negotiations Committee. This arrangement, however, has little hope of heading off developing countries from exchanging concessions in services for concessions in the trade of goods.

Other negotiating groups were to deal with: tariffs; nontariff measures; products based on natural resources; textiles and clothing; agriculture; tropical products; GATT articles; MTN agreements and arrangements; safeguards, subsidies, and countervailing measures; trade-related aspects of intellectual property rights, including trade in counterfeit goods; trade-related investment measures; dispute settlement; and functioning of the GATT system.

The results of two years of negotiations were presented to the Montreal Mid-Term Ministerial meeting of December 1988 (see GATT 1988a, 1988b). The meeting ended deadlocked on four issues: agriculture, intellectual property, textiles and clothing, and reform of the safeguards system.

On *agriculture*, the U.S. position that all trade-distorting subsidies affecting agricultural products should be eliminated within a specified time frame was unacceptable to the EC (predictably, in view of earlier French-inspired intransigence on export subsidies, and continuing EC insistence on maintaining a dual price system with different prices for exports and home consumption). The deadlock in agriculture galvanized Argentina and the other Latin American members of the Cairns group of agricultural free traders (see section III) into action. Their activities eventually achieved agreement to shelve the results so far obtained by eleven negotiating groups, pending the results of further consultations and negotiations to be held in early April 1989. In April the deadlock on agriculture was broken by U.S. acceptance of the EC refusal to commit themselves to ending subsidies, and more flexibility from the EC on the freezing of protection in the short term.

On *intellectual property*, as on agriculture, the gap between the extreme positions after Montreal was wide. The industrial countries continued to urge that GATT's rules and disciplines in this area be enlarged, and enforcement as well as dispute settlement improved, while the large developing countries—Brazil and India—insisted that WIPO was the proper forum to deal with the matter. The industrial countries' views prevailed in April 1989: it was decided that negotiations should proceed in the GATT, and that discussion of which international organization would be in charge would be postponed to the end of the Round.

As the *safeguard issue* was disposed of through an agreement on the negotiating group's program of work, pressure mounted on the developing countries to reach agreement on textiles and clothing.

The outcome of negotiations on *textiles and clothing* was disappointing: it was agreed that within the time frame of the Uruguay Round a decision will be reached on modalities of integration of this sector into the GATT. This is to include the MFA (see *News of the Uruguay Round* 1989, pp. 8, 21).

Ironically, divergences among industrial countries at Montreal over agriculture troubled the negotiations more than the differing stands of developed and developing countries at Montreal on the new themes. On the prime bone of contention—services—negotiations advanced steadily, to the visible delight of the director general of GATT (interview, *MOCI* 1989). The inclusion of the principle of national treatment of foreign suppliers in the agreed Mid-Term text is a major breakthrough and an important concession by the developing-country G-10 coalition on services. The developed countries for their part have toned down their insistence on a multilateral framework for trade in services by accepting the proviso that before such a framework is accepted "concepts, principles and rules will have to be examined with regard to their applicability to individual sectors and types of transactions to be covered by the multilateral framework" (see *News of the Uruguay Round* 1988, pp. 40–43).

Results in Montreal in other groups under the Group of Negotiations on Goods were mixed. Some of the "successful" groups owed their achievement more to the elaborate ambiguity of agreed drafts than to any substantive advance in negotiations. Main results of interest to developing countries seem to be taking shape in relation to tropical products involving $25 billion (all dollars are U.S. dollars; billion = 1,000 million) in trade, tariff reduction on the order of 30 percent, and the transformation of nontariff into tariff barriers. Some advance is to be expected on more institutional GATT issues, such as the improvement of dispute settlement machinery and the functioning of the GATT system. The latter will involve efforts to improve the GATT trade policy review mechanism and to strengthen its links with other multilateral organizations such as the World Bank and the International Monetary Fund (IMF) and will entail greater ministerial involvement in the GATT (see *News of the Uruguay Round* 1988, pp. 26–39).

III. THE ECONOMIC INTERESTS AT STAKE: THE COSTS OF PROTECTION

The most relevant costs of protection for developing countries as a whole relate to the value of forgone exports, displaced by protection in industrial countries, and the deadweight losses entailed by protection of their own domestic markets, which distorts production and consumption decisions. (See Bhagwati 1987a on why the computation of deadweight losses is likely to underestimate the costs of protection.) But specific issues raise differing concerns for different developing countries. The discussion is thus organized thematically in subsections covering the main issues that affect the interests of developing countries, and the main areas where concessions might be exchanged.

Tariffs, Tariff Escalation, and Preferences

Tariffs have become less important in industrial countries owing to agreed reductions in previous MTNs—they now average around 5 percent. But this decline has been at least partly offset by the rise in nontariff barriers, and the average nominal tariff hides important variations that in general tend to hurt the trade interests of developing countries most. The effect of tariff peaks, high internal taxes, and tariff escalation on processed tropical products is well known.

If a 10 percent ceiling were set for tariffs, imports of developed countries would rise by 1.5 percent, as against 4.9 percent if all tariffs were eliminated (see Erzan and Karsenty 1987). Internal taxes on tropical products in developed countries amounted to $5 billion in 1983, excluding $22 billion on tobacco (see Commonwealth Secretariat 1987, p. 14). The processing of tropical products in developing countries is heavily penalized by the escalation of tariffs (and nontariff measures) in developed countries. The result is increased protection of value added, which twists the worldwide distribution of value added along processing chains in favor of the industrial countries. This has prompted compensating export taxation by developing-country exporters in a cumulative trend that restricts the market for tropical goods (see Cable 1987b, tables 22-1 and 22-2; Yeats 1987). Trade and welfare gains related to some processed tropical products such as roasted coffee are likely to be significant (see Valdés and Zietz 1980, p. 34).

Many exporters of tropical products enjoy preferential entry in developed markets. Tariff reduction, which erodes these advantages, may thus be opposed by participants in preferential arrangements, though concessions such as those on internal taxes in the EC may avoid such difficulties.

Despite its institutional drawbacks (for example, its limited inclusion of textiles and agricultural products and its restrictive safeguards and rules of origin) the General System of Preferences (GSP) is important to the expansion of developing-country exports—more because it creates trade than because it diverts it (see Karsenty and Laird 1986). It mainly benefits the larger developing economies such as Brazil, Hong Kong, Korea, and Taiwan. The major donor countries have instituted a policy of graduating country-product pairs as a direct consequence of the enabling clause of the framework agreement of 1979. Their argument is that the distribution of GSP should be equitable and that, as some developing countries become competitive, their preferential treatment should be withdrawn in favor of the least developed countries. The argument is contradicted by the evidence that trade in graduated products tends to be diverted either to developed countries or to the more advanced developing countries (see MacPhee 1986, pp. 10–12). Experience has repeatedly (and not surprisingly) shown that the developing countries who enjoy best access to developed markets are those relatively less able to supply the products, and vice versa. As developed countries increasingly emphasize full reciprocity, some of the large developing countries seem to be reconsidering their interest in GSP, as they feel the balance of benefits and costs shifting against them.

The proliferation of preferential trade agreements among the major trading nations is increasingly undermining the GATT. Such arrangements are traditional EC policy, and have spread over former colonies, the Mediterranean Basin, and countries of the European Free Trade Association (EFTA). U.S. preferential agreements have been with Caribbean countries, and the more recently negotiated free trade area with Canada. The possibility looms of preferential arrangements between the United States, Japan, and the Asian newly industrialized economies as an alternative to a stalemate in the GATT. These would probably provoke defensive preferential arrangements by the EC and other major trading blocs, and they could lead to the disintegration of the multilateral system (see Fritsch 1989; Luyten 1988).

Levels of tariff protection in developing countries are generally very high (see Laird and Yeats 1987, table 13-2), but consideration of these costs is deferred to the section on quantitative restrictions and administrative controls below, because these play a much more important role than tariffs.

Agricultural Protectionism

In the current negotiations, the discussion of agricultural protectionism centers on industrial-country policies that disrupt trade in temperate agricultural goods. Developing-country exports of agricultural raw materials and tropical agricultural commodities which do not compete with the output of developed countries are relatively unaffected by such measures and thus fall outside the area of agriculture in the GATT. The highly protectionist agricultural policies of the developed countries strangle efficient agriculture not only by providing closed markets for inefficient producers—mainly through variable levies and quantitative restrictions—but also through export subsidies required to dispose of surplus production. These policies depress world prices of agricultural products significantly. Their costs in the large countries belonging to the Organisation for Economic Co-operation and Development (OECD) in 1984–86 averaged $216 billion yearly; the United States and the EC spent about $80 billion each and Japan $50 billion. Consumers mostly bear these costs in the EC and Japan; in the United States it is mainly the taxpayer who pays the bill (see OECD estimates quoted in Kelly and others 1988, p. 140).

Nominal rates of protection in developed countries are high, especially in Europe and Japan. Weighted averages for consumer prices yield nominal protection coefficients of 1.56 for the EC, 1.81 for other European countries, 2.08 for Japan, and 1.17 for the United States (see World Bank 1986, pp. 112–113). Recent estimates of producer subsidy equivalents (PSEs) (which try to encompass a wide spectrum of distorting measures to calculate the subsidy required to maintain constant farmers' incomes) were 14.5 percent for Australia, 68.9 percent for Canada, 40.1 percent for the EC, and 28.3 percent for the United States (see Kelly and others 1988, p. 141; on PSEs and variants see Josling and Tangermann 1988).

Inefficient agriculture is endemic in the EC, Japan, and many small European economies, but the United States is also far from blameless in its protection of inefficient production of rice, sugar, wool, cotton, certain processed meats, and dairy products. And the United States has a long-standing bad record of market disrupting activities, recently worsened by the introduction of the Export Enhancement Program in answer to competitive pressures from EC agricultural exports.[1]

By contrast, economic policy in developing countries tends to have an antiagricultural bias. The distortions come from a variety of policies: artificially low prices paid by marketing boards, taxation of exports, inefficient domestic production of inputs, and overvalued exchange rates that reduce the cost of competitive imports. This bias is the rule in many small developing economies, and is reflected in the PSEs of Argentina (50.1 percent) and Nigeria (44 percent) (World Bank 1986). Some of the more advanced developing countries, for instance Brazil (PSE 4.2 percent), have adopted more balanced policies, or even policies biased, like those of developed countries, in the opposite direction (for instance, Indonesia, Korea, and Mexico with PSEs of 38.3, 58.5, and 39.5 percent respectively).

Agricultural protectionism in developed countries has serious consequences for prices, trade volume, and welfare, as does the very different intervention of the developing countries. (Estimates of these impacts are known to be very sensitive to model specifications, but the general picture of what liberalization would bring is nevertheless clear. See Valdés 1987, p. 575). The impact on prices and trade volumes of a hypothetical end to intervention in certain commodities (table 1) illustrates the point.

The figures on how the trade benefits and losses from agricultural liberalization in the developed countries will be distributed among developing countries

---

1. Warley's remark (Warley 1976, p.322) remains valid: "America's enthusiasm for a liberal trade regime for farm products is not only a late conversion but is also highly selective. It focuses on those commodities in which the United States is an exporter."

Table 1. *The Effects of Liberalization of Selected Commodities on International Prices and Trade Volume in Specific Countries or Groups of Countries, 1985*
(percent)

Impact	Wheat	Coarse grains	Rice	Beef and veal	Dairy	Sugar
Price change						
EC	1	3	1	10	12	3
Japan	0	0	4	4	12	3
United States	1	3	0	0	5	1
OECD	2	1	5	16	27	5
Developing countries	7	3	12	0	36	3
All	9	4	8	16	67	8
Trade-volume change						
EC	0	4	0	107	34	5
Japan	0	3	30	57	28	1
United States	0	14	2	14	50	3
OECD	1	19	32	195	95	2
Developing countries	7	12	75	68	330	60
All	6	30	97	235	190	60

Note: This includes the effect of an end of intervention in agricultural markets and not only trade intervention.
Source: World Bank (1986, p. 129).

are fragile and not necessarily compatible with the best aggregate estimates. If developed countries liberalized all trade measures affecting agriculture, agricultural exports by developing countries of beef, wheat, sugar, and maize would increase by 533 percent, 146 percent, 103 percent, and 52 percent, respectively (Zietz and Valdés 1986, p. 43). Estimates for a 50 percent reduction by developed countries of trade barriers on temperate agricultural products other than those mentioned above suggest that the impact is not very significant, except for wine (see Valdés and Zietz 1980, p. 34).

Table 2. *Efficiency Gains of Different Economic Blocs from Different Agricultural Liberalizations of Selected Commodities, 1985*
(billions of dollars)

	Liberalization in:		
Efficiency gains in	Industrial countries	Developing countries	All countries
Developing countries	11.8	28.2	18.3
Industrial countries	48.5	10.2	45.9
East European nonmarket economies	11.1	13.1	23.1
All	25.6	4.9	41.1

Source: World Bank (1986, p. 131).

But the gains are not evenly distributed. A crucial finding of recent research is that liberalization of trade in agriculture, if restricted to developed countries, would hurt the developing countries as a whole (table 2). The winners when liberalization is restricted to developed countries are a few of the large developing countries, such as Argentina and Brazil; the main losers are Korea, Sub-Saharan Africa, and some countries of the Middle East. It is liberalization in developing countries themselves that improves their welfare as a group.

How a country—developed or developing—stands on the issue of protection for temperate products will vary according to its efficiency, income per capita, whether it is a net importer or a net exporter, and the importance of such goods in its total exports. Australia and New Zealand—efficient developed agricultural producers—are hurt by the rise of protection. The United States is a mixed case, inefficient in some agricultural activities and competitive in others. Developed economies that are inefficient producers can be classified into two types: those that protect domestic output and disrupt world agricultural markets by heavily subsidizing exports (for instance, the EC and, for rice, Japan) and those that do not export their inefficient output (typically, EFTA members).

Developing countries too can be roughly divided into two groups: net exporters (of varying degrees of efficiency and dependence on agricultural exports, ranging from such efficient and dependent countries as Argentina to such less efficient and less dependent ones as Brazil) and net importers, which will continue to enjoy low import prices if agricultural protection remains unassailed.

The Cairns group of "free trading" developing and developed countries formed in August 1986 is one manifestation of this fragmentation of interests. The members—Argentina, Australia, Brazil, Canada, Chile, Colombia, Fiji, Hungary, Indonesia, Malaysia, New Zealand, Philippines, Thailand, and Uruguay—are mainly net exporters of temperate agricultural products that have consistently pressed to dismantle agricultural protectionism.

Textiles and Clothing

The present Multifibre Arrangement (MFA IV), to run until 1991, has a long history. Since 1959, successive arrangements in the GATT have de facto legitimized textile and clothing protection, allowing industrial countries to impose quantitative restrictions on an increasing range of such exports from developing countries. The justification was that these exports were damaging output and employment in the developed countries. In fact, capital deepening, made possible by economic rents generated by import restraints and investment subsidies, is more to blame for contraction of these industries (see Silberston 1984, chap. 7).

Even inhibited by the MFA, the share of exports of textiles and clothing from developing countries in the relevant world markets has increased. The share of textile exports has increased less than that of clothing because the competitive position of developed countries in the more capital-intensive textile industry is much stronger. Developing countries (including China) in 1985 supplied $29.5 billion in textiles and clothing to the developed countries, that is, roughly 40 percent of the latter's imports (gross of intra-EC and intra-EFTA trade). MFA rules have been circumvented by upgrading exports or "quota hopping"—investing in nonquota developing countries. Developing countries imported about $30 billion in 1985, of which 40 percent was from developed countries. The high tariffs or quantitative restrictions generally imposed on these imports are based on claims of balance of payments difficulties. (See Cable 1987a, especially p. 620; 631–32 on imports into developed countries; and Kelly and others 1988, pp. 74–75 for protection in developing countries.)

The protectionist lobby in the importing countries is helped by the fact that some developing countries are often lukewarm about a return to competition. In countries where quotas are distributed according to past performance, or where export licenses are auctioned, exporters or governments reap the rents generated by artificial scarcity. This freezing of potential comparative advantage means that some developing countries actually oppose a return to competition, fearing reductions in market shares that have been sustained by the inertial rules of the MFA.

Considerable empirical work on the impact of the MFA, mainly based on partial equilibrium analysis, suggests substantial benefits from liberalizing trade in textiles and clothing. Kirmani, Molajoni, and Mayer (1984) estimated that, if all trade barriers were removed, developing-country exports would expand by 82 percent (textiles) and 93 percent (clothing)—results roughly in line with those obtained by UNCTAD. About half the trade expansion generated by removing restrictions in developed countries would be in textile and clothing products (Laird and Yeats 1986, p. 29). Consumer costs of protection in the United States alone, including losses in consumer surpluses and higher prices for imports as well as domestic output, were estimated at nearly $20 billion, and net welfare costs at about $8.1 billion in 1985 (see Cline 1987, p. 191; for other estimates, see World Bank 1987, p. 151).

Traditionally, analysts have suggested, on the basis of comparative production costs, that dismantling MFA restrictions would hurt relatively high-wage, middle-income countries without well-developed textile and clothing industries. Production would become concentrated in countries with low labor costs, locational advantages (the Mediterranean and Eastern Europe for the EC; the Caribbean and Central America for the United States), or with high technology complemented by relatively low labor costs and flexibility in fashion updating (Hong Kong) (see Cable 1986, pp. 29–30). But the empirical basis for these arguments is tenuous: experiments with a free market for textile and clothing products have been few. For example, Norway did not participate in MFA II and MFA III, and textile and clothing imports were regulated only by global (not country-specific) arrangements: it is interesting that Hong Kong maintained its market share in Norway between 1978 and 1982 (around 7–8 percent) and that the only other developing country to have a market share above 1 percent during this period was China.

More recent "general equilibrium" work suggests that such views should be dramatically revised: developing economies as a group would gain from an abolition of MFA (see Trela and Whalley 1988, especially tables 5 and 6). For several economies, welfare gains would exceed $1 billion: Brazil ($1.03 billion), China ($2.34 billion), Korea ($2.09 billion), and Taiwan ($1.4 billion). India's and Sri Lanka's gains would be surprisingly insignificant, and if liberalization were restricted to MFA quotas, Hong Kong would suffer substantial welfare losses, and Macao, Pakistan, Singapore, and Thailand very minor ones.

The implication is that countries that fear absolute export contraction and displacement from the dismantling of the MFA would in fact experience welfare gains. So textile and clothing protectionism tends to depend for survival on domestic rent reapers in developed countries and not on the fears of high-cost textile and clothing exporters among the developing countries.

Speedy dismantling of the MFA is politically unrealistic. But liberalization could begin with globalization of quotas across countries or products or (through different methods) a gradual (but scheduled) liberalization of small suppliers first (see Raffaelli 1989).

GATT Article XVIII: Balance of Payments Difficulties and Infant Industry Protection

Article XVIII(b) of the GATT allows developing countries to impose quantitative import restrictions if they face balance of payments difficulties. The use of this provision to block imports has been facilitated by rather perfunctory GATT surveillance of whether such measures were indeed warranted by balance of payments difficulties or were disguising a virtually permanent absolute protection of inefficient sectors (see Anjaria 1987, sections I and II). So easy has it been for developing countries to use article XVIII(b) that in recent years they have rarely had to resort to actions under article XVIII(c) (protecting infant industries).

Under this umbrella, protectionism in developing countries has flourished. Nontariff measures affect 40 percent of tariff lines in developing countries (see Kelly and others 1988), in comparison with 22.6 percent for nonoil imports in developed countries. The literature tends to present the costs of protection in developing countries in terms of forgone economic growth. Such evaluations are flawed by the difficulty of disentangling the costs of protection from the costs of other economic policies, and of comparing different national experiences in different historical moments. Another method of evaluating costs is the measurement of effective protection rates which underline the distortions in existence in developing countries (see World Bank 1987, pp. 88–89). The results from both methods of estimation show clearly that many developing countries protected their domestic industry well beyond the time needed to make infant industries competitive.

The well-established GATT principle of special and differential treatment (S&D) has been much criticized recently. (For a guarded condemnation, see the Leutwiler Report, GATT 1985, pp. 44–45. For more radical critical views, see Wolf

1987.) The critics argue that the S&D principle does developing countries a disservice first in allowing them to avoid making reciprocal concessions to developed countries and thus not participate in the GATT system; and second in enabling them to block imports on balance of payments or infant industry grounds.

The argument is based on the contention that liberalization, even if unilateral, is better than protection. Its proponents suggest that the advantages for developing countries of removing the S&D principle would not come from reciprocal concessions by industrial countries as their "influence . . . is transparently negligible": they should strive for "a fuller and more equal participation" in the GATT, but the main advantage would be to make it easier to liberalize at home (see Wolf 1987, pp. 661–65).

"Modernization" of article XVIII has been urged, to take into account the "new role" of fluctuating exchange rates since the early 1970s. If this reasoning were accepted with no qualification, it would mean erasing article XVIII(b), and if it were applied to other GATT articles in order to make them compatible with economic theory very little of the present charter would be left standing. Radical reform of the charter was not on the Punta del Este agenda, and it is not in the cards in the foreseeable future.

Market Access

The access of exports of developing-country manufactures to industrial countries' markets is hindered by many barriers: antidumping duties (ADs), subsidy countervailing duties (CVDs), safeguards, and indeterminate measures such as voluntary export restraints (VERs).

The increasing use of ADs and CVDs against developing-country exports since the early 1980s is well documented (see Finger and Nogués 1987; Nam 1987; Laird and Nogués 1988). There is wide agreement that ADs and CVs are used in place of safeguard measures, that their harassment content is important, and that at least in the United States preliminary determinations may be biased toward affirmative findings. The concept of constructed price is open to criticism (see Kelly and others 1988, pp. 10–11). Filing an unfair trade petition is commonly a first step in a process which leads to a U.S. demand that a VER be imposed. The economics of the legislation is faulty in concentrating on injury to domestic producers rather than the advantage to consumers of cheaper imports. In practice, it favors pricing policies based on full cost, and thus it fosters rather than prevents predatory pricing policies. And the argument that the legislation prevents pricing policies that might in the future exploit consumers in industrial countries is unconvincing in a world with a plurality of prospective suppliers (see Finger 1987, p. 156ff.)

Article XIX of the GATT states the rules for emergency action on imports of products that are injuring or threatening to injure domestic producers. Restrictions that apply under the most favored nation principle (MFN) are allowed, but affected suppliers should be compensated. These legal safeguards have rarely been applied. Instead, arrangements such as voluntary export restrictions are used, which formally preserve GATT legality by apparently being voluntary rather than being initiated by the "injured party."

There are a great many VERs: 95 in September 1986, of which 30 affected developing-country exports. The percentage of imports of developed countries from all sources affected by VERs increased between 1981 and 1986 from 6.6 percent to 45.2 percent for iron and steel products, and it remained more or less unchanged at about 9 percent for other manufactures. The cost of VERs to consumers is well documented. Less is known about the net costs to exporters because contraction of import volume is offset by rents. For clothing alone, the rents of VERs were as high as 1.4 percent of Hong Kong's gross domestic product (GDP) in 1981–83 (see Sampson 1988b, pp. 139–40; World Bank 1987, pp. 149–50).

ADs, CVDs, and VERs affect the more industrialized developing economies: Brazil, Hong Kong, Korea, Mexico, and Taiwan. The least developed countries are much less interested in such issues, because their main constraint is supply response rather than market availability.

These arrangements create vested interests—protected inefficient domestic producers obviously, but also export quota holders who prefer a stable market unrelated to dynamic comparative advantage and enjoy the economic rents generated by the restrictions. In fact, the developing countries may be better off with VERs than without them: restricting countries may, for instance, be willing to pay enough for a VER to make exporters better off than in the pre-VER situation, because the alternative article XIX safeguard would have to be applied to all suppliers (see Hindley 1987, pp. 698–99).

The industrial countries have consistently made their return to GATT discipline away from "gray area" protective devices conditional on "selectivity." Selectivity—authorization to apply safeguards to specific suppliers—would blatantly undermine the GATT; the only alternative suggested (loosening the disciplines of article XIX, including abolishing compensation) would entail the loss of rents by exporters and lessen market access (see Hindley 1987).

A revival of the Uruguay-Brazil Plan of the 1960s may be an effective replacement for the cumbersome retaliation provision of article XIX if VERs are to be discontinued. The proposal established the principle of financial payments by developed to developing countries for violations of the General Agreement. While the number and incidence of trade restrictions will stay much the same whether the loss is paid for by the party causing it or the party suffering it, exporters will benefit from the former approach (see Dam 1970, pp. 268–70).

The New Themes: TRIPS, TRIMS, and Trade in Services

Of the three new themes, TRIPs (trade-related intellectual property rights) have vied with services for first place as the principal bone of contention between industrial and developing countries. Developing-country resistance to discussion of new themes has mostly been a reaction to U.S. pressure to bring trade and foreign investment rules applicable to services into the GATT, but since the stalemate on services was broken, TRIPS have been leading the field by a narrow margin. TRIMS (trade-related investment measures) now seem the least likely candidate for a sustained confrontation, partly because the political and technical costs of enlarging the GATT to deal with them seem prohibitive and partly because some of the TRIM issues would in any case be covered by negotiations on trade in services. This discussion of the new themes will therefore be confined to TRIPS and trade in services.[2]

TRIPS. Intellectual property rights are crucial to developed countries for the strategic reasons already mentioned. The United States has increasingly used the issue to justify unilateral pressure, especially on the more advanced developing countries, to obtain (preferential) changes in their property rights legislation. (A recent example is the imposition by the United States of trade-restrictive measures on Brazilian products following an investigation under Section 301 of the U.S. Trade Act concerning alleged infringement of U.S. pharmaceutical patents.)

Developed countries are increasingly dissatisfied with the shortcomings of the regime for regulating intellectual property, both in its coverage and enforcement in general, and in its inadequate protection of patent and copyright, particularly in new fields like biotechnology, semiconductor chips, and software (see Benko 1988, p. 221ff.)

At stake is whether regulation of intellectual property rights will be transferred to the GATT from such organizations as the World Intellectual Property Organization (WIPO) or UNESCO. Developed countries see the Punta del Este negotiations mandate as justifying the transfer; developing countries have stressed that the trade-related aspects are limited. Beyond their political opposition to a transfer they consider against their interests, the developing countries feel that property rights legislation overprotects monopoly rights at the expense of issues vital to themselves, such as access to technology and limitation of exports.

The interests of the several groups of developing countries differ on the TRIPS issue. Some, like Hong Kong, favor policies similar to those advocated by developed countries. Among those more disposed to negotiate some, such as Argentina and Colombia, are mainly interested in the issue as a pawn in other negotiations; for others (Korea and Mexico) the issue is important in itself. Brazil, Egypt, and India are particularly reluctant to see the GATT setting and enforcing rules in this field.

As with services, discussion of the issue is hampered by the lack of reliable estimates of the economic impacts: the principal U.S. document on the issue (U.S. ITC 1988) reports total "losses" of $23.8 billion—an unchecked figure reported by U.S. firms using unknown procedures. Lack of credible evidence tends to concentrate the negotiations on principles and frustrates any progress towards consensus.

---

2. For a detailed treatment of the TRIMS issues at stake in the Uruguay Round, see Commonwealth Secretariat (1988).

It has been suggested that developing countries, rather than resisting the proposed intellectual property agenda and trying to maintain the present position as one of equilibrium, should take into account that, if there is no GATT agreement on TRIPs, the present position will deteriorate, because developed countries will become much more aggressive in their rule-enforcing bilateral efforts. A closely related argument is that a new arrangement will be reached irrespective of developing-country resistance, if need be on the fringes of GATT and based on conditional MFN rules. Such initiatives must menace progress in other negotiating groups and, more generally, further threaten the major GATT principles. Breakthrough in this difficult area probably depends on cross-issue negotiations, since developing countries stand to gain little otherwise.

Services. The U.S. emphasis on liberalizing trade in services arises from significant structural changes taking place in industrial countries in the producer services—telecommunications; engineering; financial and legal consultancy; insurance, banking, and other financial services; advertising; distribution; and data processing. Advances in communication and information technology have had a profound impact on the competitiveness and foreign expansion of firms that provide such services. U.S. firms want to expand and compete abroad, and they can only do so by being near the customer (U.S. Congress 1986, p. 43). But most countries restrict the foreign provision of services.

The misgivings of the developing countries—particularly those G-10 countries such as Brazil, Egypt, India, and Yugoslavia that have a substantive and immediate interest in the issue, both as importers and exporters—are rooted in two distinct sets of arguments. The first set concerns the backlog of unfinished business on trade in goods. Developing countries argue that this backlog should be tackled before proceeding to the services negotiation, so as to avoid cross bargains which are bound to weaken their bargaining position on the traditional themes. And the G-10 countries point out that discussion of services (apart from the strictly legal point that services are clearly outside the scope of the General Agreement), is bound to raise questions about right of establishment, national treatment, and other complex and politically sensitive issues. In fact, the introduction of the discussion on services in the GATT was seen as a blatantly one-sided approach to issues relating to foreign direct investment crucial to developing countries, such as right of access to technology in the developed countries and a code on restrictive business practices by transnational corporations. The contradictory U.S. stance on these themes in the United Nations, where the United States has effectively blocked discussion of a code of conduct for transnational corporations, has also been noted (see Maciel 1986, p. 90). Last but not least, the agenda initially proposed by developed countries concentrated unduly on capital-related services and excluded labor-intensive services that are of much more interest for developing countries.

The second set of arguments put forward by G-10 countries (see Batista 1987, p. 1) is that too little is known about transactions in international services to predict the implications of trade liberalization. Trade and industrial policies toward the rapidly changing producer-services sectors are clearly crucial for economic development. First, as intermediate inputs, the provision of these services at internationally competitive prices is important to maintain efficiency and export growth. Second, these new activities have important backward linkages with the production of hardware and technological capability in the domestic industrial sector.

Assessing the benefits a particular country might gain from liberalizing transactions in services is hampered by conceptual problems and the paucity of data on the structure of protection and the prevalence of nonprice restraints. The developing countries' stand against trade liberalization in this area has been built on the assumption that static gains will be unevenly distributed, since comparative advantage is concentrated in a few developed countries and developing countries would be thwarted from realizing their comparative advantage (see Nayyar 1986).

Understanding of what is at stake has advanced in the last few years: the stand of countries such as Brazil and India is no longer seen as mere filibuster. The opposing views have acted as a powerful stimulant to clearer thinking on how to advance negotiations. But empirical work on the advantages of liberalization has not kept pace with these advances. Estimates of the costs of protection are almost as fragmentary and incomplete as they were when the United States started to press for inclusion of the issue in the agenda of the new round.

Sectoral lobbies in the developed countries, especially the United States, responding positively to the initiative of a handful of more active developing countries, have begun to lay the groundwork for the developed countries to develop a more balanced proposal, in line with the Punta del Este decision that the multilateral rules on trade in services should promote economic growth for all and contribute to the growth of developing countries (see Richardson 1988, p. 9). Signs of receptiveness in developed countries to proposals freeing the flow of labor services, and proposals mentioning the need to assure an adequate flow of technologies, suggest that there are grounds for developing countries to begin to believe that there is something to negotiate.

Developing countries may, as many have noted, pay a high price for abstaining from negotiating (see Bhagwati 1987b, p. 565ff.). As merely obstructive negotiating tactics began to lose momentum, through repeated use or flagging support in the capitals, and the uncompromising stand of developed countries began to thaw, the idea that developing countries should assume a position of *demandeurs* gained strength (see Sampson 1988a, p. 108). The demands in question relate to specific sectors, such as the possibility of technological absorption through joint ventures as well as improved market access. The advantages of improved availability of services for competitiveness in the supply of goods could be another basis for negotiation. There is scope for cooperation in establishing new rules that would fulfill the Punta del Este mandate in its entirety. (See, for instance, for proposed principles of behavior by producers, appropriate regulation, and development compatibility, Richardson 1988, pp. 8–10.)

IV. Coalitions: Old and New

Together, developing countries constitute a more important market than the United States: if united, they would obviously be a force to reckon with in the GATT negotiations. But though coalition formation by developing countries has a long history in other multilateral agencies, coalitions have been less common in the GATT, where informal consensus rather than United Nations–style divided vote is the usual procedure for reaching a decision. And a coalition encompassing all developing countries would be harder to achieve than in the past, when the interests of developing countries were much more homogeneous than they are today. In fact, the only defined coalition of exclusively developing countries to emerge in the 1980s has been the G-10 Group, whose objective was to block the inclusion of services in the new Round's agenda.

An active coalition since Punta del Este, as noted above, has been the Cairns Group of countries against agricultural protectionism, an issue-based group of both industrial and developing countries.[3] But hopes that other issue-based coalitions would follow this example have proved unfounded. The so-called Hotel de la Paix group, whose membership roughly coincides with the group supporting the Swiss-Colombian draft in 1986, is by no means based on issues, and while joint proposals have been presented in certain GATT negotiating groups (those on safeguards and natural resources), these initiatives do not seem to presage more formal coalition formation. (See Hamilton and Whalley 1988, pp. 36–37.)

The prospects for developing-country coalitions based on concrete economic aims can be gauged by examining their convergent interests (for a previous attempt, see Kahler and Odell 1988). Developing countries are *demandeurs* in four major GATT fields: textiles, tropical products, agriculture, and market access; they may become *demandeurs* in services but are unlikely to do so for the other new themes. As *demandeurs* in services, the core G-10 countries probably have reasons to revive their coalition.

Textile liberalization is the only issue that, according to new evidence, would interest all developing countries (though not with the same intensity). Major economies to benefit include Brazil, China, Indonesia, Korea, Singapore, and Taiwan, but surprisingly not India. Unfortunately, substantive discussion of this vital issue has been delayed by the renewal of MFA to 1991.

Developing countries are divided on both tropical products and agriculture. Countries that are members of preferential trading areas are less interested in liberalizing tropical products than nonmembers, since liberalization would erode their preferences. Interests diverge even more over agriculture. Food importers such as Korea, Sub-Saharan Africa, and some countries of the Middle East would lose from liberalization. Their trade losses are not very significant if compared

---

3. Differences of views within the Cairns Group should not be underestimated, especially in connection with S&D.

with gains by major suppliers, but net welfare losses in connection with grains are substantial. Liberalizing trade in agriculture would benefit a few large developing countries such as Argentina and Brazil.

Improving market access in developed countries for imports of manufactures from developing countries interests mainly the Asian newly industrialized economies and a few Latin American countries (for instance, Brazil and Mexico). But even here interests are not necessarily entirely convergent, since the products affected tend to differ, the Asian exports being concentrated in more technologically sophisticated goods.

A GATT-related issue of interest for a large group of developing countries is the foreign debt constraint. Trade-debt links in the current negotiations are now restricted to the awkward issue of article XVIII(b) and tangentially to the monitoring of commercial policies being discussed in relation to the functioning of the GATT system. Highly indebted countries, especially in Latin America and Africa, would like to see their foreign debt servicing eased by debtor-country concessions over market access, but such developments are unlikely.

Such fragmentation of interests makes a strong coalition of developing countries unlikely, unless the more advanced developing countries decide that the advantages of such a coalition are worth the costs of making some concessions. The more diversified the interests of a country, the more active it is likely to be in searching for such a coalition.

V. GATT Negotiations in a Global Perspective

Developing-country commitment to trade policies that enhance market efficiency is growing, partly as a result of conviction, partly in response to conditions imposed by multilateral agencies. Developed countries emphasize liberalization of obstacles to the flow of services and foreign investment, rather than to trade in goods. Only for agricultural goods is there a major trading country—the United States—with a special interest in liberalizing trade, and even here the U.S. initiative is likely to be impeded by the protectionist interests of the EC, Japan, and the smaller European economies.

Besides showing a patent disinclination to tackle the backlog of unresolved GATT issues, developed countries, especially the United States, have been shifting their policy in a direction that short-circuits the multilateral trade system through a net of bilaterally negotiated preferential arrangements. Conversely, the idea of a "level playing field" for all GATT members raises the specter of full reciprocity—as opposed to what has been called first-difference reciprocity (see Bhagwati 1987b, p. 564)—with S&D as a main target, and it threatens developing countries' claims that, since so much of the protection backlog consists of de facto disrespect of GATT law by developed countries, it should be rolled back at no cost in terms of new concessions by developing countries.

The present multilateral system is a direct consequence of U.S. trade policies since 1934, and U.S. emphasis on the most favored nation clause. The system is far from perfect, but has on balance permitted considerable reduction of trade barriers and fast growth of trade. A host of illegal, barely legal, and legal exceptions to the rules have been allowed from the start. At present, the multilateral system is under serious threat from the U.S. Omnibus Trade Bill, with its mercantilist emphasis on the need to redress unbalanced trade through bilateral trade instruments that do not conform with GATT rules. Unless the U.S. government modifies this legislation, the multilateral system is in grave danger.

The interest of developing countries is best served by strengthening the GATT, not undermining it. Developing-country commitment to GATT's legal framework is not, as is sometimes claimed, lip service. It is in line with their fragile bargaining position with their major industrialized trade partners.

Uneven distribution of gains and losses among different developing countries creates vested interests against negotiating liberalizing policies in the GATT. Such difficulties can only be surmounted if all parties gain something in the process.

Developing countries are *demandeurs* in tropical products, and likely to obtain concessions. Substantial advance in reducing agricultural protectionism is essential for advance in negotiations as a whole. The losses suffered by the small developing countries will have to be considered and compensated either directly or indirectly. Textiles and clothing are too important to be left out of the negotiations. The developed countries are in a very weak position to ask developing countries to liberalize tariffs if they are not prepared to reciprocate with a long-term commitment to discontinue the MFA and reduce the relevant tariffs. In a constructive negotiation, developed countries would need to concede something on article XVIII over the market access issue—certainly on disciplines concerning parts (b) and (c) and possibly a time restriction on the use of quantitative restrictions and a legalization of the use of nondiscriminatory tariff surcharges. Article XIX is perhaps the most intriguing pending issue in the GATT, since the avoidance of safeguards has consolidated a low-level equilibrium and no party feels strongly enough to press for the reform of the rules.

It is not altogether clear how to evaluate changes in GATT institutional matters. In principle, improvement in enforcement and dispute settlement should assure balanced application of such new provisions and consequently the support of those contracting parties more interested in strengthening the GATT.

In TRIPs and TRIMs, the developed countries are *demandeurs*, and it is difficult to see how developing countries could be lured from their defensive position since they do not stand to gain from rule setting and enforcement. Much will depend on how much developed countries offer concessions in other negotiating groups. Services, however, seem to leave scope for an exchange of concessions involving detailed negotiations on a sector by sector basis.

A trade liberalization in developed countries in 1983 would have increased their imports by about 12 percent (roughly $30 billion) (Laird and Yeats 1986, p. 29). It is easy to imagine fluctuations of exchange rates, interest rates, and the level of economic activity in the developed countries having a similar impact on the exports of developing countries. The drawbacks of restricting negotiations to trade topics, to the exclusion of related issues (such as the debt problem) that are crucial to many developing countries, need to be considered.

The matter of linking trade and debt questions is certainly vexing. In 1985 the authoritative Leutwiler Report (GATT 1985, p. 49) stated that "the health and even the maintenance of the trading system . . . are linked to a satisfactory resolution of the world debt problem . . ." In the early days of the debt crisis it was naively thought that the debtors' leverage in obtaining access to the creditor countries' markets would increase. In the event, commercial banks not only refrained from lobbying to improve market access for debtor countries' exports, they even turned initial ideas about the trade-debt link upside down by backing U.S. insistence on obtaining rights to establish service industries in developing countries. Another trade-debt complication is the apparent contradiction between GATT's traditional reciprocal basis of negotiation, and unilateral liberalization arising from conditions imposed on borrowers by multilateral lending agencies. These tariff reductions even if not bound are unlikely to be taken into account as concessions in the future. Export performance in some of these indebted economies since the beginning of the decade has been at least as good as those of the Asian newly industrializing economies, but their GDP per capita stagnated.

Views on liberalization tend to differ over timing and sectoral distribution rather than its inherent validity. Trade liberalization by highly indebted developing countries without a corresponding liberalization by developed countries requires bigger devaluations than a concerted move by both. (Sachs 1987 has cogently advanced the prior claims of fiscal equilibrium and price stability over trade liberalization, stressing the impact of devaluation on the public deficit and on the level of inflation.) Or the reduction in trade surpluses could be compensated by much larger transitory financial support for liberalization reform than is envisaged at present. (Anjaria 1987 finds trade liberalization a worthy justification for conceding fresh foreign finance, but he believes that this role is already played by the IMF.) The debt question is paramount for many GATT members. For them to participate meaningfully in the Round, the present unstable debt position needs to be settled in such a way as to segregate old and new debt and start the process of restoring normalcy to world financial markets.

Fragmentation of the GATT and the multilateral trading system based on the MFN principle would not be in the interest of developing countries. The weakest have most to fear from the abandonment of rule. To strengthen the GATT, developing countries need to launch more positive negotiating programs, and more often adopt the position of *demandeurs*. The need to liberalize and restructure is by no means restricted to developing countries. There is scope for mutually beneficial negotiation.

References

Abreu, Marcelo de Paiva, and W. Fritsch. 1987. "Brazil, Latin America and the Caribbean." In J. Whalley, ed., *Dealing with the North: Developing Countries and the Global Trading System*. London, Canada: University of Western Ontario.

———. 1988. "New Themes and Agriculture in the New Round: A View from the South." *Texto para Discussao* 188. Rio de Janeiro, Brazil: Department of Economics, Catholic University.

Anjaria, S. J. 1987. "Balance of Payments and Related Issues in the Uruguay Round of Trade Negotiations." *World Bank Economic Review* 1, no. 4 (September): 669–88.

Batista, P. N. 1987. "Trade in Services: Brazilian View of the Negotiating Process." Statement Made at the General Debate in the Group of Negotiations on Services by Head of the Brazilian Delegation, Geneva, GATT. Processed.

Benko, R. P. 1988. "Intellectual Property Rights and the Uruguay Round." *World Economy* 11, no. 2: 217–32.

Bhagwati, J. N. 1987a. "Economic Costs of Trade Restrictions." In J. Michael Finger and Andrzej Olechowski, eds., *The Uruguay Round: A Handbook for the Multilateral Trade Negotiations*. Washington, D.C.: World Bank.

———. 1987b. "Trade in Services and the Multilateral Trade Negotiations." *World Bank Economic Review* 1, no. 4 (September): 549–69.

Cable, V. 1986. "Textiles and Clothing in a New Trade Round." London: Commonwealth Secretariat. Processed.

———. 1987a. "Textiles and Clothing in a New Round of Trade Negotiations." *World Bank Economic Review* 1, no. 4 (September): 619–46.

———. 1987b. "Tropical Products." In J. Michael Finger and Andrzej Olechowski, eds., *The Uruguay Round: A Handbook for the Multilateral Trade Negotiations*. Washington, D.C.: World Bank.

Cline, W. R. 1987. *The Future of World Trade in Textiles and Apparel*. Washington, D.C.: Institute of International Economics.

Commonwealth Secretariat. 1987. "Tropical Products in the Uruguay Round: An Overview." London. Processed.

———. 1988. "Trade-Related Investment Measures in the Uruguay Round: Some Issues for Consideration." London. Processed.

Dam, K. W. 1970. *The GATT: Law and the International Economic Organization*. Chicago: University of Chicago Press.

Erzan, R., and G. Karsenty. 1987. *Products Facing High Tariffs in Major Developed Market Economy Countries: An Area of Priority for Developing Countries in the Uruguay Round?* UNCTAD Discussion Paper 22. Geneva.

Finger, J. Michael. 1987. "Antidumping and Antisubsidy Measures." In J. Michael Finger and Andrzej Olechowski, eds., *The Uruguay Round: A Handbook for the Multilateral Trade Negotiations*. Washington, D.C.: World Bank.

Finger, J. Michael, and Julio Nogués. 1987. "International Control of Subsidies and Countervailing Duties." *World Bank Economic Review* 1, no. 4 (September): 707–25.

Fritsch, W. 1989. "The New Minilateralism and Developing Countries." In J. J. Scott, ed., *Free Trade Areas and U.S. Trade Policy*. Washington, D.C.: Institute for International Economics.

Gardner, R. N. 1979. *Sterling-Dollar Diplomacy*. New York: Oxford University Press.

GATT (General Agreement on Tariffs and Trade). 1958. *Trends in International Trade*. A Report by a Panel of Experts. Geneva.

———. 1979. *The Tokyo Round of Multilateral Trade Negotiations*. Geneva: GATT.

———. 1985. *Trade Policies for a Better Future [The Leutwiler Report]. Proposals for Action*. Geneva.

———. 1986. Press Release 1396, September 25.

———. 1988a. *Multilateral Trade Negotiations. The Uruguay Round. Group of Negotiations on Goods, Report to the Trade Negotiations Committee Meeting at Ministerial Level, Montreal, December 1988*. MTN.GNG/13. Geneva.

———. 1988b. *Multilateral Trade Negotiations. The Uruguay Round. Group of Negotiations in Services, Report on the Trade Negotiations Meeting at Ministerial Level, Montreal, December 1988*. MTN.GNG/21. Geneva.

Hamilton, C., and J. Whalley. 1988. *Coalitions in the Uruguay Round: The Extent, Pros and Cons of Developing Country Participation*. National Bureau of Economic Research Working Paper 2751. Cambridge, Mass.

Hindley, B. 1987. "GATT Safeguards and Voluntary Export Restraints: What Are the Interests of Developing Countries?" *World Bank Economic Review* 1, no. 4 (September): 689–705.

Hudec, R. 1987. *Developing Countries in the GATT Legal System*. London: Gower for the Trade Policy Research Centre.

Josling, T., and S. Tangermann. 1988. "Measuring Levels of Protection in Agriculture." Twentieth International Conference of Agricultural Economists, Invited Papers, volume 2. August 24–31, Buenos Aires. Processed.

Kahler, M., and J. Odell. 1988. "Developing-Country Coalition Building and International Trade Negotiations." In J. Whalley, ed., *Rules, Power and Credibility*. London, Canada: University of Western Ontario.

Karsenty, G., and S. Laird. 1986. *The Generalized System of Preferences: A Quantitative Assessment of Direct Trade Effects and Policy Options*. UNCTAD Discussion Papers 18. Geneva.

Kelly, M., N. Kirmany, M. Xafa, C. Boonekamp, and P. Winglee. 1988. *Issues and Developments in International Trade Policy*. International Monetary Fund Occasional Paper 63. Washington, D.C.

Kirmani, N., P. Molajoni, and T. Mayer. 1984. "Effects of Increased Market Access on Selected Developing Countries' Export Earnings: An Illustrative Exercise." International Monetary Fund DM 84/54. Washington, D.C. Processed.

Laird, S., and Julio Nogués. 1988. "Trade Policies and the Debt Crisis." World Bank International Economics Department. Washington, D.C. Processed.

Laird, S., and A. Yeats. 1986. *The UNCTAD Trade Policy Simulation Model: A Note on the Methodology, Data and Uses*. UNCTAD Discussion Papers. Geneva.

———. 1987. "Tariff Cutting Formulas—and Complications." In J. Michael Finger and Andrzej Olechowski, eds., *The Uruguay Round: A Handbook for the Multilateral Trade Negotiations*. Washington, D.C.: World Bank.

Luyten, P. 1988. "Multilateralism versus Preferential Bilateralism: A European View." In J. J. Scott, ed., *Free Trade Areas and U.S. Trade Policy*. Washington D.C. Institute for International Economics.

Maciel, G. A. 1989. "O Brasil e o GATT." *Contexto Internacional* 3 (January/July).

MacPhee, C. R. 1986. "Effect of Competitive Need Exclusions and Redesignation under the U.S. Scheme of Generalized Preferences." UNCTAD/ST/MD/29. Geneva. Processed.

MOCI (Switzerland). 1989. No. 849, January 2.

Nam, G. 1987. "Export-Promoting Subsidies, Countervailing Threats, and the General Agreement on Trade and Tariffs." *World Bank Economic Review* 1, no. 4 (September): 727–43.

Nayyar, D. 1986. "International Trade in Services: Implications for Developing Countries." Exim Bank Commencement Day Annual Lecture. Bombay.

News of the Uruguay Round. 1988. "Text adopted by Ministers in Montreal." MTN.TNC/7(MIN), December 9. Reproduced in *News of the Uruguay Round* 23 (December 14).

News of the Uruguay Round. 1989. "Text adopted by Ministers in Montreal." TNC/11, April 21. Reproduced in *News of the Uruguay Round* 27 (April 24).

Raffaelli, M. 1989. "Some Considerations on the Multi-Fibre Arrangement: Past, Present and Future." Geneva: GATT. Processed.

Richardson, J. B. 1988. "Some Thoughts on Dealing with Development in an Agreement on Trade in Services." Paper presented to the Roundtable on the Role of the Service Sector in the Development Process, Schloss Fuschl, Austria, July 1–3.

Sachs, J. D. 1987. "Trade and Exchange Rate Policies in Growth-Oriented Adjustment Programs." IMF-World Bank Symposium on Growth-Oriented Adjustment Programs. Washington D.C., February. Processed.

Sampson, G. 1988a. "Developing Countries and the Liberalization of Trade in Services." In J. Whalley, ed., *Rules, Power and Credibility*. London, Canada: University of Western Ontario.

———. 1988b. "Nontariff Barriers Facing Developing Country Exports." In J. Whalley, ed., *Rules, Power and Credibility*. London, Canada: University of Western Ontario.

Silberston, A. 1984. *The MFA and the UK Economy*. London: Her Majesty's Stationery Office.

Trela, I., and J. Whalley. 1988. "Do Developing Countries Lose from the MFA?" Department of Economics, University of Western Ontario. Working Paper 8804C. London, Canada. Processed.

U. S. Congress Office of Technological Assessment. 1986. *Trade in Services, Exports and Foreign Revenues.* Washington, D.C.

U. S. International Trade Commission. 1988. *Foreign Protection of Intellectual Property Rights and the Effect on U.S. Industry and Trade.* Washington, D.C.

UNCTAD (U.N. Conference on Trade and Development) Secretariat. 1968. *The Kennedy Round Estimated Effects on Tariff Barriers.* Doc. TD/6/rev.1. New York.

Valdés, Alberto. 1987. "Agriculture in the Uruguay Round: Interests of Developing Countries." *World Bank Economic Review* 1, no. 4 (September): 571–93.

Valdés, Alberto, and J. Zietz. 1980. *Agricultural Protection in OECD Countries: Its Cost to Less-Developed Countries.* International Food Policy Research Institute, Research Report 21. Washington, D.C.

Warley, T. K. 1976. "Western Trade in Agricultural Problems." In A. Shonfield, ed., *International Economic Relations of the Western World 1959–1971. Volume 1. Politics and Trade.* London: Royal Institute of International Affairs and Oxford University Press.

Winham, G. R. 1986. *International Trade and the Tokyo Round Negotiations.* Princeton, N.J.: Princeton University Press.

Wolf, Martin. 1987. "Differential and More Favorable Treatment of Developing Countries and the International Trading System." *World Bank Economic Review* 1, no. 4 (September): 647–68.

World Bank. 1986. *World Development Report 1986*. New York: Oxford University Press.

———. 1987. *World Development Report 1987*. New York: Oxford University Press.

Yeats, A. 1987. "The Escalation of Trade Barriers." In J. Michael Finger and Andrzej Olechowski, eds., *The Uruguay Round: A Handbook for the Multilateral Trade Negotiations*. Washington, D.C: World Bank.

Zietz, J., and Alberto Valdés. 1986. *The Costs of Protectionism to Developing Countries: An Analysis for Selected Agricultural Products*. World Bank Staff Working Paper 769. Washington, D.C.

Comment on "Developing Countries and the Uruguay Round of Trade Negotiations," by Abreu

Andrzej Olechowski

I always find it very exciting to discuss the GATT and the Uruguay Round, and I do so whenever I am in Geneva or Washington. I rarely do it in Warsaw. The irony is that I am heading a department which in the Polish administration is responsible for GATT issues.

This observation sets the tenor of my intervention. I would like in these brief comments to look at the issues cogently discussed by Professor Abreu specifically from the point of view of Poland—that is, from the point of view of a country that is medium-size, developing, heavily indebted, and undergoing a major political and economic reform aimed at internal and external liberalization.

Given the above characteristics, the GATT should be very important for Poland. First, it should secure free access for Polish products to the major export markets. Second, through article XIX it should protect our exporters from unrestrained protective actions in the importing countries—a feature particularly important for a middle-income country, which, to a large extent, exports products and services considered "sensitive" by the importing countries (such as steel, shipbuilding, petrochemicals). Third, it should provide guidelines for domestic policies and regulations, and impose discipline on the ways trade policy is carried out.

Thus, in Poland we see the GATT the same way as its founding fathers—as a strong commitment by each participating country to keep its markets open to imports. The safeguard clause provides a way to maintain this general commitment in the face of unusual trade developments affecting isolated industries.

In practice, the GATT is not effective in fulfilling its role. Owing to certain features of Poland's protocol of accession, the most favored nation (MFN) treatment in some countries—notably the United States and the European Community countries, or major trading partners—is viewed as a unilateral concession and therefore open to political maneuvering. Secondly, the GATT safeguard procedures do not shield our exports from import-restrictive actions in the form of "voluntary" export restraints (VERs). Poland, after Japan, is subject to the largest number of VERs, which cover many agricultural, textile, steel, and other industrial

---

Andrzej Olechowski is Director, Ministry of Foreign Economic Relations, Government of Poland. The views expressed are the author's and not those of the Government of Poland.

© 1990 The International Bank for Reconstruction and Development / THE WORLD BANK.

products. Finally, because of these restrictions and the general lack of international discipline, "GATT consistency" is not a persuasive argument when decisions on domestic policies and regulations are made. It is often adhered to only superficially, while substance and practice remain in conflict with GATT principles.

How, in this context, do the politicians and the general public in Poland view the Uruguay Round? I believe that the prime minister has only a vague idea of what the Round is about, not to mention the president or the public. But two issues could attract considerable attention and make a significant impact on the Polish economy: agriculture and services.

Both sectors are facing radical reform in Poland in the shape of a thorough demonopolization and extensive privatization. The reform is meeting strong resistance from pressure groups who cite short-term decline in production and uncertainty about external conditions as the main grounds for their opposition. Their resistance would be much easier to overcome if there were (even tentative) Uruguay Round agreements as to the principal future conditions for international trade in these sectors. The agreements would need to be accompanied by strengthened commitment to the safeguard rules. Otherwise, guided by past experience, politicians would hesitate to risk opening domestic markets for agricultural products and services to external competition, with no guarantee that other countries would do the same.

These considerations are also germane to some other developing countries. Many of them, faced by the collapse of the central planning concept and attracted by the successes of the market economies, are rethinking their economic systems and development strategies. In many respects, many developing countries are now at the same stage that industrial countries were when the GATT was formulated. Unfortunately, the developed countries have moved on to a stage where (often very narrow) reciprocity has become the dominant issue.

Comment on "Developing Countries and the Uruguay Round of Trade Negotiations," by Abreu

Gary P. Sampson

As mentioned in Professor Abreu's useful and comprehensive review, the December 1988 Mid-Term Ministerial Review in Montreal did not reach consensus in four of the fifteen Uruguay Round negotiating groups: agriculture, textiles, intellectual property, and safeguards. All these areas are important to developing countries for different reasons. Because the Uruguay Round is a political undertaking, the process was put "on hold." Agreement in the outstanding areas was finally reached at a meeting of the Trade Negotiations Committee in April 1989. Since Professor Abreu completed his paper before the April meeting, my comments supplement his paper and report on the current state of play.

With respect to agriculture, at Montreal, the United States and the Cairns Group (four developed and ten developing countries) proposed the long-term elimination of restrictions on market access and other trade-distorting policies, such as subsidies. The Cairns Group also proposed that in 1989 and 1990, short-term measures should be adopted to freeze and gradually reduce farm support measures. The European Community, however, emphasized the need for short-term measures based on existing policies to reduce support for agriculture. For the United States, agreement on long-term measures to eliminate farm support was a prerequisite for any discussion of such short-term measures. As for the long term, the European Community proposed to stabilize world markets by reducing the negative effects of agricultural support measures and rebalancing external protection policies. This fell short of the U.S. proposal for long-term elimination of farm support.

Not surprisingly, the agreement reached in April represents a compromise: in the long term, the objective is a "substantial progressive reduction in agricultural support." Commitments are to be negotiated for import access, subsidies and export competition, and export prohibitions and restrictions. In the short term, farm support is to be frozen at current levels of domestic and export support and protection.

Gary Sampson is Director, Group of Negotiations on Services Division, GATT. The views expressed are those of the author and not necessarily those of the organization for which he works.

© 1990 The International Bank for Reconstruction and Development / THE WORLD BANK.

Governments are to come forward with negotiating proposals by the end of 1989 on a list of topics that represents a formidable research agenda for policy-oriented agricultural economists. Topics include ways to adapt existing farm support (for instance, moving to tariffs and decoupling income support from production levels), how to take account of the possible harm the reform process might do to developing countries that are net importers of food, and the form of and use to which measures of aggregate farm support will be put. The task is daunting. The complexity of interest groups involved within and across countries is staggering, and most known intervention measures are currently being employed in this sector.

It seems fair to say that there were four breakthroughs in the negotiations on agriculture. First, for the first time in the negotiating history of the General Agreement on Tariffs and Trade (GATT) all forms of agricultural protection are now on the table. Second, there is definitely scope for the special status of agriculture to disappear over time. Third, there is agreement to freeze existing levels of protection and reduce them in the future. Fourth, and in some respects most important, governments are now engaged in a permanent state of negotiation.

As for textiles, negotiators at Montreal faced the issue of how far governments were prepared to commit themselves to dismantling the Multifibre Arrangement (MFA) and in what period of time. In the April agreement there is, for the first time, a clear commitment to negotiate an end to the MFA and to start phasing out the network of bilateral restraint arrangements in 1991.

I would tend to take issue with Abreu's assessment that textiles are unlikely to play a prominent role in the Uruguay Round because the present Multi-Fibre Arrangement is to end only in 1991. It could be argued that the expiration date of the present MFA allows countries to make a negotiated removal of the MFA part of the total negotiating package. In fact this was a consideration when the last expiration date was negotiated.

The challenge is to find a mechanism that would permit the gradual undoing of the damage from three decades of bilateral restraint arrangements and the return of textile trade to an open, liberal trading system in which decisions to produce and consume respond to relative prices rather than bilaterally negotiated limits on quantitative restraints. This may seem a good topic for an undergraduate term paper, but the issues are complex. Many participating countries see the existing arrangement as representing some balance of perceived interests in the importing and exporting countries. To be acceptable, the proposed mechanism should maintain this balance during the phaseout period.

As Abreu notes, a principal issue in negotiations about trade-related aspects of intellectual property rights (including trade in counterfeit goods) is the institutional question of whether a new set of rules involving enforcement and settlement of disputes will be negotiated in the GATT in spite of the previous role of organizations such as the World Intellectual Property Organization. The fundamental point is that different countries see their interests as better represented in one institution or the other. The compromise struck in April was to continue the GATT negotiations but to decide at the end of the Uruguay Round which institutions should implement the rules.

I agree with Professor Abreu that in many ways negotiating a new safeguards clause (Article XIX) is "the most intriguing pending issue in GATT." Indeed, for any self-respecting economist the goal should be to establish under what circumstances sudden surges of imports may be legitimately restrained for a short period without damaging the long-term interests of the economy. The procedures should avoid insulating producers from market forces that herald the need for healthy changes in patterns of production and consumption. The management of world trade in textile products provides clear evidence that such insulation only creates vested interest groups and exacerbates long-term adjustment problems. As Abreu notes, issues such as selectivity (selective application of safeguard protection to specific countries) prevail, and are a major concern for some developing countries that see themselves as potential candidates for such selective treatment. The compromise in the April Mid-Term text is largely procedural; it was agreed that a draft text was to be prepared by the chairman of the Negotiating Group on Safeguards in conjunction with the GATT Secretariat and presented to the Negotiating Group by June 1989.

It is hard to think of new theoretical or empirical research on safeguards which would be useful. Generations of economists have argued that market disturbances reflecting changing patterns of comparative advantage are all part of the normal workings of the market, while market disturbances related to dumping and subsidies can be dealt with through other procedures. If there is to be government intervention on import surges, it should be designed to facilitate rather than retard the process of market-led structural change.

I would like to make a few comments on the area of my own responsibility in GATT: negotiations to create a multilateral framework for trade in services in order to progressively liberalize this trade and promote the economic growth of all trading partners and the growth of developing countries. I will concentrate on three issues of importance to developing countries that emerged in the Montreal discussions.

First, there is no clear definition of what constitutes trade in services (variously described as trade in invisibles, intangibles, and so on), so the nature of transactions to which the multilateral framework will apply is something to be negotiated. One way of defining trade in services is to draw a parallel with trade in goods—that is, something (presumably the service itself) must cross the border for trade to take place (as when some telecommunications services are traded). A definition at the other end of the spectrum would embrace those service transactions that require a foreign presence and a cross-border movement of factors of production (labor and capital) to be marketed internationally (for example, retail banking services). Some developing countries seem to have been of two minds. Opting for a narrow definition would meet some concerns. For example, it would minimize the impact of foreign firms on nascent infrastructural industries that for a variety of reasons some countries wish to maintain even if they are internationally uncompetitive. At the same time, only a broad definition would ensure the flow of resources and technology necessary to promote development and therefore fulfill the negotiating objectives of the Punta del Este Declaration. Not surprisingly, lines tended to be drawn according to whether individual countries preferred outward or inward development strategies. The question was not settled at Montreal, but the door was certainly opened to a broad definition of trade in services. The text provides that future work in the negotiating group will proceed on the basis of trade in services involving cross-border movement of services, of consumers (as in tourism), and of factors of production, where this is essential to sell the service abroad.

A second issue important to developing countries is sectoral coverage of the multilateral framework in services. Some developing countries have been under the impression that sectors in which they possess a comparative advantage will not be covered either because of sensitivities (for example, about labor mobility in construction services) or because little can be done in such an arrangement to help expand their trade (such as tourism). In Montreal, the question of coverage was dealt with by agreeing not only that no sector would be excluded from the arrangement but also that sectors of export interest to developing countries should be specifically included in the arrangement.

Third, with respect to a point raised in the paper, some developing countries have been reluctant to engage in negotiations to liberalize trade in services. I agree that "opposing views concerning trade in services negotiations acted as a powerful stimulant to clearer thinking concerning ways to advance the negotiations." Abreu points out some reasons for this resistance, but basically the varying degrees of enthusiasm probably reflect the fact that some countries consider the link between liberalization and development to be tenuous at best. In the view of these countries, a framework supportive of development would need provisions that take account of the difficulties developing countries face in immediately implementing full obligations under the arrangement, and that introduce concepts that would strengthen the link between liberalization and development.

The Montreal text opens the way for introducing concepts that will minimize the damage of rapid liberalization in developing countries. It recognizes, for example, the need for rules and procedures for developing countries to extend market access progressively in line with their development situation. And the door is also open for provisions to increase the developing countries' participation in world trade in services and expand their own exports of services by strengthening their domestic capacity in services and making the sector more efficient and competitive.

The challenge facing negotiators from developing countries today is clear. What provisions can be written into the multilateral framework to ensure that developing countries become more efficient and competitive in providing services via the negotiated progressive liberalization of service activities in their countries?

Given the dearth of information on which to base conclusions, there is certainly scope for imaginative thinking.

Finally, the diversity of developing countries' interests, which Professor Abreu stresses in a more general context, is also apparent in the services negotiations. But all developing countries seem to agree on one important point: any development provisions should be an integral part of the agreement itself and not an addendum (as with Part IV of the GATT) or a list of exemptions from obligations (such as special and differential provisions).

Floor Discussion of Abreu Paper

One participant suggested that making debt an essential element of the GATT negotiations would overload already complex negotiations. Presumably the debt crisis will be resolved by another mechanism (guided by the World Bank and the International Monetary Fund) in the next two or three years, he said. The point of the Uruguay Round negotiations, on the other hand, is to establish rules governing trade in the last years of this century and the first years of the next. Abreu responded that steps taken to coordinate efforts in the Bank and the IMF were inadequate in an explosive situation.

Abreu's paper maintained that tariff reductions as part of conditionalities imposed on countries borrowing from the World Bank are unlikely to be considered as concessions later. To the participant who suggested that this is not true if the tariffs are bound, Abreu pointed out that in many countries tariffs cannot be bound because the governments committing themselves to liberalization are not credible. Another participant suggested that if nontariff barriers aren't addressed, it doesn't matter if tariffs are bound. Abreu agreed that it is useless to bind tariffs if GATT Article 18-B provides developing countries an easy way out. To discuss protectionism in the developing countries, he said, something must be done about Article 18-B. As for the thorny question of a tradeoff between Articles 18 and 19, Abreu said it is unclear what Article 19 offers or how that deadlock will be broken, because of vested interests in maintaining voluntary export restraints.

Sampson (discussant) said that solutions proposed to deal with the problem of nontariff barriers include (1) retariffication to replace voluntary export restraints and (2) temporary tariff quotas with a quantitative restriction (imports could be brought in if the penalty tariff were paid, but the penalty tariff would eventually be phased out and replaced by a tariff-based system that would eventually be bound).

On the points raised by Sampson in his comments on Abreu's paper, Abreu agreed that something is being done about textiles in the GATT—but too little and too late. He reemphasized that new evidence suggests that all developing countries would gain from a termination of the Multifibre Arrangement (MFA). A member of the audience commented that it is a big jump from the observation that everybody has something to gain from abolishing the MFA to the conclusion that there is room for a coalition.

This session was chaired by Herminio Blanco, undersecretary of trade, government of Mexico.

© 1990 The International Bank for Reconstruction and Development / THE WORLD BANK.

Abreu said that the evidence about textiles breaks new ground but is still controversial, and even he wonders whether Brazil would benefit from a phaseout of the MFA. He noted that this represented an opportunity for somebody to do some careful empirical work that would suggest a more traditional division of interests on textiles—for example, with China and India for, and Hong Kong, the Republic of Korea, and Taiwan against dismantling the MFA.

On the point about the prospects for a timed phaseout of the MFA, one participant stated that only the threat of other kinds of measures—typically safeguard actions—propel developing countries into these voluntarily negotiated agreements. To make predictions about something concrete happening in textiles, he said, we must look at what else is happening in the trading system in the safeguards area—so observing what happens to safeguards such as steel antidumping measures becomes important.

Phasing the MFA out in such a way that countries feel they are getting a fair deal is crucial to the phaseout's success, said Sampson. For example, some countries extract rent in the trading transaction. Giving that up means trading it off against something else, such as expanded market access elsewhere. Those devising a plan to phase out the MFA are trying to find an objective way to estimate the value of nontariff measures as a basis for negotiating change. The ultimate objective—a bound, nondiscriminatory, most-favored-nation tariff—would be considerably less restrictive than the voluntary export restraint arrangements now in place.

One participant commented on how much more active developing countries had been in this Round compared with the Kennedy and Tokyo Rounds, and how much they had been able to influence the agenda. Sampson agreed, saying that five developing countries—Argentina, Brazil, Chile, Colombia, and Peru—were able to put the negotiations on hold in Montreal. In the services-negotiating group Sampson thought this an important development, because a number of developed countries think that over time the developing countries will be unable to live up to the obligations that come out of the agreed text and will drop out. Sampson did not think that was the way the negotiations would develop. If they do, it would be a bitter fight, because the developing countries were wedded to the Montreal Text—and the far-reaching Montreal Text on services was not put on hold.

Several members of the audience were less optimistic than Abreu and (especially) Sampson about the results of the Uruguay Round. One asked what global mechanisms were being put in place to ensure that all of this was not an exercise in futility—observing that little seemed to have changed since the Tokyo and Kennedy Rounds. Another asked what would happen if the real action took place among the United States, Japan, and the European Community (EC). In the same vein, a third suggested that actions speak louder than words and that the actions of the three major actors in the game suggested that regional trading arrangements are going to be more important than a multilateral trading arrangement within GATT.

Sampson admitted that discipline of the multilateral trading system could be eroded by actions of the Super-301 type, Europe in 1992, the U.S.-Canada bilateral trade agreement, regional liberalization, and an equivalent of the Organisation for Economic Co-operation and Development for the Pacific Rim countries. But he felt that many people believed these possibilities were one way to apply pressure to revive the multilateral trading system. Only time would tell. According to Sampson, in the negotiating group on services the real fight would probably not be about North-South issues but about such issues as whether liberalization in financial services will be on the basis of reciprocity or national treatment between the United States and the EC; or whether the major telecommunication country suppliers will be able to maintain their state monopolies; or, in civil aviation, whether the extensive network of bilateral restraint arrangements will remain or will be replaced by some sort of multilateral agreement. We have signs, Sampson said, that the fight will be fought at a high political level. But he also thought that everyone, at least in the services talks, hoped to make existing agreements conform with whatever emerges successfully from the Uruguay Round.

Olechowski (discussant) said that he was not particularly optimistic about the outcome of the negotiations. Furthermore, he had difficulty in reconciling what one participant said about the Uruguay Round framing rules for the next century and Sampson's comment that once the rules are agreed upon, the current policies will be made to conform to them.

Responding to participants' comments about misplaced optimism, Abreu said that his paper implies that the behavior of the U.S. trade negotiators is slightly schizophrenic and that their bilateral and multilateral policies are contradictory. He exhorted the United States to lead the way toward multilateral trade liberalization, because it is too much to ask a high-inflation indebted country to adjust to unilateral liberalization.

One participant asked Abreu how all of this would help us decide the things we have to decide tomorrow, or next week, or by the end of the century? He asked Abreu to provide an analytical framework to help people at the World Bank decide which approaches on specific issues would strengthen and reform—or weaken and destroy—the GATT system.

Abreu responded that it is not easy to translate the paper into immediate policy actions, but that the World Bank could help deepen understanding of many of the issues being negotiated, particularly the so-called new themes. The basic U.S. document on intellectual property is fundamentally weak, because it is merely a summary of what the industry claims about losses incurred in counterfeiting and the like. Abreu felt that establishing an intellectual property system on the fringes of GATT might weaken GATT, but that he was walking on thin ice with this view.

Similarly, Abreu felt that a lot more had to be learned about services. In 1982, the United States had difficulty convincing people that services should have an important position on the agenda. Abreu thought GATT should include services, because no international organization was doing the job globally, although UNCTAD had been involved in some aspects of services. He believed there would probably be a big political wrangle about intellectual property rights, because the World Intellectual Property Organization would probably fight. And although the developed countries felt that GATT was the ideal venue for intellectual property, the developing countries did not.

It is not easy to know whether extending GATT discipline to services and intellectual property will advance GATT rules. The first obligation, Abreu felt, was to restore GATT legality over trade in goods. The contracting parties had, of course, decided that inclusion of new themes should not be made conditional on solution of the backlog; but Abreu nonetheless felt that the backlog must be dealt with.

Abreu suggested that the Bank should analyze the long-term effects of liberalization in a country such as Brazil, taking into account the possibility that liberalization could backfire and strengthen protectionist lobbies. This line was not being followed in the establishment of conditionalities.

One participant saw negotiations and actual liberalization in services as two very different issues. He argued that it would be extremely difficult to find meaningful criteria to selectively choose services to liberalize. If to do business globally you have to have factor mobility, national treatment, and the right to establish enterprises, and therefore services should be liberalized, then you are really changing the rules of the game and discussing something far beyond GATT. At one extreme, it could imply that the nation-state is no longer relevant in resource allocation and decisionmaking. The issue of whether nation-states should give up their sovereignty to allow national treatment and full factor mobility across all borders is much more important than GATT. What is the use of firms in developed countries having access and national treatment on services, he continued, if currencies aren't convertible, if they can't repatriate their profits, and so on. To make this workable we will have to change the conditions for doing business.

Some countries are not prepared to accept the pure application of GATT rules and principles to services, Sampson responded. For example, it makes sense, and there is a very specific reason, to apply national treatment to goods (under Article 3, a concession granted at the border, such as tariff reduction, should not be negated by a government restriction once inside the border); but services don't pass through customs houses, so offering national treatment to providers of services amounts effectively to free trade—with very different implications.

Sampson agreed that the problem of selective liberalization of services must be dealt with. The Montreal Text indicates that specificity of purpose, discreteness of transaction, and limited duration are to be considered in determining, sector by sector, what will or will not be a service transaction. Overriding all these considerations is the understanding that national policy objectives will be respected; but there is also the sense that countries should not unilaterally erect obstacles to trade that they consider appropriate for their own national objectives.

Blanco (chair) concluded that more theoretical work is needed to design ways for those countries undertaking unilateral liberalization to get automatic recognition and credit from GATT—so that a country coming to the negotiating table with a 100-percent tariff would not have more negotiating power than a country which has independently reduced its tariff to 20 percent. Trade gains would be speeded up if the reaction to unilateral liberalization efforts were automatic liberalization from other countries. Political pressures from domestic interest groups could be neutralized if a country knew it would receive automatic credit and recognition for liberalization.

Blanco recommended that the World Bank support theoretical work on the following:

- The new issues—services and intellectual property rights.
- The implications of the most-favored-nations principle for block formation, country size, and negotiating possibilities for small and large countries.
- How much have developing countries gained by special and differential treatment? What operating methods are available to make this clause work for each negotiating group?

Finally, the chair thought that GATT should be encouraged to do more theoretical work on how to cease creating acronyms such as FOGS, TRIMS, and TRIPS.

Saving in Developing Countries: Theory and Review

Angus Deaton

In the literature on economic development, much of the interest in saving has been focused on the relation between saving and growth. But saving is not only about accumulation. It is about smoothing consumption in the face of volatile and unpredictable income, and helping to ensure the living standards of poor people whose lives are difficult and uncertain. This paper develops a model of households which cannot borrow but which accumulate assets as a buffer stock to protect consumption when incomes are low. Such households dissave as often as they save, do not accumulate assets over the long term, and have on average very small asset holdings. But their consumption is markedly smoother than their income. Much of the evidence is as consistent with this view of saving as it is inconsistent with standard views of smoothing over the life cycle, and with explanations of the link between saving and growth in terms of life-cycle saving behavior. Consumption smoothing is also a useful way of thinking about government policy, where volatility in the world prices of taxed commodities can generate sharp fluctuations in government revenues as well as reallocations of revenue between the private and public sectors. Many important policy issues in developing countries hinge on issues of consumption and smoothing, and research on these issues is currently likely to be more productive than work on the relation between saving and growth, at least until we have a more satisfactory theory of economic growth.

I can think of four good reasons for studying saving in developing countries separately from saving behavior in developed economies.

- At the microeconomic level, developing-country households tend to be large and poor; they have a different demographic structure; more of them are likely to be engaged in agriculture; and their income prospects are much more uncertain. The problem of allocating income over time thus looks rather different in the two contexts, and the same basic models have different implications for behavior and policy.

Angus Deaton is a professor of economics and international affairs at the Woodrow Wilson School of Public and International Affairs and the Department of Economics, Princeton University. He is grateful to John Campbell, Avinash Dixit, Mark Gersovitz, Fumio Hayashi, Christina Paxson, Nicholas Stern, T. N. Srinivasan, and Steven Webb for helpful discussions and comments, and to Susan Collins, Christina Paxson, and Dwayne Benjamin for providing data. He also thanks the Bradley and McDonnell Foundation for funding some of the research reported in this paper.

©1990 The International Bank for Reconstruction and Development / THE WORLD BANK.

- At the macroeconomic level, both developing and developed countries are concerned with saving and growth, with the possible distortion of aggregate saving, and with saving as a measure of economic performance. But few developing countries possess the sort of fiscal system that permits deliberate manipulation of personal disposable income to help stabilize output and employment.
- Much of the postwar literature expresses the belief that saving is too low, and that development and growth are impeded by the shortfall. Sometimes the problem is blamed on the lack of government policy, sometimes on misguided policy.
- Saving is even more difficult to measure in developing than in advanced economies, whether at the household level or as a macroeconomic aggregate. The resulting data inadequacies are pervasive and have seriously hampered progress in answering basic questions.

The discussion is organized around these four topics. I focus on areas that are either not covered in the recent excellent survey by Gersovitz (1988), or where I wish to develop a different perspective. I make no attempt to be comprehensive where I would only be repeating Gersovitz's review.

Section I develops the microeconomic framework for household saving on which the rest of the discussion is based. The analysis is within the framework of the standard life-cycle permanent income model, but it emphasizes different features of behavior to generate results far from the standard "consumption equals permanent income" story that has so far dominated empirical work in developing countries.

Section II turns to macroeconomic saving, beginning with the relations between income growth, population growth, and saving rates predicted by some versions of the life-cycle hypothesis. The section next addresses macroeconomic stabilization. In many developing countries, protecting consumption against fluctuations in income is a public as well as a private problem. Many governments tax primary commodity exports, so that both government and external balances are sensitive to fluctuations in output levels and international commodity prices. Although the issues are perhaps well understood, there is considerable evidence that governments in many developing countries have not been able to design policies that make the appropriate adjustments.

The discussion in section III of whether saving is too low reviews the arguments based on externalities, and inquires whether government policy, by regulating interest rates, distorts patterns of saving and financial intermediations. Much of the argument here hinges on the interest elasticity of saving.

The rest of this introductory section deals with the fourth topic—the data, and how their shortcomings affect the subsequent analysis.

Perhaps the worst problem that besets data on saving is that saving is not measured directly but is the residual between two large magnitudes, each itself measured with error. The consequences show up at all levels of discussion. Household survey data often show an implausibly large fraction of households dissaving, though the implausibility may be associated with faulty theory as well as faulty data. The household survey data are often quite inconsistent with and typically less than the national income estimates—themselves possibly biased downward (see Visaria and Pal 1980; Paxson 1989) and certainly subject to substantial uncertainty.

The standard household survey may well understate saving. The concept of income is itself extraordinarily complex, and most people in developing countries have little reason to distinguish between business and personal cash transactions. A farmer who buys seeds and food in the same market at the same time may not appreciate that, when computing income, he should only deduct the expenditure on seeds from his receipts. Nor is a seller of street food likely to distinguish accurately between what is eaten by his customers and what by his family. A subsistence farmer, whose outgoings approximately equal his incomings, is quite likely to report that his income is zero. (Even in developed countries the measurement of self-employment income is notoriously inaccurate.) The problems are not entirely solved even by the detailed questioning of more sophisticated surveys, in which the surveyor, not the respondent, calculates income. And the national accounts data for household saving are not themselves reliable enough to provide a good cross-check that will show what sort of surveys do best or how they should be redesigned to do better.

In the national accounts, household saving is typically a residual among residuals. Fry (1988) notes that in many countries illegal capital outflows take place because imports are "overinvoiced" and exports are "underinvoiced," so that if saving is calculated as the sum of domestic investment, the government surplus, and the trade surplus, saving will be underestimated by the extent of the illegal capital outflow. Because household saving is not measured directly (either there are no survey data or the statisticians mistrust them), it is derived from national saving by deducting corporate and government saving, so that errors in measuring corporate saving or investment will be absorbed into this ultimate residual. Given these deficiencies, even trends over time may be incorrectly observed, while real changes, especially those that involve foreign transactions (such as increased remittances to India and Pakistan) may affect the measurement as well as the reality of saving. In India around 1980, observers were puzzled by an apparent dramatic increase in saving and investment unaccompanied by a corresponding increase in economic growth. Rakshit (1982, 1983) and a report by the Reserve Bank of India (1982) investigating the measurement issues concluded that the increases, though real, were greatly overstated by the accounting practices.

Data problems also preclude testing even the most basic hypotheses, for example, the classical (Lewis) model in which saving is done almost exclusively by capitalists. If capitalists belong exclusively to the corporate sector, the model is almost certainly false, but in most developing countries we have no way of sorting out the "capitalistic" pockets in the household sector, where a great deal of accumulation may take place within small household-owned business.

Finally, statistical practices for measuring saving are far from uniform across countries—not even between the United States and Japan (see Hayashi 1986), let alone across developing countries. Conventions for calculating depreciation are good examples of practices that are largely arbitrary and vary widely. The (very extensive) literature that makes comparisons between countries thus rests on peculiarly shaky ground. (Good reviews of these and other data problems are contained in Berry 1985, Fry 1988, and Gersovitz 1988.)

I. Household Saving Behavior in Poor Countries

A Simple Theoretical Model

The basic framework of the simple stylized model of household saving developed here—intertemporal utility maximization—is standard in the literature. But it does not deliver the standard result, that consumption should be proportional to permanent income. The special assumptions under which the standard result is derived seem to me to be unusually inappropriate for most households in developing countries. My model therefore diverges from the textbook in four important respects.

First, households in developing countries tend to be larger than households in the United States or Europe, and there is a much greater tendency for several generations to live together. At the extreme, a household might have a stationary demographic structure: old people, as they die, are replaced by those a little younger, and everyone "shifts up"—down to the youngest children, who are replaced by new births. Such a household has no need for "hump" or retirement saving, either as a vehicle for transferring income from high-productivity to low-productivity phases of the life cycle or as a means of transferring wealth between generations. Resources are shared between workers and dependents, and ownership is passed from parents to children. As emphasized by Kotlikoff and Spivak (1981), this kind of household can internalize many of the insurance activities that would otherwise require saving. Transfers within the household can insure individuals against health risk and old age by providing what are effectively annuities, and the close relationships between the individuals concerned may mean not only that moral hazard issues are less severe than in a more individualistic society but also that the *quality* of the protection is very high. Note also that this kind of household lives much longer than any individual and thus gives some substance to the idea of a "dynasty" of consumers.

Second, income derived from agriculture is inherently uncertain, an uncertainty that spreads from agriculture to related occupations and affects most of the population in predominantly agricultural economies. Uncertainty at low income poses a real threat to consumption levels, a threat that is likely to exert a powerful influence on the way in which income is saved and spent. The poorer consumers are, the more risk averse they are generally supposed to be. Declining (absolute) risk aversion has important implications for the shape of the consumption function (see Leland 1968, Zeldes 1989b, and most recently Kimball 1988; forthcoming). The standard model in which consumption equals permanent income cannot be derived from utility maximization in such a context. Note also that the household insurance arrangements discussed in the previous paragraph are unlikely to be able to deal with income uncertainty, particularly in an agricultural setting. Even multiple earners will not provide much protection if all are dependent on local agriculture.

The third divergence from the standard model is the assumption that borrowing is not permitted. This is an extreme simplifying assumption, but more appropriate than its opposite, that households are free to borrow and lend at a fixed real rate of interest. For the present, the fact of borrowing constraints is more important than the reason behind them, although it is not difficult to think of plausible scenarios. In a world of financial repression, there may be no credit available to nonfavored borrowers. Or borrowing rates may be so much greater than lending rates that credit is only a last resort in dire emergency. Even where there are financial intermediaries, they may be unwilling to lend for consumption purposes to individuals who have no collateral or to lend across agricultural seasons rather than within them. The analysis of borrowing constraints under uncertainty is the main theoretical innovation of the section, even though much of the analytical apparatus can be borrowed from elsewhere.

The fourth distinction between household saving in developed and developing countries is a consequence of the previous three. In the model developed here, saving provides a buffer between uncertain and unpredictable income and an already low level of consumption. Saving here is "high-frequency," intertemporal smoothing saving, not life-cycle-hump or intergenerational saving. The analysis is different, and so are the welfare issues, which are focused on the protection of consumption, particularly among those whose consumption levels may not be far above subsistence. The buffer analogy is also technically useful, since the model here is formally identical to the model of optimal commodity stockpiling (see Gustafson 1958 for an early treatment; also see Samuelson 1971, Newbery and Stiglitz 1981, 1982, and Deaton and Laroque 1989 for modern versions). As far as the consumption literature is concerned, the model developed here is essentially the same as that developed by Schechtman and Escudero (1977).

I begin from the standard specification without borrowing restrictions whereby the household maximizes an intertemporal utility function of the form

$$(1) \qquad u = E_t \left[\sum_t (1 + \delta)^{-t} v(c_t) \right]$$

where $\delta > 0$ is the rate of time preference, c is total household consumption, and $v(c_t)$ is the instantaneous utility associated with consumption c_t. In keeping with the dynastic view of the household, the time horizon is taken to be infinite. The expectation operator, E, is taken with respect to information at time t. The budget constraint evolves in the usual way, so that for real nonhuman wealth A_t, real income y_t, and fixed real interest rate r,

$$(2) \qquad A_{t+1} = (1 + r)(A_t + y_t - c_t)$$

The fixed real interest rate is assumed to make later computation more tractable; the assumption in any case may be reasonable in many of the contexts with which I am concerned.

Dynamic programming arguments applied to equations 1 and 2 yield the Euler equation,

$$(3) \qquad \lambda(c_t) = E_t\left[\frac{(1+r)\lambda(c_{t+1})}{(1+\delta)}\right]$$

where $\lambda(c_t) = v'(c_t)$ is the instantaneous marginal utility of consumption in period t. Often, $\lambda(c_t)$ may be taken as a price or value: when $\lambda(c_t)$ is high, consumption is low, and goods are scarce and valuable.

The concavity of the instantaneous utility function implies that $\lambda(c_t)$ is monotonically decreasing, or in terms of the price interpretation, that price rises with scarcity. I shall also be concerned with the case where $\lambda(c_t)$ is (strictly) convex, so that the scarcer the commodity, the steeper the price rise, flattening out as consumption increases. At a technical level, the convexity of $\lambda(c_t)$ is guaranteed by the usual assumption of declining absolute risk aversion. More intuitively, the convexity of the marginal utility function guarantees a *precautionary* motive for saving. In bad times, when consumption is low, the consequences are much worse than they are better in the good times, when consumption is high. The marginal disutility of losses in consumption near subsistence is greater than the marginal utility of gains in times of relative abundance. Individuals will therefore give up high consumption when it is possible so as to prepare for possible disasters, even if those disasters are few and far between. As can be seen from equation 3, an increase in the riskiness of future consumption will increase the right-hand side of the Euler equation, so that to restore equilibrium, the left-hand side must increase, and current consumption fall (see Sibley 1975). A precautionary motive for saving seems a necessary ingredient in modeling poor households which have the additional misfortune of facing considerable uncertainty in their incomes.

Perhaps the most popular solution to the Euler equation is one which assumes away the precautionary motive by working with quadratic preferences. In this case $\lambda(c_t)$ is a declining linear function but is not strictly convex. Given this linearity, and the additional assumption that the rate of interest r is equal to the rate of time preference δ, equation 3 is satisfied by the permanent income consumption function whereby consumption is the annuity value of the sum of assets and expected future income. In the form consumption equals permanent income, it has been widely applied to household behavior in developing countries, (Bhalla 1979, 1980; Musgrove 1979, 1980; Wolpin 1982; Muellbauer 1982). For present purposes, however, the assumption of certainty equivalence (linear marginal utility) is unattractive because it rules out the sort of precautionary behavior described in the previous paragraph. Unfortunately, apart from some special cases, the Euler equation is a good deal harder to solve in cases when utility is not quadratic. For econometric work this need not be a problem;

Hansen and Singleton (1983) and a host of subsequent studies have used generalized methods of moments techniques to estimate equation 3 directly, conditional on some specification of the instantaneous utility function. However, I need to develop the theory more before I can turn to empirical evidence.

In important papers, Skinner (1988) and Zeldes (1989b) have shown that with a *finite* horizon, precautionary saving can cause major deviations from the certainty equivalent formulation in which consumption equals permanent income. Since borrowings must be repaid in the finite future, possibly at a time when consumption is already low and its marginal utility high, individuals with low nonhuman wealth will be hesitant to borrow at all. This consideration influences even relatively well-off households who own land, who fear having to sell and so face permanently lower incomes thereafter. In many ways, this is an attractive formulation for the analysis of low-income household behavior.

Here I follow another tack and assume that households cannot borrow. I choose this approach partly because the resulting model is easier to handle (largely because it generates a stationary stochastic equilibrium in which consumption is not constant) but also because, at least for some households, borrowing restrictions are real and necessary to explain what we observe. Households in developing countries are often quite long-lived, and many face income processes that are stationary and well understood. But they do not have constant consumption—I suspect because they do not have access to infinite credit and do not therefore make plans that rely upon its availability, particularly when they most need it.

Another motive for adopting a new approach is the "excess sensitivity" literature on the United States (particularly Flavin 1981, Hall and Mishkin 1982, and Hayashi 1987) which has exposed a closer link between actual income and consumption than can be explained by permanent income theory.

Suppose then that the basic model is extended to incorporate borrowing restrictions by adding to the utility function (equation 1) and the budget constraint (equation 2) the inequality constraint, that for all periods t, real wealth cannot be negative:

$$(4) \qquad A_t \geq 0$$

For most households, I also assume that $\delta > r$ (the rate of time preference is greater than the rate of interest). Otherwise, as shown by Schechtman (1976) and by Bewley (1977), the borrowing constraints ultimately have no effect; households eventually accumulate infinite amounts of nonhuman wealth, at which point they never need to borrow, and consumption once again settles down to a constant fixed number. The assumption that δ is greater than r has substantive *economic* content; it takes people to be impatient, unwilling to accumulate, even "feckless," though not of course irrational. With such preferences, assets are a lost opportunity for consumption and would ideally be run down quickly. But there is a benefit to holding assets: they are the insurance against having to reduce consumption to unacceptably low levels when times are bad. Even so, the Schechtman and Bewley results indicate that in this model it is the high level of impatience that keeps people poor. Even without the ability to borrow, patient consumers will eventually become rich, at least as long as r is not driven below δ. I leave such people aside for the moment but will return to them at the end of the next section.

In contrast to the simple Euler equation (3), there are now two possible cases in each time period. In case 1, the consumer would like to borrow but cannot; even if all wealth and current income are consumed, the marginal utility of an additional unit of current consumption is greater than the expected marginal utility to be derived by saving that rupee until tomorrow. In this case, consumption is the sum of assets and income, saving is zero or negative, no assets are carried forward, and marginal utility is not equated across periods. Formally, we have

$$(5) \quad \lambda(A_t + y_t) > E_t\left[\frac{(1+r)\lambda(c_{t+1})}{(1+\delta)}\right]$$

$$c_t = A_t + y_t, \; s_t = y_t - c_t \leq 0, \; A_{t+1} = 0$$

In case 2, the consumer does not want to borrow, consumption is less than total cash on hand, and the original Euler equation (3) is satisfied. Of course, this does not mean that the borrowing constraints have no effect. The expected marginal utility of future consumption is different from the unconstrained case because the future contains the possibility of being unable to borrow when it would be desirable to do so.

The two cases of the Euler equation can be combined into a single expression:

$$(6) \quad \lambda(c_t) = \max\left\{\lambda(A + y_t), E_t\left[\frac{(1+r)\lambda(c_{t+1})}{(1+\delta)}\right]\right\}$$

In the appendix, I derive the consumption function characterized by the modified Euler equation (6) in the simplest case where income is always positive and is independently and identically distributed over time. This is reasonable enough for a poor agricultural household in a stagnant economy, but it would require substantial modification for a worker facing an increasing nonstationary income stream (see Deaton 1989 for details). The solution takes the form

$$(7) \quad c_t = f(x_t)$$

where $x_t = A_t + y_t$ is the amount of cash on hand that is available either for spending today or for keeping for tomorrow. The function $f(x)$ as characterized by equation 7 is determined by the process determining income, for example by its mean and its variance, and by the parameters of the utility function. If any of these change, so will the shape of the function. Although it is not possible to derive an explicit functional form for this consumption function, it can be computed for a range of values of x given a utility function and a stochastic process for income. The appendix explains the calculations; the next subsection uses the calculations to explore the implications of the model.

Implications and Relation to the Evidence

In the consumption functions calculated from equation A-5 in the appendix, I have assumed that income is drawn from a (truncated) normal distribution with mean μ and variance σ^2, truncated at $(\mu - 5\sigma, \mu + 5\sigma)$. The truncation has little or no practical effect, but it ensures that the marginal utility cannot become infinite. The instantaneous utility function reflects the assumption of constant relative risk aversion, that is, it is of the power form, so that the marginal utility of money function $\lambda(c)$ takes the form $c^{-\rho}$. For $\rho > 0$, this marginal utility function is convex, thus guaranteeing a precautionary motive for saving. Figure 1 shows the relation between consumption and cash on hand (assets plus income) for $\rho = 2$ and $\rho = 3$ given that $\mu = 100$, $\sigma = 10$, $r = 0.05$, and $\delta = 0.10$.

When cash is scarce, all of it is spent. At some critical point, which depends on the parameters of the problem but is rarely far from mean income, the slope of the consumption function has a discontinuity, and for higher values of cash on hand, the marginal propensity to consume is lower and continues to fall as the wealth position improves. For consumers with large assets, the liquidity constraints cease to matter, and we are back in the standard case. However, it can be shown that the slope of the consumption function will always remain greater than $r/(1 + r)$; with $\delta > r$, there is always an incentive to consume assets rather than to hold them. Bear in mind that these multiperiod models do not imply that liquidity constraints mean that poor consumers simply consume their

Figure 1. *Liquidity-Constrained Consumption Functions*

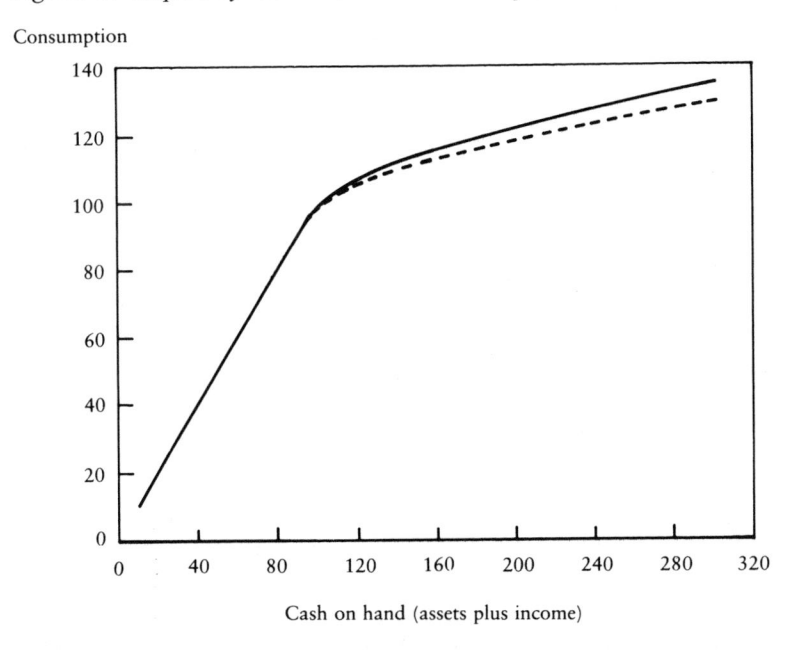

Key: ———— coefficient of relative risk aversion, $\rho = 2$; - - - - - $\rho = 3$.
Note: Assumes mean income = 100, standard deviation = 10, interest rate, $r = 0.05$, rate of time preference, $\delta = 0.10$.
Source: Calculated from equation A-5 in appendix.

incomes. Rather they consume all their available resources, which typically will include some assets accumulated in the past. Saving can be negative, and often is. And even when the liquidity constraints are not binding, so that the consumer does not wish to borrow, the consumption function is quite different from what it would be without the possibility of future liquidity constraints. Consumers in this model take precautions against bad years in which they know they will not be able to borrow. The resulting saving behavior is determined by the interaction of the liquidity constraints and the degree of precautionary saving, as controlled by the parameter ρ. These points have been well emphasized by Zeldes (1989a, 1989b).

Figure 1 shows how the consumption function shifts downward when the precautionary motive is stronger. Similar downward shifts occur as the riskiness of income increases, although increasing the standard deviation (coefficient of variation) from 10 to 15 (10–15 percent) has only a very small effect on the position of the curve. Higher interest rates also shift the function downward; in this model, assets are a buffer stock, and the cost of holding the buffer in terms of utility forgone depends on the excess of δ over r. Higher interest rates make it cheaper to hold (this sort of) buffer stock, and so there will be more saving and higher asset levels associated with higher interest rates.

Perhaps the most important feature of figure 1 is the prediction that saving will increase with "permanent income" as conventionally defined, so that the elasticity of consumption with respect to measured permanent income will be less than unity. The literature on household saving in developing countries has almost uniformly found this result (see in particular Bhalla 1979, 1980 for India; Musgrove 1979 for Latin America; Muellbauer 1982 for Sri Lanka; Betancourt 1971 for Chile; and Paxson 1989 for Thailand). The exception is Wolpin (1982) who, as Gersovitz (1988) points out, has a rather odd measure of permanent income—he assumes, in the Indian context, that permanent income is positively spatially correlated with permanent differences in rainfall, which may not be true in the presence of migration. According to the theory behind figure 1, consumption is not a function of any simple concept of wealth such as permanent income, but a nonlinear function of cash on hand, the function itself depending on characteristics of incomes and preferences. But clearly the propensity for any given household to consume out of assets will be much lower when assets are high than when assets are low, which is one interpretation of the findings.

To the (limited) extent that a cross section can be interpreted as identical households with different income draws from the same distribution, saving will rise with assets, and thus with conventionally measured permanent income. Of course, different individuals in any cross section will have different income processes, and different versions of the consumption functions shown in figure 1. In the simplest case, where the distribution of income "rescales" as the mean changes, all the consumption functions will be scaled versions of the original, and saving rates will be independent of scale. But since the income and asset processes will not be perfectly correlated across individuals, saving rates will still be positively correlated with assets across all individuals. More complicated stories can be told if there is a systematic relation between the level of income and its variability. Note also that many of the richest households are likely to be those for whom $\delta \leq r$, who have (eventually) accumulated assets and broken out of the liquidity constraints. For members of this group, consumption is growing over time, but so are assets, at least for the group as a whole. Unlike the households in figure 1, these households are responsible for net accumulation over time, and thus for household saving in the aggregate, even in a stationary income environment. The presence of some of these households in the cross section will further enhance the positive correlation between saving and asset levels.

The dynamic behavior of the liquidity-constrained consumers in this model can be seen by looking at figures 2 through 6 which plot a typical 200-period (year) simulation for, respectively, income (normally distributed white noise), consumption, saving, assets, and the marginal utility of consumption. These simulations correspond to the broken line in figure 1, where the coefficient of relative risk aversion is 3. The simple nonautocorrelated behavior of income in figure 2 results in a much more complex time-series process for consumption in figure 3. Note first that stationariness is preserved, that is, that its stochastic characteristics do not vary with time, again (and essentially) because $\delta > r$. Assets are accumulated to spread income over time, but since they are costly to hold, a time will always arrive when it is optimal to use them—that is, to consume

Figure 2. *Simulated Income*

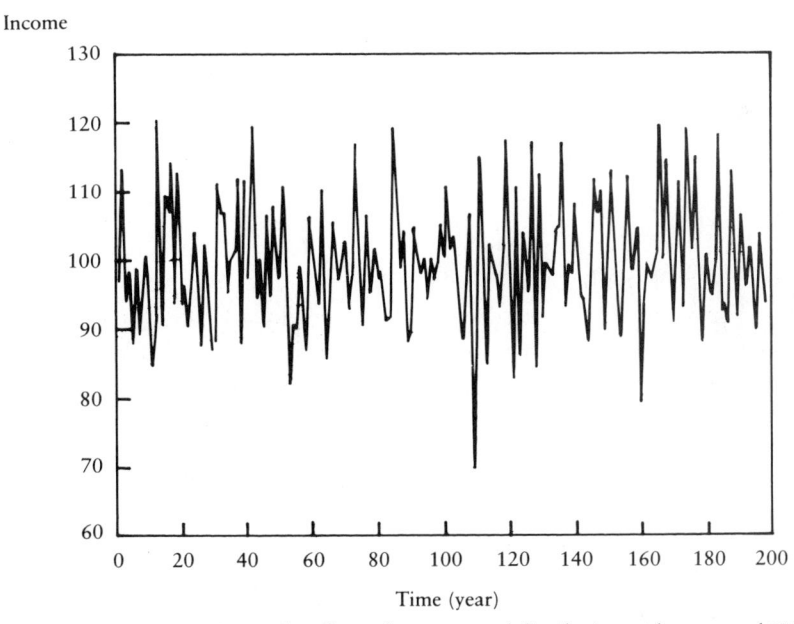

Note: Income is successive random draws from a normal distribution with a mean of 100 and standard deviation of 10.

72 *Saving in Developing Countries*

Figure 3. *Simulated Optimal Consumption Path*

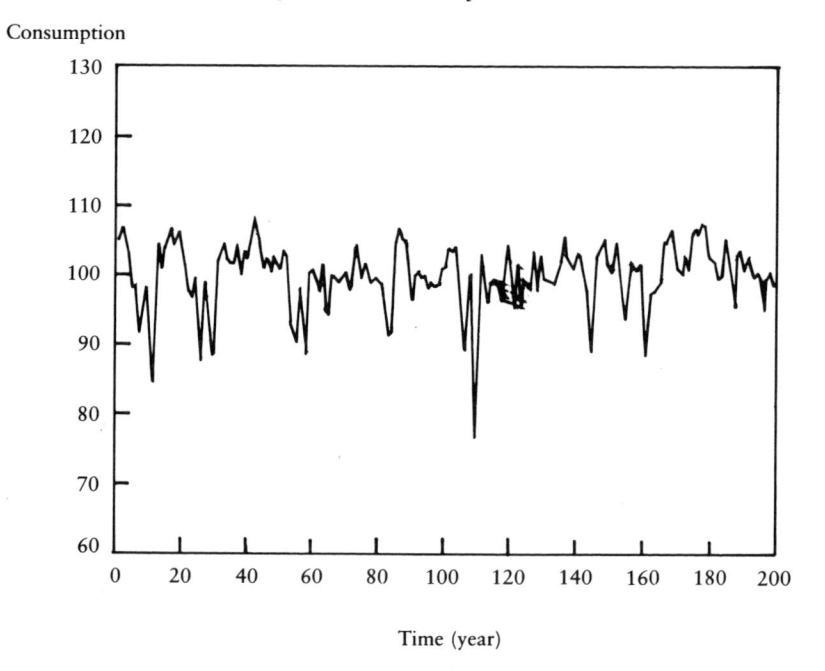

Note: Based on simulated income from figure 2, and consumption determined as in figure 1.

Figure 4. *Simulated Optimal Saving Path*

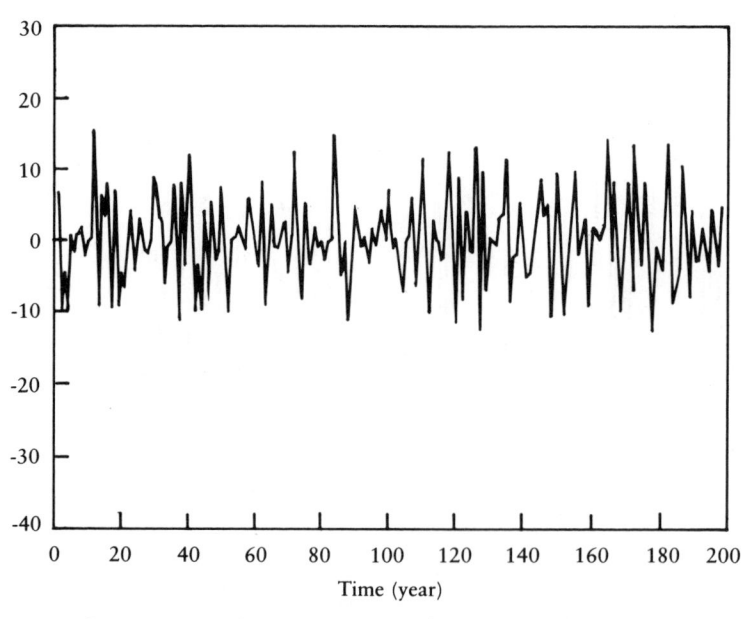

Note: Income plus asset income less consumption is derived from figures 2, 3, and 5.

Figure 5. *Simulated Optimal Asset Path*

End of period asset stock

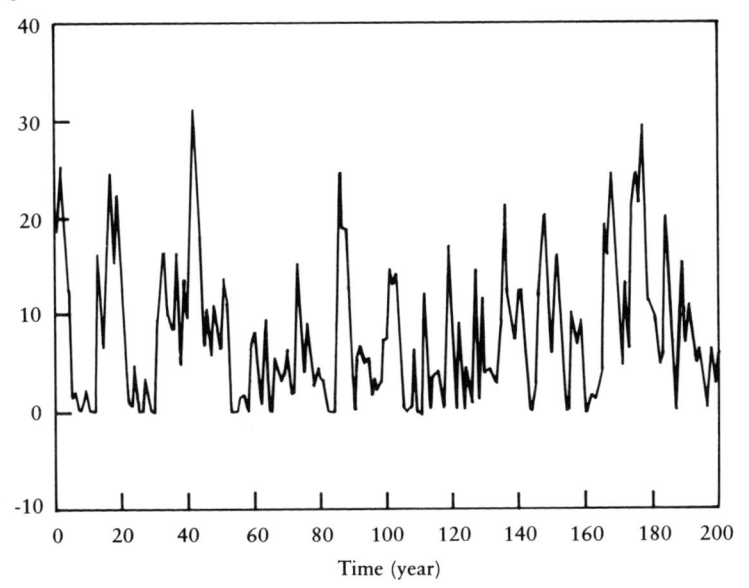

Note: Derived as $A(t + 1) = (1 + r) \{[A(t) + y(t)] f[A(t) + y(t)]\}$ where A is real nonhuman wealth, r is the fixed real interest rate, and y is real income.

Figure 6. *Marginal Utility of Consumption*

Marginal utility ($\times 10^{-6}$)

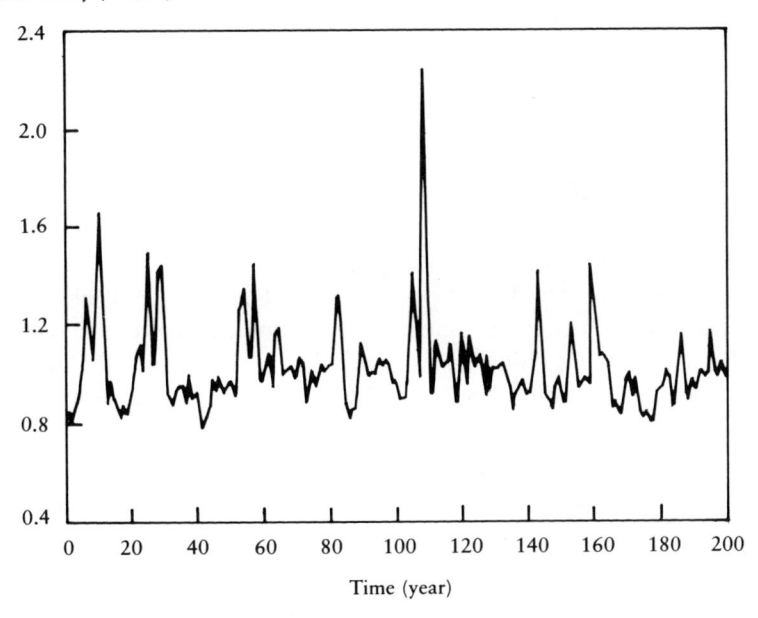

Note: Coefficient of relative risk aversion, $\rho = 3$.

everything. If things are bad enough, the consumption value of even the last rupee is more valuable than it is ever expected to be again, and so all income and assets will be used. As soon as this happens, the link between the present and the past is broken, and the consumer begins the next period with no assets and a new income draw. Such "stock-outs" can be made arbitrarily rare if a suitable income process is chosen (for example, one in which with very low probability income is very small), but they must happen eventually. Again, these seem attractive features of the model, at least for the poorest countries. The possibility of extended drought or famine is an important motive for precautionary saving, and in such periods, assets will be converted to food, although they may be far from sufficient to avoid serious consequences for consumption and its marginal utility.

Figure 5 shows that asset levels are typically low, and even at their peak do not reach one-third of mean income, in spite of the inherent variability in income and the strong precautionary element in preference. Again this accords well with the facts, not only as far as we know them in developing countries, but also in developed countries such as the United States (see, for example, Venti and Wise 1989, who report that—apart from housing and pension wealth, which are not available to buffer consumption—median family wealth in 1985 was only $600). Even so, modest amounts of asset holding can significantly smooth consumption; consumption is much smoother than income (compare figures 2 and 3) and is strongly autocorrelated over time. The literature quoted above also provides overwhelming evidence that consumption is indeed smoothed in developing countries, Paxson's results for Thailand being only the cleanest and most convincing example.

Note also that the fluctuations in consumption are not symmetric; saving can always prevent consumption from being too high, but when assets are exhausted, nothing can be done to soften the effects of low incomes. Perfect smoothing is neither possible nor optimal, and there is less than perfect protection against bad times—see in particular the downward spike in consumption around period 110, and the much more severe associated spike in marginal utility. Interestingly, although income was low in that period, the effects on consumption and on utility are much more exceptional than appear to be warranted by the behavior of income alone. A bad income draw is not in itself the cause of disaster; much depends on the state of assets before the triggering event. Such extreme responses appear to be characteristic of this sort of nonlinear time series, and they seem to account well for the sort of events labeled "panics," "runs," "manias," and perhaps even for some features of famines.

Finally, note the behavior of saving in figure 4, and especially the fact that it is as often negative as positive, as must be the case given the absence of net asset accumulation. The model here predicts the frequently lamented finding from household survey data that "implausibly" large numbers of households appear to dissave. I would not wish to claim that the data are correct; the measurement problems are real enough. But the fact that half the sample is dissaving in any given year is not theoretically implausible. Indeed, by choosing an asymmetrical density function for income, with very occasional bumper harvests, it would presumably be possible to generate time series in which dissaving occurs in nearly every period. But recall that an inability to borrow does not imply that consumers spend their incomes, and so is entirely consistent with frequent dissaving.

The results in the figures are consistent with the "excess sensitivity" findings in the U.S. literature. When the change in consumption is regressed on the change in income, the simulation results generate a coefficient of 0.291 with a standard error of 0.016—a coefficient much too large to be accounted for by the permanent income theory. Similarly, in the regression of the change in consumption on lagged income, the significant negative coefficient ought instead to be zero for an unconstrained, forward-looking consumer. Such a negative correlation exists in the microdata from the "Panel Study of Income Dynamics in the United States" (Hall and Mishkin 1982). We do not yet know whether similar phenomena exist in developing countries, although work on this and other aspects of the model is currently under way using the World Bank's "Living Standards Survey" for Côte d'Ivoire.

One aspect of reality that is *not* consistent with the model is that there should always be aggregate saving in the household sector as a whole. The model is one of income smoothing with assets acting as a buffer stock; there is no motive for accumulation, and over a long enough run of years total household saving would be expected to average to zero. But even if many household surveys show something like this, most observers would allow some credence to the national income accounts, and suppose that there is some saving to be explained. Population growth would help explain some accumulation. If there are more households, each will need its own buffer stock of assets, so that increasing population will require positive saving as the stocks are built up. Income growth is harder to handle, since the basic model assumes a stationary income process and is not easily modified to accommodate nonstationariness. One possibility is that each individual faces a stationary income stream for his or her life, but that each new generation faces a higher mean process. Such a model would tend to reinforce the population growth effect as each generation holds a larger stock of assets on average.

A more interesting hypothesis is that the preference parameter δ varies from person to person. Some are patient and willing to wait for higher consumption; others are not. For the majority, for whom ($\delta > r$), the model applies, and they spend their lives smoothing consumption, holding few assets, and always subject to liquidity constraints. The minority, with ($\delta \leq r$), are also unable to borrow, but their optimal consumption plans, which typically involve saving now to support higher consumption in the future, also have the characteristic that the stochastic process governing their assets is such as to guarantee that assets will exceed any finite level given enough time to do so. This accumulation, which is stochastic, is an almost accidental outcome of optimal consumption plans for patient consumers who can never borrow. The distribution of preferences thus divides the population into two groups, one of which lives a little better than hand to mouth but never has more than enough to meet emergencies, while the other, as a group, saves and steadily accumulates assets. Such a dichotomy recalls the classic models of saving in which "capitalists" do all the saving (see Lewis 1954; Kaldor 1955–56), but here the capitalists are created willy-nilly as a long-run consequence of their taste for future over present consumption. The preference-based dichotomy also suggests an explanation for the division of consumers into two groups—liquidity-constrained or "rule-of-thumb" consumers and "life-cyclers"—that has recently become popular in the U.S. literature (see Hall and Mishkin 1982; Campbell and Mankiw 1989a, 1989b; Flavin 1988). The theory here explains how the two groups arise, why each is behaving optimally, and why some are liquidity-constrained and others are not. But in its present form it does not do any of this when individual consumers expect their incomes to grow.

II. Macroeconomic Aspects of Saving in Developing Countries

The Life Cycle, Saving, and Growth

One of the most celebrated and most investigated predictions of the life-cycle model is that there should be a relation between aggregate saving and the rates of population and income growth. If saving is hump saving, accumulated during the working years to finance retirement, then population growth provides more savers than dissavers, and positive aggregate saving. Per capita income growth has a similar effect because workers are saving on a larger scale than the retirees are dissaving. For many people, population growth is *the* issue in economic development, and the relation between population growth and capital accumulation is one of the most important of the possible links between population policy and economic welfare (see, in particular, National Academy of Sciences 1986; and Mason 1987, 1988).

Even at the theoretical level, however, there are complications. If young consumers anticipate a steady growth in income, and can and will borrow against that increase, their dissaving in the early years of the life cycle may induce a *negative* relation between saving and growth. The standard positive relation works best if each worker experiences a stationary income stream over his or her own life cycle, with growth taking place between rather than within generations. The effects of population growth are similarly ambiguous. Even if adults would like their own consumption stream to be constant over the life cycle, their expenditures may exceed income, not only during retirement but also when there are children in the household. Population growth expands the ratio of workers to retirees, but also the ratio of children to adults, and saving may be decreased more by the latter than it is increased by the former. The net effect depends on the costs and benefits of children, a balance that may itself change (from net benefit to net cost) with economic growth (see Caldwell 1982). And do households really want to have flat consumption streams in any case? Cautious young people may not want to borrow against future income growth, even if that growth is extremely likely. And old people, faced with daunting uncertainties about health and death, may not run down their assets in the prescribed manner—a supposition strongly supported by the balance of empirical evidence from developed countries. To these lacunae in the standard argument may be added my own doubts, expressed in the previous section, about the general applicability of the hump-saving concept in developing countries.

The cross-country empirical evidence (well reviewed by Gersovitz 1988) generally supports a positive effect of per capita income growth on saving rates, variously defined; however, the results are rarely well-determined and are uncomfortably reliant on the treatment of the simultaneity between saving (investment) and growth, and on the sample of countries selected. The even more ambiguous role of population growth can perhaps be interpreted as negative dependency effects more or less offsetting the positive effects of population growth. Figures 7 and 8 illustrate fairly typical findings for the relation between saving and the total growth of gross national product (GNP).

Both figures show a positive slope, with the saving rate increasing 1–1.5 percentage points for every percentage increase in the growth rate. The t-values are modest but significant at conventional levels. Of course, there are outliers (they happen not to have much effect on the results), and the scatter yields plenty of scope for obtaining different results by suitable sample selections or choice of instrumental variables—all this quite apart from whether the countries should be given the same weight, whatever their population size, data reliability, or anything else.

The fundamental problem is the direction of causality: from growth to saving (the life-cycle explanation) or from saving to growth? The problem is tackled by several authors with various instrumental variables, but these efforts are hardly convincing in the absence of an adequate theory of growth. Summers and Carroll (1989) have argued that, whatever produces the positive correlation between saving and growth, it cannot be life-cycle saving. They point out that the life-cycle explanation assumes common preferences across countries, but that differences in economic growth generate differences in the relative lifetime economic standing of young and old in different countries. To use Lucas's (1988) graphic example of the power of compound growth: if a grandchild is fifty years younger than its grandfather, using 1965–86 per capita growth rates, then a citizen of the Republic of Korea is 26 times as rich as his or her grandfather, while an Indian is only 2.4 times as rich. These enormous differences should show up in profiles of the relation between age and consumption—if Korea is compared with India, the profile should be relatively higher among the younger cohorts in the faster growing economy. But Summers and Carroll's (1989) age-consumption profiles for Japan, the Unites States, and Canada are essentially identical in spite of the differences in growth rates; the differences predicated by the life-cycle growth effects are simply not present.

78 Saving in Developing Countries

Figure 7. *Gross Domestic Saving and Growth: World Bank Data*

Gross domestic saving ratio, 1986

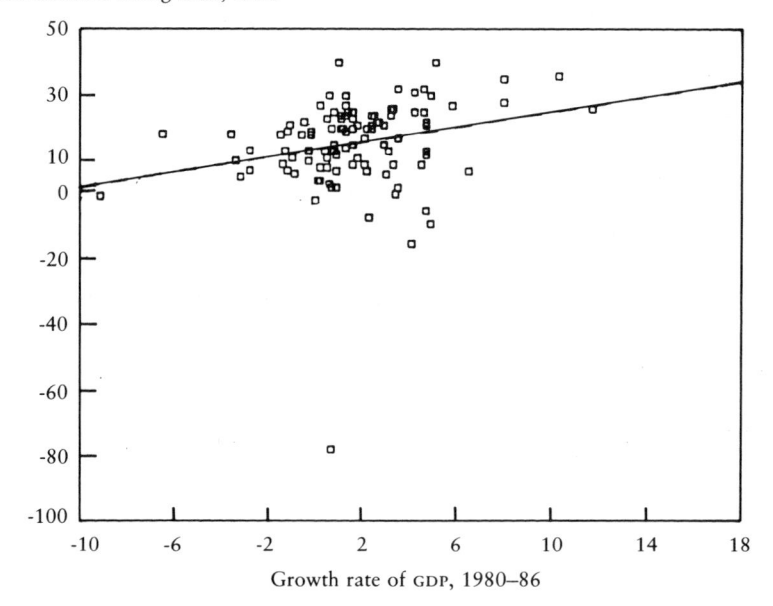

Growth rate of GDP, 1980–86

Source: World Bank (1988).

Figure 8. *Saving and Growth: Summers and Heston data*

Consumption ratio, 1980

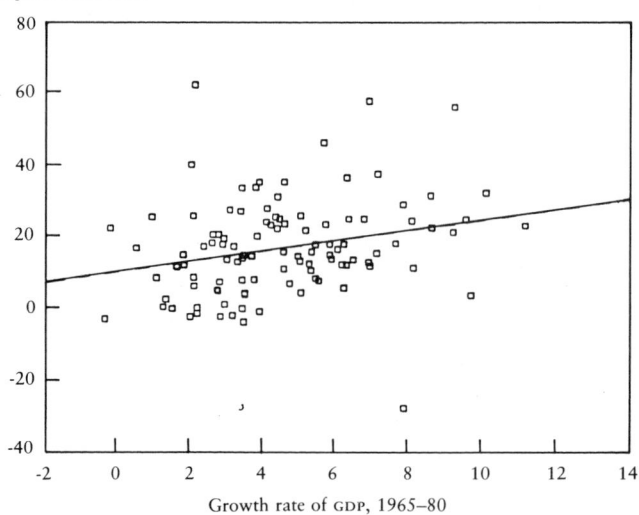

Growth rate of GDP, 1965–80

Note: On the vertical axis, the variable is one minus the sum of the shares of government and private consumption in total GDP, measured in current international prices. The horizontal axis shows the growth rate of per capita gross national product in constant 1980 international prices multiplied by population. Points for 106 countries are shown.
Source: Summers and Heston (1988).

I have been able to obtain data on age-consumption profiles for five countries: Côte d'Ivoire, Hong Kong, Indonesia (rural Java), Korea (cities only), and Thailand (see figures 9–11). The growth rates of real GNP per capita given in table 1 are from both World Bank (1988) and Summers and Heston (1988) data. The right-hand panel shows the ratios of incomes twenty years apart at these growth rates, in which, for example, the numerator could reflect the relative lifetime income of thirty-year-olds and the denominator that for fifty-year-olds. Except for Côte d'Ivoire, where the Summers-Heston growth figure is 0.2 percent a year instead of the 1.2 percent from World Bank (1988), the two sets of estimates agree closely. Both sets of rankings have Côte d'Ivoire growing most slowly, Thailand and Indonesia rapidly, and Hong Kong and Korea very rapidly. The corresponding age-consumption profiles (figures 9–11) show how far the prediction is from reality. In slow-growing Côte d'Ivoire the consumption profile is heavily tipped toward the young; in urban and rural Thailand and in Korean cities, where thirty-year-olds are two to four times richer than fifty-year-olds, the profile peaks for households with heads in their fifties. In rural Java, which is growing about as fast as Thailand, the peak is somewhat earlier, in the mid-forties. For Hong Kong, the published data points are sparse, but household expenditure levels seem not to vary very much with age from the late twenties to the late fifties. For Thailand, Korea, and Côte d'Ivoire, where I have data from more than one year, or for Thailand for more than one sector, profiles from the same country are much more similar than profiles across countries. But the differences across countries are not easily explicable by life-cycle growth effects.

The results should not be overstated. A more sophisticated analysis would take into account the differing family sizes in the different countries as well as the marked declines in fertility in several countries that have meant that older households typically had more children than households of the next generation. Even so, it is hard to see that these considerations could affect the basic point. Note too that the graphs *do not* show that households do not look ahead when planning their consumption, nor that they do not smooth out short-term fluc-

Table 1. *Growth Rates and Twenty-Year Growth Factors*

Country	growth rate 1965–1986 WDR	SH	20-year growth factor WDR	SH
	percent per year			
Côte d'Ivoire	1.2	0.2	1.27	1.04
Hong Kong	6.2	6.3	3.33	3.39
Indonesia	4.6	5.1	2.46	2.70
Korea (cities)	6.7	7.0	3.65	3.87
Thailand	4.0	4.2	2.19	2.28

Note: WDR is *World Development Report 1988* (World Bank 1988); SH is Summers and Heston (1988). The SH data are average growth rates from 1965 to 1985. The growth factor is the $(1 + g)^{20}$, where g is the growth rate.

Sources: World Bank (1988); Summers and Heston (1988).

Figure 9. *Age-Consumption Profiles for Java and Côte d'Ivoire*

Expenditure divided by average expenditure

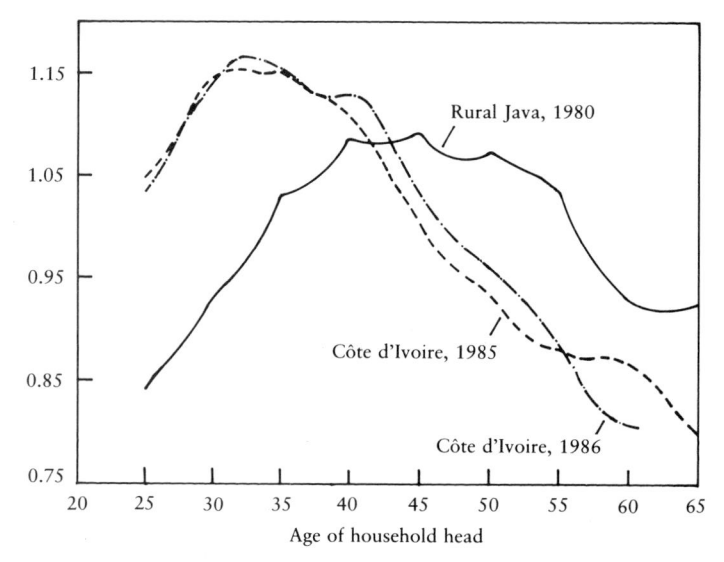

[Figure showing age-consumption profiles with curves for Rural Java, 1980; Côte d'Ivoire, 1985; and Côte d'Ivoire, 1986. X-axis: Age of household head (20 to 65). Y-axis: 0.75 to 1.15.]

Source: Calculations based on data from La Direction des Etudes et de la Recherche de l'Office National de Formation Professionelle, an agency of the government of Côte d'Ivoire; and on data from the Indonesian National Socioeconomic Survey, Central Bureau of Statistics, Government of Indonesia.

Figure 10. *Age-Consumption Profiles: Villages and Urban Areas of Thailand*

Expenditure divided by average expenditure

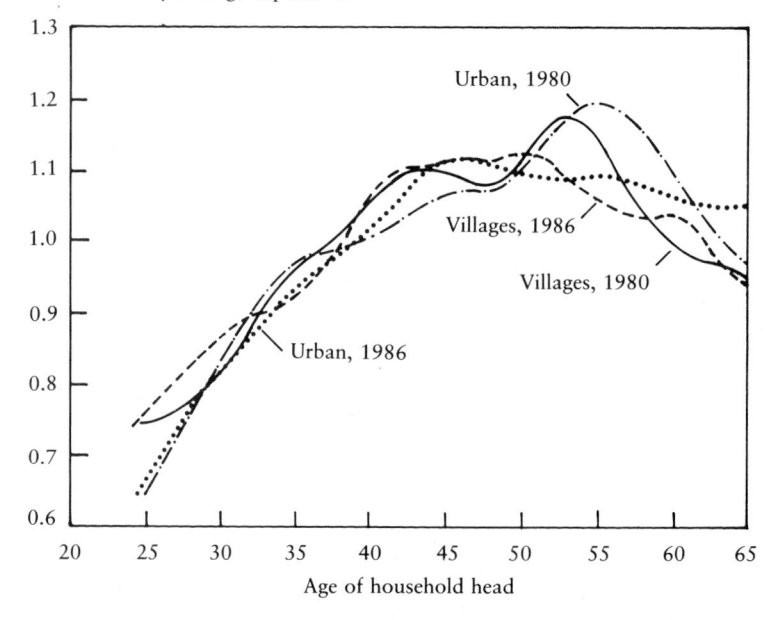

[Figure showing age-consumption profiles with curves for Urban, 1980; Urban, 1986; Villages, 1980; and Villages, 1986. X-axis: Age of household head (20 to 65). Y-axis: 0.6 to 1.3.]

Source: Calculations based on the 1980 and 1986 Socioeconomic Surveys, National Statistical Office, Government of Thailand.

Figure 11. *Age-Consumption Profiles for Korean Cities and Hong Kong*

Expenditure divided by average expenditure

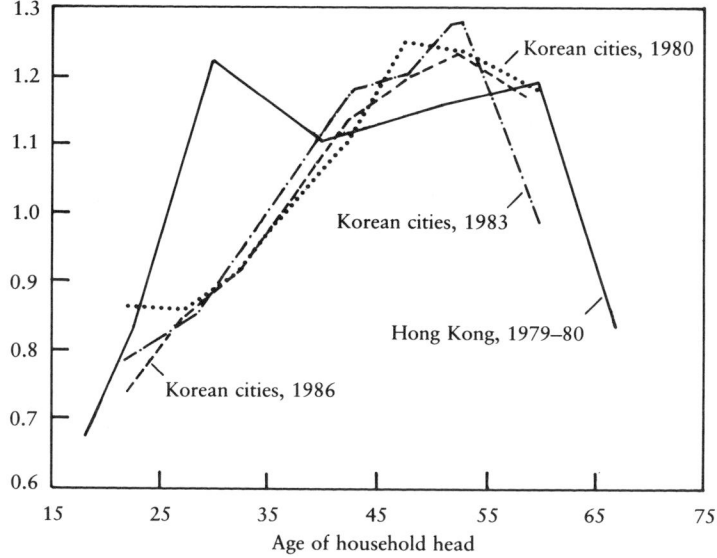

[Figure: Line graph showing age-consumption profiles with x-axis "Age of household head" from 15 to 75, and y-axis from 0.6 to 1.3. Four curves labeled: Korean cities, 1980; Korean cities, 1983; Korean cities, 1986; Hong Kong, 1979–80.]

Sources: Hong Kong (1980); and Korea (1980, 1983, 1986).

tuations in income. But they do show that the relative lifetime economic status of different age groups does not directly determine their current consumption levels. Given this, the standard explanation of life-cycle rate of growth effects, that younger cohorts are saving and spending on a larger scale, simply does not work. Why not is unclear. Even if the life-cycle model is false, there may be strong precautionary motives or constraints that prevent young consumers from borrowing against their expected future incomes. Note finally that all these data show systematic variation of consumption patterns with the age of the household head, so that the model of the infinitely lived demographically stationary household in section I cannot be literally true.

Where this leaves us is anyone's guess. My own feeling is that the cross-country correlations exist, if only weakly, but that we have very little idea of why, or at any rate no way of separating out the many possible explanations. But the support our results give to the Summers and Carroll challenge to the life-cycle explanation suggests that a great deal of the literature needs to be rethought.

Some Stabilization Issues

In developed countries, concern about the nature of the consumption function has centered on its implications for government policy, in particular the extent to which short-term fiscal policy, by manipulating household disposable income, can affect consumption and thus the level of economic activity. If most of consumption is determined by permanent income, short-term fluctuations in income will have less effect on consumption than if liquidity is constrained for a sizable fraction of consumers. Few developing countries have income tax systems that permit fine-tuning of disposable incomes; nevertheless, fiscal arrangements do have important effects on income fluctuations, on the distribution of income, and most likely on the level of national saving. I have in mind various agricultural taxation schemes prevalent in developing countries, particularly in those where there are substantial exports of primary commodities.

Prices of primary commodities are extremely volatile, so that the incomes of countries that sell them fluctuate widely. Such fluctuations are generally considered undesirable in themselves, but their undesirable effects would seem to arise from their translation into fluctuations in consumption. If so, developing countries ought to save and dissave in order to ride out the fluctuations in income. My impression is that this particular saving problem has been rather neglected until very recently. (See Gelb 1988 for a discussion of the effects of oil windfalls, and Bevan, Collier, and Gunning 1987 and Balassa 1988 for discussion of the macroeconomic problems created by the windfalls and losses that accompany commodity price fluctuations.)

Agricultural pricing and tax policies. Agricultural taxation affects the way income fluctuations are shared between government and farmers, and so determines who must save to smooth consumption. To give some examples, as detailed by Bevan, Collier, and Gunning (1987), coffee was not taxed in Kenya at the time of the coffee boom in 1975–76, so that the windfall went directly to the coffee farmers, who apparently succeeded in saving a good deal of it. Arrangements are almost the polar opposite in Côte d'Ivoire, where the government, to guarantee a constant real internal price, sets procurement prices for both coffee and cocoa at levels which bear little relation to world prices—a state of affairs common for most export crops in most of Africa (see Gersovitz and Paxson 1989). With such arrangements, all income fluctuations (and hence the responsibility for smoothing) accrue to the public sector. Between these extremes, the Thai government has varied the rice "premium" in such a way as to allow the domestic price of rice to fluctuate with the world price, though with a smaller amplitude. The government takes a larger share in tax when the world price is high, and vice versa, so that the smoothing problem is shared between the public and private sectors.

The effects of these schemes on total domestic saving depend on how public and private saving differ. One (unlikely) possibility is that there is no difference. Another is that households and farmers do not save, either because of lack of suitable instruments or because they lack foresight. In such a world, the government would have a custodial role both as guardian of future generations and as an insurance company, to protect farmers' consumption against the volatility of commodity prices (see Mirrlees 1988). The custodial role for government was prominent in most of the development literature in the 1960s and 1970s, and it is embedded in most of the standard cost-benefit procedures. A more skeptical attitude toward the ability of governments to handle these problems better than the private sector has prevailed recently, and although there is undoubtedly an element of fashion in these beliefs, there is plenty of evidence of apparently perverse government responses to temporary income shocks (see Balassa 1988). Some governments may find it hard to resist pressures to spend in the face of mounting revenues, and equally hard to make cuts when revenues fall. The result may be that all positive shocks are treated as permanent and all negative shocks as transitory. Even when the temporary revenue gains have been used to finance investment, which is one way of smoothing consumption, there have been problems. Large investment projects are not easy to reverse, and they generate commitments that may be hard to meet once the boom is over. A case in point is the Côte d'Ivoire investment program that required overseas borrowing in addition to the sums available from the boom in coffee and cocoa prices. And the quality of investment projects implemented in response to such revenue booms may be questionable.

In contrast to this evidence on government behavior, the theory and empirical results quoted in section I, although ambiguous on the applicability of simple versions of the permanent income theory, seem quite unambiguous in their finding that farmers can and do save and dissave so as to smooth consumption over time. Much more work needs to be done, on both private saving behavior and government saving, consumption, and investment patterns, to reach a realistic assessment of the effects of pricing schemes, of how to redesign them to avoid the most serious pitfalls, and of the potential value of the sort of international compensatory schemes advocated by Balassa (1988).

Fluctuations in commodity prices. How ought consumers and governments to respond to commodity price fluctuations? I shall take the simplest view, that price fluctuations induce income fluctuations, and that consumption, at least in the aggregate, ought to respond to permanent but not transitory innovations. We therefore need a mechanism for sorting out permanent fluctuations from transitory ones. Ideally, it is income that ought to be decomposed into permanent and transitory components, but the relation between prices and incomes is complicated and differs from country to country. Instead, I focus on commodity prices themselves.

The standard theory of commodity price determination is one of speculative demand for inventories interacting with agricultural supply and demand (see the references on optimal commodity stockpiling given in section I). Typically, the underlying supply and demand conditions are assumed to be stationary, so that, although the theory is consistent with extreme volatility and nonlinearity in the stochastic process which determines prices, the price process is stationary. As a consequence, price booms and slumps are transitory, and price shocks convey no useful information about prices in the far future. But this is theory, not necessarily fact, and although actual commodity prices do indeed go up and

84 *Saving in Developing Countries*

down, it is far from clear that shocks invariably die away and that booms and slumps are always temporary. Indeed, several analysts of commodity prices, for example Labys and Granger (1970) or Ghosh, Gilbert, and Hughes-Hallett (1987), treat the first difference of commodity prices as stationary (the standard prescription of the time-series analyst faced with the very high and slowly diminishing autocorrelations in most commodity prices). Many of these formulations imply that shocks are infinitely persistent and that there are no forces that act to bring prices back to some fundamental level. While this position does not seem to be sustainable, it is plausible that some part of commodity price shocks reflects shocks to fundamentals, not just temporary shortages or gluts associated with bad or good harvests and the actions of profit-maximizing speculators.

Fortunately, the extent to which price shocks are permanent is a topic amenable to empirical investigation. The precise question to be answered is how much of an innovation in the price can be expected to persist indefinitely, and how much to evaporate, at least eventually. Cochrane (1988) and Campbell and Mankiw (1987) have developed an estimate of persistence based on the successive autocorrelations in the first differences of the time series. If the time series is anchored, either to a constant base or a deterministic trend, then innovations must eventually be followed by compensating changes in the opposite directions, and there will eventually be a predominant pattern of negative autocorrelations in the first differences. Consider, for example, a white noise series ($\mu + \epsilon_t$). The first difference is ($\epsilon_t - \epsilon_{t-1}$), which has autocorrelations at all leads and lags of (. . . 0, 0, 0, -0.5, 1, -0.5, 0, 0, . . .) where the 1 is the autocorrelation at lag 0, and the -0.5s at lead and lag one. These autocorrelations add to zero, and the series has zero persistence. By contrast, a random walk with drift $\Delta y_t = \theta + \epsilon_t$ has a first difference which is white noise, and the sum of all its autocorrelations is unity, so that a random walk has a persistence measure of 1; all shocks are permanent. Any stationary series has a persistence measure of zero, but not all series with unit roots are necessarily very persistent. For example, the sum of a random walk and white noise has a persistence measure less than unity, while a unit root series that is positively autocorrelated in first differences has a persistence measure greater than unity.

Table 2 lists summary statistics and persistence measures for thirteen commodity prices important for developing-country exports and incomes. The data come from the World Bank and are monthly from January 1960 through February 1988. The Bank routinely deflates these prices by an index of import prices for developing countries; here I have deflated by the U.S. consumer price index. The difference in the deflator is insignificant compared with the fluctuations in the series. The coefficients of variation show the volatility of the series. The sugar price is by far the most volatile, and the banana price by far the least; neither commodity is traded in anything like a free competitive market. The second and third columns show the autocorrelation coefficients of the prices themselves at lags of one and twelve months. Apart from bananas, which alone

Table 2. *Monthly Commodity Prices: Summary Statistics*

Commodity	Coefficient of variation	Autocorrelation[a] 1 month	Autocorrelation[a] 12 months	Persistence measures[b] 60 months	Persistence measures[b] 120 months
Arabica coffee	0.42	0.98	0.53	0.81	0.41
Bananas	0.18	0.80	0.58	0.07	0.02
Cocoa	0.51	0.99	0.74	1.26	0.67
Copper	0.41	0.97	0.60	0.41	0.28
Cotton	0.26	0.98	0.50	0.92	0.62
Iron ore	0.31	0.99	0.85	0.31	0.16
Jute	0.36	0.97	0.62	0.37	0.14
Maize	0.27	0.98	0.70	0.70	0.35
Palm oil	0.34	0.97	0.49	0.44	0.23
Rice	0.43	0.99	0.55	0.85	0.60
Sugar	0.92	0.97	0.42	0.43	0.22
Tea	0.32	0.95	0.64	0.15	0.08
Tin	0.36	0.99	0.79	1.79	1.62

[a] The first and twelfth autocorrelation coefficients of the deflated series.

[b] Campbell/Mankiw-Cochrane measures of persistence, that is, the normalized spectral density at frequency zero, estimated using a triangular (Bartlett) window with window widths of 60 and 120 months respectively.

Source: Calculations based on World Bank data.

among these commodities are perishable and show seasonal price variation, all the first-order autocorrelations are more than 0.95, and only one is less than 0.97; even after twelve months, most of the autocorrelation remains.

These kinds of statistics are characteristic of integrated, nonstationary processes. Nevertheless, the persistence measures show considerable variability from commodity to commodity. Two estimates are shown, corresponding to "window widths" of 60 and 120 months respectively. The need for the window width arises from the impossibility of adding all terms in an infinite series; here I calculate the weighted average of either 60 or 120 autocorrelations with weights declining linearly with the length of the lag. There is a standard tradeoff here between bias and variance. Small window widths are relatively precise but, by omitting higher-order autocorrelations, run the risk of bias, especially if the price reverts only slowly to its base. Wide windows lead to imprecise estimates, and at extreme lengths are biased toward zero. The asymptotic *t*-values for the two estimates are 2.1 and 1.5 respectively.

For most of the commodities, particularly bananas, copper, iron ore, jute, palm oil, sugar, and tea, the persistence estimates are small; it would probably make sense to accept the standard view that shocks are not persistent. For a second group—coffee, cocoa, cotton, maize, and rice—the estimates are a good deal larger, so that there is some evidence that some fraction of actual, historical shocks has been permanent. For one commodity, tin, the persistence estimate is very large, even at the wider bandwidth. A country facing fluctuations in the price of tin would be justified in taking the view not only that price changes are permanent, but that it makes sense to expect further movements in the same direction. For commodities with low persistence estimates (the first group), price booms are times to save, and slumps times to dissave. For those in the second group, price booms would justify at least some increase in consumption levels. For tin, a rise in price would justify a country borrowing so as to spend more than the current increase in income. If commodity income is more than unit persistent, consumption levels should be *more* volatile than income.

The commodity boom in the 1970s appeared to trigger exactly this sort of behavior, with some countries *borrowing* internationally during the boom. Of course, the evidence here would not support such a strategy in general; indeed the lack of persistence for most of the commodities helps explain why those policies had such disastrous consequences. But it is much easier after the event to assess the transitoriness of a price boom, and the figures in the table show that it is far from obvious in advance how saving ought to respond to fluctuations in commodity prices, even when governments can and will implement the correct policies.

III. Is There Too Little Saving?

The idea that underdevelopment is a problem of too little saving is deeply embedded in the history of development economics. The argument seems simple enough: capital accumulation is a necessary and sufficient condition for growth, and capital accumulation is almost synonymous with saving; the route to development is then one of raising saving ratios. But since Lewis's (1954) statement of this "central problem of economic development," the argument has been assailed by the standard economist's question of what prevents the market from working without outside interference, and further eroded by questioning of the link between saving and growth. Solow's (1956) model does not generate any relation between saving and growth in long-run equilibrium, although increases in saving will generate increases in growth over a transition path that may be very long-lived. Recently, there has been a renewed interest in "increasing returns" models of growth (see particularly Arrow 1962; Romer 1986, 1988; and Lucas 1988; reviewed splendidly by Romer forthcoming). But these models emphasize, not so much saving, but the role of *human* capital formation, so that while such models predict a relation between the willingness to wait and the rate of growth, there is no necessary relation between growth and the rate of *physical* capital accumulation.

Nor has the empirical evidence suggested any straightforward link between growth and either saving or investment. Figures 7 and 8, with the axes reversed, show the same weak relations that, in the previous section, were interpreted the other way round. There is also a very high cross-country correlation between saving and investment, so that the picture would not be different if the latter were substituted for the former. The point is not that there has not been growth, nor that there have not been much higher saving ratios. Even after recent events, postwar growth in the developing world has been very high by all historical standards, and there are now many developing countries with saving rates that would have seemed unimaginably high to the development economists of the 1950s. In 1986, China's gross domestic saving was 36 percent of gross domestic product (GDP), India's 21 percent, Kenya's 26 percent, Thailand's 25 percent, and the People's Republic of the Congo's 30 percent. The point is that across countries there is at best only a very weak relation between saving and growth, perhaps because it is the productivity of investment that is crucial, not its volume.

Nevertheless, there are substantive issues about the "right" amount of saving. If there are positive externalities to saving by each individual, too little of it will be done, an argument formalized in Sen's (1967) "Isolation Paradox." It can also be argued that future generations will not be adequately represented by their currently living ancestors, so that governments must act on their behalf. Alternatively, it might simply be that optimal intertemporal choice under uncertainty is difficult in that it requires a degree of calculation and sophistication that is too difficult for individuals and can reasonably be expected only of a planning agency. Whatever the virtues (and vices) of planning agencies, the evidence that households make good intertemporal allocations is far from overwhelming. The ability of households and farmers to smooth out short-term income fluctuations is well established, but that is not the same as being able to make ideal provision for the long-term future. The empirical literature on life-cycle models, although successful in many respects, has repeatedly failed to observe the sorts of lifetime profiles of consumption and labor supply that would be expected from long-term intertemporal optimization (see Browning, Deaton, and Irish 1985; and Mankiw, Rotemberg, and Summers 1985).

In opposition to the view that governments need to step in to remedy the deficiencies of private-sector saving is the contention that government interference, not market failure, is responsible for inadequate saving in many developing countries. The "financial repression" literature (associated with the work of McKinnon 1973 and Shaw 1973; see Fry 1988 for an extensive review and references), argues that governments have reasons for keeping domestic interest rates low and for repressing financial intermediation in general. Low interest rates keep down the cost of domestic borrowing, and the lack of alternative borrowers allows the government to exploit its monopoly as a seller of financial securities. Low interest rates and lack of investment opportunities are then held to be responsible for low domestic saving. According to this view, financial liberalization is the recipe for higher saving ratios and higher growth. These arguments tend to parallel the similar arguments in developed economies that government policies, particularly tax policy, lower the return to saving and hamper capital accumulation.

Apart from the connection between saving and growth, which I have already discussed, these arguments take it as axiomatic that saving responds positively to interest rates. Once again, there is no theoretical basis whatsoever for this presumption. Changes in interest rates have both income and substitution effects, and can increase or decrease current consumption depending on the balance between the two. Higher (real) interest rates do indeed increase the incentive to postpone consumption and tend to make the planned consumption profile grow more rapidly over time, but the current starting point of that profile can move either up or down. There is also an enormous body of research, mostly but not exclusively in developed economies, that has singularly failed to show *any* empirical relation between interest rates and the rate of saving.

The empirical work can be divided into two classes: those studies that look for a direct effect of interest rates on saving, and those, following the more recent "Euler equation" approach, that look for a relation between the *rate of growth* of consumption and the interest rate. Theory predicts nothing in the first case and is consistent with any finding; in the second case, the effect ought to be positive, at least in the simplest models of infinitely lived consumers. Perhaps the most frequently cited of the first kind of study is Boskin (1978), who finds a very strong positive interest elasticity of saving. However, this study stands almost alone, and it is also notable for the very nonstandard data series that are used. Much more typical is the time-series study by Blinder and Deaton (1985), which finds some interest rate effects in some specifications but whose results are not robust either to changes in the sample period or to the inclusion or exclusion of other variables. Indeed, the consumption function literature abounds in studies that include, in addition to income, some favorite "exotic" variable, which does well in that particular study. However, attempts to estimate more comprehensive models rarely support the original studies. For developing countries, studies have usually been on pooled cross-section time-series data for a range of countries over some span of years. A number of early studies by Maxwell Fry reported high interest elasticities. Giovannini (1983, 1985), in what appear to be careful studies, was unable to find any positive effects in similar data for the 1970s rather than the 1960s. My reading of Gupta (1987) too is that well-defined robust estimates are very hard to obtain. Fry's (1988) review and update of his earlier studies once again finds positive interest elasticities. However, I find this latest evidence unconvincing, largely because Fry does not give enough information for me to tell how the equations were estimated. The literature as a whole is not very enlightening: the value of these sorts of cross-country studies is in any case dubious, particularly given the data problems, and several of the studies do not reach econometric standards that would allow the reader to take their results at face value.

Studies of the second type, linking consumption growth to real interest rates or, better, to *expected* real interest rates, have been, if anything, even more unsuccessful. In the U.S. data, whether prewar or postwar, there is no relation whatever between consumption growth and real interest rates, whether or not the latter are expected or realized, and however sophisticated or careful the estimation technique. Even at the most obvious level, post-tax real interest rates in the United States have been negative as often as positive, and yet consumption growth has nearly always been positive, a finding that would require a *negative* rate of time preference (see Deaton 1987). Other, more sophisticated studies, come to the same conclusion (see Hall 1988; Campbell and Mankiw 1989 and forthcoming; and Hotz, Kydland, and Sedlacek 1988). There have been few recent studies for developing economies, but Giovannini (1985) has examined the effects of expected real interest rates on consumption growth in eighteen developing economies. He finds some nonzero effect in five (India, Jamaica, Greece, Myanmar, and Turkey), and no effects in the other thirteen (Argentina, Brazil, Colombia, Indonesia, Kenya, Korea, Malaysia, Mexico, Philippines, Portugal, Singapore, Taiwan, and Thailand).

The last two figures, 12 and 13, show the cross-economy scatter of real interest rates and consumption growth. Clearly, the treatment of expectations in these figures could be much improved, but I should still expect any important patterns to show up. An important point to note is what is *not* on the figures, that is, the set of fourteen economies (thirteen in figure 13) whose real interest rates were less than −10 percent (Argentina, Bolivia, Ghana, Israel, Madagascar, Mexico, Nicaragua, Sierra Leone, Somalia, Tanzania, Turkey, Uganda, Zambia, and in figure 12, Yugoslavia). Several of these have negative rates of several hundred percent, and their inclusion would dominate the figures, as well as producing regression lines with slope zero. The (insignificant) positive slopes in the two figures should be interpreted with that exclusion in mind. There is certainly no evidence here of any well-defined relation between interest rates and consumption growth, particularly in the Summers-Heston data. If we were to believe that preferences are common across countries, these results would be prima facie evidence against the supposition that consumption is being optimally allocated over time. By the standards of a decade or so ago, such evidence would be taken as favoring some form of state planning. We are nowadays much more skeptical about the ability of planning agencies to solve these problems, but that does not mean that saving is being optimally done. Indeed, the evidence reviewed in this section does not point to any simple policy solution for the saving problem, if problem it is. Apart from the ambiguity of the empirical results, one of the main difficulties is our lack of an accepted and well-supported theory of economic growth.

IV. Conclusions

My view is that the research priorities for the immediate future lie with the topics covered in sections I and II. I think the literature has sufficiently belabored the problems of physical accumulation. The issues are certainly important, but I cannot see useful ways forward without major theoretical advances, particularly in the theory of growth. The recent developments reviewed in Romer (1989) hold promise of such an advance, but, if that promise is fulfilled, research is likely to be redirected, perhaps toward a more intensive study of human capital formation.

The rather negative results of section III should at least serve as a warning to those who like to make glib generalizations on the basis of the experiences of

90 *Saving in Developing Countries*

Figure 12. *Consumption Growth and Interest Rates: World Bank Data*

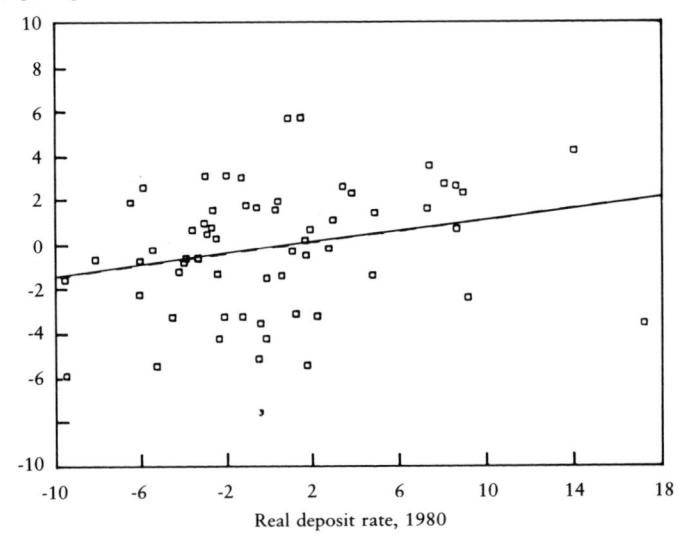

Consumption growth rate, 1980–86

Note: 60 countries excluding 14 with real deposit rates less than −10 percent.
Source: World Bank (1988). Consumption growth is from table 4, column 2, deflated by population growth from table 27, column 2. Interest rates are the nominal deposit rate in 1980 (table 25, column 7) less the actual rate of inflation for 1980–86 (table 25, column 6).

Figure 13. *Private Consumption Growth and Interest Rates: Summers and Heston Data*

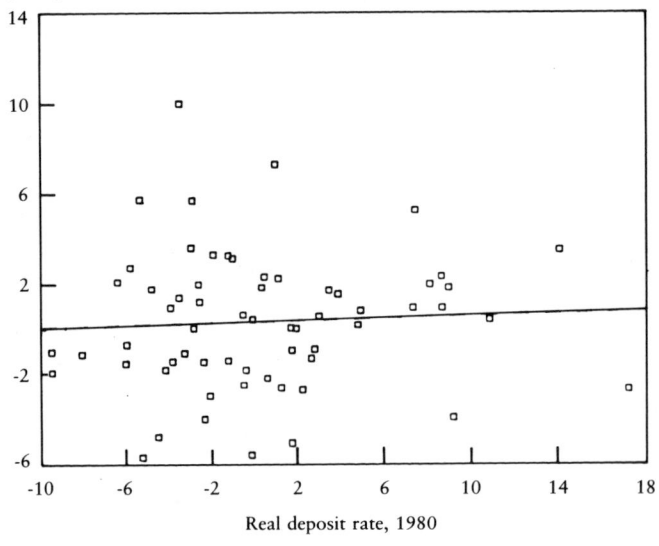

Consumption growth rate, 1980–85

Note: 62 countries, excluding 13 with real deposit rates less than −10 percent.
Sources: Interest rates: World Bank (1988, table 25); consumption growth: Summers and Heston (1988).

a few carefully selected countries: saving is not only about accumulation, but about consumption smoothing in the face of volatile incomes, and about providing insurance for poor people whose lives are difficult and uncertain. I think that the data exist that would help us understand more about how poor households use saving and assets, and I think we need a more positive understanding of how governments respond to fluctuations in their revenues.

Finally, and this is an area in which the World Bank should be taking the lead, we need to know more about the data, what they mean, and how to improve them. Useful work could be done by bringing together national income accountants and survey statisticians in a few countries where there is extensive experience in both areas. We also need experimental household surveys that will track cash flows within households, perhaps in quite small samples more akin to village studies, so that we can learn whether the apparent patterns of saving and dissaving are real, and if not, how to improve the survey questionnaires. Without such studies, and without these data improvements, our understanding is likely to remain precarious.

APPENDIX: THE CONSUMPTION FUNCTION WITH LIQUIDITY CONSTRAINTS

Section I deals with two cases of the Euler equation with a borrowing constraint. In the first case, which satisfies equation 3, the consumer is spending less than the total of his cash on hand (assets and current income), while in the second, equation 5, everything is being spent, and there may be dissaving. The two branches of the Euler equation can be combined into a single expression by writing

$$(\text{A-1}) \qquad \lambda(c_t) = \max\left\{\lambda(A_t + y_t), E_t\left[\frac{(1 + r)\lambda(c_{t+1})}{(1 + \delta)}\right]\right\}$$

In order to derive a solution to equation A-1 and for computational reasons, I will work with the simplest case, in which income is independently and identically distributed over time. I also require an assumption that prevents the marginal utility of money from becoming infinite in the worst possible case, which is when the individual has no assets and receives the lowest possible value of income. To this end, I assume that the income process is such that y_t always falls in the interval (y_0, y_1), with $y_1 > y_0 > 0$, y_1 possibly infinite but $\lambda(y_0) < \infty$. Income level y_0 is income in the "workhouse," and it is sufficient to sustain life. Define the "state" variable x_t as $A_t + y_t$; x_t is the amount of cash on hand. Given x_t, the consumer knows all that he or she needs to know; the interest rate is fixed, and because of the assumption that incomes are independent over time, income tomorrow is unpredictable by past events. As a consequence, consumption must be a function of x_t, and I write the consumption function

$$(\text{A-2}) \qquad c_t = f(x_t)$$

and the modified Euler equation (A-1) can be used to characterize the function $f(x)$. Note that if income were serially correlated, consumption would be a function of at least two state variables.

From the budget constraint (equation 2 in the main text) x_t evolves according to

$$(A\text{-}3) \qquad x_{t+1} = (1 + r)[x_t - f(x_t)] + y_{t+1}$$

From A-1 and A-3, inverting the monotonically decreasing function $\lambda(c_t)$ gives

$$(A\text{-}4) \qquad f(x_t) = \min\left(x_t, \lambda^{-1}\left\{E_t \frac{(1 + r)\lambda[f(x_{t+1})]}{1 + \delta}\right\}\right)$$

Substituting from A-3, and replacing the expectation by an integral,

$$(A\text{-}5) \quad f(x_t) = \min\left\{x_t, \lambda^{-1}\left[\int \frac{(1 + r)}{(1 + \delta)} \lambda[f\{(1 + r)[x_t - f(x_t)] + y\}]dF(y)\right]\right\}$$

where $F(y)$ is the distribution function of income y. Although A-5 is far from being an explicit functional form, it is straightforward to calculate the function from this expression, provided again that $\delta > r$. Given values of the two parameters, a marginal utility function, and a density function for income, an initial guess is made for $f(x_t)$, for example the piecewise linear form

$$(A\text{-}6) \qquad f_0(x) = \min\left[x, \frac{(rx + \mu)}{(1 + r)}\right]$$

where $\mu = E(y)$. The guess is substituted into the right-hand side of A-5, and a new function $f_1(x)$ is calculated using numerical integration to evaluate the expectation. After the first guess, only numerical solutions are possible, and the function must be evaluated over some suitable grid for x. Deaton and Laroque (1989) show that, provided $\delta > r$, this procedure defines a contraction mapping from one function to the next, so that the numerical calculations will be convergent.

References

Arrow, K. J. 1962. "The Economic Implications of Learning by Doing." *Review of Economic Studies* 29: 155–73.

Balassa, B. 1988. "Temporary Windfalls and Compensation Agreements." World Bank PPR Working Paper 28. Washington, D.C. Processed.

Berry, A. 1985. "On Trends in the Gap between Rich and Poor in Less Developed Countries: Why We Know so Little." *Review of Income and Wealth* 31: 337–54.

Betancourt, R. 1971. "The Normal Income Hypothesis in Chile." *Journal of the American Statistical Association* 66: 258–263.

Bevan, D. L., P. Collier, and J. W. Gunning. 1987. "Consequences of a Commodity Boom in a Controlled Economy: Accumulation and Redistribution in Kenya 1975–83." *World Bank Economic Review* 1 (3): 489–513.

Bewley, T. 1977. "The Permanent Income Hypothesis: A Theoretical Formulation." *Journal of Economic Theory* 16: 252–292.

Bhalla, S. S. 1979. "Measurement Errors and the Permanent Income Hypothesis: Evidence from Rural India." *American Economic Review* 69: 295–307.

———. 1980. "The Measurement of Permanent Income and Its Application to Saving Behavior." *Journal of Political Economy* 88: 722–43.

Blinder, A. S., and A. Deaton. 1985. "The Time Series Consumption Function Revisited." *Brookings Papers on Economic Activity* 2: 465–511.

Boskin, M. J. 1978. "Taxation, Saving and the Rate of Interest." *Journal of Political Economy* 86: S3–27.

Browning, M. J., A. Deaton, and M. J. Irish. 1985. "A Profitable Approach to Labor Supply and Commodity Demands over the Life Cycle." *Econometrica* 53: 503–43.

Caldwell, J. C. 1982. *Theory of Fertility Decline*. London: Academic Press.

Campbell, J. Y., and N. G. Mankiw. 1987. "Are Output Fluctuations Transitory?" *Quarterly Journal of Economics* 102: 857–80.

———. 1989. "Permanent Income, Current Income, and Consumption." Princeton University, Woodrow Wilson School of Public and International Affairs. Princeton, N.J. Processed.

———. Forthcoming. "Consumption, Income, and Interest Rates: the Euler Equation Approach Ten Years Later." NBER *Macroeconomics Annual 1989*.

Cochrane, J. H. 1988. "How Big Is the Random Walk in GNP?" *Journal of Political Economy* 96: 893–920.

Deaton, A. 1987. "Life-Cycle Models of Consumption: Is the Evidence Consistent with the Theory?" In T. F. Bewley, ed., *Advances in Econometrics: 5th World Congress*, vol. 2. New York: Cambridge University Press.

———. 1989. "Saving and Liquidity Constraints." Princeton University, Woodrow Wilson School of Public and International Affairs. Princeton, N.J. Processed.

Deaton, A., and G. Laroque. 1989. "On the Behavior of Commodity Prices." Princeton University, Research Program in Development Studies. Princeton, N.J. Processed.

Flavin, M. 1981. "The Adjustment of Consumption to Changing Expectations about Future Income." *Journal of Political Economy* 89: 974–1009.

———. 1988. "The Excess Smoothness of Consumption: Identification and Interpretation." NBER Working Paper 2807. National Bureau of Economic Research. Cambridge, Mass. Processed.

Friedman, M. 1957. *A Theory of the Consumption Function*. Princeton, N.J.: Princeton University Press.

Fry, M. J. 1988. *Money, Interest, and Banking in Economic Development*. Baltimore, Md.: Johns Hopkins University Press.

Gelb, A. 1988. *Oil Windfalls: Blessing or Curse?* New York: Oxford University Press.

Gersovitz, M. 1988. "Saving and Development." In H. Chenery and T. N. Srinivasan, eds., *Handbook of Development Economics*, vol. 1. Amsterdam: Elsevier.

Gersovitz, M., and C. H. Paxson. 1989. "The Economies of Africa and the Prices of Their Exports." Princeton University, Research Program in Development Studies. Princeton, N.J. Processed.

Ghosh, S., C. L. Gilbert, and A. J. Hughes-Hallett. 1987. *Stabilizing Speculative Commodity Markets*. Oxford: Clarendon.

Giovannini, A. 1983. "The Interest Rate Elasticity of Savings in Developing Countries: The Existing Evidence." *World Development* 11: 601–07.

———. 1985. "Saving and the Real Interest Rate in LDCs." *Journal of Development Economics* 18: 197–217.

Gupta, K. L. 1987. "Aggregate Savings, Financial Intermediation, and Interest Rate." *Review of Economics and Statistics* 69: 303–11.

Gustafson, R. L. 1958. *Carryover Levels for Grains*. U.S. Department of Agriculture, Technical Bulletin 1178. Washington, D.C.: U.S. Government Printing Office.

Hall, R. E. 1988. "Intertemporal Substitution in Consumption." *Journal of Political Economy* 96: 339–57.

Hall, R. E., and F. S. Mishkin. 1982. "The Sensitivity of Consumption to Transitory Income: Estimates from Panel Data on Households." *Econometrica* 50: 461–81.

Hansen, L. P., and K. J. Singleton. 1982. "Generalized Instrumental Variables Estimation of Non-linear Rational Expectations Models." *Econometrica* 50: 1269–86.

Hayashi, F. 1986. "Why Is Japan's Saving Rate So Apparently High?" *NBER Macroeconomics Annual 1986*: 147–210.

———. 1987. "Tests for Liquidity Constraints: A Critical Survey." In T. Bewley, ed., *Advances in Econometrics Fifth World Congress*, vol. 2. New York: Cambridge University Press.

Hong Kong, British Crown Colony of. 1980. *Household Expenditure Survey*.

Hotz, V. J., F. Kydland, and G. Sedlacek. 1988. "Intertemporal Preferences and Labor Supply." *Econometrica* 56: 335–60.

Kaldor, N. 1955–6. "Alternative Theories of Distribution." *Review of Economic Studies* 23: 83–100.

Kimball, M. S. 1988. "Precautionary Saving and the Marginal Propensity to Consume." University of Michigan. Ann Arbor, Mich. Processed.

———. Forthcoming. "Precautionary Saving in the Small and in the Large." *Econometrica*.

Korea, Government of the Republic of. Various years. *Annual Reports on the Family Income and Expenditure Survey*. Seoul.

Kotlikoff, L. J., and A. Spivak. 1981. "The Family as an Incomplete Annuities Market." *Journal of Political Economy* 89: 372–91.

Labys, W., and C. W. J. Granger. 1970. *Speculation, Hedging and Forecasts of Commodity Prices*. Lexington, Mass.: Heath.

Leland, H. E. 1968. "Savings and Uncertainty: The Precautionary Demand for Saving." *Quarterly Journal of Economics* 82: 465–73.

Lewis, W. A. 1954. "Economic Development with Unlimited Supplies of Labor." *Manchester School* 22: 139–91.

Lucas, R. E. 1988. "On the Mechanics of Economic Development." *Journal of Monetary Economics* 22: 3–42.

McKinnon, R. I. 1973. *Money and Capital in Economic Development*. Washington, D.C.: Brookings.

Mankiw, N. G., J. J. Rotemberg, and L. H. Summers. 1985. "Intertemporal Substitution in Macroeconomics." *Quarterly Journal of Economics* 100: 225–51.

Mason, A. 1987. "National Savings Rates and Population Growth: A New Model and

New Evidence." In D. G. Johnson and R. Lee, eds., *Population Growth and Economic Development: Issues and Evidence*. Madison: University of Wisconsin Press.

———. 1988. "Saving, Economic Growth, and Demographic Change." *Population and Development Review* 14: 113–44.

Mirrlees, J. A. 1988. "Optimal Commodity Price Intervention." Nuffield College, Oxford. Processed.

Muellbauer, J. 1982. "The Measurement of Long-Run Living Standards: An Application and Evaluation of the Permanent Income Hypothesis." World Bank Living Standards Measurement Study. Washington, D.C. Processed.

Musgrove, P. 1979. "Permanent Household Income and Consumption in Urban South America." *American Economic Review* 69: 355–68.

———. 1980. "Income Distribution and the Aggregate Consumption Function." *Journal of Political Economy* 88: 504–25.

National Academy of Sciences. 1986. *Population Growth and Economic Development: Policy Questions*. Washington, D.C.: National Academy Press.

Newbery, D. and J. E. Stiglitz. 1981. *The Theory of Commodity Price Stabilization: A Study in the Economics of Risk*. Oxford: Oxford University Press.

———. 1982. "Optimal Commodity Stockpiling Rules." *Oxford Economic Papers* 34: 403–27.

Paxson, C. H. 1989. "Household Savings in Thailand: Responses to Income Shocks." Princeton University Research Program in Development Studies. Princeton, N.J. Processed.

Rakshit, M. 1982. "Income, Saving, and Capital Formation in India: A Step Towards a Solution of the Saving-Investment Puzzle." *Economic and Political Weekly* 17 (annual).

———. 1983. "On Assessment and Interpretation of Savings-Investment Estimates in India." *Economic and Political Weekly* 18.

Reserve Bank of India. 1982. *Capital Formation and Saving in India 1950–51 to 1979–80*. Report of the Working Group on Savings. Bombay.

Romer, P. M. 1986. "Increasing Returns and Long-Run Growth." *Journal of Political Economy* 94: 1002–37.

Romer, P. M. 1988. "Endogenous Technical Change." University of Chicago and University of Rochester. Processed. (May).

———. Forthcoming. "Capital Accumulation in the Theory of Long-Run Growth." In R. J. Barro, ed., *Modern Business Cycle Theory*. Cambridge, Mass.: Harvard University Press.

Samuelson, P. A. 1971. "Stochastic Speculative Price." *Proceedings of the National Academy of Sciences* 68: 335–37.

Schechtman, J. 1976. "An Income Fluctuation Problem." *Journal of Economic Theory* 12: 218–41.

Schechtman, J., and V. Escudero. 1977. "Some Results on 'An Income Fluctuation Problem'." *Journal of Economic Theory* 16: 151–66.

Sen, A. K. 1967. "Isolation, Assurance, and the Social Rate of Discount." *Quarterly Journal of Economics* 81: 112–24.

Shaw, E. S. 1973. *Financial Deepening in Economic Development*. New York: Oxford University Press.

Sibley, D. S. 1975. "Permanent and Transitory Income Effects on a Model of Optimal Consumption with Wage Income Uncertainty." *Journal of Economic Theory* 11: 68–82.

Skinner, J. 1988. "Risky Income, Life-Cycle Consumption, and Precautionary Saving." *Journal of Monetary Economics* 25: 237–55.

Solow, R. M. 1956. "A Contribution to the Theory of Economic Growth." *Quarterly Journal of Economics* 70: 65–94.

Summers, L. H., and C. Carroll. 1989. "The Growth-Saving Nexus." Paper presented to National Bureau of Economic Research Conference on Savings, Maui, Hawaii, January.

Summers, R., and A. Heston. 1988. "A New Set of International Comparisons of Real Product and Prices for 130 Countries, 1950–1985." *Review of Income and Wealth* 34: 1–26.

Venti, S. F., and D. A. Wise. 1989. "The Saving Effect of Tax-Deferred Retirement Accounts: Evidence from SIPP." Paper presented to National Bureau of Economic Research Conference on Savings, Maui, Hawaii, January.

Visaria, P., and S. Pal. 1980. *Poverty and Living Standards in Asia: An Overview of the Main Results and Lessons of Selected Household Surveys*. World Bank Living Standards Measurement Study Working Paper 2. Washington, D.C.

Wolpin, K. I. 1982. "A New Test of the Permanent Income Hypothesis: The Impact of Weather on the Income and Consumption of Farm Households in India." *International Economic Review* 23: 583–94.

World Bank. 1988. *World Development Report 1988*. New York: Oxford University Press.

Zeldes, S. 1989a. "Consumption and Liquidity Constraints: An Empirical Investigation." *Journal of Political Economy* 97: 305–46.

———. 1989b. "Optimal Consumption with Stochastic Income: Deviations from Certainty Equivalence." *Quarterly Journal of Economics* 104: 275–98.

COMMENT ON "SAVING IN DEVELOPING COUNTRIES: THEORY AND REVIEW,"
BY DEATON

Fumio Hayashi

Professor Deaton's paper covers a wide range of issues related to saving. Given my background and comparative advantage in empirical studies of saving, it is perhaps appropriate for me to focus on his theoretical and empirical discussions of household saving, the topics to which the author says future research efforts should be directed.

The paper starts out by setting out a theoretical model of saving. In this model, the immortal family is the basic decision unit. The two crucial ingredients are, first, that the family is impatient and, second, that it lacks the option of borrowing. If borrowing were possible in this infinite-horizon model, it would be almost as good as having access to fair income insurance. With borrowing constraints, the impatient household elects to hold on to assets during high-income periods, not because it wants to shift resources from the present to the future for increased future consumption, but because it wants to insure itself against bad draws of income. Thus the household consumption/saving behavior has two regimes, as described in figure 1 of the paper: the zero-saving regime and the self-insurance regime. I should perhaps note that this type of consumption function has been derived (from different settings) by Helpman (1981).

The author argues that the model's predictions are consistent with several pieces of empirical evidence, including the nonunitary elasticity of consumption with respect to permanent income, the prevalence of households with negative saving, and the "excess sensitivity" findings in the U.S. literature.

The claim that the model does not deliver the standard result of unitary elasticity with respect to permanent income is somewhat misleading. Except for the certainty equivalence case, consumption cannot be related to a single-scalar indicator like permanent income. In the present model, consumption depends on two indicators (or, to be more precise, three, if the variance of income is included) of the household's resources, cash on hand, and mean earnings. As pointed out in the paper, the model does deliver the proportionality result that consumption is homogeneous in those multiple indicators. This homogeneity property of the model is not inconsistent with the empirical finding that rich households tend to save disproportionately more than poor households, if the

---

Fumio Hayashi is a professor of economics at the University of Pennsylvania.

© 1990 The International Bank for Reconstruction and Development / THE WORLD BANK.

earning process over generations is regressive. In wealthier households, the offspring are less likely to have as much earning capacity as the current adult generation. If so, the current high-earning generation will save a higher fraction of its wealth than the next generation.

Let me also note that the case for the excess sensitivity for the United States is rather shaky. Recent work by Runkle (1989) using the Panel Study of Income Dynamics micro data (compiled by the Survey Research Center of the University of Michigan) finds no evidence for excess sensitivity.

My impression is that for most East Asian countries, negative saving is relatively rare. For Japan and the Republic of Korea, it is difficult to find a cohort that dissaves (see Collins 1989; Hayashi, Ando, and Ferris 1988). The present model may be applicable to less developed countries, but not to East Asian developing countries. Furthermore, the model has an uneasy prediction that poor countries will be eternally poor. It also cannot explain why saving and growth rates differ between countries.

This brings me to the issue addressed in section II of the paper: the inability of the alternative theory—the life-cycle hypothesis—to explain the international differences in the age profile of consumption. The paper reinforces the finding in Summers and Carroll (1989) that the international differences in the distribution of lifetime resources between generations brought about by the differences in growth rates are not reflected in the age profile of consumption. Although I agree that this finding probably is fundamentally inconsistent with the life-cycle hypothesis, my reaction to the evidence presented in the paper is a cautionary note that the age of the household head does not necessarily correspond to the generation or cohort of that age when the household consists of many generations.

To pursue the point, imagine that there are only two generations, young and old, and that the age-earnings profile is flat. Suppose all households are extended families, so that household consumption is the sum of consumption by the two generations. Let w_y and w_o be earnings of the young and the old living in the same household. Since the average age-earnings profile is flat, the mean of w_y equals the mean of w_o. Suppose that w_y and w_o are uncorrelated, so that both the young and the old in the same household have an equal chance to be the head, that is, the main income earner. Then it is easy to see that the age-consumption profile will also be flat irrespective of the growth rate of the economy. Another qualification I would like to make about the Summers-Carroll finding is that the relatively flat age-consumption profile for rapidly growing countries may be (partly) due to government income redistribution programs, such as social security, that shift resources from the young to the old. It must be granted, however, that under the life-cycle hypothesis, it is not clear why people have agreed to such income redistributions.

What about the two pieces of evidence presented in the paper against the infinite-horizon model? One is the macroeconomic evidence that there is no international and time-series correlation between consumption growth and the real interest rate. The other is systematic variation of saving rates with the age of the household head. But the latter evidence seems to be consistent with the infinite-horizon models. Expenditures on, say, sporting goods depend on the age of the head. One wouldn't take this as evidence against the infinite-horizon models. By the same token, that the aggregate saving rate depends on the age distribution of people (not on resources) seems to be consistent with those models. And, on the lack of correlation between consumption growth and real interest rates, it is not clear that the deposit rate or even the interest rate on short-term government securities is the appropriate interest rate to use, because those rates may reflect transaction services.

References

Collins, S. 1989. "Savings Behavior in Ten Developing Countries." Harvard University Economics Department. Processed.

Hayashi, Fumio, A. Ando, and R. Ferris. 1988. "Life Cycle and Bequest Savings." *Journal of the Japanese and International Economies* 2, no. 4: 450–91.

Helpman, Elhanan. 1981. "Optimal Spending and Money Holdings in the Presence of Liquidity Constraints." *Econometrica* 49, no. 6: 1559–70.

Runkle, D. 1989. "Consumption and Liquidity Constraints." Research Department, Federal Reserve Bank of Minneapolis. Processed.

Summers, L. H., and C. Carroll. 1989. "The Growth-Saving Nexus." Harvard University Economics Department. Processed.

COMMENT ON "SAVING IN DEVELOPING COUNTRIES: THEORY AND REVIEW,"
BY DEATON

Steven B. Webb

Angus Deaton's useful and thought-provoking discussion breaks new ground, as well as reviewing what others have done. He sets out a new and promising model for saving in developing countries. I will briefly comment on this precautionary saving model and suggest how some features of it are also relevant to the more conventional issues raised in the latter parts of the analysis.

Deaton's household model for explaining much of the saving by poor agricultural households is convincing: the constraint of no *net* borrowing strikes me as entirely plausible. Net borrowing is uncollateralized lending, which is like lending to sovereign nations—for which a vast literature now attests to the problems in motivating repayment.

The model explains many of the stylized facts about the saving and asset-management behavior of common people in developing countries. It will be interesting to see the results of applying Deaton's model to actual income estimates for commodity producers in developing countries, as he plans to do for Côte d'Ivoire. Will plausible assumptions of parameter values yield simulations that show a time series of asset accumulation, decumulation, and famines consistent with other evidence for the economies examined?

One nexus of stylized facts about saving that Deaton's model does not seem to address is the tenacity with which people save for and hold on to their own land and housing. Farmers also own their animals, trees, tools, and seeds. Implicitly, this production side of saving behavior is left out of his model. In the face of absolute starvation, people do of course sell off or consume these core assets. But the decision to do so seems a lot more drastic than running down a savings account or a precautionary stockpile of grain. Ownership of core assets, like land and housing, defines one's socioeconomic category. Changing one's wealth status within a category would seem to be much less serious and easier to reverse than changing from one category to another. Some economics is probably also involved in the distinction between holding core assets and other assets. Agency problems in the rental markets imply a higher rate of return on saving for ownership of core assets than on other assets, and higher than the rate of time preference. Saving to acquire core assets is another channel through

---

Steven Webb is on the staff of the Country Economics Department of the World Bank.

© 1990 The International Bank for Reconstruction and Development / THE WORLD BANK.

which an increase in the number of households would lead to net saving in the aggregate.

Deaton points out that some households seem to have a lower rate of time preference, below the interest rate, and therefore accumulate assets and become the capitalist accumulators of the society. If the rate of time preference declines as wealth and income increase, a class of capitalist savers could develop endogenously from a population with identical basic utility functions. Households that start out saving only for precautionary motives (and for purchase of land and housing for their own use) might get a sequence of good draws at the income lottery, which would raise their assets and current consumption to a point where their rate of time preference would be less than the interest rate. Then they would become capitalists with trend accumulation of assets.

Of course, this could work the other way if the economy were hit by a series of negative shocks. More households would be falling out of the capitalist class than were being bumped up into it. This might explain some of the observed correlations between income growth and saving rates.

Development involves the long-run expansion of urban sectors, at the expense of agriculture. It would be useful to consider the economics of saving during the process of the urbanization of the poor, who still have a high rate of time preference and need to smooth consumption. For instance, what is the economics of saving when one's income depends heavily on government spending, and when the main available asset for saving—money—is a prime target for taxation in fiscal emergencies that also depress government spending?

The third and fourth sections of Deaton's paper mostly address conventional issues on their own terms. He rightly criticizes much of the literature for using inappropriate theories and methods, carried over from the study of industrial economies.

Deaton's discussion of the issue of how the government should react to fluctuations of commodity export prices does draw on his model of precautionary saving at the household level. If households are better than governments at saving to smooth the effects of fluctuating export commodity prices, as Deaton suggests, then we should think further about how the World Bank's lending programs to commodity exporters might be designed to discourage procyclical government fiscal policy.

In the discussion of life-cycle saving, Deaton effectively rebuts the notion that households in developing countries try to smooth and level consumption fully, and aim to run assets down to zero at death. But some of Deaton's model might usefully be carried over to the issue of life-cycle saving—carried over in the sense of using the nonnegative asset constraint and the high rate of time preference. One would need to drop or modify Deaton's assumption of extended-family households, in favor of nuclear households, which become more prevalent during urbanization and industrialization. No net borrowing would mean that consumption by nuclear families (headed by workers) would almost equal average earnings in the parents' younger years, when the presence of children would increase the demand for consumption. They would do only precautionary saving, like Deaton's rural extended families. Nuclear households would start to save for future consumption on a life-cycle scale only after the children left home. Having a rate of time preference above the interest rate would mean that people would tilt consumption toward the present, but would still save some for old age, aiming to have a smooth, albeit declining, consumption path.

Deaton notes that efforts to detect the influence of real interest rates on the saving rate have failed to come up with robust results. Strong risk aversion and the predominance of the precautionary motive for saving could help explain why the level of real interest rates is not monotonically related to saving rates. Risk-averse, precautionary savers like those in Deaton's households would worry at least as much about the variance of real interest rates as about the level. Any time the ex post real interest rate is (or has recently been) more than ten points below or above zero, people probably become uneasy about the real interest rate. Firms and wealthy individuals may happily and warily keep their money in the domestic financial system when real interest rates are 25 or 50 percent, because they have the means to move assets abroad quickly. But common people can move assets only slowly from a bank account into farm animals or consumer durables. They will be much more cautious in responding to changes in real interest rates. A real interest rate above 10 percent would probably not be sustainable for long enough to attract such savers into the financial system. Their saving in the informal sector would probably not be well measured.

The World Bank tells people in developing countries that they should save in order to grow. And Bank programs try to tell people how to save in ways that will provide more resources for investment. Deaton is telling us that people in developing countries behave as if their primary motive for saving is to protect consumption against disasters. Perhaps the Bank should reprogram its priorities to match theirs. Suppose, for instance, that the first priority in reform of the financial sector were to provide people with more secure and convenient instruments for precautionary saving. Would precautionary priorities lead to recommendations different from when the priority is to promote investment or close the fiscal gap? Would the design of instruments to suit the desires of precautionary savers raise the amount of saving available for investment? How could the assets of precautionary savers be made available for the most productive investment while still respecting the priority of security?

FLOOR DISCUSSION OF DEATON PAPER

Deaton agreed partially with Hayashi's (discussant) comments about "dynasties" in his model, but he didn't want people to believe that his model was committed to a dynastic, infinitely lived family of consumers. That is a mathematical convenience. These households often run out of assets altogether. The real horizon is the period until they run out of assets. For a shorter horizon, the behavior would look much the same.

More serious for Deaton was the question of whether these people are "doomed" and whether we should feel sorry for them because they are caught forever in this liquidity trap. Deaton mentioned that this was not the case. First, they are doomed partly by assumption, because for simplicity's sake he had assumed that the income process is stationary, that the harvest never gets better, that incomes are constant—and of course if you assume no growth, you never get growth. You need more complicated models to handle that. Second, Deaton said that Webb's (discussant) point that the patient consumers in this model do accumulate wealth and get rich, so that wealth is being accumulated in these societies, was also important. It is just that a lot of the saving is being done by very few people, and most people are saving very little (an idea he still endorsed, though it had gone out of fashion).

One participant observed that Deaton, like Irving Fisher, sees poorer households as more impatient than the richer households—unlike Hirofumi Uzawa, who believes that impatience is a property of richer households. Deaton was happy to be associated with Fisher in this view.

Commenting on the relation between uncertainty in income and saving, one participant said it is not enough to assume that the households are risk averse. You have to assume more about the nature of the risk aversion before you can say anything about how saving would respond to changes in uncertainty.

Another participant congratulated Deaton for formally taking up the implication of covariance of risks in rural areas for at least some kinds of rural behavior. He found the implications to be much broader—to include, for example, how land markets behave in such economies. Deaton agreed with the participant's observation that the reason this model works well in rural areas is that rural labor markets are tied to harvest outcomes, so when you have a bad harvest both your output and labor markets collapse. The model would not

This session was chaired by Yung Chul Park, professor of economics, Korea University.

© 1990 The International Bank for Reconstruction and Development / THE WORLD BANK.

work well for urban areas, where you can simply make intersectoral switches if one sector has a worse year than another.

One participant suspected Deaton's model was also unable to explain saving behavior in urban areas because it did not incorporate technological change in the income function. If family income increased over time because of technological changes, saving behavior might change to serve both precautionary and investment purposes. Deaton's response was that the model could be extended—he was in fact extending it in another paper—but it would look very different when income processes were growing.

Deaton's type of model is likely to miss what one participant saw as the most important form of household saving: own-account investment by a rural household that is both a consuming and producing unit. Own-account investment by rural households—in everything from tree crops to buildings—is an important form of saving which is typically not measured at all. Deaton accepted this as a legitimate criticism of his paper, explaining that such saving did not easily fit into his framework. A rural household has both production and consumption sides, and his was a theory of smoothing consumption over time. He agreed that accumulation within the household firm was as important; however, the question remained: why not dump some firm assets when the consumption going gets tough? The answer might be, as Webb had stated earlier, that the consequences of doing so were much more serious than shedding your financial assets. Selling land or capital stock, for instance, might be irreversible. Although Deaton had not tried to build a formal theory that would answer these objections, he agreed that it was important to try to do so.

Moving from the household to the aggregate level, Webb suggested that if you are applying this model to agricultural households that save by, say, stockpiling grain, each household operates independently so you don't have to worry about how it all adds up. But if households are saving cash, then when they're on the low side they have to use the cash for purchases, so someone else out there must be holding the stockpiles of grain. Maybe that is the capitalist class that takes advantage of famines or almost-famines once households are holding financial rather than consumable assets—but then there is an adding-up problem. In a nationwide drought do they import grain, or is someone in the domestic economy holding it? Deaton felt that some of the grain could come from outside and some from other people. He thought of such outcomes as being highly correlated within the village but not so highly correlated across the whole economy.

During the discussion, one participant said that he could see the asset-income ratio going down if financial institutions were to develop that allowed for a transfer of funds to less covariant regions. He wondered if Deaton thought the saving rate would also go down.

Because the question could be interpreted in different ways, Deaton ended up providing two answers. First, under some circumstances development of the financial system, by increasing the rate of interest and increasing people's options across regions, would increase the saving ratio. This model doesn't produce a high saving ratio, he said, but a higher interest rate would. It is like a commodity model in which people are holding assets as buffers and if the higher interest rate means it is cheaper to hold the assets, people will buffer more. Second, and perhaps more directly addressing the participant's point, would it reduce saving if you opened banks that could invest in other parts of the economy, so that the banks could act as agents spreading risk across the economy? Deaton thought it would, although it would be hard to see them as banks, because only if they could develop instruments for explicitly insuring against bad crops—another issue altogether—would saving decrease and there be less incentive to hold precautionary assets.

A participant asked Deaton what moves the aggregate saving rate. If you have a kink at 80 or 100 (see figure 1 in Deaton paper), and behavior to the left of it (essentially precautionary saving) accounts for more saving than behavior to the right of it, whatever determines that kink presumably has a tremendous impact on the overall saving rate. What in the real world corresponds to that point in Deaton's model? According to Deaton that point, or kink, is essentially the mean of the income process or close to it. The participant cited Stephen Zeldes as putting that level somewhere around a low U.S. income, but Deaton obviously puts it at a low "Côte d'Ivoire" income. The question is, what is moving it? Deaton clarified that below the kink people don't save at all and probably dissave, using everything they have to buy food and the like. Above that, they save some. In the aggregate, flashes of temporary income—a good harvest—will produce high aggregate saving and a bad harvest will produce dissaving or a low saving ratio. By itself this model is not suited to explain aggregate saving in countries where saving is positive. For that, said Deaton, you must turn to more traditional explanations such as patient consumers who behave more like standard life-cycle consumers.

Another World Bank participant pursued the question, suggesting that if the interest rate affects saving at all, one would expect it would do so after the kink (in figure 1). But since Deaton had seen no evidence that the interest rate affected saving, what else would explain the slope after the kink? The investment climate? Deaton said he had no answer to the question of whether there is some point in the income distribution at which saving behavior changes. His figure represents a single household, not aggregate saving, he explained. To the left of the kink, you have no saving at all; to the right of it, some income would be retained for precautionary saving. The individual is behaving in a precautionary manner at all points; there is no distinction between precautionary and nonprecautionary saving. Everything about that curve—except of course the 45-degree line that stays fixed—is determined by everything else, including the interest rate and the kink point. If the implicit question is whether there is some break in income distribution, below which people don't save and above which they do, the answer might be yes and might be no, but his model could not answer that directly.

Do households dissave or not? Deaton felt that data problems make it difficult to answer that question. The Korean evidence Hayashi had cited in his comments was data on Korean cities; household surveys show positive saving in cities in other countries as well, but Deaton's is a theory about agricultural households, and he thought a number of surveys show saving in rural areas to be unreasonably low or negative. Deaton mentioned that empirical work is being done on the model; the World Bank is funding a project to examine panel data from Côte d'Ivoire, which is now available for three successive years.

The theme of inadequate data on saving came up repeatedly. One participant went so far as to say the data in the World Bank's *World Development Report* are often not worth the paper they are printed on. Half the tables in the *World Development Report*, he claimed, give data on income distribution, infant mortality, and population for countries for which in living memory there has been no census. Sometimes a bad number is worse than no number at all. He bemoaned the Bank's methodology for computing GDP rates and its reluctance to give ranges for estimates.

A Bank participant agreed about the seriousness of the data problem, pointing out, for example, the divergence in saving rates between U.S. flow of funds and national income data. He believed the problem would require vast resources. It would not make sense to put ranges on the estimates; if the Bank didn't know the numbers, it certainly didn't know the ranges.

At the outset, Park (chair) had observed that ten years ago a U.S. economist had written a paper about why Koreans save so little—and now people wonder why they save so much. Despite learning a lot from the discussion, Park felt he was still unable to explain why Koreans save too much, if they do. Now we had two competing models to explain saving behavior in developing countries. But we still have a long way to go to understand saving behavior, and there are many data problems.

PROCEEDINGS OF THE WORLD BANK ANNUAL CONFERENCE
ON DEVELOPMENT ECONOMICS 1989

Social Sector Pricing Policy Revisited: A Survey of Some Recent Controversies

Emmanuel Jimenez

Some developing countries have begun to reevaluate the traditional policy of charging uniformly low (or zero) prices for such social services as education and health. But the reform of social service pricing has been controversial. Some disagreements are ideologically based and inherently irreconcilable. Others are about the empirical evidence concerning the impact of raising prices on efficiency and equity. Simulations of behavioral models show that the price elasticity of demand is generally low and that prices can be raised from present levels without significantly affecting consumption. But this responsiveness varies by price level and income category, underlining the need to protect the very poor. There has been some debate about the sensitivity of the parameters estimated, and the technical, administrative, and economic costs of targeting have not been researched. What is needed is more empirical evidence that proposed measures to protect the poor are feasible as well as effective; estimates of the magnitude of the efficiency gain; and systematic evaluations of actual attempts at social sector price reform. Other questions to be considered in further research are: Have alternative forms of financing been adequately compared with price reform? Can and should there be operational rules of thumb about social sector pricing, comparable to the marginal cost approach to public sector pricing? How can noneconomic objectives be incorporated into pricing policy?

Traditionally, the public sector has dominated social services in most countries. Government provides most of these services free, or almost free, and has often restricted the fees private providers can charge users.

Subsidized education and health services have dramatically improved basic indicators of well-being, such as literacy and child mortality rates, during the past three decades. But some governments in developing countries, with active support from the World Bank, are beginning to reevaluate the policy of uniform and heavy public subsidization, for three reasons:

Emmanuel Jimenez is a senior economist in the Country Economics Department of The World Bank. He is grateful for the useful comments on an earlier version from Nancy Birdsall, Dennis de Tray, Stanley Fischer, Johannes Linn, Benno Ndulu, Javad Khalilzadeh-Shirazi, Nicholas Stern, and several colleagues from the Public Economics Division. John Brondolo and Fiona Mackintosh provided research and editorial assistance.

© 1990 The International Bank for Reconstruction and Development / THE WORLD BANK.

First, though more investment in education and health would still be socially profitable, the outlook is bleak for tapping central government resources, which are under more and more strain from recent macroeconomic setbacks. Additional sources of funding have to be found.

Second, uniformly low prices for social services mean that expensive services are much more subsidized than cheaper ones. Yet the poorest people often have least access to these high-cost services for a variety of reasons, including the high private cost of consumption and built-in biases when services are rationed.

Third, the limited resources devoted to social services are badly used. Too little goes to cheaper, more cost-effective alternatives—partly because there is no pricing mechanism to impose discipline either on users or providers.

Out of these problems have come proposals to revamp the traditional pricing structures.[1] These proposals, and consequently this review, focus on publicly provided education and health services—sectors in which pricing policies have traditionally been ignored. The common link across their recommendations is the idea that policies that differentiate prices by type of service and by type of consumer are generally more efficient and equitable than low and uniform price policies (or slogans, such as free education and health for all).

Though few question the diagnosis, many have debated the prescription that better pricing policy will improve the situation. This review addresses the controversies under three headings: ideological, empirical, and conceptual.

I. The "New" View: Ideology and Interpretation

Charging for social services is not a new idea. Both education and health services have, until this century, been provided privately on a fee-for-service basis in many countries (see Roth 1987). None of the papers reviewed here advocated a return to this system. Most analysts recognize that externalities, lack of information about benefits, equity considerations, and failure in complementary financial markets mean there is a continuing role for government.

What Is the New View?

The "new" idea is that governments should reexamine whether, given budgetary allocations too low to finance socially productive spending in the social sectors, selectively increasing some user fees leads to greater efficiency and equity.[2] The focus has tended to be on second-best allocation.

The basic premise is that investments in social services, like most other long-term investments, are particularly at risk during periods of adjustment. Yet in many countries where the needs are greatest, social sector subsidies (that is,

---

1. See, for example, World Bank (1986, 1987); Akin and Birdsall (1987); de Ferranti (1985); Griffin (1988); Jimenez (1986b, 1987); and Psacharopoulos, Tan, and Jimenez (1989).
2. The word "new" is in quotation marks because the ideas are not original—they are applications of optimal tax models with nonresalable commodities (for theoretical expositions, see Besley 1989; Jimenez 1987; Heady 1989; Katz 1987; and Thobani 1983).

public provision at a price less than social cost) are wasted. Revising pricing policy, while not a panacea, may be an effective antidote. The principal recommendations[3] are to:

- *Increase prices for some social services* that have large private benefits and are consumed mostly by high-income people—to raise revenue, direct implicit subsidies away from the rich, and to assist in demand management. For many countries, these services include higher education and curative care in urban hospitals.
- *Target subsidies toward poor households.*[4] To protect the poor's consumption of services whose prices are increased, subsidies, in the form of fee exemptions as well as outright payments, should be better targeted—if possible, distributed on the basis of income or wealth criteria.
- *Invest revenues in socially profitable services.* In education, this often means expanding or improving primary education or expanding secondary and tertiary-level disciplines for which skills are in short supply; in health, primary health care, particularly in rural areas, is frequently a priority.
- *Develop credit and insurance markets.* In practice, the low level of development of these markets precludes raising prices, particularly for high-cost services such as higher education and in-patient hospital care. Expanding these financial markets also serves as an important allocative device because they allow mobilization of resources when payoffs are in the future (education) or involve the pooling of risk (health).
- *Liberalize overly centralized provision.* Alternatives to central government providers, such as local communities or private groups, should be allowed to compete with public providers. This will increase private financing as well as encourage supplier efficiency.

Some Conflicting Interpretations

The view that market-based incentives have a role to play in allocating social sector resources is not universal. Advocacy of price reform has been attacked for its "assumption of essentially selfish individual behavior" (see Gilson 1988, p. 16, on health) or for being "too short-sighted and economistic" (see Dempster 1987 on education.) Similar views are expressed by Bray (1986); Klees (1984); Abel-Smith (1987); Cornia, Jolly, and Stewart (1987); and various commentators in Pan American Health Organization (1988); and Neave (1988).

The heat of the debate has fueled misunderstanding of the intent, content, and logic of the proposals. Three prevalent misconceptions are that the proposals advocate wholesale cuts in health and education, that they intend full cost recovery, and that they entail drastic downgrading of universities and hospitals.

---

3. These recommendations are summarized from the works cited in footnote 1.

4. Subsidy is defined as public expenditure less private payment. The public expenditure may accrue to an individual through a transfer of purchasing power (for example, a social security payment or a scholarship check) or through access to a public service at a price less than the cost of provision (for example, free health care at a public clinic).

Do the proposals advocate wholesale cuts in health and education? The proposed policy packages are clear that prices should be raised only selectively. Services with fewer "public good" characteristics, such as positive externalities, are first on the list for price increases. These tend to be the services consumed least by the poor. The proposals generally exclude charges for primary education and basic rural health care or some types of preventive care from the proposed increases—and in fact call for increased subsidies for these basic services. Only when it is clear that central governments are unable or unwilling to direct adequate resources to social priorities should prices for basic services be increased. Then, the money raised should be spent on basic supplies that are often the first to be cut when budgets are tight, such as school books or medicines. Experience has shown that many people, even the relatively poor, are willing to pay for a service if they know that their access or the quality will be consequently improved.

Do the proposals advocate full cost recovery?[5] For university education or hospital care generally not; the recommendation generally differs in this respect from the traditional pricing suggestions for infrastructure sectors, like electricity, water, and housing (see Julius and Alicbusan 1988 for a review of their implementation record). Even services not characterized by severe externalities or not otherwise considered true public goods cannot necessarily be bound by standard public sector pricing rules because of imperfections in credit and insurance markets. The proponents of user charges are careful to make pricing recommendations contingent on the success of complementary markets. One possible source of confusion may be that the papers on pricing policies did not develop operationally oriented rules of thumb (for example, what percentage of costs to recover) to correspond with marginal cost pricing in other sectors.

Are the policy packages meant to cut back university education and the provision of hospital care? Concern over this issue has sometimes meant dismissal of the whole policy package. But, although the fee advocates do argue that some subsidies can be cut, they stipulate that this should be done only when present subsidies produce few benefits, consumption is not going to be severely affected, and the poor can be adequately protected. For example, in many countries there is currently excess demand for student places at the same time that graduates are finding it hard to get jobs. Moreover, current rationing schemes do not encourage use by the poor. Rather than indiscriminately dispensing allowances, low tuition, and grants across all activities, these and other subsidies should be directed toward high-return activities and toward the poor. Primary education is an obvious priority, but some activities in higher education research or even teaching may also have high returns.

---

5. Cost recovery is defined as the amount of public expenditure that is financed by user payments. It generally does not imply setting price equivalent to marginal cost. (See Jimenez 1987 for a fuller discussion of average versus marginal cost pricing in this connection.)

II. Empirically Based Controversies

The empirical evidence that uniformly high subsidies across all social services meet neither equity nor efficiency objectives is fairly strong. But can user charges improve the situation? The principal empirical bones of contention are: the impact of user fees on the poor's access to public subsidies; the impact of user fees on efficiency and allocation; and the administrative and political feasibility of implementing major reforms.

Do User Fees Impede the Poor's Access to Social Services?

In many countries, poor consumers do not generally have good access to publicly subsidized social services, despite uniformly low fee levels. But would increased user fees help?

Present subsidies are not directed toward the poor. Free or almost free provision does not ensure that the poor will get more or even their proportionate share of the subsidies. Uniformly low prices mean that high-cost services are subsidized more heavily than low-cost services. The relatively rich consume more of the high-cost services, for several reasons.

First, high subsidies are usually financed from general revenues. When budgets are constrained, services often have to be rationed. Unless carefully and deliberately targeted, rationing often favors high-income categories. For example, rationing of school places, nominally by ability, may in fact favor richer households which can afford to pay for tutoring or to repeat a grade.[6] The same may be true of rationing through providing the service only in urban areas. Population densities are high in urban areas and the services are cheaper to provide, but urban incomes are also likely to be higher than rural incomes.

Second, even with a zero or very low price, social services are costly to use. The private cost includes payments for transport, materials (medicines or school books), and opportunity cost. For education, the opportunity cost alone can amount to 25-50 percent of the total social (private plus public) cost of education (Jimenez 1987, p. 19). Even though poor adults generally have a lower opportunity cost of time than richer adults, this relationship may be reversed for children. Poor children tend to work at home and in the marketplace and may find it more difficult to attend school. Also, other costs (particularly transport) may be higher for the poor.

Table 1 shows the distribution of education and health subsidies in several countries. Students from the highest quartile of the income distribution profile in Chile, Colombia, Indonesia, and Malaysia receive between 51 and 83 percent

---

6. Rationing through waiting for a service such as health care can favor the relatively poor if the price of a wait is higher to those with a higher opportunity cost of time. But the benefits from redistributing resources in this way (as opposed to the benefits of improved access but at a higher tax) may not exceed the costs if the government can redistribute income effectively by direct transfers that can be used to finance higher prices (see Bucovetsky 1984); other allocation mechanisms are available (Sah 1987); or the benefits are unevenly distributed among those who wait.

Table 1. *Who Gets Social Sector Subsidies?*

		Percentage of government subsidy received by income group		
Country and sector	Year of survey	Lower 40 percent	Middle 40 percent	Upper 20 percent
All education				
Argentina	1983	48	35	17
Chile	1983	48	34	17
Colombia	1974	40	39	21
Costa Rica	1983	42	38	20
Dominican Republic	1976–77	24	43	14
Uruguay	1983	52	34	14
Indonesia	1978	46	25[a]	29[a]
Malaysia	1974	41	41	18
Higher education				
Argentina	1983	17	45	38
Chile	1983	12	34	54
Colombia	1974	6	35	60
Costa Rica	1983	17	41	42
Dominican Republic	1976–77	2	22	76
Uruguay	1980	14	52	34
Indonesia	1978	7	10[a]	83[b]
Malaysia	1974	10	38	51
Public health				
Argentina	1980	69	27	4
Colombia	1974	42	40	20
Costa Rica	1983	49	38	13
Chile	1983	51	47	11
Dominican Republic	1984	57	44	9
Uruguay	1983	64	25	12
Indonesia	1978	19	36[a]	45[b]
Iran	1977	51	37	13
Malaysia	1974	47	37	17
Philippines	1975	27	33	40
Sri Lanka	1978	46	39	14
Hospitals				
Colombia	1974	23	53	23
Malaysia	1974	36	34	20

a. These figures are for the middle 30 percent.
b. These figures are for the upper 30 percent.
Sources: Jimenez (1987); Petrei (1987); World Bank (1986).

of all public expenditures on higher education, whereas those from the lowest 40 percent receive between 6 and 15 percent. This effect is only partly counterbalanced by the concentration of primary education subsidies among poor families, which have most of a country's younger school-age children. The net result is a distribution of overall educational subsidies roughly proportional to each income group's population share, with the exception of the Dominican Republic, where the poor's share is still less.

The income bias is less for health. Health subsidies for Colombia and Malaysia are roughly proportional to each income group's population share. But in Indonesia, the poorest 40 percent capture only about 19 percent from public health centers and hospitals.

These figures need to be replicated for a wider group of countries and to be updated, particularly for African countries. But conditions are likely to be even worse for the poorest countries, where greater scarcity means greater rationing. For example, with lower primary and secondary enrollment rates than in other countries, African university systems have a much smaller applicant pool from which to draw. Poor income groups would have self-selected themselves out before applying.

Subsidies may be targeted through differential pricing of services. Can a more efficient pricing policy—one that generates enough revenue and encourages appropriate use—also ensure access for all? The popular method for ensuring access has been to provide all social services at a heavy per unit subsidy through uniformly low or zero prices, accompanied by quantity rationing when budgets are tight. This has not worked. The "new" view of social sector pricing advocates targeting primarily by differential pricing: increase prices for those services consumed by the rich, and increase subsidies (lower the private cost) for those consumed by the poor.

The estimates of the potential effectiveness of this policy are often dramatic. For example, if those engaged in higher education paid its public cost, and the resources thus freed were used to expand the lower levels of education, the Gini coefficient measuring the distribution of public subsidies would move from 0.60 to 0.27 (Mingat and Tan 1985, p. 306). Similar distributional benefits are predicted for health services (World Bank 1987, p. 26).

With a price-differentiating strategy, would the poor (or other vulnerable groups) have to be protected? Would the poor's use be affected by raising prices for higher levels of education and curative care?

It depends, first, on whether the poor use any of the service whose price is to be raised. In some countries, access may already be so restricted that few if any poor people use the service; prices of zero may be insufficient to overcome other obstacles, such as high private costs or a bias in the rationing scheme. Some urban-based specialty hospitals, for instance, cater solely to diseases that afflict the relatively wealthy. In Africa the steep education pyramid means that many children have already been selected out at lower levels, so that by the tertiary level the elite form a majority of all applicants (World Bank 1987).

In other countries, however, the poor may represent a minor but still significant portion of students, particularly at primary and secondary levels and for moderately priced services. For example, evidence indicates that they make substantial use of publicly provided health services (see table 1).

A second determinant of the impact of differential pricing on the poor's use of services is the set of behavioral parameters, such as the elasticity of demand. Studies on this topic differ in methodology and in measurement, particularly of the price variable. Nevertheless, there are some consistent findings. The demand for education and medical care is generally responsive to price changes. But the magnitude of this response varies, although most studies indicate that the elasticity, at current prices, is significantly less than one for almost all services (table 2). The implication is that a 1.0 percent increase in price, say, will amount to a decline in consumption of less than 1.0 percent, leading to a rise in revenue.

Table 2. *Price Elasticities of Demand for Health and Education Services*

Year of data	Country and service	Price range (U.S. dollars)	Overall	Price elasticity by income group — Lowest quartile	Highest quartile
	Health				
1985	Côte d'Ivoire[a]				
	Clinic	Free–$.11	n.a.	−0.61	−0.38
		$.11–$.22	n.a.	−1.16	−0.05
	Hospital	Free–$.11	n.a.	−0.47	−0.29
		$.11–$.22	n.a.	−0.86	−0.51
1985	Peru[a]				
	Private doctor	Free–$1.56	−0.14	−0.20	−0.06
		$1.56–$3.12	−0.29	−0.44	−0.12
	Hospital	Free–$1.56	−0.41	−0.67	−0.33
		$1.56–$3.12	−0.64	−1.18	−0.05
	Clinic	Free–$1.56	−0.46	−0.76	−0.03
		$1.56–$3.12	−0.68	−1.28	−0.06
1975	Malaysia				
	Outpatient visits	n.a.	−0.01	n.a.	n.a.
1981	Philippines				
	Prenatal child care	n.a.	−0.01	n.a.	n.a.
1980–81	Kenya	$5.80	inelastic[b]	n.a.	n.a.
1985	Ethiopia	n.a.			
	Outpatient care	−0.05–−0.50		n.a.	
1986	Sudan	n.a.			
	Outpatient services	n.a.	−0.37	n.a.	n.a.
	Education				
1985	Peru[a]				
	Secondary education	Free–$1.56	−0.14	−0.18	−0.20
1982	Mali[c]	n.a.	−0.98	n.a.	n.a.
1983	Malawi[d]	n.a.	−0.52	n.a.	n.a.

n.a. Not available.
a. These are arc price elasticities, which is why price ranges are relevant.
b. Magnitude could not be computed from available data.
c. Uses distance as price variable.
d. Uses household enrollment ratio as dependent variable.
Sources: Health in Côte d'Ivoire and Peru: Gertler and van der Gaag (1988). Education in Peru: Gertler and Glewwe (1989). Philippines: Akin and others (1986). Kenya: Mwabu (1986). Ethiopia: Dunlop (1987). Mali: Birdsall and others (1983). Malawi: Tan, Lee, and Mingat (1984). Sudan: Schwabe (n.d.).

Equally important for these point estimates, especially for large price changes, are assumptions about the structure and shape of the demand curve over the entire range of feasible consumption levels. For example, if the elasticity of demand increases as price rises or as consumption falls (as it would for a straight line demand curve), then the magnitude of the price response depends on where elasticity is computed along that curve.[7] Specification tests are also important, yet most analysts are content with imposing a predetermined structure on the curve (see Jimenez 1987 for a review).

Moreover, demand elasticity may vary by income with important consequences for the consumption of the poor. A series of recent microeconometric studies (Gertler, Locay, and Sanderson 1987; Gertler and van der Gaag 1988; Gertler and Glewwe 1989) show that, in Côte d'Ivoire and Peru, the price elasticity of demand rises with falling income (table 2). Thus the consumption of poor people falls proportionately more than that of richer people for a given price increase. One piece of corroborative evidence from experience is in Ghana, where urban-based health stations that raised fees saw an initial drop in attendance but recovered quickly, whereas attendance at small, rural-based health stations was much lower after two and a half years (Ennimayew, cited in Gertler and van der Gaag 1988).

These research results support the view that special consideration ought to be given to poor people when prices are raised by relatively large increments (in this connection, see World Bank 1986, p. 24, on loan and credit schemes for education; and World Bank 1987, pp. 31–32, on community insurance and differential pricing for health). The critical question is whether schemes to protect the poor can be implemented effectively.

Subsidies may be targeted by consumer characteristics. Governments have to evaluate fundamental tradeoffs in choosing: whether to target at all; to target through differential pricing (or per unit subsidies) of services; or to target through direct identification of consumer characteristics. Subsidy schemes that are less costly to administer, such as a general subsidy of commodities or services that the poor are likely to consume, may be more costly in terms of "leakage." Although it is possible to design self-targeted schemes in which poor income groups are given a greater incentive to participate than others, such schemes may be socially unacceptable. In the Philippines, for example, a plan to subsidize low-quality four-year public colleges, where poor students are more heavily represented, while further restricting access to the prestigious national university, ran into opposition because of the fear that it would institutionalize a two-tiered educational system (World Bank 1988b).

Unfortunately, there are few systematic evaluations in developing countries of targeted health or education programs—countries are only beginning to im-

---

7. This point is controversial. Several authors (Dor, Gertler, and van der Gaag 1986; Gertler, Locay, and Sanderson 1987; and Gertler and van der Gaag 1988) argue that demand for health services is very responsive over large price increases. Akin and others (1986) argue that small changes in prices have no impact. Both sides can be technically right but have different policy recommendations.

plement such policies, and documenting such experiences is a priority task. However, preliminary reviews of analogous experiences in other sectors, such as food (Namor 1987), and from developed countries (Sawhill 1988) show that promising targeting alternatives exist. Some important lessons emerging from this literature are:

1. Program size matters: the effectiveness and administrative cost of targeting by recognizable income group depends on the size of the group. This in turn is partly determined by the inequality of the income distribution. A highly skewed income distribution means that a large proportion of the population may be classified as "poor" and that, within that group, incomes are roughly similar. In this case, it may be easier to target by pricing specific services because the administrative costs of collecting information on a large proportion of the population are large and the tastes of the targeted group are likely to vary from the untargeted group.

The size of the targeted group also varies according to the program goals—how different members of the targeted group are to be treated; whether all members of the targeted group should be raised above a certain threshold, and so on (see Besley and Kanbur 1988). Food subsidies are usually meant for broad groups: the bottom x-percentile of the income distribution, or all those who fail to meet a certain threshold nutrition level. However, targeted scholarship schemes in universities are for a much smaller pool—those who apply from among the graduates of secondary education. This number, and the consequent administrative cost, is generally small for the poorest developing countries. Such a scheme is being tried in the University of the Philippines in its "Socialized Tuition and Financial Assistance Program." Fees are being raised overall, but certain income categories are being exempted because a university study found that, despite very low tuition charges and merit scholarships, "the higher a student's annual family income, the greater are his chances of being admitted into the University" (University of the Philippines, n.d., p. 8).

Program size and consequently the cost of targeting will change over time. It is essential to monitor the program's growth, and how this affects the ability of government to use means-testing devices to target effectively.

2. When income criteria are inappropriate, proxies can be used. Using income criteria has been cost-effective in countries where beneficiaries are reasonably well educated and are concentrated in urban areas, and where income taxes are successfully collected. For example, in the United States the administrative cost of most poverty programs ranges from 5 to 10 percent of program benefits. Overpayments to ineligible applicants were about 3 percent of program benefits for both Medicaid and supplemental social insurance (Mackintosh 1989). There are few studies of the effectiveness and cost of using income criteria in other circumstances. The costs are bound to be higher. However, there are proven alternatives to using income criteria that approximate their benefits without incurring the costs.

Studies of food subsidies have found that physical criteria, such as nutrition level, are generally more effective in reaching target populations and in keeping out others than income criteria (Timmons and others 1983; Edirisinghe 1987; Garcia and Pinstrup-Andersen 1987; Namor 1987). In education and health, these kinds of data would probably be costly to collect. Two criteria that have been applied in developing countries (see Griffin 1989, who mentions twelve countries; and Pfeffermann and Griffin 1989) are health status (or incidence of certain diseases) or adult literacy (children of illiterate parents are given full scholarship). A drawback of the health criterion would be that it would rule out subsidies for preventive care where broad population groups are at risk.

Other proxies for income are already widely used in education and health. In Chile, education levels are used to identify potential program recipients (Chile 1988). But again these measures are generally effective only in middle-income countries that have adequate record keeping, relatively high literacy levels, and a high rate of participation in formal sector jobs. For others, coverage will likely be limited; Zaire, for instance, has a sliding fee scale for hospitals by broad occupational category, with students and the handicapped paying the lowest rates and enterprise employees the highest (Griffin 1988, p. 65).

An alternative to targeting by individual or household characteristics is to target by geographic location. The simplest division, by rural and urban areas, is used in many developing countries in the distribution of food subsidies. For example, food subsidies distributed in ration shops have been judged to be more effective and less costly than vouchers in Mexico and Sri Lanka (Namor 1987; Edirisinghe 1987). The experience in health and education is more limited (see Griffin 1989), but the rule of exempting institutions from fees in urban slums or poor rural areas would probably be easy to implement. The one drawback is that, if the locations with different rates are close enough, people may seek the cheapest alternative.

3. Welfare stigma may be a cost—individuals do not like to be classified as needy and may even turn down some subsidies as a result.

Recent evidence, however, indicates that in the United States, although the decision not to participate in a welfare program may be affected by stigma, the probability varies with the size of the potential benefit. Nor does the stigma seem to affect the amount of the benefit, once someone has decided to be on welfare (Moffit 1983). Moreover, the United Kingdom experience suggests that the importance of stigma may reflect prevailing political trends. In the 1940s "the strength of popular objection to any kind of means test" (Lord Beveridge quoted in Ahmed 1989) pushed the United Kingdom from targeted programs to an untargeted social security system, but this trend was reversed in the 1980s with Prime Minister Margaret Thatcher's reform of major U.K. social programs. These issues can be studied in more depth for developing countries.

4. Incentive effects of subsidies may affect incidence and efficiency. The full economic costs of the alternative subsidy scheme mentioned above have yet to

be assessed. Subsidy schemes may exact incentive costs. Do those who do not initially belong in the targeted population distort their behavior so as to obtain the benefit? What disincentive effects are there for the potential beneficiaries?

Another research question is: can the benefit be traded? Some benefits of targeted subsidized services, such as education or medical care, cannot generally be traded by poor beneficiaries. But medicine or school books can. It is probably impossible to prevent the sale and resale of education or health vouchers—such bartering has been evident in housing programs (Mayo and Gross 1987). Although such sales are not necessarily bad since targeted recipients receive the proceeds, questions must be raised about how the subsidies are shared. There may be more efficient means of distributing the subsidies.

Can Increased User Fees Make People Better Off?

The conceptual argument that selectively increasing user fees can improve welfare is compelling. The combination of tighter budgets and low or zero prices for publicly provided services has led to rationing or a deterioration in quality. Increased prices will generate more revenue. This will, in turn, improve welfare by financing the expansion of a previously rationed service, or an improvement in quality of a deteriorated service, or the expansion of another service with higher social returns (see Besley 1989b, Jimenez 1987, or Katz 1987 for a more detailed and rigorous treatment). In addition, increased fees may induce consumers to use the service more carefully, thus freeing up capacity for those who value the service the most.

Are these conceptual arguments supported by facts? The empirical record is uneven.

User fees, revenues, and service availability: actual experience. Few developing countries have dramatically changed their financing of social services in the past twenty years. Many newly independent countries in the 1950s and 1960s nationalized schools and health systems, but before/after comparisons have little value for policy judgments now because the preindependence systems were generally so limited and colonial in nature. Large-scale subsidized expansions occurred when systems were small and budgets were not as tight. Reforms of social sector pricing structures beginning in some countries are mostly too recent to generate much information.[8]

One country where evidence is beginning to be collected is Chile. During the early 1980s, Chile moved from a centrally directed social service system, heavily subsidized and untargeted, to a decentralized system more reliant for its finance on users and local communities. Preliminary evaluations are that this system has allowed Chile to maintain its impressive record in improving a variety of social sector indicators even while economic growth has lagged. The nutrition and housing programs in particular have been cited in recent World Bank reports

---

8. Between 1984 and 1988, thirteen education and six health projects have incorporated new financing ideas in World Bank operations. A list is available from the author.

as possible models for other countries on how to target scarce spending. Evaluations of the education reforms, which include selective scholarship schemes at universities, were not available for this analysis (see Castaneda 1986 and Chile 1988 for program descriptions).

Chile's experience with health financing has been less encouraging. The 1981 reforms were meant to shift some of the burden from the general budget to user fees, employee payroll deductions, and the sale of vouchers to patients. Recent World Bank reports indicate that although central government budgetary allocations have indeed fallen, the other financing sources have not filled the gap. The reasons appear to be that fee structures for vouchers and direct use have not been adjusted to keep up with rising costs; high-income employees have been opting out of the payroll-payment plan and transferring to private providers; and "eligibility creep" has meant a tremendous expansion in the number of beneficiaries exempted from voucher or fee payments. This expansion has arisen from underreporting of income and ambiguities about the definition of what constitutes a household.

Another way of drawing on experience is to make cross-section comparisons. Some countries rely more heavily on user financed social services than others. In the 1960s, the Tanzanian government reduced the share of public spending allocated to secondary schooling and, until recently, also restricted the establishment of private and community schools. In contrast, the Kenyan government encouraged the growth of both public and self-financing private secondary education. By 1980, secondary school enrollment ratios were six times greater in Kenya than in Tanzania. A World Bank study has concluded that the overly restrictive and rationed educational system in Tanzania contributed to its relatively poor economic performance (Knight and Sabot 1986).

User fees, revenues, and service availability: simulations. In the absence of the data afforded by actual experience, a strong case for pricing policy reform has often been based on predictions of its probable impact on revenue mobilization, use, and even welfare.

The impact of increased user fees on revenue depends on the price elasticity of demand for the service and whether, at current prices, there is excess demand for the service. On the evidence cited earlier—that, on average, the demand for many education and health services is relatively price inelastic—an increase in price will cause the quantity demanded to drop, but less than proportionately. So revenue can be expected to rise, at least with modest price increases. If the choice is between a service that is low-priced but heavily rationed or low-quality and one that is inaccessible, evidence indicates that many households are willing to pay for the service, even in poor areas.

Some innovative studies showing this result have been done in Côte d'Ivoire and Peru, where high-quality household data are available (Gertler, Locay, and Sanderson 1987; Gertler and van der Gaag 1988; Gertler and Glewwe 1989). The methodology follows the logic of revealed preference. The estimated parameters of a utility function are used to calculate the welfare of a hypothetical nonuser, if that nonuser were then given the option of an increased access at increased prices. (Access is measured by travel time to the public facility.) The price level that makes the consumer indifferent between a low price–low accessibility scenario and a high price–high probability of access scenario is then compared with the marginal cost of providing the service. This price can be interpreted as the marginal "willingness to pay" for a service.

The results for Peru and Côte d'Ivoire (table 3) indicate that, although the estimated willingness to pay is less than the estimated marginal cost price, the amount that can be recovered is still substantial. For example, in Peru, if the school is one hour away, the average student's willingness to pay for a place in a secondary school at his or her own village would be roughly equal to about half of the cost of providing that place (assuming constant marginal cost and a class size of about sixty students).

The willingness to pay for education and health might be even greater if the users felt that the funds were going to be used to improve quality, such as in the provision of school materials and medicines. Birdsall and others (1983) found this to be true for households in Mali; Mwabu (1986) found similar results for Kenya.

Fee-generated revenues can be used to make rationed services more readily available. For services with low costs and relatively large benefits, the impact can be dramatic. A report on financing education (World Bank 1986) estimated that merely eliminating living allowances to university students in several African countries could finance an 18 percent average expansion in the yearly primary education budget (table 4). In countries where higher education enrollment and

Table 3. *Individual Willingness to Pay for Access to Social Services and the Cost of Provision*
(1985 U.S. dollars)

Country and service	Willingness to pay for obtaining access to a nearby facility when the alternative is: One hour away	Two hours away	Marginal cost
Côte d'Ivoire			
West Forest Health Clinic[a]	0.10	0.17	1.30
Savannah Health Clinic[a]	0.03	0.06	1.30
Peru			
Coastal Health Clinic[a]	0.09	0.17	2.73
Sierra Health Clinic[a]	0.00	0.02	2.73
Secondary School[b]	14.29	104.64	35.71

a. Dollars per visit.
b. Dollars per academic year.

Sources: Health: Gertler and van der Gaag (1988, tables 5 and 6). Education: Gertler and Glewwe (1989).

Table 4. *Potential Impact on Primary Education in Africa of Increasing Fees in Higher Education*
(percent)

Country	Increase in primary education budget if higher education students bear entire cost of: Living expenses	Operating cost	Both	Current enrollment ratio	Potential primary enrollment ratio with full cost recovery in higher education[a]
Benin	19	5	24	65	81
Burkina Faso	19	8	27	20	25
Central African Republic	12	4	16	68	79
Congo	18	6	23	n.a.	n.a.
Côte d'Ivoire	21	19	40	76	100
Malawi	9	46	54	59	91
Mali	22	9	30	27	35
Niger	10	2	12	23	26
Senegal	20	49	68	48	81
Sudan	3	40	43	51	73
Tanzania	24	31	55	n.a.	n.a.
Togo	40	52	92	n.a.	n.a.
Average	18	23	41	49	66

n.a. Not available.
a. Full cost recovery refers to the elimination of university student allowances and introduction of tuition payments to cover operating costs.
Source: World Bank (1986, pp. 22, 23).

unit subsidies are large, such as Côte d'Ivoire, Malawi, Senegal, Sudan, Tanzania, and Togo, the scope for expansion is even greater.

The approach taken by the studies is very promising but has some significant limitations. First, the data requirements are substantial. The present studies, for example, have only a rudimentary data base on the quality of the various schools. An integrated household-institution data base is required.

Second, the revealed preference approach assumes that households, not institutions, choose to obtain access. In many cases, a model in which institutions, as well as households, choose who obtains access is more appropriate. These choices are unlikely to be independent of one another. For example, students who believe they have very little chance of passing stringent entry requirements may be discouraged from even applying.

Third, analysis of the supply side is simplistic. The impact on the provision of social services depends on the cost elasticity of supply. Cost estimates are very rough, and marginal cost is assumed to equal average cost for the system. The assumption is restrictive, but often necessary, because there are very few studies of the level and structure of provider cost in developing countries, either in education or health (see Jimenez 1986b for one such on education, Jimenez

1987 and Vitialano 1987 for reviews of the sparse studies that exist). There is little consensus, for example, on whether or not educational and health institutions currently operate at a size at which scale economies are still possible. The empirical work is complicated by: the need to see providers as multiproduct facilities in which some inputs can be used for a variety of outputs; the need to measure and to control for quality; the need to have specifications consistent with behavioral assumptions, such as cost-minimization; and the need to control for incentives by looking at private sector observations.

Demand-side efficiency. Demand-side efficiency involves allocation of a fixed quantity among competing uses. Increased user fees will depress demand, more for those who value the service least, in this way releasing greater access to those who value the service more, for example, the rich. For those who do obtain access, the increased price will make them more wary of wasted consumption.

But equally, increased user fees might discourage those who value the service but who are confronted by a liquidity constraint. This would be particularly true for expensive services, such as higher education and hospital care. Subsidized access may be more efficient with an appropriate rationing scheme, such as scholarships or queuing—but these too have their drawbacks, as discussed above.

So the efficiency gain on the demand side is an empirical issue. It remains to be rigorously evaluated. Although most of the estimated models have found demand for many social services to be relatively price inelastic (see table 2), these models generally use, as the dependent variable, the decision to use a service at all or not. The decision of how much to consume may be more sensitive to price changes.

Supply-side efficiency. Supply-side efficiency involves the provision of a service at least cost. Providers who have to rely more heavily on fee revenue for their survival are more likely to be subject to pressures from their clients to be efficient. This might lower unit costs.

This argument hinges on the effect of competitive forces in making providers accountable for their actions. Fees alone may not bring greater pressures from consumers; the users have to have alternative services to which they can choose to transfer.

The limited evidence available indicates that institutions confronted by competition are more efficient. For example, some recent research shows that, at the secondary level, with background and selection held constant, students in private unsubsidized schools generally score better than their public school counterparts. At the same time, average (per student) costs in private schools are generally less (table 5). There is also some evidence in the Philippines that, among public schools, those that rely more heavily on community contributions have lower costs, given average achievement levels within those schools (Jimenez, Paqueo, and Lourdes de Vera 1988). Cost estimates in these and other comparisons need further refinement.

Table 5. *Efficiency of Private Unsubsidized Secondary Schools Relative to Subsidized Public Schools*

Country	Year of data	Achievement indicator: average score on standardized test	Corrected private score as proportion of public score[a]	Private cost as proportion of public cost
Colombia	1981	Mathematics and verbal	1.12	0.69
Philippines	1983	Mathematics	0.99	0.55
		Verbal	1.20	
Tanzania	1981	Mathematics and verbal	1.77	0.69
Thailand	1981–82	Mathematics	2.63	0.39

a. Proportional gain (loss) in achievement score if a randomly selected student, with the characteristics of the average public school student, attends private rather than public school, holding constant for that student's background.

Source: Computed from Jimenez, Lockheed, and Paqueo (1988) and recent World Bank data.

Are Increased User Fees Feasible Administratively and Politically?

Many critics claim that the administrative and political costs of increasing user fees are prohibitive. But countries are already beginning to implement some of these policies. This suggests that, important as they are, these factors can be assimilated in the design of policy changes.

Administrative and collection costs. The public administration of many developing countries is weak: personnel are poorly paid, trained, and motivated. Will this lead to poor collection and administration of fees?

The few case studies indicate that, with some exceptions, the administrative cost of implementing user fees is not excessive. For example, in Senegal, the direct cost of collecting fees for primary health care, which includes incentive payments to ticket clerks, amounted to less than 10 percent of collections in 1979. In larger hospitals, the administration netted about 75 percent of fees. In the Sudan, the annual cost of collecting user fees as a percentage of revenues for clinics, pharmacies, and hospital services amounted to 5 percent or less (see Griffin 1988, p. 78.) Many countries in eastern and southern Africa already collect fees or community levies to finance the building of public primary and secondary schools (World Bank 1988a). These costs are probably lower than the estimated collection and economic cost of the alternative method of generating revenue—general taxes (World Bank 1988c). Precise estimates would be useful.

One general lesson on collection is that, to give the institution an incentive to collect the fees and to limit the cost of handling the funds, the revenue should remain with that institution. In Senegal, for example, a fee structure, in place since 1968, was not enforced until 1982, when newly created hospitals were allowed to retain proceeds collected from nonindigent users (Vogel 1988, p. 166). Retaining revenue has the added advantage that users may be more willing to pay if they know how their funds are being spent, particularly when small amounts are frequently being collected for a variety of services and materials, such as drugs. In Ghana, for example, the government is linking increased university fees with a program to improve the availability of books and supplies (World Bank 1988c).

Another important problem is the administration of effective educational credit and health insurance. The unit costs are particularly large for smaller schemes. In Latin America, the only region in the developing world where student loan schemes are widespread, administration amounted to 12–23 percent of total outlay, compared with 1.5–2.0 percent in larger schemes in developed countries (World Bank 1986, p. 28). But the financial viability of many student loan institutions is also at risk because of overly generous terms. Subsidized student loans may be necessary to make the schemes initially viable but, if the institutions are not allowed to be self-financing, they become just another way to subsidize consumption—and a particularly inefficient way, as the eventual recipients are probably not those who should be targeted for such subsidies. If subsidies are necessary, they should be given directly. The same situation holds for health. Latin America is also the region in which social insurance, funded mostly by payroll taxes, has most been used to finance health care. The cost of these schemes is beginning to be a burden on governments, as their traditional sources of finance have either been poached by other sectors or have been insufficient to cover costs because no copayments are collected (World Bank 1987, pp. 36–7). In addition, coverage tends to be limited to relatively well-off workers in the formal sector (Zschock 1986).

The economic and administrative issues are beyond the scope of the present paper. However, most of the proponents of the "new view" of social sector financing recognize that, until countries successfully implement credit and insurance schemes, full cost recovery for higher education and hospital care, even for those who can afford it, cannot be implemented. But, in the meantime, this does not preclude some partial cost recovery scheme, along with more research on workable ways to introduce student loans and health insurance to the system.

Political economy. When there are losers as well as winners from a policy change, even if the net social benefit is positive, problems can arise. Winners will not necessarily compensate losers, and losers, if they happen to be powerful, may block the policy change. The conceptual problems involved are discussed more fully in the next section.

What Have We Learned and What More Do We Need to Know?

Despite some obvious gaps, the empirical research shows solid support for the following conclusions:

- Free or heavily subsidized provision of social services has not led to adequate access for the poor. Subsidies tend to be available across the board for all

types of social services, even when they are being rationed ineffectively and people are willing to pay for some of them.
- Moderate increases in fees will raise revenue because, as most studies show, demand for many social services is relatively price inelastic. But these fees should not be set to recover full costs, particularly of expensive services such as tertiary education and inpatient hospital care, because of: positive externalities (for example, research at universities); the lack of adequate credit or insurance markets; little evidence on the cost-structure of facilities; and fees so low that cost recovery would require unsustainable price increases.
- Demand elasticities are lower for the rich than for the poor. Thus, the poor have to be protected when prices are raised.
- Practical schemes have been tried to target subsidies toward the poor. Their benefits often exceed the high costs of implementation.

At the same time, much more work needs to be done. First on the research agenda are the following:

- The robustness of the above results has to be tested. The distribution of social sector subsidies has yet to be calculated for many countries, particularly in Africa, along the lines of Meerman's (1979) study for Malaysia, Rodriguez-Grossi's (1985) study for Chile, and Selowsky's (1979) for Colombia. The innovative models of demand for social services should also be applied to other countries, and they should be extended to study the demand for the intensity of use, rather than just participation.
- Little is known about the cost structure of social service provision. Most studies simply assume that marginal costs are constant. Cost functions that are consistent with economic theory should be estimated. The supply side should not be ignored because practical advice on how much fees should be raised depends partly on what determines cost: scale, scope, joint production, and so on.
- Given that the ability to protect the poor is a central theme in the literature, social experiments on alternative means-testing schemes that apply specifically to education and health services should also be evaluated. Actual administrative costs should be estimated, as well as economic costs in terms of incentives.
- More work on the economics of educational credit and health insurance has to be undertaken. Under what conditions can these institutions be made to work in developing countries?

III. THE CONCEPTUAL CHALLENGE

The literature has yet to address systematically, from the conceptual as well as the empirical standpoint, such topics as: ways other than price rises or general taxation of providing additional resources; and improving implementation through consideration of political constraints.

Increasing Budgetary Allocations

Most of the recent literature on pricing education and health services takes a sectoral perspective: given tight budgets, how should these sectors cope? This view is undoubtedly valid for many countries. But a broader approach that considers both budgetary allocations and prices as flexible policy levers is sometimes more appropriate. Even when the budget resources are scarce, governments may maximize social welfare by making resources available from other sectors. Or governments could try to alleviate tight budgetary constraints by raising more nonprice revenue without resorting to traditional general taxes. In either case, a more complicated analytical model must underlie the pricing arguments.

Intersectoral subsidization. Even when the fiscal position is poor, funds can be made available for social services, either by cutting back subsidies destined for other sectors or, for those sectors that make net budgetary contributions, by charging more if demand is relatively price inelastic.

The traditional way of choosing among spending alternatives would be to use social rates of return. The techniques can be adapted to evaluate recurrent spending, which is more important in social spending than, say, in infrastructure expenditures that are heavily weighted by new investments. This is sound advice in theory. In practice, although there are a growing number of studies that estimate the rate of return to different levels of education (see Psacharopoulos 1985 for a review), they are not available for many countries, are of variable quality, and generally ignore some high cost-services, such as alternative disciplines in higher education. The difficulty of evaluating benefits in health services has forced analysts to turn to cost-effective analyses which do not allow intersectoral comparisons of spending options. These drawbacks, combined with the lingering view that "social" services cannot inherently be compared with "productive" services, have meant that rate-of-return comparisons are not used to guide spending decisions in the social sectors. Even among those sectors where such calculations are routine, the computation of social rates of return is an inexact science.[9] Thus, how to provide sound, practical guidance on intersectoral spending choices remains an important item on the conceptual agenda.

Cross-sectoral pricing can, in principle, be tackled using the modern theory of optimal taxation (see Atkinson and Stiglitz 1980; Newbery and Stern 1987; Besley 1989a). The problem would be to derive a set of optimal subsidies, which can be interpreted simply as negative taxes. Given costs, these would imply a set of optimal prices for all public services. These would presumably depend upon the relative elasticities of demand for the range of goods and services. If, for example, demand for transport services were less elastic than that for some health service, then cross-subsidies from transport to health might be in order. If work on the price elasticities of different public services continues to be fruitful, this could be a promising avenue for future research.

9. A recent internal report of the Bank reviewing public expenditure–public investment studies shows that most fail to derive a set of objective criteria to make investment decisions.

Other means of raising revenue. Community financing and the payroll tax have been prominent in discussion of ways of financing services other than general taxation or user fees. Many local communities may already be doing more than aggregate data indicate. For example, in education, communities have a heavy hand in funding capital and sometimes recurrent spending in eastern and southern Africa and in Asia (Bray and Lillis 1988). But the experience varies within and across countries. An important research topic would be to use this variation to explain the ability of some communities to finance and provide social services.

Communities that finance and provide their own social services have incentives similar to those for individuals who pay for the use of services. They can provide the quality of service they prefer and have incentives to do so at least cost.[10] But in societies that want to provide a homogeneous type of service, particularly in education, and to equalize opportunities across communities, the central government must play a regulatory role. The tradeoffs in the balance between local and central authorities have yet to be fully addressed (see Winkler 1989 for a review of the education cases).

Payroll taxes are already being used to finance many health programs in Latin America through the social security system, and to finance training programs. Should they be more widely used? The answer probably varies from country to country. Poor countries with small urban labor forces may find it difficult to levy payroll taxes, whereas low-middle-income countries find them attractive because they are relatively easy to collect and rates can be targeted by sector. Their efficiency effects depend on coverage of the labor force and on the incidence of the tax. Most studies of developed countries assume that employers are able to pass on the burden of the tax's effects to labor (Whalley and Ziderman 1989). Whether this is likely to hold for developing countries remains a research question. Most evaluations of health insurance schemes in Latin America also find that the tax does not obviate the need for pricing through copayments and other means to raise revenue and gain efficiency (Zschock 1986).

Other schemes include poll taxes (levied on graduates) and schemes to generate income by having students work. Data on the impacts on efficiency or equity of these schemes or whether they are generally effective are limited at present.

Making Service Provision More Efficient

The key question in making service provision more efficient is how to lower unit costs without sacrificing quality, particularly for the most expensive services such as universities and big-city hospitals. One way is to improve input mixes, technology, managerial procedures, and technical skills among service providers in developing countries. This work is already the focus of much foreign assistance to developing countries. But the expertise, the new technology, and the skills

---

10. A study in the Philippines shows that schools that rely more heavily on community-level financing have lower costs than those that rely more on central government financing (Jimenez and others 1988).

will not solve efficiency problems if providers are not also given appropriate incentives.

Do we really know what input mixes are more efficient? Production-function studies of education and health services have produced conflicting results (see Hanushek 1986 for a review of the education production-function literature in developed countries, and Fuller 1987 for developing countries.) Researchers have begun to see that the parameter values and ensuing policy recommendations are likely to differ for countries that have different characteristics (Fuller 1987).

Even with trustworthy estimates of the effectiveness of various public interventions, costs also have to be evaluated. Lack of data for solid empirical analysis partly accounts for the paucity of research on these costs, but part of the problem is conceptual: estimating a cost function means assuming that minimizing costs is the goal. If public providers are guided by other motives, those other motives would have to be modeled. Otherwise, the analysis would have to be conducted on a sample of private (and presumably competitive) providers. If the providers are heavily regulated or restricted to serve only a narrow market, these complications would also have to be addressed.

Incentives to be efficient. Showing educational and medical personnel more effective ways of operating may not improve efficiency unless incentives are also changed. In most instances competitive pressures to produce the required high-quality services at least cost simply do not exist. More work needs to be done on finding out which incentives work.

A greater reliance on self-finance through pricing may improve efficiency if administrators are held accountable for their actions. But in centralized systems, accountability is not transparent. And when consumers are uninformed about benefits and do not have to pay each time they use a service, they have an incentive to go along with expensive interventions prescribed by the more knowledgeable provider. In such instances, decentralization may be appropriate. But the proper balance of responsibility between traditional central authorities and decentralized institutions is difficult to determine.

Models of Political Economy

Even those governments in favor of pricing reform may be deterred from taking the necessary steps. They may simply not have the necessary information or skills to make the necessary budgetary allocations and intersectoral tradeoffs. Alternatively, those in government may be acting not in the public interest but in their own interest—they may not want to make the necessary policy corrections if they themselves stand to lose by them (see Mills 1986; Birdsall 1988). Another possibility is that some governments may be unable to withstand pressure from powerful minority interests. This is what Birdsall (1988) calls "the Robin Hood failure"—taking from the poor and giving to the rich.

Such pressures might explain the Chilean government's reluctance to adjust the fee structure in their health reform program. They could also account for the findings of Mingat and Tan (1986) that white collar workers in francophone

Africa (6 percent of the population) appropriate over a third of all education subsidies, while farmers (three-quarters of the population) get less than half—a discrepancy due primarily to the heavy subsidy of tertiary education. The white collar workers live in urban areas, and many of them are in government. So their influence on government is greater than their proportionate numbers.

The influence of pressure groups may also partly explain the systematic underfunding of certain services. For example, social and political pressures have made schools more accessible, but often at the expense of quality. Quality is particularly easy to neglect because it is difficult to detect small changes and citizens have little information about it.

For similar reasons, policymakers may not only resist reforms but may take measures to counteract reforms already under way. For example, user fee revenues will not be of much use to social services if they are outweighed by cuts in budgetary allocations. More work is thus needed on countervailing measures. Two possibilities are to identify and compensate losers, and to replace government discretionary authority with rules.

Compensating the losers and mobilizing the winners. At the very least, when social sector reforms are proposed, potential winners and losers have to be identified by documenting who benefits from social sector subsidies. A more complex incidence analysis of the proposed program would be based on this information (as yet available for only a few countries; see table 1). Who is likely to benefit? Can benefits be passed on to others in the free market?

The next step is to assess whether and how to compensate the losers. Losers could be directly compensated or even protected by "grandfathering" a fee increase. Or the support of the winners could be mobilized. If winners can "outmuscle" the losers, then compensation may not be needed. For example, in support of extensive educational reforms which will hit subsidized tertiary levels of education hardest, the government of Ghana is mounting a massive public education campaign to alert the population to the inequities of the present distribution of subsidies (World Bank 1988c). This is being accompanied by a media campaign which stresses that the funds now spent on boarding privileged students could provide many more places for others. Public opinion matters, even in countries that do not have Western-style democracies.

Finally the complicated issue of designing and implementing compensation systems must be tackled. Even if it were possible to devise a compensation scheme that would make everyone better off, the winners and losers might not be able to agree on the amount of compensation. This problem is addressed conceptually by the vast literature on the design of incentive compatible mechanisms (see Groves and Ledyard 1985).

Rules versus discretion. Political pressure works best on "discretionary" spending items. It is often harder to change laws, rules, or institutions. When the portion allocated to nondiscretionary spending—for instance, interest payments on foreign debt—has to increase, pressure on the discretionary portion correspondingly heightens. For developing countries (excluding highly indebted ones) interest payments on foreign debt have been increasing from an average of about 1 percent of gross domestic product in 1975 to 3 percent in 1985. For the seventeen highly indebted countries (see World Bank 1988, p. 11) this average percentage has risen from about 1 to over 8 percent over the same time period. Discretionary budget items that have few political backers, such as spending on nonsalary operations and maintenance of schools and health facilities, are most at risk.

When discretionary public policy does not work to improve social welfare, rules and institutions may. Earmarking—assigning revenues from specific sources, by statute or by constitutional fiat, to finance some areas of government activity—may be an effective way of ensuring that some funds continue to go to some specified services and that fee revenue stays with the collecting institution. But the net effect on the collecting institution could be ambiguous. If earmarked revenues must be supplemented by some significant amounts from discretionary funds, governments could still manipulate those funds to counteract the nondiscretionary portion.

Earmarking also incurs costs in terms of the lack of budgetary control and inflexibility of budgets—costs that fall most heavily on governments that are able, for the most part, to behave in the public interest. But this mechanism may be fruitful for tackling the problem of regimes overly influenced by minority private interest groups, particularly if the incidence of the tax falls heavily on the beneficiaries of the expenditures for which revenues are earmarked (McCleary 1988).

Other "rules" can be equally effective in reducing the discretionary power of governments that do not act in the public interest—for instance freezing expenditures on such items of chronic overspending as expensive hospital care or university teaching. But all such action is likely to have only short-term or medium-term effects. In the long run, the laws, rules, or constitutions themselves may be subject to the same pressures that confront discretionary budgets.

The Agenda for Conceptual Research

The literature to date has assumed a fixed budgetary allocation to the social sector; has focused on user fees as a solution to the financing, efficiency, and equity problems; and has used a "public interest" welfare economics model of analysis. This section has discussed how these assumptions may be relaxed in order to address broader questions. They could be ordered in ascending order of difficulty, as follows: increasing efficiency as an alternative to raising prices; accounting for flexible budgetary allocations in the model; and taking the "private interest" view into account.

One area of work, not purely research, deserves some mention. The proponents of social sector pricing have so far been writing sweeping policy documents. Their objective has been to change a way of thinking, away from social services as entitlements and toward reaching social objectives with efficient policy instruments. They have not tried to furnish detailed guidelines on what practitioners should be doing in the field. Although it is probably not feasible or even perhaps useful to codify guidelines for the education and health sectors (see Julius and Alicbusan 1988 for an account of how public pricing rules have been implemented in other sectors) it may be time for researchers to address more detailed issues, specifically: Under what conditions can a specific price level be computed and recommended (most recommendations are on the direction and not the magnitude of change)? How can different types of prices (for example, copayments versus premiums in insurance or registration versus tuition fees in education) relate to one another?

IV. Conclusions

Recent proposals that traditional low- and uniform-price policies for education and health services be replaced by policies that differentiate prices by type of service and by type of consumer have generated considerable debate. Some of the disagreements are ideological and have led to misunderstandings about the extent and scope of cost recovery being proposed.

A substantial part of the debate has also focused on the empirical evidence. There is strong evidence that free or highly subsidized social services have not led to adequate access for the poor. But because countries are only beginning the process of reform, rigorous evaluations of the experience of policy reform have yet to be made. The evidence that selective user charges will improve efficiency and equity is partly based on simulations—the price elasticity of demand is generally low and prices can be raised without significantly affecting consumption. The responsiveness does vary by price level and income category, underlining the need to couple price increases with measures to protect the poorest income groups. The critical missing link in such research is assessment of the technical, administrative, and economic costs of targeting education and health subsidies in developing countries. Lessons can be learned from other sectors and developed countries on questions such as the costs of means-testing and the alternatives to using income as a criterion for targeting.

Research should also look at the unresolved conceptual problems. These include seeking ways other than price reform to direct funds to the social services (such as reallocating funds among sectors and raising revenues through means other than pricing) and ways to increase the efficiency of current provision, incorporating incentive effects. And the broader perspective encompassing political-economy arguments, particularly the "private interest" view of government, might offer ways to ensure that policy reform is undertaken and sustained.

Finally, more work should be devoted to the details of price reform. Most of the debate has been about generalities—the direction, rather than the magnitude, of change—and rightly so, for the tradition of free or highly subsidized provision has been so firmly entrenched. Detailed work is now needed to inform operational activities that are trying to put these ideas into practice. Such policy work should distinguish clearly among groups of countries with different characteristics and tailor the recommendations accordingly.

In sum, there is much merit in the proposals to increase user charges selectively. Aside from ideologically based challenges, the conceptual framework has not been undermined. There is also strong empirical evidence to support many of the arguments, particularly the present distribution of public subsidies and the raising of revenues through pricing reforms for high-cost social services. But there are still some weak links. Research is needed on the feasibility of measures to protect the poor, on estimates of the magnitude of the efficiency gain, and on the cost structure of service provision. More systematic evaluations of actual attempts at social sector price reform are also crucial. Unless these links are forged soon, the momentum for price reform in the social sectors may falter.

References

Abel-Smith, Brian. 1987. "Book Review" of *Financing Health Services in Developing Countries: An Agenda for Reform* [World Bank 1987]. *Health Policy and Planning* 2, no. 4: 355–58.

Ahmed, Ehtisham. 1989. "Social Security and Poverty Alleviation: Issues for Developing Countries." World Bank Country Economics Department. Washington, D.C. Processed.

Ainsworth, Martha. 1984. "User Charges for Cost Recovery in the Social Sectors: Current Practices." World Bank Country Policy Department Discussion Paper 1984–6. Washington, D.C. Processed.

Akin, John C., and Nancy Birdsall. 1987. "Financing Health Services in LDCs." *Finance and Development* (June): 40–43.

Akin, John C., Charles Griffin, David K. Guilkey, and Barry M. Popkin. 1986. "The Demand for Primary Health Care Services in the Bicol Region of the Philippines." *Economic Development and Cultural Change* 34: 755–82.

Atkinson, A. B., and Joseph E. Stiglitz. 1980. *Lectures on Public Economics.* London: McGraw-Hill.

Besley, Timothy. 1989a. "Reforming Public Expenditures: Some Methodological Issues." World Bank Country Economics Department. Washington, D.C. Processed.

———. 1989b. "Welfare-Improving User Charges for Publicly Provided Private Goods." Woodrow Wilson School of Public and International Affairs, Princeton University. Processed.

Besley, Timothy, and Ravi Kanbur. 1988. "Food Subsidies and Poverty Alleviation." *Economic Journal* 98 (September): 701–19.

Birdsall, Nancy. 1988. "Pragmatism, Robin Hood, and Other Themes: Good Government and Social Well-Being in Developing Countries." World Bank and Rockefeller Foundation. Washington, D.C. Processed.

Birdsall, Nancy, François Orivel, Martha Ainsworth, and Punam Chuhan. 1983. "Three Studies on Cost Recovery in Social Projects." World Bank Country Policy Department Discussion Paper 1983–8. Washington, D.C. Processed.

Bray, Mark. 1986. "Book Review" of *Financing Education in Developing Countries: An Exploration of Policy Options* [World Bank 1986]. *International Journal of Ed-*

ucational Development 7, no. 2: 147–48.

Bray, Mark, and Kevin Lillis, eds. 1988. *Community Financing of Education: Issues and Policy Implications in Less Developed Countries*. Oxford: Pergamon Press.

Bucovetsky, Sam. 1984. "On the Use of Distributional Waits." *Canadian Journal of Economics* 11, no. 4: 699–717.

Castaneda, Tarsicio. 1986. "Innovations in the Financing of Education: The Case of Chile." World Bank Education and Training Department Discussion Paper 35. Washington, D.C. Processed.

Chile, Government of. 1988. "Evolución de la Extrema Pobreza en Chile." Santiago.

Cornia, Giovanni A., Richard Jolly, and Frances Stewart. 1987. *Adjustment with a Human Face*. Oxford: Clarendon Press.

de Ferranti, David. 1985. *Paying for Health Services in Developing Countries: An Overview*. World Bank Staff Working Paper 721. Washington, D.C.

Dempster, Carolyn. 1987. "African Heads Attack World Bank Plan." *The Times (London) Higher Education Supplement*. April 24.

Dor, Avi, Paul Gertler, and Jacques van der Gaag. 1987. "Non-price Rationing and Medical Care Provides Choice in Rural Côte d'Ivoire." *Journal of Health Economics* 6: 291–304.

Dunlop, David. 1987. "A Study of Health Financing: Issues and Options, Ethiopia." *World Bank Sector Review*. Washington, D.C. Processed.

Edirisinghe, Neville. 1987. "The Food Stamp Program in Sri Lanka: Costs, Benefits, and Policy Options." International Food Policy Research Institute Research Report 58. Washington, D.C.

Fuller, Bruce. 1987. *Raising School Quality in Developing Countries*. World Bank Discussion Paper 2. Washington, D.C.

Garcia, Marito, and Per Pinstrup-Andersen. 1987. "The Pilot Food Price Subsidy Scheme in the Philippines: Its Impact on Income, Food Consumption, and Nutrition Status." International Food Policy Research Institute Research Report 61. Washington, D.C. Processed.

Gertler, Paul, and Paul Glewwe. 1989. *The Willingness to Pay for Education in Developing Countries*. Living Standards Measurement Study Working Paper 54. Washington, D.C.: World Bank.

Gertler, Paul, Luis Locay, and Warren Sanderson. 1987. "Are User Fees Regressive?: The Welfare Implications of Health Care Financing Proposals in Peru." *Journal of Econometrics* 33: 67–88.

Gertler, Paul, and Jacques van der Gaag. 1988. "The Willingness to Pay for Medical Care: Evidence from Two Developing Countries." World Bank Population and Human Resources Department. Washington, D.C. Processed.

Gilson, Lucy. 1988. *Government Health Care Charges: Is Equity Being Abandoned?—A Discussion Paper*. EPC Publication 15. London: School of Hygiene and Tropical Medicine.

Griffin, Charles C. 1988. *User Charges for Health Care in Principle and Practice*. Economic Development Institute Seminar Paper 37. Washington, D.C.: World Bank.

———. 1989. "Means Testing in Developing Countries." Eugene: Department of Economics, University of Oregon. Processed.

Groves, T., and Ledyard, J. O. 1985. "Incentive Compatibility Ten Years Later." Department of Economics, Northwestern University Discussion Paper 648. Evanston, Ill.

Hanushek, Eric A.. 1986. "The Economics of Schooling: Production and Efficiency in the Public Schools." *Journal of Economic Literature* 24, no. 3: 1141–77.

Heady, Christopher. 1989. "Public Sector Pricing in a Fiscal Context." World Bank Policy, Planning, and Research Working Paper 179. Washington, D.C. Processed.

Jimenez, Emmanuel. 1986a. "The Public Subsidization of Education and Health in Developing Countries: The Impact of Equity and Efficiency." *World Bank Research Observer* 1, no. 1: 111–29.

———. 1986b. "The Structure of Educational Costs: Multiproduct Cost Functions for Primary and Secondary Schools in Latin America." *Economics of Education Review* 5: 25–40.

———. 1987. *Pricing Policy in the Social Sectors: Cost Recovery for Education and Health in Developing Countries*. Baltimore, Md.: Johns Hopkins University Press.

Jimenez, Emmanuel, Marlaine Lockheed, and Vicente Paqueo. 1988. "The Relative Efficiency of Public and Private Schools in Developing Countries." World Bank Policy, Planning, and Research Working Paper 72. Washington D.C. Processed.

Jimenez, Emmanuel, Vicente Paqueo, and M. Lourdes de Vera. 1988. "Does Local Financing Make Primary Schools More Efficient?: The Philippine Case." World Bank Policy, Planning, and Research Working Paper 69. Washington D.C. Processed.

Julius, DeAnne, and A. P. Alicbusan. 1988. "Public Sector Pricing Policies: A Review of Bank Policy and Practice." World Bank Policy, Planning, and Research Working Paper 49. Washington, D.C. Processed.

Katz, Michael. 1987. "Pricing Publicly Supplied Goods and Services." In David Newbery and Nicholas Stern, eds., *The Theory of Taxation for Developing Countries*. New York: Oxford University Press.

Klees, Steven J. 1984. "The Need for a Political Economy of Educational Finance: A Response to Thobani." *Comparative Education Review* 28, no. 3: 424–40.

Knight, John B., and Richard H. Sabot. 1986. "Overview of Educational Expansion, Productivity, and Inequality: A Comparative Analysis of the East African Natural Experiment." World Bank Education and Training Department Discussion Paper 48. Washington, D.C. Processed.

Mackintosh, Fiona, J. 1989. "Notes on Means-Tested Poverty Programs in the U.S." World Bank Country Economics Department. Washington, D.C. Processed.

Mayo, Stephen K., and David J. Gross. 1987. "Sites and Services—and Subsidies: The Economics of Low-Cost Housing in Developing Countries." *World Bank Economic Review* 1, no. 2: 301–35.

McCleary, William A. 1988. "Notes on the Principles and Practice of Earmarking." World Bank Country Economics Department. Washington, D.C. Processed.

Meerman, Jacob. 1979. *Public Expenditure in Malaysia: Who Benefits and Why*. New York: Oxford University Press.

Mills, Edwin S. 1986. *The Burdens of Government*. Stanford, Calif.: Hoover Institution Press.

Mingat, Alain, and Jee-Peng Tan. 1985. "On Equity in Education Again: An International Comparison." *Journal of Human Resources* 20, no. 2: 298–308.

———. 1986. "Who Profits from the Public Funding of Education? A Comparison by World Regions." *Comparative Education Review* 30: 260–70.

Moffit, Robert. 1983. "An Economic Model of Welfare Stigma." *American Economic Review* 73, no. 5 (December): 1023–35.

Mwabu, Germano. 1986. "Health Care Financing in Kenya: A Simulation of Welfare Effects of User Fees." *Social Science and Medicine* 22, no. 7: 763–67.

Namor, Eugenio. 1987. *Issues in the Targeting of Food Subsidies for the Poor: A Survey of the Literature*. International Monetary Fund Working Paper WP/87/75. Washington, D.C.

Neave, Guy, ed. 1988. "Higher Education and Development: A Reappraisal. *Higher Education Policy* (special issue) 1, no. 1 (March): 7–36.

Newbery, David, and Nicholas Stern. 1987. *The Theory of Taxation in Developing Countries*. New York: Oxford University Press.

Pan American Health Organization. 1988. "Financing Health Services in Developing Countries: An Agenda for Reform." *Bulletin* 22, no. 4.

Petrei, A. Humberto. 1987. *El Gasto Publico Social y sus Efectos Distributivos*. Rio de Janeiro: Estudios Conjuntos de Integracao Economia da America Latina.

Pfeffermann, Guy, and Charles C. Griffin. 1989. *Nutrition and Health Programs in Latin America: Targeting Social Expenditures*. Washington, D.C., and Panama City: World Bank and International Center for Economic Growth.

Psacharopoulos, George. 1985. "Returns to Education: A Further International Update and Implications." *Journal of Human Resources* (Fall): 583–604.

Psacharopoulos, George, Jee-Peng Tan, and Emmanuel Jimenez. 1989. "Financing Education in Developing Countries." *IDS Bulletin* 20, no. 1 (January): 59–71.

Psacharopoulos, George, and Maureen Woodhall. 1985. *Education for Development: An Analysis of Investment Choices*. New York: Oxford University Press.

Rodriguez-Grossi, Jorge. 1985. *La Distribución del Ingreso y el Gasto Social en Chile, 1983*. Santiago: Instituto Latinoamericano de Estudios Sociales.

Roth, Gabriel. 1987. *The Private Provision of Public Services in Developing Countries*. New York: Oxford University Press.

Sah, Raaj Kumar. 1987. "Queues, Rations, and Markets." *American Economic Review* 77, no. 1 (March): 69–77.

Sawhill, Isabel V. 1988. "Poverty in the U.S.: Why Is It So Persistent?" *Journal of Economic Literature* 26, no. 3 (September): 1073–119.

Schwabe, Christopher. Nondated. "The Demand for Curative Health Services in Juba, Sudan: An Empirical Investigation into the Potential for Introducing User Fees." Graduate Research Paper, Syracuse University. Syracuse, N.Y.

Selowsky, Marcelo. 1979. *Who Benefits from Government Expenditure? A Case Study of Colombia*. New York: Oxford University Press.

Tan, Jee-Peng, Kiong Hock Lee, and Alain Mingat. 1984. *User Charges for Education: The Ability and Willingness to Pay in Malawi*. World Bank Staff Working Paper 661. Washington, D.C.

Thobani, Mateen. 1983. *Charging User Fees for Social Services: The Malawi Education Case*. World Bank Staff Working Paper 572. Washington, D.C.

Timmons, Robert J., Roy I. Miller, and William D. Drake. 1983. "Targeting: A Means to Better Intervention." Report to U.S. Agency for International Development on nutrition programs in Brazil, Colombia, India, Sri Lanka, and Thailand. Washington, D.C. Processed.

University of the Philippines. Nondated. "Democratization of Admissions." Office of the Chancellor, Diliman, Quezon City, Philippines.

Vitaliano, Donald F. 1987. "On the Estimation of Hospital Cost Functions." *Journal of Health Economics* 6: 305–18.

Vogel, Ronald J. 1988. *Cost Recovery in the Health Care Sector: Selected Country Studies in West Africa*. World Bank Technical Paper 82. Washington, D.C.

Whalley, John, and Adrian Ziderman. 1989. "Payroll Taxes for Financing Training in Developing Countries." World Bank Policy, Planning, and Research Working Paper 141. Washington, D.C. Processed.

Winkler, Donald. 1989. "Decentralization in Education: An Economic Perspective." World Bank Policy, Planning, and Research Working Paper 143. Washington D.C. Processed.

World Bank. 1986. *Financing Education in Developing Countries: An Exploration of Policy Options*. Washington D.C.: World Bank.

———. 1987. *Financing Health Services in Developing Countries: An Agenda for Reform*. A World Bank Policy Study. Washington, D.C.

———. 1988a. *Education in Sub-Saharan Africa: Policies for Adjustment, Revitalization, and Expansion*. A World Bank Policy Study. Washington, D.C.

———. 1988b. *The Philippines Education Sector Study*. Report 7473-PH. Washington, D.C. Processed.

———. 1988c. *World Development Report 1988*. New York: Oxford University Press.

Zschock, Dieter. 1986. "Medical Care Under Social Insurance in Latin America." *Latin American Research Review* 21, no. 1: 99–122.

Comment on "Social Sector Pricing Policy Revisited,"
by Jimenez

Benno J. Ndulu

To look at the debate about social sector pricing clearly and objectively, it is imperative to set the issue squarely in its policy context. To do this, I need to revisit the nature of the problem confronting the providers of social services in developing countries.

I. The Nature of the Problem

The gap between objective growth in demand for social services and resources available to meet this demand is growing. This is a long-term trend to which a combination of rapid population growth and youthful structure of population is fundamental. Not only are requirements for health and education services expanding; there are also proportionately fewer people in the population to carry the growing burden. In the short to medium term these pressures have been exacerbated by economic crises. Two major sources of pressure have been: (1) erosion of the public revenue base as a result partly of a decline in real economic activity and partly, for many countries, of a reduction in the share of formal (taxable) incomes as various groups in the economy cushion decline in real incomes through tax evasion and (2) that the resultant reduction in both quantity and quality of social services has given rise to rationing, to the disadvantage of the more vulnerable groups.

To create a sustainable delivery system for social services to meet growing needs requires policies both to manage demand and to augment supply. At the same time, in the short to medium term, solutions to the problem must take into account the broader stress on macroeconomic performance brought by the impacts of economic crises. The policy action required and the adjustment costs involved are clearly more intense and complex currently than before the crises. The overlap of pressure from long-term trends and pressures from crises demands that measures to restore normalcy be carefully separated from those tackling the sustainability problem in the long term.

Benno Ndulu is research coordinator for the African Economic Research Consortium, Nairobi, Kenya.

© 1990 The International Bank for Reconstruction and Development / THE WORLD BANK.

II. Latitude for Policy Action

The aggregate demand side for social services, dominated as it is by population pressures and state guarantees of some socially desirable minimum provision of services, seems to leave much less room for policy maneuvering. Demand structure and supply augmentation seem more susceptible to policy manipulation.

For demand structure, there is some latitude for internalization of benefits and for distinguishing between basic and nonbasic services. But to the extent that most services are still rudimentary, and social returns from their provision are still relatively high, the room for policy maneuvering is still very limited. Pricing reforms to influence demand structure face a particular constraint in the case of education. The relatively slower growth in absorptive capacity, especially for higher education output, may reduce prospective private benefits relative to private investment. This may dampen private demand, further constricting the effective room for modifying the structure of demand.

As is apparent from the set of studies Jimenez reviews, resource gaps are large at the aggregate level. Price measures alone will probably generate insufficient revenues to fill the gap. Other measures—including a stopgap inflow of external resources—may have to be regarded as complementary, rather than as alternative.

The political calculus of adjustment cost incidence across various interest groups is important for implementing reforms. As the paper correctly points out, the poor suffer most under relative scarcity, while those currently benefiting from the status quo command significant political resources to maintain it. The process of reform then inevitably becomes political and has to be resolved internally. Well-grounded studies for each particular situation may facilitate, but can never replace, this process.

The costs of reforms are more visible than the benefits because of the empirical weaknesses of the studies reviewed. Uncertainty about benefits could hinder the adoption of the reforms. The expected magnitude of the impacts of policy measures matters at least as much for implementation as their direction.

III. The Role of Pricing

Jimenez's discussion assigns a threefold role to pricing in tackling the problem described above: resource mobilization, promotion of efficiency, and equity.

Resource Mobilization

The case for pricing as an effective instrument for reducing revenue gaps is perhaps the most convincing. The basic hypothesis is for cost-sharing in line with the proportions of private to social benefits derived from services. The workability of this proposal hinges on resolving the liquidity constraints associated with the nonexistence or inadequacy of capital markets, especially in Africa. The prevalence of such constraints may reduce levels of supply to socially inefficient levels. Empirical information on what level of consumption and private demand would be best for the society is required before pricing can be determined.

Scarcities have already brought implicit (albeit tacit) implementation of user charges in some countries. Where public supply has fallen below private demand, private enterprise has tended to fill the gaps. Whether through increased use of private services, or through supplementing public services (for example, purchasing medicines after consultation with public medical personnel or supplementing shortfalls of educational materials in public schools), costs of social services over and above the normal access costs are partly privately borne. Measuring the extent to which private expenditures have cushioned the drop in quantity and quality of public social services would furnish some indication of private willingness and ability to contribute toward costs. This would provide information on the scope for pricing action that brings into the open implicit charges and necessary targeting for those without the ability to pay.

To estimate revenue yields from pricing it is critical to obtain relevant demand estimates that incorporate intensity of service utilization in addition to participation ratios (for example, attendance or enrollment). The wide variations of characteristics across income groups and types of services make this imperative. Methods of generating revenue other than pricing are referred to passim, but in my opinion more detailed work on the comparative efficacy of the various instruments is needed. Because operational pricing strongly suggests budgetary earmarking, contrary to current broad budgetary practice, the strong case for relative efficacy will have to be a good one.

Promotion of Efficiency

The case for pricing as an instrument of allocative efficiency is perhaps the weakest. Prevalence of externalities, current inadequacy of services supplied, the issue of institutional legitimacy and complementary requirements (competitiveness, capital market efficiency, and efficiency of sectors competing for access to the same resources) make this function close to untenable. Several "second-best" scenarios have been suggested, but none of them is definitive.

This is not by any means to say that efficiency of the social service delivery system is unimportant. Cost minimization (in this case not necessarily the "standard dual") is important. Research should emphasize methods for making delivery systems more cost-effective to alleviate the pressure of budget constraint. Here, the paper lacks review of relevant cost studies.

Equity

Pricing addresses the equity issue indirectly through revenue generation, which reduces relative scarcity and hence the impetus for potentially inequitable rationing. To the extent that a general increase in access reduces the need for rationing, inequality of accessibility is reduced, if we accept the author's arguments about unequal access via rationing. But, as argued earlier, because any measures to ease the budgetary constraint would have the same impacts, pricing has no intrinsic superiority, from the equity point of view, over any other method.

On the contrary—increased prices, given income distribution, are as likely to have a negative as a positive impact on equity by constricting access for the poorer segment of the population. Price rises flanked by programs targeted to offset disadvantages to the poor need to be carefully compared with other schemes for their effectiveness in generating revenue while preserving equity.

The paper by Jimenez has no doubt raised some important issues concerning the role of pricing in the provision of social services for long-term sustainability and in response to short-term resource shortfalls. But significant empirical gaps remain. The superiority of pricing over other instruments to achieve the combined targets of revenue generation, cost effectiveness, and equity needs to be established. In view of the wide variations in characteristics across different types of social services and countries, the prevalence of externalities, and the inadequacy of complementary capital markets, the need for such empirical studies cannot be overemphasized.

COMMENT ON "SOCIAL SECTOR PRICING POLICY REVISITED," BY JIMENEZ

Nicholas Stern

My comments concern, first, theory; second, empirical questions (though the latter are guided by and suggest further theoretical questions); and third, further work.

I. Theory

Early World Bank manuals apparently recommended that public sector pricing be based on "efficiency prices" modified appropriately for "non-economic objectives." The health and education sectors were specifically exempted from this prescription. The "new view" analyzed in Jimenez's paper may be seen as in part an attempt to bring health and education into the fold of standard public sector pricing. Thus one way of thinking about the subject is to examine whether we *should* bring them under that rubric. In other words, we ask what is different about health and education from the point of view of pricing policy.

But before doing this we must note in passing that the correct price for public sector pricing is not marginal cost. In an economy that is revenue constrained in the sense that lump-sum taxes are not possible (and this applies to all real economies) the correct public sector price is marginal cost plus an element of indirect taxation to contribute to revenue. What precisely that extra contribution should be will depend on the revenue requirement, the distributional pattern of consumption of the good, value judgments about distribution, and the pattern of demand elasticities. However crudely the problems of calculation are resolved, the central question of revenue cannot be overlooked, and it is simply wrong to say that economic theory points to marginal cost pricing in this context. It does not, and the World Bank would be making a serious error if it encouraged countries with real revenue difficulties to overlook revenue generation in public sector pricing.

To return to the ways in which health and education differ from the standard publicly supplied private goods: the first of the different features of health and education is that they cannot easily be resold. This means that the public sector can charge different prices to different individuals. Such a scheme would not

---

Nicholas Stern is a professor of economics and chairman of the Suntory-Toyota International Center for Economics and Related Disciplines at the London School of Economics and Political Science.

© 1990 The International Bank for Reconstruction and Development / THE WORLD BANK.

work with standard private goods because reselling would mean that people who were charged a higher price would simply buy from others who had been charged a lower price rather than from the public sector. If, however, women are charged lower prices than men for chest X rays, then it makes little sense for me, observing this low price, to ask my wife to go and have the chest X ray for me. It is easy to show that, if personalized prices are to replace uniform prices, welfare would be improved if the reform is in the direction which, for equal revenue, raises prices to the richer person and lowers prices to the poorer person (provided that demand patterns and other taxes are such that a small price increase to richer households does not result in sharp revenue losses elsewhere).

Whatever the method used to calculate the personalized prices, the central issues to be resolved—revenue, the ability to charge personalized prices, and a lower valuation on increases in income for the rich relative to increases for the poor—would combine to call for a solution where the rich pay more than the poor.

The second difference between health, education, and ordinary private goods concerns externalities. It may be our view that better education and better health confer positive externalities on other members of the community. These positive externalities might lead to the suggestion that the goods be subsidized, for the standard reasons, and that the measurement of these externalities would thus be useful for applied policy analysis. I doubt that the measuring can be done with enough precision to act as a direct input into policy, but the consideration does point unambiguously toward a subsidy.

A third peculiarity of the health and education services concerns the consumer's lack of knowledge about quality. (This was a central feature of Arrow's justly famous article on the economics of medical care; Arrow 1963). Lack of knowledge might better be addressed through government programs to disseminate information and regulate quality rather than through a subsidy. But there might still be a case for a subsidy if consumers systematically underestimate quality despite information and regulation.

Fourth, in education at least, the decisionmaker—the parent—is not necessarily the only relevant consumer. Children consume education too, and the interests of parent and child may not always exactly coincide. Indeed, in most countries, the state is seen to have a role, in extremis, in protecting children from the parent. Such considerations lie in part behind the idea of compulsory education up to a certain age. The level of prices charged may have serious effects on the ability to enforce such regulation, and this should be taken into account in considering the appropriate pricing policy.

Fifth, the government may consider that education and health are what Musgrave (1959) terms "merit goods"—in other words, the consumer is deemed unable or unwilling to understand what is good for her or him, and the government might charge lower prices to offset this partial self-neglect.

Finally, and related to the previous two points, the government may see that it has a responsibility to provide universal access to health and education of a certain quality, and that individuals have rights to such access. This may not accord directly with our standard welfare economic approach, which is based largely on individual sovereignty and individual judgment of own best interest. But the view that policy should take into account responsibilities and rights should not be lightly dismissed. For many aspects of economic policy this consideration may not be central, but in this case we have to consider the possibility that it might be.

II. Empirical Issues

The first proposition arising from the empirical work discussed by Jimenez is that existing cheap provisioning with rationing can lead to substantial use of the provided services by the middle and upper classes. The finding—often referred to as "middle class capture"—is well documented in both developed and developing countries. The common inference that the service is not particularly egalitarian or well targeted is often seen as a partial indictment of the system itself. The charge is not necessarily appropriate for two reasons. First, from the standpoint of rights and responsibilities, all should consume regardless of income. Second, the participation of middle and upper classes in the service can often improve its quality for everyone because they may be better capable of translating complaints into action than less privileged groups—though they might, by the same token, use their articulateness and influence to divert resources to themselves. The first proposition seems more firmly based than the other five, which follow.

The second stylized fact discussed is that total supply may be higher in an unrestricted private market. Jimenez uses the examples of Kenya and Tanzania here. We do not know, however, whether this is a reliable empirical phenomenon, and if so how much it matters. Higher supply strongly biased toward more privileged groups may be worse than lower supply.

Third, the cost of supply may be too high. As is pointed out in the paper, this may be hard to judge because the outputs of health and education systems are multidimensional. Moreover, the tests of output may be biased. For example, the ability to pass certain tests into a higher level of education may be an exaggerated focus of attention for a private school, whereas a public school may have broader objectives that are less measurable and do not appear in output measures. Nevertheless, one does have the feeling that cost minimization does encourage the husbanding of resources, and that it may be only desultorily applied in the public sector.

Fourth, what has been supplied may not be well allocated. This idea raises interesting theoretical and empirical questions that deserve further research. What do we mean by resources being allocated well in the health and education sector? What criteria should we use and how can we measure them? No doubt these issues have been the central concern of education and health economists, but one does not have the impression that workable yardsticks are easy to come by.

Fifth, the wrong things may be supplied by the system. Again, this raises an interesting question of what should be supplied and raises similar problems of how to formulate criteria.

Sixth, it seems that price-elasticities of demand may decrease with income. The paper's conclusion on the policy consequences of this observation is wrong according to standard applied welfare economic theory. The author argues that the observed decrease of price-elasticities with income implies that the poor are hit more by the price increase. According to standard theory, the higher the elasticity of demand, the less I am hurt by a unit price increase, because essentially I can substitute toward other goods. The paper's divergence from standard theory here is revealing: it shows that the commentator is concerned with the distribution of the good itself, which in turn indicates that something more than simply individual perception of welfare is involved. We would, I think, attach no special welfare significance to the distribution of the consumption of croissants or chewing gum, whereas it appears from the inference in the paper that we do attach significance to the distribution of health and education. The last two or three of the differences between health and education indicated in the preceding theory section do indeed seem to be relevant, at least for the author of the paper.

III. Further Work

The research agenda provided in the paper is sensible, and it need not be repeated here. Similarly, I need not belabor the theoretical issues mentioned in the first section of my remarks, since the research agenda arising from them is self-explanatory. What I want to bring out here is the need for more precisely formulated and researched policy proposals that embody some of the ideas of the "new view." It is simply not enough to attack the existing state of affairs as a shambles, nor to denounce opposition to the new view as consisting merely of slogans. Furthermore, to protest that one does care about the poor is not persuasive unless the protestation is supported by specific and workable programs that will, demonstrably, not only meet goals described in the new view but at the same time protect the poor. As with the standard analysis of tax and price reform, we should show who will be the gainers and who the losers from a policy change. This information is critical not only to our standard procedures of applied welfare economics, but also to any analysis of political economy that seeks to identify which groups would try to lobby for or oppose which policy. Prediction of winners and losers is a critical issue, not just for this particular problem but for almost all problems of policy. And it is the most difficult aspect of most applied policy research.

The severe difficulties of researching and designing workable policies bring with them the temptation to assume problems away—to say, for example, that problems of credit and insurance should be resolved in those markets and not in the market for health and education. The problems of credit and insurance markets cannot simply be assumed away; they are deeply rooted both theoretically and empirically and must be taken as central to those of health and education. Similarly, we should ask whether we can really target effectively without running into dangers of both fraud and disincentive. And, aside from those dangers, there are major difficulties in defining eligibility. Income-based tests bring all the problems of defining and measuring income. But if tests are not income-based, then are they well targeted? Further, means-testing can cause real personal difficulties of self-esteem, and doubtless contributes to poor take-up. Measuring success or failure for policies should not be confined to assessing gainers and losers simply in monetary terms. We must ask directly about outcomes in terms of literacy and standard of health, rather than simply looking at who consumes what service and at what price. Thus we must ask of any health and education delivery systems how they have affected, for example, literacy and infant mortality in different parts of the community. Some important examples exist of countries, such as China, that have followed policies very different from those suggested by the new view yet seem to have achieved impressive advances in increasing literacy and reducing infant mortality in vulnerable communities.

Social sector pricing is a fundamental area of policy, presenting difficult intellectual and empirical challenges. This is surely a priority for research at the World Bank, which should mount the appropriate research programs to meet and respond to these challenges. Without further research, and in particular the testing of the effects of specific programs, we should be cautious about widescale advocacy of a particular line of reform.

References

Arrow, Kenneth J. 1963. "Uncertainty and the Welfare Economics of Medical Care." *American Economic Review* 53, no. 5 (December): 941–73.

Musgrave, R. A. 1959. *The Theory of Public Finance.* New York: McGraw-Hill.

Floor Discussion of Jimenez Paper

One participant felt that the paper may be posing the wrong question by emphasizing pricing of social services rather than first examining the allocative decisions and framework—the relative merits of, say, spending money on defense or on health and education—within which pricing decisions are made. You need to conclude that public funds are allocated efficiently; only then do you address the question: Within a sector, how do you compensate the losers—the poor—with higher price elasticities of demand?

A participant pointed out that China had performed better than India in providing social services and, put very simply, China had not used pricing, whereas India had. Is rationing better than pricing as a way of allocating social services? The answer, he thought, depended not just on price elasticities but on the distribution of needs that society places a value on satisfying. Jimenez agreed with the speaker, that governments want to provide some services universally, but was not sure that many governments would want to provide equal access, regardless of economic status, to all social services. For example, would governments in Africa currently want to provide universal higher education?

One member of the audience asked if the purpose of making user-cost pricing an element of conditionality wasn't deficit reduction more than effective resource allocation. And if so, in the typical developing country, where so few people participate in postsecondary education, would not the potential savings be small? Jimenez responded that potential revenues from pricing schemes vary by country. Studies in Africa show, for example, that if you raise user fees in universities and use those funds to increase subsidies in primary education, the potential impact on primary school enrollment can vary a lot depending on the number of higher education students in the system and the relative costs for the two levels of education. Another participant agreed that the fiscal implications of delivering social services are exaggerated—that social sectors account for only about 5 percent of most government budgets. Subsidies for higher education were introduced in many developing countries because the expected returns to education were such that if you priced these services at the notional marginal cost plus, you would drive higher education out of business. The World Bank, he felt, needs to do more research on the implications of different ways of arriving at an optimal pricing strategy.

A participant noted that the treatment of these issues seemed to be quite

---

This session was chaired by Nancy Birdsall, chief, Population and Human Resources Division, Brazil Country Department, World Bank.

© 1990 The International Bank for Reconstruction and Development / THE WORLD BANK.

different, at least in the public finance literature, for the countries that belong to the Organisation for Economic Co-operation and Development (OECD) than in the development literature discussed in Jimenez's paper. The OECD-oriented literature rationalizes certain types of activity in the public sector in very traditional public goods terms, including rationalizing zero- or low-cost pricing for education, health-care, urban transit, and so on, on a case-by-case basis. For example, there is a lot written on education as a quasi-public good, where you enforce uniform consumption but there is a cost of exclusion. The participant felt that the development literature, on the other hand, seems to be taking a very broad approach of recommending pricing of all social services on a user-cost basis. Jimenez responded that some of the literature approaches the question of public goods from the point of view that perhaps some levels of education or some services within education are "more public than others," and similarly in health.

A participant emphasized the weakness of the conceptual and empirical foundation on which social sector price reform was building. In his opinion, the agency that wants to spread this gospel should be responsible for stating what is needed, so that analysts can reliably estimate the critical parameters on which price reforms would proceed, and evaluate the consequences. He emphasized certain problems. For price reform to work, we have to identify those parts of the population for which withdrawing a subsidy and charging a higher price would not discourage desirable behavior. Rural-urban and regional differences may make for viable market segmentation, but he doubted that separating people by income testing was viable in many parts of the world. Then, we need to see if such differential pricing schemes can be administered. Finally we need to understand much more about the political difficulty of charging certain parts of the population for services that are provided free to other parts of the population. Intuitively, he doubted these sorts of problems were as easily dealt with as the original World Bank publications implied, and deserved intensive study.

A Bank participant suggested that although it is difficult to estimate the "exact" price to charge for social sector services, there is empirical evidence that *something* should be charged. In a systematic study, the Rand Corporation had examined the effect on demand for health insurance of different co-insurance rates. Rand found that the biggest change in demand for services came at the step from a zero rate to something, not the step from a positive rate to something higher. Charging a little made a big difference in efficiency. In most public sector goods and services—and primary education may be an exception—it may make sense to charge a little simply to make people aware that resources are not free. So he firmly believed that there were significant pricing, accountability, competition, and related issues that could be discussed without getting into ideological arguments. Ndulu (discussant) pointed out that in some economies during periods of economic crises when the public supply has declined in quality or quantity, some individuals have been willing and able to pay extra for the free services they had gotten used to.

In designing policy on user charges, it is important to research both equity issues and political costs, commented one participant. It is not enough to just show what proportion of a subsidy goes to what income groups—say, for instance, that the bottom 40 percent of the population gets only 10 to 15 percent of the total subsidy. Targeting is important because that 10 to 15 percent may be a large part of household income for the poor and may make a big difference to them. As for political costs: we always distinguish too simplistically between the poor and the nonpoor, but the urban lower middle class is a politically important beneficiary of services. It is important to find measures that are politically acceptable to this group.

Stern (discussant) argued for a practical approach. He did not see the point of computing optimal prices. We are interested in reform and we can see the direction we want reform to take—with the rich paying a bit more for these services. What we want to be sure about is that we have schemes that actually work. We should look at the impact on, say, literacy and infant mortality, of different schemes—not just at who pays more or less or consumes more or less. Stern found the public goods argument made by a participant earlier in the discussion inappropriate in this context. These were private goods, on the whole, with externalities—and price elasticities were probably not as important as the size of the externalities, in his view.

A Bank participant noted that we should first deal with the problem of financial discipline and financial incentives and then talk about introducing user fees, rather than the other way around, as the paper did. Without fiscal discipline, evasion, avoidance, and leakage from user-fee revenues would be substantial. He recollected that a study of hospital finances in Malaysia, which has a system of user fees, had found that revenues amounted to only 7 percent of what was collectible. The people who do not end up paying the user fees are predominantly the rich and the influential—the very people from whom you are trying to capture the fees. With financial discipline and the ability to collect revenue, we can make sure that any user fees that are introduced actually work.

Wrapping up the discussion, Birdsall (chair) observed that, not surprisingly, there had been some agreement on the notion that because of equity concerns and externalities associated with providing these services, policymakers must look beyond the market mechanism and treat social services as more than private goods. Disagreement about whether pricing reform is worth it, or would work, seemed to be related to confusion and disagreement about the primary purpose of pricing reform. Is it to achieve fiscal gains, efficiency gains, or better equity? In her opinion, the discussion did not address an important point raised in the paper—that you can probably improve equity with pricing reform, particularly if you focus on selective, not across-the-board, user charges.

She observed that the participants agreed that more research was needed about reforms now being undertaken—their outcomes, use of services, and issues of political economy; and about which groups lose, which gain, and how it is that some pricing reforms go ahead and others do not.

The Role of Institutions in Development

Brian Van Arkadie

Economists interpret "institutions" in at least two ways. Institutions can be the "rules of the game" (which provide the context—such as markets—in which actors make decisions), or they can be organizations (typically, systems of nonmarket relations). What is the role of public policy in influencing the rules of the game, and what is its role in public sector economic organizations? Informal conventions and informal rules of the game make institutions function differently than their formal structure might lead us to expect. Governments can intervene and influence the rules of the game, but their interventions should be based on an adequate perception of existing formal and informal arrangements and on processes of adaptation that were under way before intervention was initiated. The literature does not adequately explore the normative arguments for public economic organizations, nor has there been enough rigorous analysis of the causes of public sector failure. Many institutions are dysfunctional in terms of development, however, not because they are inefficient but because their intended purposes conflict with the requirements of economic growth. Diagnosing the causes of good or bad performance by public organizations could provide the basis for exploring a rational public sector organizational strategy.

Which government institutions and institutional interventions seem essential to growth, which can be helpful, and which are likely to obstruct growth? Such questions cannot be answered definitively, and answers cannot be applied universally: the observed failure or success of an institution in one national setting may reveal little about its potential performance elsewhere. But short of a checklist of "good" and "bad" institutions, a good deal of light can be thrown on what should be considered in appraising them. Strong institutional assumptions are often implicit in the design of programs and projects. The logical and empirical basis for such assumptions should be explored, even if the result is far from a cook book of recipes for effective institutions.

I. INSTITUTIONS: TWO DEFINITIONS

Two different, although related, meanings are given to the term "institutions" in discussions of development. The first is as rules of the game. The second is as organizations.

Brian Van Arkadie is a professor of economics at the University of Dar es Salaam, Tanzania.

© 1990 The International Bank for Reconstruction and Development / THE WORLD BANK.

Rules of the Game

The general meaning that informs much of the academic discussion of institutions is captured by Ruttan and Hayami (1984):

> Institutions are the rules of a society or of organizations that facilitate coordination among people by helping them form expectations which each person can reasonably hold in dealing with each other. They reflect the conventions that have evolved in different societies regarding the behavior of individuals and groups relative to their own behavior and the behavior of others. In the area of economic relations they have a crucial role in establishing expectations about the rights to use resources in economic activities and about the partitioning of income streams resulting from economic activity.

Similarly, Feeny (1988) quotes Douglas North (1981):

> Institutions are a set of rules, compliance procedures, and moral and ethical behavioral norms designed to constrain the behavior of individuals.

In this definition "institutions" encompass the fundamental rules of the game within which the economic system operates. Economic historians have been particularly concerned with the broad changes in these rules that accompanied the emergence of modern capitalism—for example, the change in land tenure systems, the decline of serfdom, and the emergence of "free" labor.

Such broad issues might seem to have little operational interest for contemporary policymakers. But in fact the institutional context determining access to land, and relationships between farmers, landlords, workers, traders, and moneylenders has been long recognized as critical for rural project design. And the current fashionable concern with an "enabling environment" in which nongovernment actors can contribute to development emphasizes the importance of institutional factors in this sense (see Aga Khan Foundation 1987).

Organizations

Donor agencies tend to define institutions somewhat more narrowly, essentially as synonyms for organizations—government departments, state enterprises, banks, armies, hospitals, and the like (see van Rennin and Waisfisz 1988). Discussions of "institutional development" and "institution building" are therefore typically concerned with how to make organizations work.

The difference between the concepts has some interest from an analytical as well as a semantic point of view. Institutions in the "rules of the game" sense provide the context in which markets operate—influencing both their efficiency and distributive impact. Institutions define the terms under which the various actors in the market confront each other, molding their expectations and defining their rights. In this sense, economists should be very much at home with institutional questions, relating as they do to the central concern of neoclassical economics: the operation of markets.

The institution as organization is another matter. From the point of view of an economist an organization can be usefully defined as an area of activity within which the market does *not* coordinate the activities of the participants. An organization may be externally constrained by market factors, but its internal arrangements are coordinated by nonmarket instruments. Internal decision rules and incentive systems may be chosen to simulate the market, but even then the relationship between the actors is inherently different from that between independent actors in the marketplace.

The principal strengths of neoclassical economics derive from propositions of widespread applicability about markets. Not only is the underlying assumption of maximizing behavior plausible, but also the pressures of competitive markets force actors to perform in ways approximating such behavior as a condition for survival.

The tools of neoclassical economics cannot, however, be readily used to explain behavior *within* organizations. Bureaucratic (or organization) man is not different in inherent motivation or psychology, but the incentives and constraints he faces differ from those facing the actor in the market. (Hence, Israel 1987 seeks a prescription for improving institutional performance by creating a "competitive" institutional character.)

This being so, it is not surprising that early models used in the development of the study of business administration were borrowed from engineering (Turnerism), the military (line and staff organizational structures), and the social psychology of nonmarket behavior (Elton Mayo) rather than from economics, and that subsequent explorations by economists took account of nonmaximizing managerial behavior within the large firm.

The Influence of Informal Factors

In either definition of institutions there are both formal and informal characteristics to be considered. Access to land, tenant-landlord arrangements, and so on may be subject to legal provisions, but they may also incorporate informal conventions and understandings either not incorporated in the law or even at variance with formal legal provisions. And the behavior of organizations with the same formal structure (chain of command, job descriptions, and so on) may vary enormously depending on the informal environment.

Those of us who had the experience of working in the postcolonial twilight know that the operational characteristics of systems changed often when the formal structure did not because informal assumptions altered. Colonial civil servants were bound together by an "old boy" network from "home," informally exchanged information in the club, were little dependent on status in the local society, and had no family responsibilities in the local community. The local bureaucracy were connected by a different "old boy" network (although often a copy of the metropolitan model), were able to exchange information informally in a different social setting, were dependent on local society for status, and were faced with a network of extended family obligations.

Assumptions or expectations of behavior, in general currency but informally based, influence organizational behavior. In a system with little or no corruption, it will be equally difficult to ask for or to offer a bribe; in one where corruption is the norm it becomes routine to ask for a bribe and impossible to conduct business without offering one.

The influence of informal factors makes the transfer of organizational models from one setting to another risky. A particular "success" may be based on a successful congruence between the formal model and the informal setting, or it may even result from particularly propitious informal circumstances actually transcending inadequacies in the formal structure (for instance, charismatic leadership sustaining a flawed organization).

The same formal model may mean very different things in different settings. Cooperatives, for example, with a fairly standard legal constitution, perform quite differently in terms of operational efficiency and distributional consequences not only between countries but even within the same country.

This suggests that the design of programs on the basis of successful models should be approached with caution, be it the Kenya Tea Development Authority, the Grameen Bank, the Uganda Development Corporation (of the early 1960s)—all of which at one time or another have been proposed or used as organizational models. This caveat is particularly relevant for itinerant advisers, who may be well informed about "success stories" but not about the specific origin of the observed success or the relevant informal characteristics of the setting to which the model is to be transferred.

The absence of any single driving force (analogous to the market) determining organizational behavior plus the impact of informal factors on formal structures makes generalization difficult. It is therefore, as Nellis (1980, p. 413) notes, not surprising that early efforts to create a general theory of development administration failed.

The best line of attack, therefore, is probably not to seek out a grand theory of the role of institutions but to sort out the questions about that role relevant to the design and implementation of development programs. This is done here by first considering the general approach of economists to the role of institutions (section II). A discussion of institutions in the two senses defined above follows, with consideration of the rules of the game that influence and constrain the behavior of the various actors in the economy (section III) and of the effectiveness of government organizations (section IV). The discussion concludes with a commentary on the political economy of government approaches to institutional issues (section V).

II. Some Economic Interpretations of Institutions

Broadly, economists' questions about institutions cluster around four themes. The first concerns the origins of institutions. How far can economists offer an endogenous explanation of the origins of institutions? Explanation of origin may in turn relate to the identification of current function, although there is no necessary connection. Institutions may in their actual operation serve purposes quite different from those intended by their creators. Moreover, their role may change in response to a changing environment.

Economic institutions as rules of the game can be seen as defining the terrain over which economic actors maneuver. The second theme concerns how economic actors behave in a particular institutional setting, and how their behavior, as affected by that setting, determines the economic outcomes.

The third theme is normative. How does one evaluate the economic effectiveness of institutions? A straightforward response would be to apply the normal criteria of welfare economics. However, insofar as some institutions exist to meet social objectives which transcend, or are separate from individual welfare maximization, evaluation against individualist, utilitarian criteria is not uncontroversial.

The fourth theme relates to the practical concerns of policymaking. How can institutions be changed to perform better according to chosen criteria of evaluation? Exploration of the first three issues—the origins of institutions, the motivation and behavior of economic actors in the existing institutional setting, and institutional effectiveness—provides a foundation on which to tackle the fourth: institutional engineering.

The initial brief for this conference paper asked what light the various paradigms in economics throw on the role of institutions in development. An adequate answer to that question would demand a long essay on the history of ideas outside the competence of this author, but there is room to locate the issues in the context of at least some economists' ideas. Because, in a Kuhnian sense (Kuhn 1970), most of the literature usually identified in the World Bank milieu as "economics" falls within the neoclassical paradigm, approaches from within that paradigm are emphasized.

The issue of "institutions" was raised by the U.S. institutionalists, following an earlier tradition of the German historical school, arguing that propositions of economic theory (that is, of mainstream neoclassical economics) were highly relative and were based upon unstated institutional assumptions much less universal than implied by the theorizing. "Institutionalism" therefore challenged economic theory in its dominant form.

The Neoclassical Positions

In contrast to the institutionalist view, the "purist" defense of neoclassical economics, set out in great clarity over fifty years ago by Lionel Robbins (1931), defined economics as the study of the interrelation between means and ends through theories of choice of general applicability—potentially useful in exploring economic decisionmaking in all institutional settings. Within that vision, the concept of "institutions" can be applied to aspects of human organization that may be accepted as important but are not the subject of economic analysis as such. Like technology, tastes, or resource endowments, they were seen as exogenous to the economic model—data that influence parameters, constraints, or the definition of a social welfare function without themselves being a subject of study by the economist.

No economist would have claimed that political institutions or social attitudes are unimportant; the argument was rather that in the intellectual division of labor they were not the appropriate subject of study for the economist. The approach might be seen either as modest in the limited scope it claims for economics, or arrogant in its view of "economic analysis" as being sufficient to handle the "hard" issues.

There continues to be a great deal of work—even some practical analysis of policy and projects—within that "purist" tradition,[1] but neoclassical economics has also vigorously developed beyond the overly restrictive boundaries envisaged by Robbins, through what Jack Hirshleifer (1985) has described as "imperialist economics" (an unintended double entendre in this context).

The rational choice approach has thrust neoclassical economics in the direction of issues once considered noneconomic. Thus Hirshleifer quotes Gary Becker (1976):

> The combined assumptions of maximizing behavior, market equilibrium and stable preferences, used relentlessly and unflinchingly, form the heart of the economic approach

and goes on to add:

> It is this approach that has powered the imperialist expansion of economics into the traditional domains of sociology, political science, anthropology, law and social biology—with more to come.

This approach has both a positive and a normative element. Positively, it attempts to explain the behavior of a wide range of institutions in terms of the maximizing pursuit of self-interest by the actors in those institutional settings. Normatively, in light of such behavior, institutional performance is evaluated against the individualistic and utilitarian objectives that underpin neoclassical welfare economics.

In the development literature, the rational choice approach has informed the discussion of rent seeking in general and the analysis of state agricultural marketing in particular, and it has been extended to the analysis of household behavior, and so on.

Although its adherents are often drawn from the other end of the political spectrum, rational choice explanations of political and social behavior share many of the strengths and weaknesses of Marxist analysis. In particular, the attempt to endogenize institutional factors through explanations based on a

---

1. An important part of the thrust of Gunnar Myrdal's critique of the work of economists in Asia was concerned with economists' neglect of institutional questions. It is not difficult to find work equally subject to that earlier criticism.

strong element of economic determinism are shared characteristics of rational choice and Marxist analysis.

At its best, this sort of analysis provides powerful insights into the ways economic actors pursue their interests both through the market and through nonmarket institutions, and how this in turn affects the institutional context in which markets operate. It may, however, claim too much, taking too little account of factors other than the pursuit of economic self-interest that determine political and social behavior.

Another contribution within the neoclassical tradition is the market-failure—transactions-cost approach, which sees the existence and behavior of a number of economic institutions as resulting not from the effective operation of markets but from market failures that require nonmarket institutions (and sometimes nonmaximizing behavior) for their resolution. (On this point, see the discussion of institutions below and Bardhan 1988.)

This approach was developed in the context of the theory of the firm, following R. H. Coase, and has been used to explore such issues as vertical integration and antitrust policy in the context of the U.S. economy (see Williamson 1985, 1986). It has also provided the intellectual underpinnings for a burst of recent literature on rural institutions.

Some economists faced with institutional questions have called on other disciplines for a joint attack on the problem. In some heroic cases, the economist has taken on the task of acquiring the skills of those other professions (see, for instance, Hill 1986). Whether, in practice, multidisciplinary work has typically meant cross-fertilization or cross-sterilization of ideas can be debated. But it would take a very robust imperialist of economics to believe that the economist's tools are uniquely appropriate for analyzing all important development institutions.

Structuralist and Marxist Challenges

In the development debate, the earlier institutionalist criticisms of neoclassical economics were echoed in the structuralist[2] critique. Two observations were particularly influential: (1) that "Western" economics had many implicit assumptions regarding institutions, among other things, that undermined its applicability to economies in the developing world; and (2) that insofar as certain institutional factors constrained the effectiveness of policies, such rigidities had to be either incorporated into the analysis of policy or tackled by political or social reform.

Some aspects of the structural approach have similarities with, or even roots in, Keynesian economics. The structuralist differs from the strict neoclassicist in

---

2. This imprecise designation covers an enormous potential range of literature. Meier identifies Lewis, Myrdal, Prebisch, Singer, and Rosenstein-Rodan—six of the ten authors covered in *Pioneers in Development* (Meier and Seers 1984) as "introducing elements of structural analysis into their work." See also Furtado (1964) and Seers (1963).

regarding what the latter sees as transitory "market distortions" as fundamental characteristics of the system, for which neoclassical solutions are impracticable, at least in the absence of profound structural change (for a neoclassicist's view, see Little 1982).

Structuralists have been concerned with the persistence of archaic rural institutions (for instance, in the Latin American literature of the 1960s a backward rural institutional structure was seen to inhibit response to price incentives and thus contribute to inflation), which suggests the need for active land reform; with skewed distribution of wealth, which requires active redistributive policies; and with weak entrepreneurial institutions, which justify strong state intervention and protectionism.

Central to the structuralist policy agenda was the need for deep-seated institutional reform. The reforms in question demanded explicit examination of the political conditions in which they would be implemented. But when conducted, such analyses often revealed a pessimistic outlook for the reform agenda. (See de Janvry 1981, p. 146, for a succinct criticism of the structuralist thesis on agricultural stagnation in Latin America.)

Evidently the term "structuralist" as used here covers a wide range of ideas, united more by a common deviation from tenets of neoclassical economics than by a shared theoretical approach. In such terms, much early development economics (say 1945–65) could be described as structuralist (see Meier and Seers 1984). Since the mid-1960s there has been a revival and consolidation of a neoclassical approach to the subject (see Little 1982).

The other main challenge to the neoclassical paradigm is from Marxist analysis. Its strength lies precisely in its holistic ambitions, which have never allowed it to accept the boundaries traditionally defined for neoclassical economics.

Four strands of Marxist thought throw light on the question:[3] (1) the emphasis on the historical setting and the historical process of change; (2) the exploration of the interaction between institutions (superstructure), economic forces (forces of production), and social relations (the relations of production); (3) the focus on class interests and class struggles (rather than individual interest and welfare maximization through exchange); and (4) explicit consideration of the role of ideology.

Yet there is no more unanimity in the Marxist than in the neoclassical paradigm on any of the basic issues facing development economists. Thus Marxism, as much as neoclassicism, can inform both an activist and a deeply skeptical view of the potential role of the state in the reality of the developing world (see Baran 1957). In this regard, the neoconservative critique of the rent-seeking bureaucracy resembles that of Marxists who emphasize the corruption of the

---

3. The quick characterization of paradigms demanded by limits of space runs the obvious risk of vulgarization. The only way to do justice to each of the paradigms is to illustrate their use in tackling the problems discussed here: for instance, de Janvry's (1981) study of the agrarian questions in Latin America demonstrates the sensitive use of Marxist concepts.

neocolonial state: the pessimism of both is based on an economically determined explanation of political behavior, although for one the mainspring is individual or pressure group interest, and for the other the pursuit of class interest and the international context.

III. GOVERNMENT, INSTITUTIONS, AND THE MARKET

It is by now generally accepted that a critical task of government, neglected in earlier models of economic planning, is to provide the "right" incentives to stimulate and guide the various actors in the economy—though views may differ as to what the right incentives are. A corollary to this view is that development policy must focus on the institutional arrangements that provide the setting in which the incentive system will operate.

Rules of the game which stand out as susceptible to government influence include: (1) rules defining private property rights and their allocation; (2) other rules and conventions governing the relationships between participants in the economic process (for example, those affecting the operation of the labor market); (3) rules and conventions defining the economic role of a hierarchy of social institutions (for example, local governments, trade unions, cooperatives and peasant associations, and churches); and (4) rules and conventions restricting participation in the economic process.

Potential government influence on the rules of the game is illustrated by reference to three important areas: property rights and rural development, institutional pluralism in decisionmaking, and the promotion of entrepreneurship.

Property Rights and Rural Development

Property rights (land rights and their interrelations with other institutional arrangements) have figured prominently in the discussions of agricultural development (Bardhan 1988). Changes in rural property rights, encompassing such issues as the decline (or survival) of serfdom and the enclosure of common land, have been central concerns for the historian, whether the neoclassicist exploring responses to changing economic opportunities and factor scarcities or the Marxist for whom relations of production in the rural sector are seen as defining the mode of production. Two questions particularly intrigue economists: (1) Why do differing property rights emerge to provide the framework within which economic decisions are made in rural areas? (2) What are the relative merits of alternative systems on both efficiency and distributive grounds?

One view is that, on the one hand, economic development has meant the displacement of one set of rural property rights by others more adapted to the emerging economic requirements, whereas, on the other hand, existing arrangements can and should be improved both in efficiency and distribution. This view has fueled the argument for rural institutional (land) reform. In reaction, the rationale of existing institutions has been explored to question whether they are as atavistic, inefficient, and disequalizing, as the reform agenda implies.

Property rights determining access to land are part of a complex of institutional arrangements providing the context for rural economic activity. These include institutional arrangements determining labor contracts and access to land, credit, and commodity markets; that is, the set of rules and conventions that define the relations between the various actors in the rural economy. A critical analytical concern is with the interlinkages between markets. Thus neoclassical economists have explored such institutions as sharecropping as part of a more general attempt to understand the role of property rights in light of transactions costs, or alternatively under conditions of imperfect information in interlinked factor markets. For the Marxists, the critical characteristic of the changing labor market, the emergence of "free" labor, is related in turn to changes in access to land and the expansion of commodity production.

There is a body of empirical literature which provides useful insights into the effectiveness of rural institutions. But the neoclassical theoretical literature has recently become so complex that it yields little policy guidance for the applied economist, other than that existing institutional arrangements are likely to be a good deal more complex, and their efficiency and distributional implications less straightforward, than at first sight.

It is particularly tricky to establish the actual status of rural institutions (see Feder and Noronha 1987). The concept of property rights in land is far from clear cut: often the requirements of rural economic activity lead to the useful development of a range of differing property rights relating to differing attributes of land; de facto practice may vary greatly from the de jure system; and the national system of statutory laws may coexist with local law and customs. The likely impact of statutory reform is therefore particularly hard to predict, since it is both difficult to delineate the existing structure to be replaced and even harder to forecast the de facto outcome of de jure proposals.

Thus while there has been a widespread presumption that a movement toward securely held registered title is economically desirable, recognition of the problems involved has been slower to emerge. For example, conferring land tenure rights on sedentary agriculturalists (already apparent occupants) may disrupt a system of pastoral seminomadism, based on rights of passage and of dry season grazing, which represented a sophisticated response to a particular ecological problem. Likewise, the allocation of land rights to an individual may misinterpret and disrupt arrangements within the family (displacing the rights of women, for example).

Views on what the best institutional structure may be for fostering growth vary and change; indeed, research on rural institutions seems to be widening the range of debate, as institutions earlier seen as barriers to progress are rehabilitated in light of a more sophisticated interpretation of their function.

Theories of endogenous institutional change, which argue that the institutions that provide the framework for the market tend to adapt themselves to changing market conditions, such as changing factor scarcity and relative factor productivity, suggest that informal institutional arrangements are likely to adjust to new conditions even without official sanction. This suggests that one official task should be to adjust formal rules to accommodate changes under way so as to improve the certainty of transactions by making them official. But there are dangers: formalizing informal arrangements—for instance, through land registration—will have its own effects, by shifting the access of different economic actors to the formal system—for instance, through land grabbing.

Institutional Pluralism

The rules of the game, besides defining property rights and acceptable contractual relationships, also define how and by whom the rules themselves are made. A recent collection of essays on institutional analysis and development (Ostrum, Feeny, and Picht 1988) argues that the institutional choice should be presented not as a dichotomy of state or market but as a pluralism of possible contractual relationships, both explicit and implicit. To quote (p. 456):

> Systems of governance can be constituted by conceptually simple but socially complex configurations of implicit or explicit contractual relationships. There is no theoretical reason why there must be a single centre that has exclusive authority to formulate and enforce rules in a society.

The volume is in the tradition of U.S. pluralism, favoring a diversity of social institutions as the desirable base for a democratic order, with a place for initiatives from many levels of society and not providing central government with undue concentration of power. Systems of decentralized decisionmaking and control might bring to bear user pressures as stimuli to performance not possible in a centralized bureaucracy.

Skepticism about the concentration of power in centralized institutions is not confined to neoconservatives: on the left, popular participation, workers' and peasants' movements, and other forms of grass-roots mobilization are seen both as virtues in themselves and as mechanisms to make institutions responsive to local conditions and needs.

Of course, while decentralized institutions may be more susceptible to local participation and control, by the same token they may be captive to the local structure of power. The drawbacks of centralized power—insensitivity to local needs and ignorance of local capacities—have their counterparts in the skewed access that can arise from local systems of power and prejudice.

The Promotion of Entrepreneurship

Another area to explore is the possible impact of government molding of the rules of the game on entrepreneurial initiatives. While not all would share the Schumpeterian view that entrepreneurship is central to capitalist development, entrepreneurial capacity is clearly important, and particular development successes seem to be associated with a concentration of entrepreneurial flair or capitalist "animal spirits."

Given their pivotal role in capitalism, entrepreneurship and entrepreneurial institutions would be expected to be central in neoclassical treatments of development. Yet entrepreneurship has found a more prominent place in the work of economic and business historians (see, for example, Iliffe 1983) than in the neoclassical theoretical tradition. This lack leaves at least some free market advocacy with a strange lacuna: the market sets the stage for successful private initiatives, but it is unclear from where the cast of characters is to be supplied.

The lack of an endogenous economic theory of entrepreneurship has made this an area in which economists have often been willing to traverse the multidisciplinary route. And in practice folk wisdom, which identifies particular social groups as being "entrepreneurial" in culture, is often influential. But folk characterization, and even learned identification of entrepreneurial groups, tends to be based on ex post recognition of performance. Stereotypes change very fast with changes in performance (see, for instance, Elkan's (1988) contrast of Tawney's negative characterization of Chinese entrepreneurship in 1932 with current perceptions). What is lacking is a good *predictive* model of entrepreneurial capacity to bring out ways of enhancing entrepreneurship through policy measures.

Theories that emphasize deep-seated psychological or cultural characteristics (see, for instance, McClelland 1961) do not seem particularly relevant for policy, as these variables are unlikely to be subject to policy influence over any useful time horizon (though McClelland's psychological interpretation of entrepreneurial capacity was incorporated in business training in India and elsewhere).

Are there specific ways in which government can influence the institutional context of entrepreneurship (other than the obvious panoply of economic policies and commercial laws that determine the broad incentives and constraints)? Elkan (1988) broadly concludes that there is none: the best policy is laissez-faire.

An acceptable role for private entrepreneurs is defined both by formal rules and informal signals. Here, not only the stated intentions of governments but the outcomes expected by the entrepreneurs are important. One interesting historical insight relates to the entrepreneurial role played by cultural, ethnic, or religious minorities, whose entry into certain entrepreneurial areas may be restricted but who, by the same token, in being politically excluded from easier avenues of advancement, are sometimes stimulated into a risk-taking innovative role.[4]

These considerations could lead to a bizarre (dialectical) conclusion about the virtues of discriminating *against* potentially entrepreneurial groups. More seriously, it would be interesting to know what conditions would be conducive to a nice balance in which a minority, pushed into entrepreneurship, is nevertheless

---

4. The East African Asians, for example, have had repeated experience as a minority community, first under British colonial rule, then in independent Africa, and now in Britain and North America, and have shown a high degree of entrepreneurial ingenuity in all three situations. At the same time, of course, the culture of a minority group may be more or less consistent with taking on a successful entrepreneurial role.

sufficiently accepted to be allowed to play the part effectively, and secure enough to take a long view of investment opportunities—as against a common situation of insecurity in which suspicion engenders precisely the short-term, capital-exporting behavior that reinforces the initial suspicion.

The view that entrepreneurship is likely to appear when other avenues of advance are blocked relates to two other observations. The first is that entrepreneurship often seems not to be highly correlated with formal educational achievement, in part because the able but uneducated are excluded from more secure avenues of social advance. Second, crises that erode bureaucratic incomes and frustrate the expectations of the educated elite may call forth considerable entrepreneurial response. This seems to be the case in the recent experience of a number of African countries.

Strangely, Marxist and related literature has tackled the long-term institutional issue of capitalist development more explicitly than neoclassical writing. The main thrust of the Marxist (and dependency) literature is to see the development of national capital and multinational enterprise as essentially antagonistic—with indigenous capital trapped in a stunted, essentially comprador role (see Baran 1957). In some Marxist writing this comprador role is extended to the state sector (Shivji 1973). But the opposite view has also been expressed in the Marxist literature (see Warren 1980; Sender and Smith 1986). It has been suggested, for example, that multinational business supported indigenous capital in the colonial period (as compared to settler colonialism; see Cowen 1979).

The propositions of neoclassical economics are most strongly developed in relation to the virtues of liberal international commodity markets. While no doubt for most neoclassical economists, the commitment to freely operating markets would extend to capital markets, there are different issues involved from those related to free trade in commodities. Albert Hirschman (1969) made the interesting point that quite different issues are at stake when a country specializes in the supply of one factor of production, labor, than when it specializes in producing a particular commodity.

The assumption implicit in much pro-free-market analysis is that there is a potentially complementary and supportive relation between multinational business and indigenous private enterprises, while in contrast the relation between state and private enterprise is likely to be competitive and antagonistic. Hence an institutional choice must be made between state and private enterprise.

Such a view is not, however, necessarily consistent with rent-seeking interpretations of political processes, which could equally well suggest that public corporations are likely to be responsive to private interests either bringing pressure through the political or administrative process, or engaging in commercial manipulation to gain access to potential rents. A large scale public sector, even if conceived in the context of a transition to socialism, can as well provide one path toward capitalism, depending on the role of the state system vis-à-vis incipient national capital.

IV. Government Economic Organizations

The discussion in *World Development Report 1983* (World Bank 1983) on "Management in Development" described the role of the state as follows:

> Some economic activities are universally recognized as the sole responsibility of the state; others, it is widely agreed, are best left to private initiative. Between these extremes governments have tended to expand their sphere of activity for a variety of reasons.

This statement implies some consensus about the state role in a considerable range of activities. Such consensus may exist from time to time, and in particular countries, but it often changes when big political shifts occur. In Britain, for example, there have been two major shifts since World War II.

Even activities on most "commonsense" lists of state responsibilities may in practice be far from universal state monopolies. Cases in point are police services, supplemented in many countries by booming private security services, and postal services, virtually displaced in some lines of business by private courier services. On the other hand, international experience yields examples of government involvement in virtually all areas of economic activity.

The origins of public economic organizations are extraordinarily diverse. Some spring from a systematic initiative to extend state influence; some emerge to handle problems of private bankruptcy, or as vehicles for political patronage; and aid donors themselves sometimes generate new institutions as a conduit for external funding. Many have probably been created for conventional reasons—in the colonial period, for example, reflecting metropolitan practice as much as local requirements or local interests. And perhaps as important as their origin is the tenacity with which public institutions, once created, defend their own survival (on this topic, see Bernard Schaffer, quoted in Lamb 1985).

Thus there is a wide diversity of government economic organizations. Among the reasons for this diversity are political factors, both ideological and, more prosaically, those that respond to the day-to-day needs of the political system.

It is surely a mistake to avoid recognizing this openly, by presenting the issue as largely technocratic—particularly since shifts in the international climate of opinion on this issue reflect shifting political winds in the industrial countries.

Nevertheless, the question of the appropriate form and role for government economic organizations cannot be sidestepped as simply political. Good or bad performance by government organizations is critical to growth, and particularly important for aid donors, because these organizations are the preponderant channel for aid. Despite the difficulties, the task of improving the performance of public economic organizations must be confronted.

The messy array of issues is tackled here by addressing three sets of questions: (1) What are the arguments for the existence of public economic organizations? (2) How should aid donors relate to institutional performance? (3) What are the factors that influence performance?

Arguments for Public Economic Organization

The most widely accepted role for public economic organizations is that of supplying goods—such as road services, public health, and agricultural extension—that the market cannot supply efficiently (because of externalities, the "free rider" problem, natural monopoly, and the like).

A second function, argued for specifically in relation to development, is for government enterprise to supplement an inadequate supply of private entrepreneurship: to demonstrate the viability of an activity so as to encourage involvement by nongovernment actors. Government enterprise here is seen as necessary to reduce the risk, lower the cost, and increase the profitability of private ventures in the context of economic backwardness.

A third view sees government organizations as an instrument for the transfer of surplus—in effect to tax or subsidize (for example, through agricultural marketing boards or state cigarette, match, and liquor monopolies). Here the justification may be administrative—that without the involvement of government organizations, the tax system would be inadequate to achieve the desired result. More cynically, it is easier to tax agriculture under the guise of providing a service, or stabilizing prices, than through overt levies.

A fourth function of public sector economic institutions is to further some policy intended to affect patterns of property holding in a society—either to encourage a general commitment to social ownership or to shift the balance of property ownership between different national or ethnic groups.

There are also regional arguments for public economic institutions, in the two different senses of promoting the development of backward regions or promoting cooperation between different nation-states in a regional grouping.

Other arguments could be listed, but these five encompass the main economic justifications for government economic organizations, and as such provide a basis for judging what is to be done about the complex array of them that exist.

Where there is a need that cannot be met by the market, the task of achieving efficient nonmarket economic management solutions must be confronted. That the state *should* undertake an activity does not guarantee that it will be able to do so effectively.

Where the objective is to change the balance of property ownership or the distribution of income, different lines of reasoning are possible. One possibility is that public economic organizations be subject to the market, along the lines of the Lange-Lerner model of market socialism: public managers having to respond to the market on the same terms as private managers, the public interest being that of a shareholder, and any deviation from a "pure" market solution being handled by explicit public subsidies or taxes.

Alternatively, the option of government intervention to achieve the intended result without the existence of a public economic organization could be explored—taxing, subsidizing, licensing, private ventures—or where the objective is wealth redistribution a once-and-for-all reallocation among private economic actors might be seen as an alternative (as in some land reforms).

Donors and Institutional Performance

Some governments command public economic organizations capable of implementing the government's intentions, others not. Bureaucracy may be reasonably effective in one ministry, parastatal, or sector, and quite ineffective in others. Why? And what determined changes in performance over time? For an institution such as the World Bank, acting as it does primarily through government institutions, appropriate answers to these questions are crucial, and errors of judgment in assessing administrative capacity are probably as important a cause of project failure as mistakes of economic calculus or technical design.

Israel (1987), analyzing the evidence on institutional performance from the World Bank's own project experience, found that institutional performance varied more across sectors and activities than among countries. He summarized the record as follows (p. 4):

> The most successful were found in industry, telecommunications, utilities and finance; the least successful in agriculture, education and services. Within institutions, technical and financial activities fared the best, while maintenance, personnel issues, and co-ordination were the least successful.

The study recounts the piecemeal explanations of differential performance found in the Bank's own operational evaluations and, finding them wanting, identifies two factors which he argues are decisive in explaining institutional performance in practice: "specificity" and "competition." Specificity is defined in terms of concreteness of objectives, means, and rewards, and the immediacy and transparency of the effects of an activity. Competition covers the influences that impel an organization to improve its performance. These are seen as including market pressure but also encompassing pressure from clients, beneficiaries, or suppliers, from the political and bureaucratic establishment, and from internal managerial measures to stimulate a competitive atmosphere within an organization.

Israel uses the empirical record of Bank projects to draw some plausible conclusions about ways to improve the performance of most institutions. But there are problems with using this evidence to judge the appropriateness of public institutions.

The first is that the evidence seems to suggest that institutions that work best more or less approximate to a modern industrial plant. Thus plantation projects in the Bank portfolio have worked better in Africa than projects that support smallholder agriculture.

Unfortunately, this does not tell us whether plantations or smallholder agriculture are the more reasonable vehicle for agricultural development in Africa. Smallholder agriculture might be (and, indeed, I believe is) superior on both efficiency and distributional grounds, although it does not respond readily to direct public institutional interventions. The fact that "modern institutions" have the characteristics of specificity and competitiveness does not mean that the best growth path is found by emphasizing such institutions, any more than the fact that wealthy countries are industrialized means that at a particular moment industrial investment should be emphasized.

A second problem is that the identified characteristics of effective institutions and the characteristics of institutions that would be considered appropriate for public sector attention often do not match—for instance, it is in the nature of some public goods that their supply lacks specificity. One is left with the awkward conclusion that the public sector is in part the residual legatee of activities that do not lend themselves to effective institutional performance.

But this need not be so alarming, as some of these activities may be quite satisfactorily handled by governments, even if they do not respond to systematic efforts to improve productivity, nor are plausible candidates for external assistance. Even though primary education is a low-specificity, low-competition activity, in most countries it is done quite well, sometimes in extremely difficult conditions. But there is no very good reason for external funding to be mobilized for primary education (except for textbook production—which can be organized in ways to meet the Israel criteria).

This brings out an important point that is sometimes overlooked: there is a difference between a worthwhile organization or activity and one that is an appropriate object for external assistance. The institutions that can productively use external support form a specialized subset of the group of viable or potentially successful institutions. Analysis is required at two stages. Is a public economic institution desirable, or likely to be effective? If so, is external assistance required, and does a candidate-funding institution have the competence (comparative advantage) to supply that assistance?

Evaluating the institutional performance of aided projects is tricky. Elaborately designed externally funded projects sometimes fail because they demand an unattainable level of managerial performance. And those that succeed might do so because they divert scarce managerial talent from other activities. If so, there are hidden costs, particularly where the response to a weak implementation structure is to use external funds to set up parallel institutions.

A Summary of Factors Affecting Performance

A bureaucracy can only be as effective as the tasks delegated to it allow: if it is called upon to undertake economic management tasks that are incoherent or inconsistent, and generate considerable potential rents, it is not surprising if its effectiveness or honesty is impaired. Declining institutional capacity can result when the state's efforts to control economic activity are overextended. Administrative performance is also likely to be correlated with a realistic system of material incentives, and with a decision system within the administrative structure that is able to locate responsibility and reward effective performance.

However, the capacity, loyalty, and honesty of bureaucracies vary for reasons that are not simply to be explained by material incentives or the availability of "rents." Organizations, including private businesses, survive because they can command a loyalty beyond what can be induced by the material incentives of a strictly market transaction.

In this regard, professionalism can be an asset to be used by public institutions. The continued delivery of some public services under the most appalling conditions is evidence of that. A professional ethic of commitment and service can generate performance in excess of that explainable by material incentives. The university at which this paper is being drafted survives, for example, through a combination of economic ingenuity and professional commitment of its academic staff in the face of a collapse in real salary levels. This is not to say that professional commitment is an inexhaustible asset, nor that professionals are impervious to material conditions. It would, however, be of interest to consider the conditions under which professional commitment can be created and nurtured, and those under which it is likely to be eroded or destroyed.

Understanding factors that affect the morale of organizations is the province of sociologists and management specialists. In practice those concerned with economic policy and the design of programs have to react to the observed operational capacity of organizations. Where there is weakness, the crucial judgment will be whether performance can be raised or not, which in turn depends on the diagnosis of sources of poor performance. Many explanations of organizational failure fall into three categories: the inadequacy of available inputs, inherent incapability, and avoidable inefficiency.

The inadequacy of available inputs. An example of the inadequacy of available inputs is that organizational weakness is often attributed to a lack of trained labor and weak management. Certainly many countries have labor shortages, and the case for training and technical assistance is unassailable—presumably most organizations in the world would perform better with more qualified personnel, and superlative management might make the most hopeless venture viable. But, after two or more decades of training and technical assistance, shortage of high-level labor is no longer so obviously the problem. For donors there is a real danger that inadequate labor supply is an attractive diagnosis because apparent cures (technical assistance and training) are readily at hand.

Inherent incapability. There are some economic tasks that public institutions may be inherently ill-adapted to handle—in particular, activities requiring decentralized risk-taking (some forms of agriculture; shopkeeping), combined with the need for considerable labor commitment. But this is no more than a casual observation. Unlike market failure, analyzed exhaustively by economists starting from the assumption that market solutions are best unless proved otherwise, "public institution failure"—identification of those activities that public economic organizations are not, a priori, likely to be able to handle efficiently—has attracted remarkably little systematic examination.

Such factors as risk, economies of scale, and standardization of the process determine the comparative advantage of public institutions. This is of some interest to donors, as the same question could be asked of their own interventions: what determines donor comparative advantage?

Avoidable inefficiency. Many activities that are properly the province of public institutions are not performed very well because of poor management. Available trained labor is used badly because of poor incentives, inefficient organization of work, inappropriate delegation of responsibility, and inadequate accountability.

Inherited civil service practices were often poorly designed to manage public economic activities in the first place and have deteriorated further under economic stress. Examples are rare of decisions to expand the role of public economic institutions that have been matched by adequate consideration of the managerial requirements.

Indeed incentive systems are often so poorly constructed and managerial practice so evidently inadequate that it is often surprising that public institutions work as well as they do. This makes it hard to use the empirical record to assess the intrinisic value of an organization, since more effective performance might be achieved with perfectly plausible managerial improvements.

V. The Political Economy of Public Institutional Interventions

The most telling case against many institutions is not that they are technically inefficient or poorly managed (although they may be) but that, in the political and administrative reality in which they operate, they end up pursuing objectives inconsistent with development.

For example, there are two quite distinct strands in the criticism of marketing boards in Africa. One is that they are expensive and inefficient, perhaps inevitably so. They are dysfunctional because they place a burden of bureaucratic overhead costs on the farmer. A quite separate argument is that their basic objective is to shift the terms of trade against agriculture, serving a political economy weighted against the farmer (see Bates 1981).

In other words, one must go beyond the assumption that government institutions are by definition pursuing the goals of national development to explore what determines the interests organizations work for in practice. This proposition applies as much to international institutions, and to bilateral donors, as to institutions in the recipient countries. "Interests" can relate to the play of foreign policy concerns of states, sectional economic interests brought to bear on aid programs, and the interests of aid officials, departments, and agencies in perpetuating their roles.

The view taken of the determinants of government behavior obviously influences normative judgment about the role appropriate for government institutions. One "rational choice" approach to the political economy of public institutions emphasizes "rent seeking" as a powerful motive force. If the main determinant of government behavior is pressure from rent seekers, it is not difficult to support a strategy of liberalization through confronting or buying out the vested interests in question (see Lal 1987).

A more structuralist (but still normative) view might explore the issue of market failure in a dynamic context, defining the appropriate role of government as promoting desirable structural change which would not spring from the unhindered play of market forces.

In the era of structural adjustment and privatization the view that the state needs to play an interventionist role in a backward economy is not fashionable, despite its respectable intellectual antecedents. And the question remains why governments would take on the task of structural transformation expected of them, rather than just using the vocabulary of "development" to cloak the practice of "rent allocation."

There is no simple answer to that question. Kleptocracies in which those who run government seem largely concerned to enrich themselves are not rare, but then again they are not typical.

Where the political process is such that leaders must satisfy competing interests to remain in power, the question to be addressed is the circumstances in which those interests coincide with a "developmentalist" rather than a parasitic rentier strategy (see Bates 1988). If leaders are more secure and enjoy some autonomy in decisionmaking, they will be much freer to make choices without reference to the short-term interests of pressure groups.

The counterpart in Marxist theory for the neoclassical concept of "rent" has been the role of "surplus" in the "accumulation process." Surplus is seen as a typical and necessary component of capitalist development, not as a transitory rent resulting from a deviation from an abstract, optimal rent-free equilibrium. The issue to be addressed is in what circumstances are surpluses likely to be channeled to productive uses. The purpose of many public sector initiatives could be seen not so much as creating rents as shifting the control of surplus from one group to another—for example, from multinational corporations to national hands, or from one national group to another.

In these terms, Marxist analysts might be roughly in agreement with neoclassical rent-seeking theorists about the interests served by particular policy initiatives, but the interpretation would differ in at least one profound respect. For the Marxist, state interventionism is understood as necessary to capitalist development. Whether capitalist development can succeed depends on whether the political and economic process is such that the surplus is at the disposal of national capital—either state or private—and as a result is used productively, or whether it is transferred outside the country or flows to domestic groups incapable of making productive investments.

John Kenneth Galbraith (1987) claims:

> Japanese who become business executives and high civil servants frequently began their lives as Marxists. There is no serious expectation of revolution, but the Marxian influence does have a significant consequence: it relieves

> Japanese economic and political thought of the notion of a social dichotomy, even conflict, between the market economy and the state, a theoretical conflict that has a strong hold on all American and British economic thinking. In Japan the state is indeed, as Marx held, the executive committee of the capitalist class; this is normal and natural. The result is an accepted cooperation between industry and government . . . that is unthinkable, to the extent that it is not thought subversive, in the American and British tradition.

Irrespective of whether this is an accurate description of the intellectual formation of the Japanese elite, the ideas are intriguing.

Examining the determinants of government policymaking leads into a related question—what are the political and institutional prerequisites for implementing a particular economic policy regime?

Advocates of free markets sometimes associate economic "freedom" with political freedom. There seems little empirical basis for such a view in poor countries where, often, the inequalities associated with freely operating markets and the austerities required for market-based macroeconomic solutions are as likely to be associated with authoritarian control as with democratic processes.

As a corollary, where pluralistic or fairly open political processes stand in the way of "correct" economic policies (removal of subsidies, devaluation, and so on) such policies could either be not politically sustainable or imply a change in political regime, which should be understood as an integral part of the policy package.

Normative assessment should take account not only of the impact of government institutions on economic outcomes, but also of the impact of economic developments on the evolution of institutions. Public economic institutions are not just to be seen as good or bad instruments for achieving an economic policy goal; they are also active in the choice of policy goals. As part of the social fabric, an institution may be seen as good or bad in itself, or in terms of social objectives not translatable into economic calculus.

The concept of "rent" depends on the acceptability of criteria for the definition of rent-free, earned factor income, in turn dependent on a view of policy as being concerned with maximization of individual welfare. While that provides a powerful tool for much policy analysis, it does not provide a basis for evaluating all social institutions.

There are also nonmaterial determinants of policy, which are not handled very well by neoclassical or Marxist analysis. Ethnicity, religion, and nationalism are much more influential than their place in the policy literature implies. This is conspicuous in dramatic events such as the breakup of Pakistan, the expulsion of the Ugandan Asians, the displacement of European farmers from the Kenya White Highlands, the recent conflict in Fiji, and the conflict in Sri Lanka; less obvious are the tensions from similar causes that underlie an often hidden political agenda in a much wider range of countries. Likewise, the relative ethnic and cultural homogeneity of the sucessful East Asian economies may be a crucial factor in their performance. Yet economists neglect these ethnic, religious, and nationalist influences, important and wide-ranging as they are. Partly, in the official literature, this is a matter of etiquette. But it is also true that economists find such matters hard to handle. Neither neoclassical economics, with its emphasis on individualism, nor Marxist economics, focusing on class interest, are well geared to analyze economic behavior motivated by awareness of ethnic or religious identities.

References

Aga Khan Foundation. 1987. *The Enabling Environment.* Report of Conference held in Nairobi, Kenya, 21–24 October 1986.

Baran, Paul A. 1957. *The Political Economy of Growth.* New York: Monthly Review Press.

Bardhan, Pranab, ed. 1988. *The Economic Theory of Agrarian Institutions.* New York: Oxford University Press.

Bates, Robert H. 1981. *Markets and States in Tropical Africa: The Political Base of Agricultural Policies.* Berkeley: University of California Press.

———, ed. 1988. *Toward a Political Economy of Development: A Rational Choice Perspective.* Berkeley: University of California Press.

Becker, Gary S. 1976. *The Economic Approach to Human Behavior.* Chicago: University of Chicago Press.

Coase, R. H. 1937. "The Nature of the Firm." *Economica.* November. Reprinted in G. J. Stigler and K. E. Boulding, eds., *Readings in the Theory of Price.* Homewood, Ill.: Irwin.

Cowen, Michael. 1979. "Capital and Household Production: The Case of Kenya Central Province, 1903–64." Ph.D. thesis, Cambridge University.

de Janvry, Alain. 1981. *The Agrarian Question and Reformism in Latin America.* Baltimore: Johns Hopkins University Press.

Elkan, Walter. 1988. "Entrepreneurs and Entrepreneurship in Africa." *World Bank Research Observer* 3, no. 2 (July): 171–88.

Feder, Gershon, and Raymond Noronha. 1987. "Lands Rights Systems and Agricultural Development in Sub-Saharan Africa." *World Bank Research Observer* 2, no. 2 (July): 143–69.

Feeny, David. 1988. "The Demand for and Supply of Institutional Arrangements." In V. Ostrum, D. Feeny, and H. Picht, eds., *Rethinking Institutional Analysis and Development.* San Francisco: International Center for Economic Growth.

Furtado, Celso. 1964. *Development and Underdevelopment.* Berkeley: University of California Press.

Galbraith, John Kenneth. 1987. *Economics in Perspective: A Critical History.* Boston: Houghton Mifflin.

Hill, Polly. 1986. *Development Economics on Trial: The Anthropological Case for a Prosecution.* Cambridge and New York: Cambridge University Press.

Hirschman, Albert O. 1969. *How to Divest in Latin America and Why.* Essays in International Finance 76. Princeton, N.J.: Department of Economics, Princeton University.

Hirshleifer, Jach. 1985. "Expanding Domain of Economics." *American Economic Review* 75, no. 8: 53–68.

Iliffe, J. 1983. *The Emergence of African Capitalism*. London: Macmillan.

Israel, Arturo. 1987. *Institutional Development: Incentives to Performance*. Baltimore: Johns Hopkins University Press.

Kuhn, Thomas S. 1970. *The Structure of Scientific Revolutions*, 2d ed. Chicago: University of Chicago Press.

Lal, Dipak. 1987. "The Political Economy of Economic Liberalization." *World Bank Economic Review* 1, no. 2 (January): 273–99.

Lamb, Geoffrey. 1985. "Bernard Schaffer: A Personal Appreciation." *Development and Change* 16, no. 3 (July): 515–20.

Little, Ian D. 1982. *Economic Development: Theory, Policy, and International Relations*. New York: Basic Books.

McClelland, David C. 1961. *The Achieving Society*. Princeton, N.J.: Van Nostrand.

Meier, Gerald M., and Dudley Seers, eds. 1984. *Pioneers in Development*. New York: Oxford University Press.

Myrdal, Gunnar. 1968. *Asian Drama: An Inquiry into the Poverty of Nations*. New York: Twentieth Century Fund.

Nellis, John R. 1980. "Maladministration: Cause or Result of Underdevelopment? An African Example." *Canadian Journal of Algerian Studies* 13, no. 3: 413.

North, Douglas. 1981. *Structure and Change in Economic History*. New York: Norton.

Ostrum, V., D. Feeny, and H. Picht, eds. 1988. *Rethinking Institutional Analysis and Development*. San Francisco: International Center for Economic Growth.

Robbins, Lionel. 1931. *An Essay on the Nature and Significance of Economic Science*. London: Macmillan. 3d ed. New York: New York University Press, 1984.

Ruttan, V. W., and Y. Hayami. 1984. "Towards a Theory of Induced Institutional Innovation." *Journal of Development Studies* 20, no. 4 (July): 203–23.

Seers, Dudley. 1963. "The Limitations of the Special Case." *Bulletin of the Institute of Economics and Statistics*, May.

Sender, John, and Sheila Smith. 1986. *The Development of Capitalism in Africa*. London and New York: Methuen.

Shivji, Issa. 1973. *The Silent Class Struggle*. Dar es Salaam: Tanzania Publishing House.

Tawney, Richard H. 1932. *Land and Labour in China*. New York: Harcourt Brace.

van Rennin, Gelt-Jan, and Robert Waisfisz. 1988. "Final Report on Institutional Development." A report by IDEAS to the Dutch Minister for Development Cooperation.

Warren, Bill. 1980. *Imperialism, Pioneer of Capitalism*. London: New Left Books.

Williamson, Oliver E. 1985. *The Economic Institutions of Capitalism: Firms, Markets, Relational Contracting*. New York: Free Press.

———. 1986. *Economic Organization: Firms, Markets and Policy Control*. New York: New York University Press.

World Bank. 1983. *World Development Report 1983*. New York: Oxford University Press.

Comment on "The Role of Institutions in Development,"
by Van Arkadie

John Nellis

Professor Van Arkadie's paper presents useful, nonobvious reflections and insights on the relation between institutions and economic development. His analysis of a range of problems confirms that the topic is at once difficult and worth wrestling with.

The first problem, cogently confronted in the paper, is the breadth of the concept of institution. At the more concrete and applied end of the spectrum is the notion of institution as a synonym for organization: a power company, a department of a ministry, a development bank, a project management unit. When governments, the World Bank, and other donor agencies speak of institutions, this is normally what they mean. Analyzing the capacity of such organizations or institutions, diagnosing their deficiencies, and proposing reinforcing or corrective measures—this has been the standard practice of "institutional development," at any rate in the World Bank.

But there is a quite distinct, more abstract definition of institutions: as rules of the game—patterns of norms specific to a society, "compliance procedures" that lend predictability to expectations and, in Professor Van Arkadie's words, define "the terrain over which economic actors maneuver." Examples of these broader sorts of institutions are land tenure patterns, property rights, and legal systems. Less easy to define and far less easy to reform, these institutions are nonetheless profoundly important.

Thus, the analyst of institutions is confronted at once by the nitty-gritty of diagnosing deficiencies and changing detailed management and production procedures at the level of the firm, *and* by sweeping, near metaphysical issues such as the extent to which cultural variables influence economic outcomes. Conclusion one: the topic is enormous.

The second problem is that the question in its entirety lacks an analytical method, a conceptual framework capable of rendering it coherent. There is no organizing mechanism, such as the market, to order the different portions of the topic. Certainly, there is a lot of thinking going on, both in and outside the discipline of economics, to derive or construct such a device, and reams of paper have been produced on what is called "organizational economics," on public

The author is on the staff of the Country Economics Department of the World Bank.

© 1990 The International Bank for Reconstruction and Development / THE WORLD BANK.

choice theories, analyses of transaction costs—various strands of "the new institutional economics." So far, by their own admission, they have produced a metaphor—suggestive, admittedly productive—but nonetheless a "metaphor for organizing thinking about technological and institutional change" (Feeny 1988, p. 162). Metaphors may be a necessary starting point, but: "If institutions matter—if they affect the performance of an economy—then . . . a theory of economic change must include a theory of institutional change" (Feeny 1988, p. 161). I believe the author and I would concur that we do not yet have such a construct. Conclusion two: the theory of the topic is underdeveloped. Whether it is "developable" remains to be seen.

The third and principal problem, very well handled in the paper, is that despite its intractability, the topic's importance is incontestable. And probably growing. The paper correctly notes that internal and external observers, from all perspectives, left, right, and center, are critical of institutional performance in developing countries. Criticisms now extend to all types of institutions, homing in more and more on the need to deal with and reform the broader, less tangible institutions—for example, the overwhelming need to ensure the enforceability of contracts; to establish operational notions of property, and how it can be used, consumed, and exchanged; the need to break the hold of excessive, counterproductive regulations, rent-seeking or otherwise.

I welcome Van Arkadie's insistence that the issue is not going to go away. It cannot be set aside by economists with the reductionist claim that institutions and their impact are someone else's concern; it cannot be ignored by developing-country governments that face increasing pressures to deliver a modicum of services to their populations; it cannot be overlooked by the World Bank in the hope that we can take the high road of defining policies and leave it to someone else—the borrower governments? the bilateral donors?—to implement them. So, a third conclusion: we in the Bank are in this messy business for the long haul, irrespective of whether we continue to emphasize adjustment or find our way back to primarily investment lending. Thus those who might prefer their development economics unsullied have been overtaken by events.

In illustration, an anecdote. In 1962, it was suggested to Arthur Lewis that a set of Indian cultural norms and institutions, the caste system, constituted a powerful and perhaps impenetrable barrier to economic development. Sir Arthur disagreed: "The love of money," he declared, "is a powerful institutional solvent. Many countries have indeed attitudes and institutions which inhibit growth, but they will rid themselves of these attitudes and institutions once their people discover that they stand in the way of economic opportunity" (Lewis 1962). The prose is splendid but the sentiment is simplistic and, alas, dated: a quarter of a century later many economists are inclined, with Van Arkadie, to admit that institutions, like prices, matter; that we have not paid sufficient attention to ways and means of improving the performance of organizations and the appropriateness of the broader institutions.

This brings me to my last point: the next and most crucial step in the process (and here, not surprisingly, the Van Arkadie paper is not too helpful) is to specify precise operational methods and tools by which to improve performance in institutions. A great deal of analytical review of how technical assistance for institutional development has been used—and misused—is about to come to fruition. Guidelines may reasonably be expected to come out of this work, a distillation of "best practice" in this subfield that will be of use to governments and donors. Such guidelines already exist for the reform of public enterprises, a *comparatively* manageable element of public sector institutional reform (see Shirley 1989 and Nellis 1989). And efforts are under way to do the same for budgeting and public expenditure (see Lacey 1989). Devising the appropriate techniques is perhaps less the job of the academic economist than of the government bureaucrat, the World Bank staff, and management specialists—though we in the practitioner community would gratefully accept any further assistance Van Arkadie and other academic economists might care to offer.

References

Feeny, David. 1988. "The Demand and Supply of Institutional Arrangements." In Vincent Ostrom, David Feeny, and Hartmut Picht, eds., *Rethinking Institutional Analysis and Development*. San Francisco: International Center for Economic Growth.

Lacey, Robert M. 1989. *Managing Public Expenditure: An Evolving World Bank Perspective*. World Bank Discussion Paper 56. Washington, D.C.

Lewis, W. Arthur. 1962. "Foreword." In T. S. Epstein, *Economic Development and Social Change in South India*. Manchester: Manchester University Press.

Nellis, John. 1989. "Public Enterprise Reform in Adjustment Lending." World Bank PPR Working Papers 223. Washington, D.C. Processed.

Shirley, Mary. 1989. *The Reform of State-Owned Enterprises: Lessons from World Bank Lending*. Policy and Research Series 4. Washington, D.C.: World Bank.

Comment on "The Role of Institutions in Development," by Van Arkadie

Pranab Bardhan

I agree with most of what is said in the paper. Essentially this critique supplements the paper, emphasizing institutional issues that Professor Van Arkadie did not go into very much—particularly from the point of view of rural development. I will try to discuss these issues in the perspective of economic theory, keeping in mind our primary focus on policy issues and empirical matters.

Until recently, mainstream economic theory has by and large ignored institutional issues—often stating central propositions with a false air of institutional neutrality. Of course, radical economists, economic historians, and other such wishy-washy characters among us have always made a noise about institutions being important, but much of mainstream economic theory has kept a safe distance from such polluting influences.

Fortunately that's no longer true. In the last ten or fifteen years, economic theory—particularly non-Walrasian neoclassical and non-neoclassical theory—is increasingly recognizing a whole range of problems that come up in analyzing institutions. We are now in the process of developing an endogenous theory of institutions that will help us understand the forces behind them. Our focus is, of course, on economic factors because our comparative advantage lies in analyzing them.

There is now a vast literature, which includes several points of view. The transactions costs theorists have taken one line, largely flowing from the seminal work of Ronald Coase; somewhat different, though related, is Oliver Williamson's work (1985). The Coase-Williamson literature on transaction costs concentrates on corporate structure and practices; more recently, the literature (see, for example, Bardhan 1989) has tended to focus on things like imperfect information, usually emphasizing the emergence of institutions as substitutes for missing markets—particularly for credit, insurance, and futures transactions—in an environment of pervasive risks, moral hazard, information asymmetries, and so on. The theme was first taken up in the literature on sharecropping, but now a whole range of rural institutions has been analyzed—in the labor, credit, and other markets.

The author is a professor of economics at the University of California, Berkeley, and editor of the *Journal of Development Economics*.

© 1990 The International Bank for Reconstruction and Development / THE WORLD BANK.

Radical economists often speak of institutional obstacles to development in poor agrarian economies and overlook the microeconomic rationale of these institutions' formation. Under certain informational constraints and missing markets, a given agrarian institution such as sharecropping may actually be serving a real economic function. Its simple abolition—often called for by radicals, who ignore the factors that gave rise to the institution in the first place—may not improve the conditions of the intended beneficiaries. The economics of what may be called "second-best reformism" may offer some important political lessons here, which are applicable to land reform, credit reform, and so on.

Although I generally favor the development in this fast-growing literature, I am increasingly doubtful about the direction it is taking. In the first place, this literature (with some notable exceptions) tends to assume the optimality of persistent institutions. That is, if you can explain an institution in terms of imperfect information and the like, something must be right with that institution, so we shouldn't tinker with it. Sometimes that is the right conclusion to draw but often it is not. It is possible to construct models in which you can show that dysfunctional institutions may persist for a very long time. All kinds of self-reinforcing processes are increasingly recognized now—not so much in development economics but in the new institutional economics literature—processes of the kind, for example, that George Akerlof (1984) has discussed in terms of social sanctions. Other self-reinforcing mechanisms have been recognized in a completely different literature, in the theory of technological innovations. There is the idea of what is called path dependence, for example, where a path chosen initially because it suited particular interests may lock the system in for a long time because of increasing returns to adoption, learning, and other kinds of bandwagon effects. These self-reinforcing mechanisms are just as important to the literature on institutional innovations as to that on technological innovations.

The new institutional literature also sometimes ignores that the new theory cannot completely supersede some of the emphasis of the earlier reformists. Much of the new literature assumes, for example, the framework of information symmetry and risk-sharing. But it cannot on that basis deny that a redistribution of assets or reorganization of the work process might lead to a superior equilibrium, since sometimes there would be less asymmetry of information and less need for risk-sharing.

The different strands in this literature share another methodological problem, having to do with functionalism—a problem not exclusive to development economics. If we can show that an institution helps a large number of people, we assume that somehow it will come about; we try to explain an institution by pointing to its benefits. The assumption of course ignores the enormous difficulty of getting the potential gainers to get their act together to somehow defeat the potential losers or vested interests. This collective action problem is familiar in the literature on the political economy of trade policy.

There are two kinds of collective action problem here. One is the well-known free-rider problem about sharing the costs of bringing about change. The other, less often talked about, has to do with bargaining about sharing not the costs but the potential benefits from the change, disputes about which may lead to a breakdown of the necessary coordination.

The collective action dilemma brings to mind another general problem of this literature: much of the focus is on efficiency-improving institutions, whereas historically considerations of efficiency have been less important than redistributive issues in processes of institutional change. Take the eighteenth-century enclosure movement in England, for example, which some literature in economic history has tried to explain. Enclosures have been explained as more efficient than the open field system that prevailed before. Now, there is no doubt that if an institution improves efficiency, pressures will be generated to bring it about—but redistribution has often been the crucial factor in this particular collective action problem. Mobilizing the relevant interest groups and tackling the bargaining and free-rider problems often turn on the redistributive effects of the particular institutional change, which are at least as important, if not more so, than the efficiency-improving effects.

There is an identification problem here. Hayami and Ruttan (1985) distinguish between demand for and supply of institutional change—demand coming from demographic and technological changes which generate pressures for institutional change; supply from political entrepreneurs who try to resolve the collective action problem. Although they recognize this distinction, Hayami and Ruttan often try to show how demographic and technological changes have brought about institutional changes in agriculture. There are several examples in the book and also in Hayami and Kikuchi (1982). Let me take just one example. The rapid expansion of labor-tying arrangements such as *kedokan* in many parts of Java in the late 1960s, which Hayami and Kikuchi attribute to population growth, can be explained from the "supply side" by reference to the drastic changes in the collective strength of the poor peasantry brought about by the bloody political changes of the 1960s. I am not saying that the supply side is more important than the demand side, but in observed historical instances sometimes it is difficult to identify whether demand for institutional change or resolution of the collective action problem in some way was responsible for the outcome. Often the two are interdependent.

Identification is a general problem in applying some of the rather sophisticated theoretical models from the institutional literature. When I was a student in development economics, one of the major issues that used to be discussed was "Are peasants rational?"—which always sounded a little silly to me. Now we have moved full circle: we have superclever peasants solving multistage, multiperiod game-theory models. I am in favor of applying more sophisticated reasoning to understanding processes we do not understand otherwise, but there are significant empirical difficulties. As we know, many of these game-theoretical results are highly model-specific and are not robust at all. An empirical testing of these models is extremely difficult: for the same observed phenomenon that you explain by one intricate game-theoretical model, you can find five other intricate or not-so-intricate models. There is a disproportion between theoretical and empirical work in this area which will crop up in all sorts of ways as we start testing the theoretical models.

Finally, on the role of the state, which is the real focus of Van Arkadie's paper: sometimes the literature is unduly preoccupied with the extent of state intervention when the more interesting subject is how, given the extent, the nature or quality of the intervention varies; even the same amount of intervention can bring about completely different outcomes.

I also think that the literature focuses too much on state versus private property regimes. In many aspects of development—including rural development and many of the looming environmental problems—we should pay more attention to "intermediate" institutions, such as small-group cooperatives, formal or informal. The history of cooperatives is by and large dismal: they have failed in many parts of the world. I am not talking about large collectives or the kind of cooperatives in Kenya discussed in Van Arkadie's paper. (In fact, one reason cooperative history is so often a history of failure is that cooperatives are often essentially the lower end of a big state bureaucracy or a front organization to milk the state cow.) I am talking about more genuine voluntary, small-group, self-help cooperatives that may get help from others but are more self-generative and self-sustaining. Successful examples of such groups exist in different countries.

Water management is one area that generates many externalities. How do village societies cope with internalizing them? How do farmers get together locally to resolve conflicts—or sometimes fail to resolve them—in allocation? East Asian history has many success stories about informal, traditional village community organizations in which all kinds of implicit cooperation have been going on for some time. Even in different parts of India I have seen scattered evidence of a remarkable amount of informal cooperation among farmers. These institutions are not listed as cooperative societies, and they often take rather soft institutional forms, but they have survived for a long time. Unfortunately, informal cooperatives are now fading away as the state, as a patronage-giver, becomes more important and intrudes into village life. Externalities of this kind are important in many other areas—environmental issues particularly come to mind.

We should study informal institutions involving cooperation to try to understand why they fail in many areas and why they succeed in some. I would urge those who are interested in these issues not to try to resolve them at general theoretical or aggregate statistical levels. I think this calls for many microlevel studies that include analyses of processes. We economists in our surveys are not very good at understanding processes. We get observation points on outcomes and analyze those outcomes. To understand processes, I think we have to give up our somewhat arrogant imperialist attitude toward other social studies and collaborate with others, such as anthropologists, and get on with more such microstudies.

References

Akerlof, George. 1984. *An Economic Theorist's Book of Tales*. Cambridge: Cambridge University Press.

Bardhan, Pranab, ed. 1989. *The Economic Theory of Agrarian Institutions*. Oxford: Oxford University Press.

Hayami, Y., and V. W. Ruttan. 1985. *Agricultural Development*. Baltimore, Md.: Johns Hopkins University Press.

Hayami, Y., and M. Kikuchi. 1982. *Asian Village Economy at the Crossroads*. Baltimore, Md.: Johns Hopkins University Press.

Williamson, O. 1985. *The Economic Institutions of Capitalism*. New York: Free Press.

FLOOR DISCUSSION OF VAN ARKADIE PAPER

Expanding on a theme in Van Arkadie's paper, one participant observed that economists tend to export into other countries organizations that do not fit the norms of people in those countries, yet expect them to succeed. Similarly, often the people are maximizing one thing and government imposes an organizational structure designed to maximize something else, producing inconsistencies. It would be more appropriate first to focus on what we are trying to maximize in a society and then to find the type of organizational structure to support that objective. Cooperatives are often well-matched to societal norms, but other institutions may not be. In a typical rural area in Africa, for example, credit and saving are linked. Individuals put their money together and give it to a person who needs capital, and it passes around. This informal system is an institution, one that links saving and investment with the objective of providing capital to generate production. Introduce a bank in a rural area where that system exists and you will get no saving, and economists will say the people and banks are risk averse—because they do not understand the system.

Acknowledging the validity of this observation, which he had also made in his paper, Van Arkadie suggested that in some situations one has to ignore or try to change the norms. The World Bank is in the business of lending to governments, for example, and does so on the assumption that the governments are not crooked. What happens when governments will not repay loans and are crooked? You could say, "That's their norm," or you could conclude that you are in the business of changing norms and trying to assert norms that may be at variance with the existing system.

Bardhan (discussant) elaborated on the subject of norms, noting their importance in the game-theoretic literature, particularly for repeated cooperative games of the prisoner's dilemma type. In repeated transactions, some codes of conduct become norms that people accept without thinking. The problem is, norms change. Economists don't have a very good theory of changing norms. They have interesting ideas about how norms change, but many economists' models of norms assume that all social norms are reducible to economic rationality, which is questionable.

One Bank participant thought that confusion about the meaning of "institutions" might be the result of historical accident, of someone somewhere using the term institutions when they meant organizations. Van Arkadie had developed

---

This session was chaired by Visvanathan Rajagopalan, vice president, Sector Policy and Research, World Bank.

© 1990 The International Bank for Reconstruction and Development / THE WORLD BANK.

the two definitions along parallel tracks—with marriage, societal norms, and the like along one track and with diagnoses of organizations along another—but perhaps there is no real link between the two meanings. Does one follow the other in terms of the sequence of development? Does the development and effectiveness of organizations—particularly the kinds of agencies the World Bank works with—depend upon a certain level of development of norms? If there is no such link, perhaps it would be more productive to discuss them separately, and we could get on with the task of considering organizational alternatives for development programs. Admitting that his work on this subject was new and transitional, Van Arkadie said he would have to think about whether the two subjects deserved separate discussion. His two definitions of "institutions" were an empirical reaction to the discourse; if separated, the question would be how the two meanings could be related at the analytical or theoretical level.

Nellis (discussant) said that the Bank working group that is producing a policy paper on institutional development is receiving many comments along two lines: (1) what you are attempting is ludicrously broad and (2) how could you have left out local government, decentralization, finance, tax administration, and so on?

A participant offered an explanation of why this field is theoretically underdeveloped and how to improve matters. Economists writing about rural institutions, for example, speak of utility-maximizing producers, production functions, risk, and asymmetric information—all elements of an urban sector theory, none of them specific to agriculture. Once you get specific about agriculture, suddenly, without a great deal of analytical apparatus, implications become apparent. In his own work, by looking at elements such as covariance of risk and the spatial dispersion of agriculture, the participant had shown that crop insurance is not likely to work and that rural financial institutions that confine their operations to agriculture would have trouble operating successfully. Introduce agroclimatic differences—for example, the high degree of covariant risk in semiarid, highly seasonal climates and the low degree of risk in humid climates that are not very seasonal—and you arrive at the differences anthropologists have long observed between the hierarchical family structures found in semiarid areas and the nonhierarchical family structures found in humid areas. Introduce differences among crops—whether the crop can be stored before being processed, for example—and you can predict which crops are suited for plantations and which are not. He strongly felt that economists writing about institutions systematically ignore simple technological and material conditions.

While agreeing with this comment, Van Arkadie felt that the difficulty lay in knowing which were the right questions for economists to look at. Take the plantation example just cited, for instance. In the 1960s Van Arkadie saw that sisal was a plantation crop, and coffee a smallholder crop in Tanzania. To him it seemed obvious and logical why this was so. Then he went to Brazil where he found coffee to be a relatively large-scale and sisal a relatively small-scale crop. As an economist one can say that some crops probably can't be produced by plantations, given various factor endowments or costs, or can only be produced inefficiently, so that under competition the plantation will not succeed and the smallholder will. But that does not explain why in some parts of the world certain crops are grown in plantations and others are not, without looking at the issues Bardhan introduced in his panel comments—about the nature of power in those societies at particular historical moments and the persistence of institutions once they're created, regardless of inefficiency or inequity.

Bardhan found covariant risks to be important for looking at rural institutions, but unlike the earlier participant, believed that many models already do use covariant risks, implicitly or explicitly. In the literature on credit markets, for example, covariant risk came up in considerations of whether the lender should be a village resident or someone from outside. This is related to the demographic question: when do we go to the village moneylender for credit and when to relatives far away who do not face the same covariant risks? In rural India (where, as in much of the world, marriage is an economic institution), it is assumed that a village bridegroom or bride will marry a distant villager, partly because in times of crisis you can fall back upon your new relatives or other relatives who are not facing the same risks.

A participant felt that institutions in the two senses that Van Arkadie had defined were clearly important, but it seemed to him unproductive to talk simultaneously about credit markets, marriage, and the way different parts of agriculture work. He recognized that there were many serious issues that needed positive analysis—for example, how the Indian caste system might function if it changed radically under economic pressure, or how people provide for social security without specific government intervention—but found it unsatisfactory to consider all of these things together, and suspected that was why Van Arkadie found it so difficult to write his paper. Economists should be more problem-oriented. He added a plea to avoid terms like "new institutional economics" or "new" anything as being pretentious, inaccurate (they were seldom new), and certain to go out of date quickly.

Bardhan concurred that concrete studies and more problem-specific discussions were preferable, but he felt that a general discussion made people more aware of the complexity of problems for which economists sometimes give simple-minded policy suggestions. Van Arkadie agreed with Bardhan, pointing out that economists attack particular problems carrying their own intellectual baggage, which every now and then they should examine.

A participant from the Bank asked Van Arkadie to elaborate on his statement that there are some things institutions can do that markets cannot do, and some things neither do well, since Van Arkadie had also talked about the importance of political economy for determining institutional purpose. Van Arkadie explained that he was talking about bias in judgment. He was amazed after twenty-five years' experience in Africa, at the persistent support for certain agricultural policies despite the lack of any empirical evidence that those policies were working. Why was that? If it was highly desirable to increase agricultural productivity, and it was evident that market forces would not do so, policymakers decide that something ought to—and therefore could—be done. The wish then fathers the support, and the persistence of support, often despite the lack of positive results.

Citing Harold Lasswell's definition of political science as the study of who gets what, when, where, and how, a participant suggested that if one accepts that institutions like the World Bank have been effective in specifying who, what, where, and when one transforms resource inputs into outputs, what the topic was addressing seemed to a political scientist to be simple: the feasibility of the question of how, which the Bank had addressed less successfully. The key variables are motivations and incentives (which, when expanded, cross over into culture, psychology, rules of the game, and so on). Institutions are simply the collective mechanism by which people pursuing their own interests transform inputs into outputs. Outcomes are more rational if the collective action is purposeful and less rational when it is the sum of anarchic activities—or something in between. If we assume that to accomplish our institutional ends we must control all the variables and come up with generic prescriptions, this may seem to be an unmanageable field. By focusing on process and recognizing that the complexity is largely in the location-specific way motivations and incentives manifest themselves, we can find out what motivates people in a particular context and come up with adaptive institutional solutions. Agreeing with this assessment, Van Arkadie observed that complaints are more often about action (or inaction) than about the analysis. As an observer of Bank policy missions he is struck by how often perfectly sensible, straightforward advice is not taken.

Another participant expressed the need for more guidance on how to conduct meaningful institutional appraisals. If in the absence of a theory of institutional change, one were to decide on a case-by-case basis whether or not to recommend institutional interventions—analyzing institutional microprocesses, the institution's political and technical purpose, its historical origins, its public and private influence, and various social, anthropological, cultural, ethnic, and political factors—what should the methodology be?

Two participants offered constructive criticism on current approaches to institutional change. The first participant suggested that economists at the World Bank and elsewhere should probably concentrate on public *economic* and *financial* organizations—concerning themselves with noneconomic organizations only to the extent of helping them use resources optimally. He believed there had not been enough empirical studies about optimal cost structures for noneconomic public organizations. When such an organization applies for grants or aid, lending institutions look at its financial profile and conclude that it is inefficient if they see that personnel costs and overheads exceed certain ratios. He felt that these ratios were drawn from the developed market economy experience and he wondered if these cost profiles can be applied without adaptation to noneconomic public organizations in developing countries. The participant also seconded Van Arkadie's recommendation that the World Bank support research into entrepreneurship, particularly studies about how to predict entrepreneurial responses to policies in developing countries.

The second participant urged a distinction between individual institutions and the structure of institutions. The performance of an individual institution depends on the structural arrangement of institutions. Under different arrangements performance will differ; this is probably one of the main reasons why an institution works in one society and not in another. He also urged more careful consideration of the cost of institutional change. A particular institutional arrangement may not appear rational, but if analysis suggests that the cost of change is prohibitive, the wiser course may be to live with inefficiency.

After observing that the Bank has paid increasing attention to institutional behavior important to policy change, Rajagopalan (chair) suggested that interdisciplinary research and analysis focus on giving development practitioners paradigms and criteria for evaluating institutional structures. Particular emphasis needs to be given to the efficient management of the public sector. Ownership was not the issue so much as performance, so he urged researchers to find ways to improve performance under different ownership patterns. Researchers should also try to identify the conditions that encourage entrepreneurs to emerge in underdeveloped economies. Analysts should clarify the effect of interactions between economic and noneconomic (including ethnic, religious, and nationalist) factors and their effect on such activities as regulation of public utilities and privatization. Finally, Rajagopalan urged more study of the implications of the increasing role of multinational corporations, trade unions, and international credit in the economies of developing countries.

The Noncompetitive Theory of International Trade and Trade Policy

Elhanan Helpman

This paper reviews recent theoretical developments in the analysis of trade structure and policy. It emphasizes how understanding monopolistic (noncompetitive) market structures and elements can help explain trade flows and the relation between trade and growth, and can be useful in evaluating tariffs, quotas, and research and development subsidies in noncompetitive markets. Noncompetitive trade theory identifies testable relations that have already received empirical support in various studies. Once their significance is recognized, it is important to take them into account in designing policy. Policies exist that raise welfare, but simple policy prescriptions do not. Theory helps to identify situations in which particular policies work, but under only slightly different circumstances opposite policies may have to be implemented. Recent studies have shown that long-run growth rates depend on an economy's structural features and the country's trading partners. So policy can affect long-run growth—but identifying useful policies requires an understanding of market structure and conduct, entry constraints, intersectoral links, and the like. More empirical studies are needed to elicit this information. Meanwhile, policy should be designed on a case-by-case basis and—because good policies improve welfare only slightly—no intervention (free trade) remains a good rule of thumb. All the more so when one takes into account the competitive pressure of a free trading world system, the probability of retaliation, and the political economy of protection.

A decade of intensive research on increasing returns to scale and market structure has generated a host of insights about their role in international trade and trade policy and narrowed the existing gap between theory and application. The new approach offers explanations for a number of empirical regularities, and provides new tools for policy analysis. Its findings underline the need for a case-by-case approach to policy design. The vitality of this work is by no means exhausted, and the research has recently been redirected to deal with dynamic concerns.

The new line of research began with models of monopolistic competition designed to explain intraindustry trade. The point of departure was the observation that many industrial products are differentiated, not homogeneous. If countries have a taste for such product differentiation—a typical example would

Elhanan Helpman is a professor of international economic relations at Tel Aviv University. He thanks June Flanders and T. N. Srinivasan for their comments.

© 1990 The International Bank for Reconstruction and Development / THE WORLD BANK.

be demand for variety in consumer electronics or cars—and if variety-specific economies of scale exist in manufacturing, we may expect intraindustry trade in differentiated products (see Balassa 1967). Variety-specific economies of scale ensure specialization in brands; the demand for a wide spectrum of products ensures a market for them in every country. Under these circumstances, every country specializes in certain brands and imports brands produced by its trading partners. This leads to intraindustry trade.

The formal theory that was developed on the basis of this insight is consistent with three observations. First, it is consistent with the factor proportions view of the factor content of net trade flows: that is, it predicts that a country exports embodied factor services of inputs with which it is relatively well endowed, and imports embodied factor services of inputs with which it is relatively poorly endowed (see Leamer 1984 for evidence). Second, the theory explains large trade volumes between similar countries—a well-documented phenomenon (see, for instance, Linnemann 1966) which the traditional theory failed to explain. Third, it explains the determinants of the composition of the volume of trade (that is, intraindustry versus intersectoral), which the traditional theory again could not address. The predictions of the new theory are supported by empirical findings (see Balassa 1986, Helpman 1987). The theory applies to consumer as well as producer goods (see Ethier 1982a and Helpman 1985).

Because space is limited, I do not review the above line of work or other theories of trade structure based on oligopolistic competition (for a recent review, see Helpman 1989). Instead, with an eye toward application, I survey the developments that followed the static theories of monopolistic and oligopolistic competition as applied to trade structure. My hope is that economists who work on applied issues of trade and development will find useful guidance in the results, though the coverage is necessarily selective.

The next section deals with recent studies of structural issues related to dynamics of international trade, long-run growth, and product cycles. Section II reviews arguments for an activist trade policy in noncompetitive economies, first in a static framework, which permits consideration of the role of one-sided market power and strategic trade policy, and second in a growth context. The paper closes with a short section of concluding comments.

I. Trade Dynamics

The static model of monopolistic competition that was designed to study intraindustry trade in a framework consistent with the factor proportions view of intersectoral trade (as described, for example, in Helpman and Krugman 1985, chapters 7–8), has been extended by Grossman and Helpman (1988) to a dynamic framework. In the static model, brand-specific fixed costs are often associated with product development and design. A proper treatment of such costs requires, however, a dynamic model in which costs are incurred before actual manufacturing takes place, and are gradually recovered over time as the entrepreneur collects monopoly profits. This Schumpeterian view of dynamic competition can be combined with Chamberlin's view of monopolistic competition to shed light on trade issues such as the dynamic evolution of trade when technology changes over time, the role of technological leadership, the role of product imitation, and the like.

The decision to develop a new product is a central ingredient in this line of inquiry. An entrepreneur needs to hire resources at cost $c_n(t)$ in order to design a product. He or she then needs to estimate the future flow of profits $\pi(\tau)$, $\tau \geq t$, that can be derived from the ownership of the exclusive knowledge or right to manufacture and market the product. (Naturally, product-specific monopoly power may be lost at some future point, as I will discuss below; at this stage assume that it lasts forever). Then the entrepreneur will choose to develop the product if, and only if, the present value of these profits does not fall short of the research and development (R&D) costs. If there is free entry into this line of business and there are no indivisibilities (strictly speaking, the number of products is a continuum), the present value of profits just equals product development costs in an equilibrium with active R&D. In this case, the instantaneous profit rate π/c_n plus the capital gain on R&D costs (the rate of increase in c_n) equals the interest rate. This dynamic relation combines pricing of the firm on the stock market together with absence of arbitrage between the cost of product development and the value of the firm. It can be embodied in a complete model in which (a) consumers use prevailing interest rates to allocate spending and saving optimally over time; (b) full employment of resources takes account of their use in R&D; and (c) all markets clear, which also implies equality of saving and investment.

Grossman and Helpman (1988) have done just that in the framework of a simple, two-country, two-sector, two-factor model with fixed coefficients of production and no factor accumulation, so that all dynamics result from product development. In their model one sector supplies differentiated products while the other supplies a homogeneous product.

The Evolution of Trade

In the dynamic framework it is useful to think about capital as human capital rather than machines and equipment, which makes it natural to suppose that R&D is the most capital-intensive activity. Also, assume manufacturing of differentiated products (that were developed) to be more capital intensive than production of the homogeneous product. Finally, assume for the moment that factor prices are the same in both countries at every instant of time (even though factor prices change over time). Then if no country begins with a relative advantage in the number of products (a) the relatively capital-rich country develops relatively more products; (b) the trade pattern at each point in time resembles the pattern that emerges in the static model of trade in differential products (that is, the capital-rich country imports the homogeneous product, it is a *net* exporter of the differentiated product, and intraindustry trade exists in differentiated products); and (c) the volume of trade grows faster than world gross domestic product (GDP) (a well-established phenomenon in the postwar period). The world converges to a steady state in which product development ceases. The steady state looks very much like an equilibrium of a static world.

In a South-North interpretation, where the North is taken to be the country relatively rich in capital, these results suggest that in a free trade environment the North's technological leadership lasts forever, as do its net exports of manufactured differentiated products. This conclusion rests on the particular model, which is restrictive in many ways, but it does point out a realistic mechanism at work. More mechanisms need, however, to be considered.

The model can also be used to predict the point at which multinational corporations will emerge. As investment in R&D declines and employment in the manufacturing of differentiated products rises, the capital-labor ratio employed in these two activities declines. For this reason, a world structure that, in the early stages of development, permits factor price equalization without multinationals may reach a point at which it can do so no longer. This happens necessarily when the capital-labor ratio in manufacturing of differentiated products exceeds the endowed capital-labor ratio of the country relatively rich in capital. Then, from the point at which total capital per worker in the differentiated product sector (R&D plus manufacturing) exceeds the capital-rich country's capital-labor ratio, multinationals emerge. The degree of multinationality—as measured by employment in subsidiaries, their volume of output, or the number of brands produced by subsidiaries—increases over time until a steady state is reached. The steady state resembles a static world with multinational corporations (see Helpman 1984b).

No long-run dynamics exist in the scenario described above. Recent research has concentrated on discovering mechanisms that generate such long-run dynamics. Trade and development theories that explore implications of economies of scale have joined forces with new approaches to economic growth (for the latter, see Romer 1986, 1988; Lucas 1988; Helpman 1988). At the heart of these approaches are *dynamic* economies of scale (such as the product development process) coupled with externalities associated with *knowledge* capital. Thus, in Grossman and Helpman (1988) growth peters out because the profit rate falls over time as more and more brands crowd the differentiated product sector. This reduces the return on R&D until it stops being profitable. If, however, knowledge capital serves as an input in R&D and this capital stock rises over time as a result of experience (that is, learning by doing à la Arrow 1962), it may counteract the effect of product crowding on the profitability of R&D and thereby sustain product development and growth in the long run.

Multiple Equilibria

Before discussing the effects of knowledge capital on long-run growth, I would like to pause to set it in the context of the emergence of multiple equilibria. The tendency of product-specific learning by doing to perpetuate every initial pattern of specialization introduces persistence into trade patterns. Krugman (1987), for example, constructed a model with product-specific learning by doing in which every historically determined pattern of trade and specialization lasts forever. Under such circumstances temporary shocks—whether from technology, policy, or other sources—have permanent effects.

The observation that temporary events have lasting effects arises from two sources that have been widely studied. One is a case in which the long-run equilibrium depends on initial conditions, for which Krugman's model of learning by doing provides an instance. Here, shocks that change initial conditions extract long-run effects. The other is a case in which more than one long-run equilibrium exists, and the economy can converge to each of them from the same initial conditions, depending on expectations. This phenomenon has been recognized in international trade at least since Graham's (1923) famous argument for tariff protection.

Graham envisioned a two-sector economy whose opening to international trade may lead to resource migration from the industry in which returns to scale are increasing, to the industry in which they are decreasing, thereby depressing GDP so much that the usual gains from trade are outweighed. This observation led to a heated debate between Graham and Knight (see Helpman 1984a for a review of the debate). Graham was vindicated by Ethier (1982a), who studied countries that have an industry with external economies of scale and perfect competition (that is, a firm's productivity depends on aggregate output, but the firm treats productivity as an exogenous parameter). In this type of economy a number of trading equilibria may differ in the degree of specialization in the increasing-returns industry. In the absence of intersectoral adjustment costs, the instantaneous allocation of resources relies entirely on expectations about factor rewards, and several sets of self-fulfilling expectations exist, each one leading to a different outcome. These outcomes can be Pareto ranked (see Helpman and Krugman 1985, chap. 3).

As an illustration, consider a two-sector economy with a single resource, say labor, that faces constant terms of trade and a constant labor-output ratio in the non-increasing-returns sector. The firm's perceived marginal product value of labor in the increasing-returns sector (sector X), depends on the industry's output level; the larger aggregate employment and output, the larger the marginal value product. Suppose also that the perceived marginal value product equals zero when the industry's output equals zero, and that the marginal value product in X is larger than in the alternative use when X employs all resources. Two self-fulfilling-expectations equilibria will then exist with complete specialization. In one, all labor works in the constant-returns-to-scale industry and the wage rate equals its marginal value product in that sector. Labor's marginal value product in X equals zero, so that there are no incentives to produce in X. In the other equilibrium, all labor works in X and the wage rate—which equals the marginal value product in X—exceeds labor's marginal value product in the constant-returns industry. The country is clearly better off in the latter equilibrium.

Recently Krugman (1989) has extended this analysis to an economy with adjustment costs in factor reallocation. As usual, the adjustment costs bring about gradual intersectoral adjustment in response to economic incentives. He finds that, given some initial conditions, the economy converges to one steady state, while with others it converges to another. In yet other initial conditions it may converge to either one of those possible steady states, depending on expectations (self-fulfilling expectations are assumed throughout). In this last case the resulting dynamics involve cycles of rising amplitude. Expectation-driven equilibria are of course not peculiar to international trade; they play a prominent role in other areas, such as macroeconomics (see, for example, Diamond 1982; Shleifer 1986; Cooper and Jones 1988; Murphy, Shleifer, and Vishny 1988).

All this implies that in certain circumstances an economy's trajectory is unpredictable, because it may follow more than one equilibrium trajectory, or that small shifts in initial conditions may have dramatic long-run effects. In either case it may be possible to use policies to shift initial conditions or to influence expectations, to force the economy to follow a desired path. An appealing feature of such policies is that often they need to be applied for only a short time. As usual, however, they are formidably difficult to design, because the required information is seldom available. The long-standing debate about infant industry protection represents well those difficulties (see Baldwin 1969).

Long-Run Growth

We now return to long-run growth. Suppose that current experience with product development reduces R&D costs to all future product developers. The product developer has thus generated a twofold output: an appropriable blueprint that can be used to acquire future monopoly rents, and a contribution to knowledge capital that is not appropriable. The contribution to knowledge may disseminate equally quickly to all future entrepreneurs, or faster to entrepreneurs from his own country. Suppose also that the differentiated-product sector provides intermediate inputs that are used in the manufacture of final consumer goods (as in Ethier 1982b). Each country has the technology to produce a different consumer good, and trades in both intermediate and final goods.

Grossman and Helpman (1989a) have studied a two-country world of this type. In their framework both countries converge to the same long-run growth rate, even if they differ in size and sectoral productivity levels. The long-run growth rate depends on the size of each country and the composition of demand for their final goods. When knowledge gets disseminated at an equal speed to both countries, the larger the country with comparative advantage in R&D and the smaller the relative demand for the final good in which it specializes, the faster the common growth rate. The growth rate may be increasing or decreasing with the size of the country that has comparative disadvantage in R&D, but it is definitely higher the larger the relative demand for the final good in which that country specializes.

The last point identifies a mechanism of more general relevance. The larger the relative demand for the final good of the country that has comparative advantage in R&D, the larger the demand for its resources and the lower the demand for resources in the other country (other things being equal). Under these circumstances, the intermediate-product sector and the R&D sector contract in the former and expand in the latter. Given the structure of comparative advantage, aggregate effective employment in product development declines in the world economy, thereby slowing growth (because the growth rate depends on the equilibrium size of the R&D sector).

If we interpret this model in a South-North context—where the country with comparative advantage in R&D is the North—this analysis suggests, for example, that the South grows faster the larger the North, but that the North's growth rate may be slowed down by a larger South. It also suggests that a shift of demand from Northern to Southern final goods raises the world's growth rate.

So far, our discussion has relied on what may be termed "natural" comparative advantage in R&D, which builds on endowed differences in technology. We have seen that it is an important determinant of long-run growth (and of policy effects, as I discuss in the next section). If, however, the diffusion of knowledge is faster within countries than across them, then natural comparative advantage does not fully determine a country's long-run comparative advantage overall—because these differing learning speeds give a country that does more R&D to begin with a lasting cost advantage. In this instance the final position of comparative advantage depends also on the relative size of the country's resource base and the derived demand for its resources for other uses. Thus, other things being equal, long-run comparative advantage in R&D is larger the larger the resource base and the smaller the demand for the country's final goods.

Innovation and Imitation

Comparative advantage in R&D has been prominent in discussion of North-South trade problems. It is manifested in an extreme form in Vernon's (1966) product cycle and its later elaborations. In this approach only the North is capable of developing new products. Immediately after a product is developed the North has also the cost advantage in its manufacturing, until the production techniques are standardized. Afterward, the cost advantage—and with it production—shift to the cheap labor region, that is, the South.

Vernon's approach was formalized by Krugman (1979; see also Dollar 1986; Jensen and Thursby 1986, 1987), who assumed that the rate of growth of new products g (rate of innovation) and the rate at which the South imitates products in which the North has monopoly power μ (rate of imitation) are constant. This specification suffices to describe the evolution of products that are manufactured in every region without specifying additional details of economic structure. In the steady state, the South produces a proportion $\mu/(\mu + g)$ of the available products. By imposing on these dynamics a model of oligopolistic price competition in differentiated products with labor as the only primary input, Krugman showed that the long-run relative wage of the South is increasing in $(\mu/g)(L_N/L_S)$, where L_S stands for the South's labor force and L_N for the North's labor force. Hence, the South's relative wage is larger the larger the rate of imitation, the smaller the rate of innovation, and the smaller its relative labor force.

Grossman and Helpman (1989b) have reexamined the long-run implications of the product cycle approach in light of the fact that both the rate of innovation and the rate of imitation result from the interaction of market forces with the explicit decisions of Northern entrepreneurs to innovate and Southern entrepreneurs to imitate. Imitators invest resources in learning and reversed engineering in expectation of future monopoly profits, just as innovators invest resources in R&D in expectation of future monopoly profits. But the innovators, uncertain as to when their product will be imitated—and hence when their monopoly profits will cease—discount profits with an interest rate that includes a risk premium, the risk premium being equal to the rate of imitation.

In this environment the long-run rates of innovation and imitation depend on country size and sectoral productivity levels. Innovation is faster the larger the North or the South (with one minor exception), whereas the rate of imitation is larger the larger the South and the smaller the North. Both regions grow faster when they trade with each other than in autarky. Now the relative wage of the South rises with the South's relative labor force (taking account of the endogenous response of innovation and imitation). This is just the opposite of Krugman's (1979) finding. It shows how crucial the explicit decisions to innovate and imitate are in bringing into full play the dynamic economies of scale.

To illustrate the point, consider Grossman and Helpman's "wide gap" case. Here the relative wage of the South is low enough for a Southern imitator to charge his monopoly price without risking undercutting by the Northern original innovator. In the wide gap case the South's relative wage is increasing in $(\mu/g)(L_N - g)/L_S - g)$ (using a suitable normalization). Hence, for constant g and μ this relative wage increases with the North's labor force and declines with the South's labor force, as in Krugman. But when the effects of labor on g and μ are taken into account, the results are reversed. That is, the indirect effects that changes in labor have on innovation and imitation are stronger than the direct effects.

II. Policy

In competitive economies two efficiency considerations may exist for trade policy: improvement in the terms of trade and a second (or third) best improvement in resource allocation in the presence of domestic distortions. Both exist in noncompetitive environments. In fact, imperfect competition necessarily involves a domestic distortion because firms do not engage in marginal cost pricing. For both objectives various different policies might be helpful (at least from the point of view of a single country). But can any broad policy conclusions be drawn, such as "whenever domestic firms compete against foreign oligopolistic firms in export markets we should subsidize their exports" or "whenever domestic import competing firms face noncompetitive foreign exporters in the domestic market we should impose import restrictions"? The answer turns out to be negative; no policy conclusion of this sort can validly be drawn. To design successful policies, instruments must be tailored to particular industries on the basis of their degree of concentration, the conduct of firms, the position of domestic firms relative to foreign, the industry's links with other sectors of the economy, and the like. In short, to exploit imperfect competition for policy purposes one requires detailed information about the economy. Such information is seldom available (see Helpman and Krugman 1989); furthermore, experiments with actual data reveal that the potential gains to be derived from such policies are rather small (see Helpman and Krugman 1989, chap. 8). On the other hand, existing tariff structures go much too far in terms of protection relative to optimal policies (see Harris and Cox 1984). The implication is that, given the current state of knowledge, a government that engages in a deliberate welfare-increasing policy takes significant risks; it stands to gain little but may cause significant losses.

The profusion of cases that need to be considered is described in figure 1 for a single market that can be either domestic or foreign (thereby immediately doubling the number of cases). There can be perfect competition, one of two cases of one-sided market power, or a case of two-sided market power. When market power is one sided, it of course makes a great deal of difference whether domestic or foreign suppliers own market power. In addition, a matrix of this sort applies to different types of conduct: one matrix for single firms with monopoly power, one for Cournot oligopolies (in which a small number of firms compete in quantities), one for Bertrand oligopolies (in which a small number of firms compete in prices), one for a cartel of a particular form (in which the allocation of benefits among members results from a particular solution to a bargaining problem), and so on. Then there are links with other industries that matter—we need to know how each policy affects entry, and so on.

The task of sorting and integrating the variables to elicit results that will be useful for policy is not as hopeless as it sounds: a number of the results described below reveal important considerations for a successful policy and indicate the information that will be required to make it effective.

In the first two subsections I discuss situations in which the number of firms is constant and all firms minimize costs. This state of affairs ensures efficiency of production (that is, output is on the transformation surface) although the composition of output need not be efficient. If we restrict attention to homo-

Figure 1. *Considerations for Trade Policy: Competitiveness and Market Power*

		Foreign	
		Competitive	Market power
Home	Competitive	Perfect competition	One-sided
	Market powers	One-sided market power	Two-sided market power

Source: Author's typology.

geneous products and trade taxes only, the change in aggregate welfare can be measured by

$$dU \equiv -m \cdot dp^* + t \cdot dm + (p - c) \cdot dX,$$

where m is the vector of net imports (a negative component represents exports), p^* stands for the foreign price vector and p for the domestic price vector (for consumers and producers), $t \equiv p - p^*$ represents the vector of trade taxes (a positive component represents an import tariff if the good is imported and an export subsidy if the good is exported), c is the vector of marginal costs, and X stands for the output vector.

The first term on the right-hand side of the equation represents the usual terms of trade effect: a country gains when the price of its exports rises or the price of its imports declines. The remaining two terms represent considerations of efficient supply. The last term says that an expansion of domestic output of goods that are priced above marginal cost raises welfare. Competitive industries price according to marginal cost, so that their contribution to this term equals zero. In noncompetitive sectors price exceeds marginal cost, which implies that expansion of their output is desirable (because domestic valuations exceed supply costs). Hence, other things being equal, policies that lead to an average expansion of noncompetitive sectors improve welfare. A similar interpretation can be applied to the second term in relation to imports. The marginal cost of imports equals the foreign price. If the domestic price exceeds the foreign price (as a result of a tariff or a quota, for example) an expansion of imports is desirable. Much of the welfare analysis of various policies concerns the tradeoffs among these three considerations.

One-Sided Market Power

Bhagwati in his famous (1965) paper analyzes a tariff in the presence of a domestic monopolist and fixed foreign supply price. He shows that in the situation depicted in figure 2—where the foreign price p^* is below the prohibitive domestic price P—gradual tariff increases (beginning from zero) that raise the domestic price toward P induce the monopolist to expand output. In this range he chooses output by equating price to marginal cost. Hence, the contribution of the third term in the equation above equals zero and welfare declines, because imports contract and the domestic price exceeds the foreign price (the contribution of the first term also equals zero because the foreign price does not change). When the domestic price reaches the prohibitive price P, imports cease and are never renewed for further tariff increases. Further tariff increases, however, induce the monopolist to reduce output, because now he equates price with demand until the monopoly price p_M is reached. In this case the second term in the equation equals zero (there are no imports), but welfare declines owing to the third term, because price exceeds marginal costs and output declines. This example also shows that with imperfect competition import protection can be effective even when imports equal zero. Here the effect of the mere threat of imports is not negligible.

In this instance a tariff is more restrictive than a quota in the following sense. Suppose we replace the tariff with a quota that equals the import volume under the tariff. The monopolist responds by cutting back output. Quotas thus lead to lower consumption and a higher price. The reasoning here needs to be clearly understood. A quota reduces the elasticity of demand perceived by the monopolist. In its absence a price increase leads him to lose sales to consumers on account of the downward-sloping demand curve and to importers who replace his sales (when imports are imperfect substitutes for his output; otherwise he loses all sales to importers). In its presence he does not lose sales to importers, and so his effective demand curve becomes steeper. This lowers his marginal revenue, and he responds by contracting output. The same reasoning applies to Cournot oligopolies. It can also be used to show that a quota equal to the free trade level of imports leads the monopolist or a Cournot oligopoly to contract output. Hence, whereas in a competitive environment a quota at the free trade level of imports has no effects, here it does. With monopoly power, moreover, quotas that *exceed* the free trade level of imports (up to a limit) also lead to lower consumption and a higher price. So for an oligopoly the quota leads to a more collusive outcome.

The question of whether quotas (or quantitative restrictions) facilitate collusion is of great interest. The previous analysis suggests that they do, and I

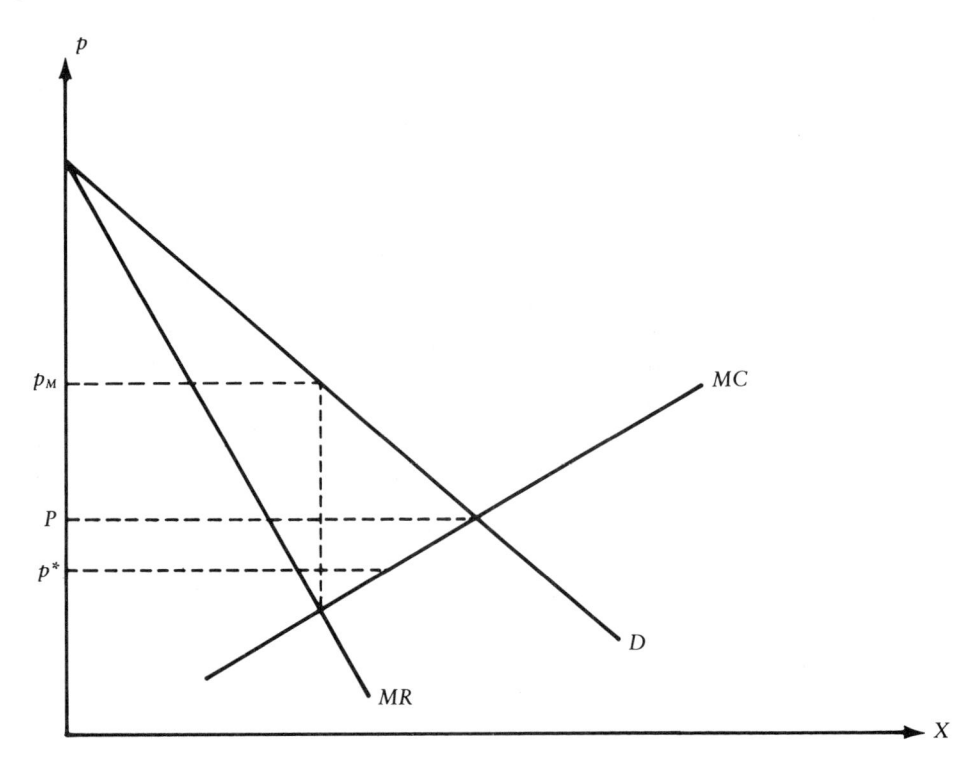

Figure 2. *Effects of Tariff Increases on Monopolistic Output*

Note: p = price, p^* = foreign price, P = domestic price, p_M = monopoly price, MR = marginal revenue, MC = marginal cost, D = demand, X = output.

think that this is a reasonable presumption. But there are exceptions, one of which serves to illustrate additional considerations.

The previous analysis relied on a static environment. Recently, however, much of oligopoly theory has been reformulated in order to allow firms to interact repeatedly. Repetition brings in important new elements, such as the possibility of implicit, as opposed to explicit, collusion. (Explicit collusion, in the form of a binding agreement, is often impossible because such a contract cannot be specified for all relevant circumstances or is illegal.)

Implicit collusion of repeatedly interacting firms may force an oligopoly to charge a price lower than the monopoly price (see Tirole 1988, chap. 6). That is, implicit collusion may not suffice to achieve the fully cooperative outcome attainable if it were possible to write a binding contract, for the following reasons.

In order to sustain an implicit agreement it has to be in the interest of each member: the present value of profits to be obtained from the cartel must not fall short of the present value of profits derived by deviating from the implicit agreement. It is then usually supposed that if a member deviates, the cartel falls apart in the next period and the noncooperative equilibrium (say, Cournot) gets established forever (this equilibrium is time-consistent in the sense that at each point in time every firm finds it desirable to follow the specified strategy). Hence, a potential deviator has to compare the one-period gains from choosing his best deviant strategy when everyone else obeys the implicit agreement with the present value of future losses that will result from the noncooperative outcome. The comparison depends on the size of the one-period gains, on how bad the noncooperative outcome is relative to the cooperative outcome, and on the rate at which future profits are discounted. Naturally, the smaller the one-period gains from a deviation and the worse the noncooperative outcome, the less likely it is that a deviation will pay off.

For these reasons an implicit agreement sometimes needs to specify a price below the monopoly price in order to sustain collusion. The lower price reduces the gains from deviation to the point at which collusion is viable, while at the monopoly price the gains from deviation are too high to sustain collusion (because when everyone restrains output in order to achieve the monopoly price, the deviant can make large one-period profits). Rotemberg and Saloner (forthcoming) have shown that under those circumstances a quota at the free trade level may *restrict* collusion rather than facilitate it. In their example, the quota raises the noncooperative equilibrium profit level (which is possible, as we have seen above, even though the quota exceeds the noncooperative import level). This forces the cartel to *reduce* price in order to prevent profitable deviation. Their example (even if not realistic) shows how important repetitive interactions can be for policy considerations (see also Davidson 1984 on tariffs).

We turn now from import-competing markets in which domestic firms have market power to those in which the domestic firms are competitive and foreign suppliers have market power. Here a desirable trade policy may consist of import subsidies rather than tariffs.

Suppose a monopolist foreign supplier who chooses a strategy that equates marginal revenue of the import demand function to his marginal costs. Now suppose that we impose a small tariff. If foreign supply were competitive and upward-sloping, the tariff would have improved the terms of trade and would have raised welfare. With the foreign supply controlled by a monopolist, there is no guarantee that a small tariff improves the terms of trade, and the terms of trade are the only relevant consideration. To illustrate the last point, observe that under those circumstances the last two terms on the right-hand side of the equation above are zero, because domestic firms price according to marginal costs and the initial tariff rate equals zero. Hence, we only need to consider the effect of a small tariff on the terms of trade. Now, the tariff, of say $1 per unit imports, raises the monopolist's marginal costs of supplying the domestic market by $1. Assume for simplicity that his tariff-exclusive marginal costs are constant. Then the contraction of sales equals the inverse of the slope of the marginal revenue curve, because he equates marginal revenue to marginal costs. The increases in the domestic price equals the contraction of sales times the slope of the demand curve. Therefore the domestic price rises by less than $1 if, and only if, the marginal revenue curve is steeper than the demand curve. If the domestic price rises by less than $1, the terms of trade improve. The terms of trade worsen when the domestic price rises by more than $1 (because the import price p^* equals $p - 1$). For example, when the demand curve is linear it is flatter than the marginal revenue curve and a tariff improves the terms of trade. Conversely, when the demand curve has a constant elasticity that exceeds 1 it is steeper than the marginal revenue curve and a tariff worsens the terms of trade. In the latter case an import *subsidy* improves the terms of trade. We have therefore a simple condition on the relative slopes of the demand and marginal revenue curves that determines whether a tariff or an import subsidy is desirable (see Brander and Spencer 1984).

An important point about this type of one-sided market power is that even in cases in which a tariff improves welfare its replacement with a quota reduces welfare below the free trade level. This does not result from differences in the level of domestic production. Indeed, if the quota equals the import level that prevails under the tariff, both policies lead to the same levels of imports, domestic production, and domestic price. The difference arises from the fact that under the quota the foreign monopolist exploits the quantitative restriction to charge the consumer price. Therefore instead of improving the terms of trade the quota worsens them. Alternately, under a quota the equivalent of the tariff revenue (which translates into quota rents under competition) accrues to the monopolist rather than to domestic owners of import licenses (see Shibata 1968). This result applies also to foreign oligopolies (which compete with imperfect substitutes) as long as the quota exceeds a minimal level. Helpman and Krugman (1989, chap. 4) show that for sufficiently small quota levels domestic owners of import licenses collect rents, but that in the linear demand case these are never sufficient to compensate for the initial losses (see also Krishna 1988a, 1988b). Whether circumstances exist in which a quota can bring about a less collusive outcome that would be preferable to free trade remains an open question.

Strategic Policy

In the presence of two-sided market power, economic policy has a strategic value as well: it changes the terms on which domestic noncompetitive firms interact with foreign noncompetitive firms. The best-known examples in international trade concern precommitment strategies. In particular, in situations in which domestic firms do not have the means to precommit to a particular course of action—even though that is desirable—the government can sometimes act to ensure (albeit indirectly) the desired precommitment. This typically requires the government to have the first-mover advantage—to be able to announce or execute a reliable policy before firms complete their strategic choices.

For instance, suppose that a domestic firm competes against a foreign firm in a third-country market. (We are concerned only with our firm's gross profits.)

Competition takes place in two stages. In the first stage, firms decide whether to enter the market. This may involve the development of a product or the settting up of a marketing network. In the second stage, the firms produce and compete in either price or quantity. Now, suppose that the market is small, so that when only one firm enters its second-stage profits exceed its first-stage entry costs, and when both enter, second-stage profits fall short of entry costs in each one of them. In this case two equilibria exist: one in which only the domestic firm enters and the other in which only the foreign firm enters. Clearly, the domestic firm and the home country prefer the former.

Because the two equilibria exist, the domestic government may want to force establishment of the preferred equilibrium. The following strategic policy could achieve this. Before the firms make their entry decisions the government provides the domestic firm with an entry subsidy that exceeds the loss that materializes when both firms enter. Under these circumstances the domestic firm chooses to enter independently of the foreign firm's decision. Consequently, the foreign firm does not enter and this is the unique equilibrium. The same can be achieved by a government commitment to a lump-sum export or production subsidy as long as the commitment is made before the entry decision and a mechanism is in place to make it good. Second-best policies in the form of ad valorem export subsidies can also be used for this purpose. Naturally, the foreign government has an equal incentive to engage in a strategic policy, and so the outcome may be a three-stage game in which governments choose policies in the first stage, firms make entry decisions in the second, and production and sales take place in the third (see Dixit and Kyle 1985).

Strategic policies do not apply exclusively to entry; they can also be used effectively when domestic and foreign firms have established themselves in a market. Consider an export market with one established domestic and one foreign firm that compete in prices with imperfectly substitutable products. Let each firm's profit maximization require a price rise in response to its rival's price increase. In this case the domestic government can raise its firm's gross profit level (and therefore welfare) by taxing exports (see Grossman and Eaton 1986). This result can be shown as follows (Helpman and Krugman 1989, chap. 5): the firm equates perceived marginal revenue to marginal costs, where perceived marginal revenue is calculated for a fixed price of the rival. When the domestic firm reduces price, however, the rival responds with a price reduction of his own. Nevertheless the home firm cannot take advantage of this information as long as both set prices simultaneously. If one could exploit this information, one would recognize that true marginal revenue is lower than perceived marginal revenue, because the foreign firm's price response to the home firm's price reduction brings about an increase in home sales that is smaller than the perceived sales increase. For this reason it is desirable to induce the home firm to charge higher prices and limit sales. An export tax achieves just that. The government can exploit the first-mover advantage by establishing an export taxation program that acts as a precommitment device. Then the firms compete with the program in place and the outcome is higher prices for both products. Here—unlike the entry promotion programs discussed previously—both countries gain higher profits, because the best response of a firm leads to higher profits the higher the rival's price. In this case a two-stage game in which both governments choose taxation programs in the first stage and firms choose prices in the second leads to a time-consistent equilibrium in which both countries are better off than under free trade.

Strategic policies thus need not lead to a conflict of interest. Although in the entry-intervention case one government's successful policy harmed the rival country, in the export-intervention case one government's successful policy brought a positive benefit to the other country. The inference to be drawn is more subtle, however, than a simple distinction between entry and export policies. In the first example entry decisions were strategic substitutes (when one firm entered, the other abstained from entering), whereas in the second prices were strategic complements (when one firm raised its price, the other responded with a price increase). The distinction between strategic substitutability and complementarity is key in understanding these results. The same distinction is also central in understanding the *direction* of desired policies.

These points can be demonstrated by means of an alternative example of two established firms that compete in an export market where governments intervene in foreign trade. But this time instead of competing in prices (à la Bertrand) the domestic and foreign firms compete in quantities (à la Cournot). Assume—as would be most likely—that a firm responds with an output contraction to an output expansion of its rival, thus ensuring strategic substitutability. The critical difference from the previous example is not the strategy space of the firms but rather the strategic relationship. Now an export *subsidy* rather than an export tax proves to be desirable (see Brander and Spencer 1985).

The argument can be made as follows (see Helpman and Krugman 1989, chap. 5). The domestic firm chooses output that equates perceived marginal revenue with marginal costs. It calculates perceived marginal revenue for a fixed output of the rival. The rival, however, responds with an output decline to an output increase of the domestic firm. Consequently, true marginal revenue exceeds perceived marginal revenue and the firm would earn higher profits if it could precommit to a larger output level. Unfortunately it cannot, because both firms play simultaneously. The government can improve the outcome by providing the necessary precommitment. To raise output the government should subsidize exports. The subsidy has to be in place (or be committed to be put into place) before the firms make their decisions. The firms can then choose outputs recognizing the existence of the export promotion program and end up in an equilibrium in which the domestic firm sells more and the foreign firm sells less.

Two points need to be underlined. First, in contrast to the Bertrand case, here export subsidies are required rather than export taxes. Second, countries face a conflict of interest in their trade policies. When one country engages in export promotion the other loses, because the policy-active country forces its rival to contract output, and output contraction as a best response to the domestic firm's output expansion leads to lower profits for the foreign firm. This conflict of interest leads to a Prisoners' Dilemma in the policy game. For suppose that there are two stages: governments choose their export policies in the first, and firms choose quantities in the second. For simplicity, also assume symmetry and constant marginal costs. Then in the resulting time-consistent equilibrium both governments subsidize exports and both firms sell more than under free trade. Observe, however, that even under free trade a Cournot duopoly produces too much, in the sense that joint output exceeds the output level of a single monopolist so that a further output expansion reduces profits per firm. Hence, the two countries are better off in the free trade equilibrium than in the equilibrium with active policies. The problem is that when one country does not promote its exports it pays the other to do so. Consequently, free trade is not an equilibrium unless policies are coordinated (that is, governments cooperate in the first stage).

We have seen that one can make a case for export taxation as well as export promotion on strategic grounds, depending on circumstances. In either set of circumstances the existence of more than one domestic firm strengthens the need for taxation—because the policymaker cares about aggregate profits of the exporting firms while each firm cares only about its own profit level (see Dixit 1984). Naturally, when a single domestic firm considers the effects of its price or output decisions on perceived marginal profits it does not take into account the effects on profits of other firms. Therefore, other things being equal, prices are too low and output levels too high when a number of domestic firms participate in the oligopolistic market. To offset this negative externality, an export tax is called for. Clearly, in the Bertrand case this strengthens the need for export taxation. In the Cournot case it conflicts with the need to subsidize exports on strategic grounds. The net result may be the need either for lower export subsidies or for taxation.

Entry

So far the discussion has concentrated on cases in which the number of firms is assumed to be fixed, or more to the point, in which firms do not enter or exit in response to policy measures. This is not, however, a safe assumption. Export subsidies may lead to entry, whereas export taxes may lead to the exit of domestic firms, independently of *conduct*. This is a significant consideration whenever there are firm-specific increasing returns to scale. For example, when fixed entry costs exist one must take account of the resource loss from entry of new firms (see Helpman and Krugman 1989, chap. 5). This consideration weakens the case for an export subsidy and strengthens the case for an export tax. In the presence of free entry that drives to zero tax- and subsidy-inclusive profits, export promotion damages welfare while a small export tax raises welfare (see Horstman and Markusen 1986).

The last point applies to all forms of conduct. If—as has been assumed so far for the industry under discussion—domestic firms export but do not sell in the local market, the change in welfare equals the change in aggregate gross profits. Conversely, aggregate gross profits equal aggregate net profits plus tax revenue minus the subsidy bill. Free entry ensures zero net profits. Therefore the change in welfare equals the change in net revenue. The imposition of a tax raises revenue, and thereby welfare. The provision of a subsidy reduces revenue, and thereby welfare.

All this suggests that if anything there is a presumption in favor of export taxation rather than export promotion. Export promotion is desirable only when a firm's choice variables are strategic substitutes, the number of firms is rather small, and the scope for entry in response to export subsidies is limited.

Intersectoral Links

To evaluate the response of resource allocation to policy we need to use correct measures of marginal costs. Much of the previous discussion relied on the assumption that firms use social marginal costs in their profitability calculations. This supposition is correct when all other sectors are competitive, but it is typically incorrect when some are noncompetitive. For this reason policymakers need to know the difference between true and perceived marginal costs as well as the difference between true and perceived marginal revenue. In other words, one cannot design a successful policy without properly taking account of intersectoral links (see Dixit and Grossman 1986). For example, when true marginal revenue in an export sector exceeds perceived marginal revenue it does not guarantee that export promotion will increase welfare. In order to see this point, suppose that the subsidized sector expands in response to the policy incentive by drawing resources from another export sector in which true marginal revenue exceeds perceived marginal revenue. If the divergence in the latter sector is large enough, the net result will be a decline in aggregate profits.

Differentiated Products

In the presence of product differentiation, a variety effect exists along with the terms of trade and the efficient supply effects that appear in the equation above, that has a bearing on policy design. Before discussing it, however, I would like to make two points.

First, the supply of many brands does not eliminate a country's market power even when the country is very small. Gros (1987) has demonstrated this in the following way (see Helpman and Krugman 1989, chap. 7, for a simple exposition). In a one-sector, one-factor, two-country world with product differentiation and a constant elasticity of substitution across brands (see Dixit and Stiglitz 1977), output per product does not depend on country size. The reason is that with Dixit-Stiglitz preferences the elasticity of demand does not change with the number of products. In addition, the number of brands is proportional to country size. Thus ad valorem trade taxes, which do not affect the elasticity of demand, cannot change the number of brands that each country produces, or output per brand. If they affect anything at all it must be the terms of trade. Calculating the optimal tariff for the home country, one finds that it equals $1/(1 - s)(e - 1)$, where s represents the share of world spending allocated to the home country's products and e represents the constant elasticity of demand. The smaller the country the smaller s and the smaller the optimal tariff. But even when the relative size of the country shrinks to zero, the optimal tariff remains positive. For no matter how small a country is, it specializes in a range of products in which it maintains monopoly power; the demand for a variety is downward sloping, and even a small country can affect its terms of trade.

The second point concerns the production efficiency effect. Consider a case in which the number of products and relative prices are constant but output per brand can change (see Helpman and Krugman 1989, chap. 7, for a model that ensures it). Then the imposition of import duties on brands that compete with domestic products shifts domestic demand from foreign to domestic varieties and shifts demand away from all varieties. Output per domestic brand may thus expand or contract and welfare may increase or decline (see Flam and Helpman 1987; Helpman 1989).

To return to the effect of variety on welfare: other things being equal, consumers prefer more variety. One can, in fact, think about a consumer price index that is lower the larger the variety choice. If a tariff reduces this price index by raising the available variety choice (as in Flam and Helpman 1987) or by changing the composition of products in favor of the home country at the expense of the foreign country (as in Venables 1987), it necessarily improves home welfare. But the increase in variety is not guaranteed (see Markusen 1988; Helpman 1989). A tariff may shift demand away from differentiated products so much that available variety is *reduced*. This contraction of variety choice may bring a decline in welfare. Conversely, in some circumstances the tariff raises available variety and welfare (for example, see Flam and Helpman 1987; Venables 1987). Consequently, it is not clear a priori whether small tariffs are desirable; all the effects mentioned above have to be taken into account. Large tariffs lead to additional welfare losses that stem from the undersupply of imports (the second term in the equation above). Moreover, even where tariffs are desirable they correct only indirectly the distortion that emerges from monopolistic or oligopolistic competition. Direct correction of the distorted price-cost margins, if feasible, would be preferable.

Promotion of Growth

In a dynamic economy the static issues reviewed so far have to be augmented by explicit consideration of the links between policy and growth. In the growth models described in section I, commercial policy and other forms of industrial policy affect long-run growth rates, exerting strong influences on welfare. But the resulting relations are far from simple. For example, in the world studied by Grossman and Helpman (1989a)—where both countries develop new intermediate products and one of them has a comparative advantage in R&D—an import tariff on final consumer goods slows down world growth if imposed by the country with a comparative advantage in R&D and speeds up world growth if imposed by the country with a comparative disadvantage in R&D. The intuition behind this result reveals a channel of influence that is not specific to the model. When a country imposes a tariff on imports of final goods, it shifts the composition of demand toward its own final goods. The expansion of the final goods sector draws resources from the manufacturing of intermediate products and product development. Opposite shifts in resource allocation take place in the other country. In particular, its product development sector expands. Whether these changes accelerate or slow down growth depends on whether the contraction of the R&D activity in the tariff-imposing country is smaller or larger than the expansion of the R&D activity in the other country. The answer depends on comparative advantage in R&D; world output of R&D declines only if the tariff-imposing country has a comparative advantage in R&D.

In this type of world one expects R&D subsidies to speed up growth—as indeed turns out to be so when the subsidy is provided by the country whose R&D is relatively more efficient, or when both countries subsidize at an equal rate. When the country with relatively less efficient R&D subsidizes product development, however, it may lead to slower growth. The outcome depends on structural features that cannot be spelled out in the available space.

Conversely, in the North-South model with a product cycle that was discussed in section I (Grossman and Helpman 1989b) innovation subsidies in the North and imitation subsidies in the South speed up growth. However, they each affect the rate of imitation differently, and thereby the average length of the first phase of the product cycle. Innovation subsidies reduce the rate of imitation and the average length of the first phase, whereas imitation subsidies raise the rate of imitation and shorten the average length of the first phase.

Grossman and Helpman (1989c) study a small-country variant of their growth models with a focus on the consequences of various policies for welfare. The resulting equilibrium differs from the first-best because, first, of markup pricing in the differentiated intermediate product industry, and second, of the externality that a product developer imposes on future product developers through his contribution to knowledge capital. Small R&D subsidies raise welfare. Larger subsidies accelerate growth more, but eventually reduce welfare. A small tariff that speeds up growth may either raise or reduce welfare. But whether it speeds up or slows down growth depends on the factor intensity of the import-competing sector relative to the exporting sector and the product development activity. Here, quotas also affect growth and welfare. They are particularly damaging relative to tariffs if they induce rent seeking that uses up entrepreneurship in which product development is relatively intensive.

III. Concluding Comments

The new theory of international trade and trade policy evidently encompasses numerous relevant elements. Although judgments may differ as to the relative importance of each, I believe there should be no controversy over the significance of the package as a whole. Existing empirical evidence on trade structure (see, for example, Havrylyshyn and Sivan 1984; Balassa 1986; and Helpman 1987) support the new view, and "calibration" studies of policy experiments (see Helpman and Krugman 1989, chap. 8, for a review) give quantitative support to many of the considerations that were discussed in section II. The most recent studies that embody those elements in a dynamic setup should make the approach even more useful.

One major conclusion emerges from both theory and the "calibration" studies: there are no simple answers to many important questions. This conclusion applies with particular force to policy concerns. Proper evaluation of outcomes requires detailed information about conduct, market structure, entry constraints, intersectoral links, and the like; we need more empirical studies designed to reveal this information. Such studies, as in the past, will also help to identify weaknesses in the theory and point out directions for future research. In any case, since (a) the information needed for a successful policy design is not available; (b) the policy recommendations are very sensitive to this information; and (c) the "calibration" studies indicate that good policies improve welfare only slightly; free trade remains a good rule of thumb—the more so given retaliation, the competitive pressure of a free trading world system, and the political economy of protection.

References

Arrow, Kenneth J. 1962. "The Economic Implications of Learning by Doing." *Review of Economic Studies* 29: 155–73.

Balassa, Bela. 1967. *Trade Liberalization among Industrial Countries*. New York: McGraw-Hill.

———. 1986. "Intra-Industry Specialization: A Cross-Country Analysis." *European Economic Review* 30: 27–42.

Baldwin, Robert E. 1969. "The Case Against Infant-Industry Protection." *Journal of Political Economy* 77: 295–305.

Bhagwati, Jagdish N. 1965. "On the Equivalence of Tariffs and Quotas." In Robert E. Baldwin and others, eds., *Trade, Growth and the Balance of Payments: Essays in Honor of Gottfried Haberler*. Chicago: Rand McNally.

Brander, James A., and Barbara J. Spencer. 1984. "Tariff Protection and Imperfect Competition." In Henryk Kierzkowski, ed., *Monopolistic Competition and International Trade*. Oxford, England: Blackwell.

———. 1985. "Export Subsidies and Market Share Rivalry." *Journal of International Economics* 18: 83–100.

Cooper, Russell, and Andrew Jones. 1988."Coordinating Coordination Failures in Keynesian Models." *Quarterly Journal of Economics* 103: 441–63.

Davidson, Carl. 1984. "Cartel Stability and Tariff Policy." *Journal of International Economics* 17: 219–37.

Diamond, Peter. 1982. "Aggregate Demand Management in Search Equilibrium." *Journal of Political Economy* 90: 881–94.

Dixit, Avinash K. 1984. "International Trade Policy for Oligopolistic Industries." *Economic Journal* (Supplement) 94: 1–16. Reprinted in Jagdish Bhagwati, ed., *International Trade: Selected Readings*. Cambridge, Mass.: MIT Press, 2d ed., 1987.

Dixit, Avinash K., and Gene M. Grossman. 1986. "Targeted Export Promotion with Several Oligopolistic Industries." *Journal of International Economics* 21: 233–50.

Dixit, Avinash K., and A. S. Kyle. 1985. "The Use of Protection and Subsidies for Entry Promotion and Deterrence." *American Economic Review* 75: 139–52.

Dixit, Avinash K., and Joseph E. Stiglitz. 1977. "Monopolistic Competition and Optimum Product Diversity." *American Economic Review* 67: 297–308.

Dollar, David. 1986. "Technological Innovation, Capital Mobility, and the Product Cycle in the North-South Trade." *American Economic Review* 76: 177–90.

Drazen, Allan. 1985. "State Dependence in Optimal Factor Accumulation." *Quarterly Journal of Economics* 100: 357–72.

Drazen, Allan, and Nils Gottfries. 1987. "Seniority Rules and the Persistence of Unemployment in a Dynamic Optimizing Model." Institute for International Economic Studies Seminar Paper 387. Stockholm.

Eaton, Jonathan, and Gene M. Grossman. 1986. "Optimal Trade and Industrial Policy under Oligopoly." *Quarterly Journal of Economics* 101: 383–406. Reprinted in Jagdish Bhagwati, ed., *International Trade: Selected Readings*. Cambridge, Mass.: MIT Press, 2d ed., 1987.

Ethier, Wilfred J. 1982a. "Decreasing Costs in International Trade and Frank Graham's Argument for Protection." *Econometrica* 50: 1242–68.

———. 1982b. "National and International Returns to Scale in the Modern Theory of International Trade." *American Economic Review* 72: 389–405.

Flam, Harry, and Elhanan Helpman. 1987. "Industrial Policy under Monopolistic Competition." *Journal of International Economics* 22: 79–102.

Graham, Frank D. 1923. "Some Aspects of Protection Further Considered." *Quarterly Journal of Economics* 37: 199–227.

Gros, Daniel. 1987. "A Note on the Optimal Tariff, Retaliation and the Welfare Loss from Tariff Wars in a Framework with Intra-Industry Trade." *Journal of International Economics* 23: 357–67.

Grossman, Gene M., and Elhanan Helpman. 1988. "Product Development and International Trade." National Bureau of Economic Research Working Paper 2540. Cambridge, Mass. Forthcoming in the *Journal of Political Economy*.

———. 1989a. "Comparative Advantage and Long-Run Growth." National Bureau of Economic Research Working Paper 2809. Cambridge, Mass. Forthcoming in *American Economic Review*.

———. 1989b. "Endogenous Product Cycles." Foerder Institute for Economic Research, Working Paper 10-89. Tel Aviv, Israel.

———. 1989c. "Growth and Welfare in a Small Open Economy." Foerder Institute for Economic Research, Working Paper 15-89. Tel Aviv, Israel.

Harris, Richard, and David Cox. 1984. *Trade, Industrial Policy, and Canadian Manufacturing*. Toronto, Canada: Ontario Economic Council.

Havrylyshyn, Oli, and E. Civan. 1984. "Intra-Industry Trade and the State of Development." In P. K. M. Tharakan, ed., *The Economics of Intra-Industry Trade*. Amsterdam: North-Holland.

Helpman, Elhanan. 1984a. "Increasing Returns, Imperfect Markets, and Trade Theory." In Ronald W. Jones and Peter B. Kenen, eds., *Handbook of International Economics*. Vol. 1. Amsterdam: North-Holland.

———. 1984b. "A Simple Theory of International Trade with Multinational Corporations." *Journal of Political Economy* 92: 451–71. Reprinted in Jagdish Bhagwati, ed., *International Trade: Selected Readings*. Cambridge, Mass.: MIT Press, 2d ed., 1987.

———. 1985. "International Trade in Differentiated Middle Products." In Donald Hague and Karl G. Jungenfelt, eds., *Structural Adjustment in Developed Open Economies*. London: Macmillan.

———. 1987. "Imperfect Competition and International Trade: Evidence from Fourteen Industrial Countries." *Journal of the Japanese and International Economies* 1: 62–81. Reprinted in Michael A. Spence and Heather A. Hazar, eds., *International Competitiveness*. Cambridge, Mass.: Ballinger, 1988.

———. 1988. "Growth, Technological Progress and Trade." *Empirica* [Austrian Economic Papers] 15: 5–25.

———. 1989. "Monopolistic Competition in Trade Theory." Frank Graham Memorial Lecture, 1989. Special Paper 16, International Finance Section, Princeton University. Princeton, N.J.

Helpman, Elhanan, and Paul R. Krugman. 1985. *Market Structure and Foreign Trade*. Cambridge, Mass.: MIT Press.

———. 1989. *Trade Policy and Market Structure*. Cambridge, Mass.: MIT Press.

Horstman, Ignatius, and James R. Markusen. 1986. "Up the Average Cost Curve: Inefficient Entry and the New Protectionism." *Journal of International Economics* 20: 225–47.

Jensen, Richard, and Marie Thursby. 1986. "A Strategic Approach to the Product Life Cycle." *Journal of International Economics* 21: 269–84.

———. 1987. "A Decision Theoretic Model of Innovation, Technology Transfer and Trade." *Review of Economic Studies* 54: 631–49.

Krishna, Kala. 1988a. "The Case of the Vanishing Revenues: Auction Quotas with Monopoly." Harvard University. Cambridge, Mass. Processed.

———. 1988b. "The Case of the Vanishing Revenues: Auction Quotas with Oligopoly." Harvard University. Cambridge, Mass. Processed.

Krugman, Paul R. 1979. "A Model of Innovation, Technology Transfer, and the World Distribution of Income." *Journal of Political Economy* 87: 253–66.

———. 1987. "The Narrow Moving Band, The Dutch Disease and the Competitive Consequences of Mrs. Thatcher: Notes on Trade in the Presence of Dynamic Scale Economies." *Journal of Development Economics* 27: 41–55.

———. 1989. "History vs. Expectations." Massachusetts Institute of Technology. Cambridge, Mass. Processed.

Leamer, Edward. 1984. *Sources of Comparative Advantages*. Cambridge, Mass.: MIT Press.

Linnemann, Hans. 1966. *An Econometric Study of International Trade Flows*. Amsterdam: North-Holland.

Lucas, Robert E., Jr. 1988. "On the Mechanics of Economic Development." *Journal of Monetary Economics* 22: 3–42.

Markusen, James R. 1988. "Specialized Intermediate Inputs and Derationalizing Tariffs." London, Canada: University of Western Ontario. Processed.

Murphy, Kevin M., Andrei Shleifer, and Robert Vishny. 1988. "Industrialization and the Big Push." National Bureau of Economic Research Working Paper 2708. Cambridge, Mass.

Romer, Paul M. 1986. "Increasing Returns and Long-Run Growth." *Journal of Political Economy* 94: 1002–37.

———. 1988. "Endogenous Technological Change." University of Chicago. Processed. Forthcoming in *Journal of Political Economy*.

Rotemberg, Julio J., and Garth Saloner. Forthcoming. "Tariffs vs. Quotas with Implicit Collusion." *Canadian Journal of Economics*.

Shibata, Hirofumi. 1968. "A Note on the Equivalence of Tariffs and Quotas." *American Economic Review* 58: 137–42.

Shleifer, Andrei. 1986. "Implementation Cycles." *Journal of Political Economy* 94: 1163–90.

Tirole, Jean. 1988. *The Theory of Industrial Organization*. Cambridge, Mass.: MIT Press.

Venables, Anthony J. 1987. "Trade and Trade Policy with Differentiated Products: A Chamberlinian-Ricardian Model." *Economic Journal* 97: 700–17.

Vernon, Raymond. 1966. "International Investment and International Trade in the Product Cycle." *Quarterly Journal of Economics* 80: 190–207.

Comment on "The Noncompetitive Theory of International Trade and Trade Policy," by Helpman

T. N. Srinivasan

Roughly a decade ago some perceptive trade theorists saw an intellectual arbitraging opportunity in applying developments in industrial organization to the theory of international trade and policy. Pioneer arbitrageurs, including Professor Helpman, reaped handsome returns by imaginatively combining insights of industrial organization and traditional factor proportions theory to explain such stylized facts as intraindustry trade, trade between countries with similar factor endowments, and a positive correlation between country size and volume of trade.

Their new theory suggested a more active role for government policy in trade. In some cases it appeared to provide an intellectually respectable economic argument for such not-so-respectable policies as protection. Those die-hard development economists who were loath to give up their intellectual investment in an inward-oriented development strategy—despite mounting evidence of its failure—latched on to the new theory in hopes of salvaging their intellectual investment.

Professor Helpman, in the manner that we have all come to expect from him, has given us a balanced, masterful survey of this literature without making any exaggerated claims for it. Since he is unlikely to make an analytical error, there is nothing that I can criticize about the internal logic of his models. I propose instead to place the inward-oriented-based theory in the perspective of traditional trade theory; to emphasize the extreme fragility of its conclusions and their lack of robustness; to point out the inherent conceptual and econometric problems that arise when you try giving the theory empirical content, or use calibration-cum-simulation methods to evaluate empirically alternative strategic policy interventions; and to argue that the fragile policy conclusions are likely to be of limited relevance to developing countries.

To begin with, almost all the problems analyzed by new trade theory have their counterparts in traditional theory: increasing returns, monopoly power, intraindustry trade, multiple equilibriums, and even the possibility that countries with access to identical technology, identical factor endowments, and identical tastes may trade in equilibrium. Traditional theory analyzes increasing returns

T. N. Srinivasan is a professor of economics at Yale University.

© 1990 The International Bank for Reconstruction and Development / THE WORLD BANK.

in a competitive equilibrium among atomistic firms and consumers by postulating that scale economies are external to a firm but internal to an industry. Similarly, market power exists only at the national level. Because firms do not perceive scale economies or national market power, they cannot reflect them in their profit maximizing decisions. A policy intervention in the form of an appropriate subsidy, tax, or tariff ensures that external scale economies or markets are reflected in the profit maximizing calculus internal to the firm. Put another way, policy in effect makes firms do what they cannot do by themselves. Traditional theorists also recognize that one government's intervention may invite retaliation by other governments. Three decades ago Harry Johnson explicitly modeled a Nash tariff policy equilibrium in a two-government world. Subsequent writers have extended his analysis to quotas.

The new theory postulates increasing returns at the firm level and hence has to consider noncompetitive market structures and equilibria. In the small group case, oligopolistic firms that perceive their market power will behave strategically. Nevertheless they may not be able to precommit themselves credibly to actions that will improve their profits given other firms' reactions. Government policy intervention in such cases achieves what the firms cannot credibly do by themselves. Once again reaction to one government's policy intervention by other governments has to be allowed for. The new theory explicitly analyzes the issues of time consistency and credibility, issues that are either irrelevant or are not raised in traditional theory. But that under these circumstances free trade is not optimal, and that suitable intervention can improve welfare over free trade, is not a particularly novel conclusion nor unique to the new theory.

The new theory explains intraindustry trade in terms of product differentiation and increasing scale economies. The traditional explanation for intraindustry trade is to trace it to one or more of three problems: aggregation over commodities, over space, or over time. Obviously, if the level of aggregation of commodities in defining an industry is high, even though two countries exchange commodities that are different at a disaggregated level, the exchange will show up as intraindustry trade in the aggregate statistics. A large country may export and import the same commodity because it is cheaper to export its production at one end of the country rather than transport and sell it to the other end where it may be cheaper to import it from abroad. Similarly, within a year a country may export a commodity in one season and import it in another. I am not entirely persuaded that, after careful disaggregation, much of what is shown in statistics as intraindustry trade will be left to explain.

The possibility of multiple equilibria in models involving nonconvexities is well-known. Let me take just two textbook examples from traditional theory. Given scale economies or externalities at an industry level, the production possibility curve of the economy may include convex and concave stretches, and multiple competitive equilibria are possible. What is more, under such circumstances it is easy to depict an equilibrium with nonzero trade between two identical countries because each is producing at a different production point even though they face the same prices. In a dynamic context, more than thirty years ago Solow showed in his famous growth model paper that if the production function is not concave, multiple steady state equilibria are possible given the same saving rate—some of which are stable, and to which the economy will converge, given the appropriate initial condition. Even an argument based on the Solow model for "big push" in savings and investment can be found in the development literature. Although hysteresis and multiple equilibria in the new theory are based on different dynamics, qualitatively the results are similar.

Let me turn now to the policy implications of the new theory. Professor Helpman points out that one of the major implications of the new theory is the need for a case-by-case approach. This is somewhat understated. In fact the policy conclusions are extremely fragile and unrobust to changes in the oligopolistic model: not only the levels at which policy instruments are set but even their signs can be changed by changes in modeling. Take the partial equilibrium, duopoly model in which the home and foreign firms have no domestic sales but compete only in the third market. Under the same set of assumptions about demands, costs, and foreign government nonintervention, if each firm has consistent conjectures about the other's response to its change in sales, optimal policy is laissez-faire. If the conjectures are Cournot, the optimal policy is an output subsidy; if the conjectures are Bertrand, the optimal policy is a tax. This lack of robustness points to the need in devising policy for empirical work on the structure of competition in the industry.

Before I turn to the empirical issues, let me point out that this literature rarely takes on board an important insight of the theory of distortions and the second best: that a policy that is optimal in the presence of a single distortion—say, a noncompetitive structure in the market for one good—need not be optimal when several other distortions are present. It goes without saying that no economy in the world, developed or developing, is characterized by a single distortion. Indeed, traditional theory has analyzed trade policy in the context of several distortions, especially factor market distortions.

A number of conceptual and econometric issues arise in attempting empirical work in this area. Conceptually, many of the game-theoretic formulations of strategic policy choice assume common knowledge among participants about payoffs, strategic space, and the like. That is to say, each participant knows the others' payoffs, the others know his payoffs, he knows that the others know his payoffs, others know that he knows their payoffs, and so on ad infinitum. In my view, common knowledge is what is called in Sanskrit *Swayam Bhava* or self-being—it comes to existence by itself. There is no process by which common knowledge can come about. It has to be viewed as an untested and untestable hypothesis.

Leaving this thorny issue aside, econometrically speaking the Lucas critique applies with great force in this context: if, before formulating policy, the necessary parameters (other than the so-called deep ones relating to technology and taste) are estimated, those parameters are virtually useless for policy change because they are by definition dependent on existing policy. Even if the Lucas critique is ignored, one has to recognize that the relevant market structure has to be part of the model specification if the estimated parameters are to be used. It is not easy to infer the strategies and responses that oligopolistic firms are using for collecting data on market outcomes.

Another empirical problem is that what constitutes an industry for the purpose of analysis is debatable, since the elasticities of substitution both for supply and demand can be substantial between products produced by different industries under any classification. What does fee entry—or for that matter, absence of entry—mean in such a context? Once again this problem was recognized long ago. Soon after Chamberlin published his *Monopolistic Competition*, Triffin (1940) examined it in a general equilibrium context. Those who avoid full-blown econometric estimates but use the so-called literature-based estimates of some parameters, while choosing others to calibrate their model to reproduce a given data set, also encounter serious problems, because there are many ways to choose the parameters for which literature estimates are to be used and those that are to be calibrated. And this choice can drastically alter the policy recommendations, as Kala Krishna recently showed by reexamining an earlier calibration exercise of Avinash Dixit (Krishna, Swagel, and Hogan, forthcoming).

As for the relevance of the new theory to development, Professor Helpman rightly noted that in neoclassical growth theory of the 1960s, the steady state growth rate of the economy equals the natural rate of growth of labor force and the rate of labor augmenting technical progress. But both these rates were assumed to be exogenous, not because there was any compelling empirical evidence to support the assumption, but because the economic determinants of fertility and technical progress, theoretical and empirical, were not well established. Considerable progress has been made since then, particularly about changes in fertility. It is fair to say that the determinants of technical progress are still unsettled. Despite considerable progress in formalizing Schumpeter's theory of innovation and market structure and testing it empirically with data from developed countries, no strong support has emerged either for or against the Schumpeterian hypothesis.

Long ago, in the framework of a neoclassical optimal growth model of an open economy, Bardhan (1970) introduced learning by doing à la Arrow. Because, except for this externality, Bardhan's model was of a small, open, competitive economy, strategic policy intervention as such did not arise. In this respect the new theory is richer.

But how important learning or, for that matter, scale economies are relative to global market demand is an empirical issue. For example, Benhabib and Jovanovic (1989) reexamined the aggregate data for the United States for the postwar period on growth of output, labor, and capital and found that the data were consistent with the absence of externalities and increasing returns to scale. Anecdotal evidence suggests that learning effects are important, but rigorous econometric studies showing economically significant learning effects are almost nonexistent. The Indian passenger automobile industry began assembling cars more than four decades ago, for example. One of the firms that began manufacturing cars (and still produces them) was established at roughly the same time as Toyota. As recently as ten years ago India was producing more passenger cars than the Republic of Korea. Yet until the entry of Suzuki was allowed recently, the industry was stagnant. There is not much evidence of learning associated with cumulative output in this industry in India! Korea, however, has achieved a significant toehold in the U.S. auto market. It seems that an industry established and nurtured by policy, heavily protected from competition from imports and from entry by other domestic firms, is not likely to generate much learning.

It is dangerously simplistic, because markets in many developing countries appear to be oligopolistic, to decide that the policy conclusions of the new theory apply. First, many of these oligopolies are creations of inappropriate public policy and not the result of increasing returns or externalities in production. Second, the capacity of governments to gather information, arrive at appropriate policies, and implement them—without at the same time unleashing resource-wasting rent seeking—is extremely limited. And the character of appropriate policies can change drastically depending on whether rent seeking is significant or not. Social welfare may be higher without government intervention than with possibly inappropriate intervention. It is therefore essential to take explicit account of a country's policymaking and rent-seeking realities. The new theory has yet to take this step, and until it does the traditional arguments for limited or no intervention in trade will remain unchallenged.

References

Bardhan, Pranab K. 1970. *Economic Growth, Development and Foreign Trade: A Study in Pure Theory.* New York: Wiley-Interscience.

Benhabib, Jess, and Boyan Jovanovic. 1989. "Growth Accounting and Externalities." Working Paper 80-10. New York: C. V. Starr Center for Applied Economics, New York University.

Krishna, Kala, Phillip Swagel, and Kathleen Hogan. 1989. *The Non-Optimality of Optimal Trade Policies: The U.S. Automobile Industry Revisited.* Working Paper. Cambridge, Mass.: National Bureau of Economic Research.

Triffin, Robert. 1940. *Monopolistic Competition and General Equilibrium Theory.* Cambridge, Mass.: Harvard University Press.

Comment on "The Noncompetitive Theory of International Trade and Trade Policy," by Helpman

Nancy Barry

When Dennis de Tray asked me to participate in this session I had to ask myself why. I've come to the conclusion that it is because of my well-known capabilities as a troublemaker and perhaps to provide some comic relief but certainly not because of my known competence as a theoretician of either the old or the new trade policy. Perhaps it is also because I am one of a number of people in this room that have been mucking about with these issues over the last fifteen years in at least fifteen countries: issues of industry, trade, and finance. So perhaps I can make some remarks about the relevance of the new trade theory. So as not to disappoint Dennis, these comments will be cantankerous and heretical and do not represent his views or those of the World Bank.

I have reviewed the new trade theory, including the paper that is being discussed today, and I find overall that the *new* trade theory seems to be a timid departure from the *old* trade theory. Most of it appears to be tinkering with the two-by-two-by-two model, usually one assumption at a time. As such, I do not find the new trade theory to be particularly better at simulating realities, predicting performance, or prescribing policy.

I also find the new trade theory literature somewhat disappointing. It seems to be a set of tremendous talents talking to each other—rather than getting closer to the realities that are being faced in both developed and developing countries. I would like to talk about a few of those realities because I think the purpose of this seminar is to deal efficiently with growth and development in the Bank's member countries.

I think it is clear that OECD countries are rapidly liberalizing everything but trade. It is also clear that most trade is taking place among *like* countries. And it is clear that a tremendous amount of game playing is taking place, with strategic alliances being formed among the main players, who recognize how much needs to be invested in research and development and how development costs quickly reap the benefits. The concept of a production function is rapidly disappearing, given rapid technology change.

The other phenomenon that seems obvious is that the real success stories of the 1980s are Japan, the Republic of Korea, and Taiwan. We may try to rewrite

Nancy Barry is chief of the Industry Development Division in the Industry and Energy Department of the World Bank.

© 1990 The International Bank for Reconstruction and Development / THE WORLD BANK.

that history, but it is clear these economies have several things in common. And one of them is that they have been factor endowment makers—not factor endowment takers. They have really sat down and said, "Where is the world going to be in the year 2000, where do we want to be in that world, and what are the pieces that we don't have that we need to get?" And that type of thinking has been in the context of using international competitiveness, present and future, as the litmus test. The strategies pursued place the East Asians apart from other developing economies—not in the level of government intervention but in the purposes of that intervention.

Now, looking at the realities of our member countries, the developing countries—be they the poorest of the poor or the next-in-line newly industrializing countries—it seems that most countries have got themselves tied in terrible knots—which means that a free trade model is not terribly informative, and that most of these countries are not in a position to do strategic game playing.

In fact, it could be argued that most countries that the Bank works in have developed comparative advantage in backing the losers. So the concept of trying to pick winners—where you have a convergence of vested interests in the public sector, business as usual in the private sector, and insulation from the dynamic processes—has very real risks.

What seems to matter in these settings? Clearly, competition matters, and progress on that front—trade liberalization, deregulation, or unraveling of all the subsectoral incentives that create rigidities and inability to respond to change—is urgently needed.

It is also clear that building capabilities matters. I have a hard time believing on a commonsense basis that we can really say that learning does not matter. What the whole East Asian experience has been about is learning, entering global markets at the low end, moving up, and taking advantages of the learning which comes with playing in the global market.

It is also clear that dynamic processes matter and that within those processes, organizations and people—the created endowments—increasingly explain who is competitive. In our research work we need to give a lot more attention to those functions.

In my view, therefore, what we should not do over the next ten years, in research and policy work, is try to figure out to what extent the new trade theory or the old trade theory applies to developing countries. We should not try to squeeze data and realities into theoretical models. We need to focus on how to unravel all of the ties that are binding our client countries; on how to combine these incentives for competition and competitiveness with the building of endowments; and on how to deal with the transitional issues—that it is less important whether you think that free trade or strategic trade is the ideal than how you get out of the mess you are in now. And we need to focus on how countries and companies get on the bandwagon of one thing leads to another—human resource development, catalysts, direct foreign investment—how countries can be in as opposed to out of what is admittedly a very unfair global game.

I agree that the last portion of Professor Helpman's discussion is potentially the most interesting because what we are really dealing with in all of our countries is market takers, technology takers, but potential endowment makers. I think that the Bank needs to understand and deal in the "missing middle"—not in firm size but in thinking about innovation systems, of closing the gap even between best and worst practice within a country.

So I am advocating that in the next five years we deal much more with the how tos—how to promote effective competition policies, capability buildup programs, and commercial links in countries at different levels of development.

Floor Discussion of Helpman Paper

Observing that it would be as unfair to take credit for all the developments in strategic trade theory in the last ten years as it would be to take the blame for them, Helpman began the discussion by responding to the panelists. He could understand Barry's (discussant) feeling that the literature was doing too little too late, and he would be the first to admit that the answers they had come up with were unsatisfactory, but, he argued, they were working in the directions she indicated. Strategic trade theorists were focusing on the very elements she had highlighted—acquired comparative advantage, dynamic competition, learning by doing, and so on.

After concurring with Srinivasan's (discussant) point about the fragility of the policy conclusions—indeed, this was a central point in Krugman's and his recent book on trade policy—Helpman observed that the fragile empirical content was not unique to the new trade theories but applied to economics in general. Conclusions depend on assumptions about conduct, and economists do not know how to pinpoint precisely behavior in a particular industry. For example, with calibration models, using the data and parameters we have, we assume one type of conduct and adjust the remaining parameters to fit the data. If we change our assumptions about conduct, we get a different remaining set of parameters, and we calculate different answers to our policy experiments. Does that mean economists should abandon their work and go home? Presumably not. It means more work is needed. Srinivasan countered that to apply the conclusions of strategic trade policy one needed far more information than one needed to apply traditional trade theory.

Responding to Srinivasan's comment about the need for common knowledge, Helpman responded that it really does not matter much. He agreed that going through the process Srinivasan described in his panel comments, one would discover that common knowledge is a stringent requirement, but he would argue that without assuming common knowledge the analytical problems would be even more severe.

Nor did Helpman consider the problem of externalities and spillovers as cited by Srinivasan unique to trade policy. It occurs also in public finance, urban economics, rural development, and so on. Data in recent studies, he felt, point to spillovers and externalities explicitly related to technology. Was this enough for the new trade theories? Probably not. But both theoretical and empirical

---

This session was chaired by Heba Handoussa, professor of economics, American University in Cairo.

© 1990 The International Bank for Reconstruction and Development / THE WORLD BANK.

work were lacking, and it was too early to rule all of this out of hand.

Finally, Helpman disagreed that there was nothing new in the new trade theories. However, he also did not argue that these developments broke entirely with tradition; he had worked hard to show continuity.

Referring to the debate between the new and old theories as a Jekyll and Hyde phenomenon, a participant said Helpman was the Dr. Jekyll in this case because his paper was so logical and precise. This was not true of everyone who tried to persuade the U.S. Congress that finally we have invented a new argument for protection and export promotion. He argued that this was not the first argument for protection—it was simply an important extension of older arguments. In confining his attention to noncompetitive product markets, Helpman had ignored the huge literature (from development economics) on factor market imperfections, sector-specific minimum wages, sticky wages, generalized sticky wages, and wage differentials—all of which apply to imperfect competition. He felt that by concentrating only on noncompetitive product markets Helpman understated the case for appropriate intervention. Helpman agreed that there were many other arguments for protection—but explained that he was asked to discuss only this particular line of research.

The participant also felt Helpman had neglected the institutional side of the problem. In presenting the case for intervention, economists should also consider the solid empirical and theoretical work done on commercial policy, rent-seeking, and tariff formation. Recommendations for intervention, in other words, should be qualified by indicating not only what they might capture, but also what possible wrong outcomes might ensue. He particularly urged the World Bank to view the theory in its entirety, not just compare the old and new.

Helpman was asked if he had general recommendations. On balance, did he feel there should be a free trade orientation, with some exceptions made according to simple decision rules? Or should we introduce a blanket policy of import substitution and let people argue for free trade on a case-by-case basis? The participant emphasized the importance of investigating what happens when you actually use strategic trade policy.

Helpman responded unequivocally to the question of policy recommendation. Krugman and he, in the last chapter of their recent book, conclude that given current knowledge about strategic trade policy—or general trade policy built on market imperfections—the best bet is not to intervene, for two reasons. First, the policy conclusions of the new theories are still fragile. Second, empirical or semiempirical studies that evaluate the consequences of optimal strategic trade policy have come up with small potential gains from those policies in the framework of calibration models using existing parametric estimates. In other words, one stood to gain little, but if one made a serious mistake, one could lose a lot.

Pursuing the question further, a participant asked Helpman to be as specific as he could about the sorts of policy conclusions he thought this literature might yield when all the empirical work he called for was done, ten or fifteen years from now. For example, one sort of policy conclusion might be that government should have a discrete, ever-changing policy for each significant industry (as had already happened with civil aviation). A second policy conclusion might be that one needs a general sort of policy rule but that the way it operates should change. Citing antidumping measures as a policy system designed largely to deal with strategic trade concerns, he asked how Helpman might design a strategic policy in the future to deal with the perceived problem of dumping. To this specific query about antidumping measures, Helpman responded that in his view the current models that support such measures are far more fragile than the others, because all the arguments rely on market segmentation supposedly brought about by the behavior of firms, and Helpman did not believe this was a reasonable description.

Another participant asked what process Helpman could imagine that would give both the rule by which you could decide on an intervention and at the same time insulate it from the political process. Many countries are persuaded to lower tariffs, but when they try, those who are adversely affected by the tariff protection find five thousand good reasons not to lower it.

Concurring with most of the views expressed by previous participants, Srinivasan felt that it was important to set up institutions and transparent rules that were as politically unmanipulable as possible, rather than deal with trade policy on a case-by-case, discretionary basis. For example, he considered strengthening multilateral trade arrangements through the Uruguay Round negotiations more important than any gains from unilateral actions of the Super 301 type introduced by the recent U.S. trade legislation, for which the new trade theory seemed to be providing a rationale. Generally, Srinivasan found that this literature assumed the oligopolistic or noncompetitive market structure as given, and then looked to see how a nation could benefit from the structure—rather than question whether the international structure itself could be changed. He regretted the tendency in U.S. trade policy to relax antitrust laws, permit mergers and acquisitions, and promote what earlier would have been considered noncompetitive behavior—in order to give U.S. firms competitive advantage in the rest of the world. It seemed to Srinivasan that one should, on the contrary, extend the antitrust laws globally rather than relax them domestically to gain perceived advantages in international competition.

A participant said he would like to raise a very specific question about the allocation of quotas. In his discussion of tariffs and quotas in the context of the new theories, Helpman had seemed to draw conclusions regardless of how quotas were allocated. It seemed to the participant that the method of allocating quotas would affect the degree of competition. The Japanese, for example, assign their beef quotas to the producers' cooperatives, which have monopoly power in Japan.

Another participant pleaded with trade theorists and empirical economists to use less technical jargon and make their results more transparent, so that policy and country analysts could have an effective policy dialogue with developing countries on the new developments in trade policy. He then asked the panel if, in line with what Singh had said in his keynote address, new capital-intensive and skill-intensive technologies and the extensive use of nontariff barriers and strategic alliances had rendered obsolete the operational notion of comparative advantage, even for such traditionally labor-intensive products as textiles. How should we apply the notion of "new comparative advantage"? Can we replace the "old" notion of comparative advantage with something else, or should economists simply fly by the seat of their pants in discussing trade policy?

Barry responded that technological change, particularly in electronics, is making traditional concepts of comparative advantage increasingly obsolete. In mature industries (automotive, textiles and garments) and in the "high-tech" industries, it is changing the entire definition of a product and dramatically increasing the possible combinations of factor use and the importance of the transformation of process technology itself. Scale economies no longer matter so much on the shop floor. Technological change requires a different kind of organization within the company, of everything from sourcing to distribution. The whole system is a product, and the issues of technology accumulation and learning make it ill-suited to modeling.

Helpman agreed that economists must look beyond traditional comparative advantage. The new trade policy literature, he felt, does exactly that. He concurred with a point made earlier about rent-seeking behavior, which he thought was even more important for Schumpeterian dynamic competition and strategic trade.

In response to the broad question about the overall policy message of strategic trade theories raised by several participants, Helpman said that the more forceful global competition is, the less room it leaves for single-economy trade policy. On average, this works in everyone's interest, because it typically reduces market power in every country—and therefore reduces the price-cost margin globally. This is good from an international point of view, so economists should try not to segment economies and isolate them from international markets. At this stage it seems reasonable to recommend a global approach, with global competition and little intervention. In any international system, however, a prisoner's dilemma situation could arise—where it is good for everybody to adopt one policy, but if everybody does, it pays one country to deviate. Therefore, it may well be that a good case for intervention could be made in some isolated industries—in which research and development are important and there are externalities within the industry, or across industries, or over time. The intervention need not be in trade policy, however. With research and development (R&D) competition, for example, the best policy might be to subsidize R&D or provide venture capital.

The Policy Response of Agriculture

Hans Binswanger

In assessing the response of agricultural production to government policies, it is necessary to look not just at output prices but at all the factors that affect real farm profits; to disentangle the effects on individual (or export) crops from the effects on aggregate output; and to distinguish the short-run aggregate response from the long-run. Individual crops respond strongly to price factors, but growth in one crop usually takes resources away from others. The price elasticity of agriculture overall is very low in the short run because the main factors of production—land, capital, and labor—are fixed. Aggregate output can grow only if more resources are devoted to agriculture or if technology changes. Output is also affected by investments in roads, markets, irrigation, infrastructure, education, and health. Research and extension increase the demand for fertilizer. As for adjustment policy: domestic food supply may not increase rapidly in response to adjustment programs, so structural adjustment programs should do more than ease the balance of payments; analysis should focus on how to make all of agriculture grow.

The policy response of agriculture has been primarily addressed in the supply response literature. Because much of agricultural price policy is made on a commodity by commodity basis, the supply response literature has concentrated on the short- and long-run supply response of individual crops to changes in (relative) output and input prices. Reviews of this literature can be found in Askari and Cummings (1976, 1977) and Bond (1983). Adjusting relative prices among farm outputs and relative to farm inputs can lead to important efficiency gains.

With the rising importance of structural adjustment, however, changes are often contemplated in the entire agricultural price regime. These changes would eliminate urban bias in the terms of trade by devaluing currency and by dismantling the structure of industrial protection. Recent studies have shown that in many developing countries indirect discrimination against agriculture via overvalued exchange rates and industrial protection is quantitatively more important than commodity-specific direct policy intervention (Krueger, Schiff, and Valdés 1988). In analyzing the response to dismantling indirect discrimination,

Hans Binswanger is chief of the Agriculture Operations Division in the Latin America and Caribbean Country Department 2 of the World Bank. He is indebted to Eileen Hanlon for developing the tables and figures and helping him write the paper. Bruce Ross-Larson edited the conference version.

© 1990 The International Bank for Reconstruction and Development / THE WORLD BANK.

it is the response of broad agricultural aggregates to the policy changes that must be examined, rather than that of individual crops. Although there are perhaps thousands of individual commodity studies, the literature on the short- and long-term response of aggregate agricultural output to price changes is small. For recent reviews of this sparse literature, see Mundlak, Cavallo, and Domenech 1988; Chhibber 1988a, 1988b; and Bond 1983. Other aggregates that must be evaluated under structural adjustment are the performance of agricultural exports and of domestic food production; for these the literature is even thinner.

A common mistake in policy analysis is to extrapolate from the short-run effects of policy changes on the production of individual crops (or small groups of crops) to the long-run effects on aggregate output. The tendency surfaces in observations of the impressive possibilities for rice, or for maize, or for tree crops, or for some other agricultural product—and in the accumulation of those observations as evidence of the impressive (and immediate) possibilities for all agriculture. The land isn't so kind. Individual crops do respond strongly to price factors. This responsiveness shows up in crop elasticities that are fairly high— and higher in the long run than the short run. But growth in one crop usually takes resources away from other crops. So the price elasticity of all agriculture is very low in the short run. The problem is that the main factors of agricultural production—land, capital, and labor—are fixed in the short run.

Unlike individual crops, aggregate agricultural output can grow only if more resources are devoted to agriculture or if technology changes. The literature shows convincingly that the long-run response of agriculture is large: higher prices will slow migration out of rural areas and increase investment in agriculture. But these responses take time to develop fully—as much as ten to twenty years. They also depend greatly on public investments in roads, markets, irrigation, infrastructure, education, and health.

In addition to the prices of agricultural inputs and outputs, real farm profits are influenced by numerous factors such as the cost and accessibility of consumer goods, farm subsidies and taxes, research, extension, road infrastructure, and services such as marketing or credit. The response of individual crops to some of these factors—research and extension, for example—has been widely studied (Huffman and Evenson, forthcoming; Birkhaeuser, Evenson, and Feder 1988). Again, however, the literature on the response of aggregate output to these factors is very sparse (exceptions are Antle 1983 and Krishna 1982). Yet adjustment policies often require large cuts in public expenditures, which may affect spending for research, extension, infrastructure, or agricultural credit. The impact of such changes on aggregate output is therefore of major importance.

Although the response of individual crops to price changes remains an important tool of policy analysis, there are few controversies in the literature on that topic; this literature will therefore not be reviewed here. Instead, this paper begins by looking at why agriculture's aggregate response to price changes is small in the short run, and what this means for structural adjustment programs. After positing that the long-run response of agriculture to policy changes can be substantial, the paper reviews recent studies of aggregate supply response with respect to public investment, research, and extension. The conclusion spells out the implications of these findings for the adjustment programs of World Bank clients.

I. Why the Aggregate Response to Price Changes Is Small in the Short Run

Individual crops respond strongly to price factors—a response that is well known. Reviews by Askari and Cummings (1976, 1977) show that one-year elasticities for individual crops can be high and that they vary depending on the characteristics of the crops or regions. (By contrast, livestock supply elasticities are usually negative in the first year, as farmers respond to high prices by first building up their herds (Reutlinger 1963). But the response of an individual crop to price changes differs fundamentally from the response of all agriculture, for individual crop production can grow by taking resources from other crops. Farmers can shift land, labor, fertilizer, and irrigation water from wheat to rice without raising their total farm output. And what is true for a farm is true for a country or region. Aggregate production can increase only if more resources are devoted to agriculture or if technical change is introduced.

The difference between individual and aggregate elasticities is a standard microeconomic lesson that World Bank staff too often ignore. The lesson is that the aggregate agricultural supply response can be very low even if individual crop responses are fairly high. Bapna, Binswanger, and Quizon (1984) estimated the short-run (one-year) elasticities for individual crops from a poor agroclimatic subregion in India: the results ranged from 0.25 to 0.77 for the main crop, sorghum. But when an elasticity matrix is used to estimate the supply elasticity of all agricultural output (see the matrix and formula in table 1), the result is only 0.05. Bapna and his associates also directly estimated an aggregate supply elasticity for a larger region, which included the subregion for which the elasticity matrix is shown. They found an aggregate elasticity of only 0.09, consistent with the implied elasticity.[1] The figure is also consistent with aggregate short-run price elasticities for various other countries. These fall mostly between 0.05 and 0.25 for the United States, several developing countries, and a cross-country sample of developed and developing countries (table 2). Interestingly, the short-run supply elasticities for Sub-Saharan Africa are no lower than for other areas. Long-run elasticities (using the Nerlove technique) tend to be higher than short-run elasticities, but they are still low.[2]

---

1. It is often believed that poor agroclimatic regions do not respond to price, but the fact that the elasticities for a poor, semiarid, tropical area in India are not much lower than those of the countries listed in table 2, dispels the idea that poor areas do not respond to price changes.

2. The Nerlove technique includes the lagged dependent variables to estimate the long-run elasticities. As argued in the appendix, these long-run elasticities are probably questionable and should not be used for policy analysis. Other econometric issues pertaining to table 2 are discussed in the appendix.

Table 1. *Semi-Arid India: Price Elasticities and Shares of Income by Crop*

	Price of wheat	Price of sorghum	Price of other coarse cereals	Price of chickpeas	Price of other crops	Price of fertilizer	Wages	Share of crop in aggregate crop revenue
Fertilizer	1.48	−1.46	−0.30	−0.46	0.64	0.03	0.08	—
Wheat	☞0.33	−0.35	−0.05	0.03	−0.12	−0.12	0.29	0.19
Sorghum	−0.39	☞0.77	0.06	0.00	−0.26	0.14	−0.32	0.23
Other coarse cereals	−0.14	0.16	☞0.23	−0.48	0.41	0.07	−0.26	0.09
Chickpeas	0.08	0.00	−0.41	☞0.46	−0.14	0.09	−0.08	0.08
Other crops	−0.07	−0.13	0.08	−0.03	☞0.25	−0.03	−0.08	0.41

Implied elasticity of supply of all crops

$$\eta = \sum_i S_i \sum_j \eta_{ij}$$

0.05

η = aggregate supply elasticity with respect to price, S_i = share of crop i in aggregate crop revenue, η_{ij} = elasticity of crop i with respect to price of crop j.

Direct econometric estimate for the elasticity of supply of all crops for a similar region

0.09

— = Not applicable.
Source: Bapna and others (1984).

Table 2. Some Econometric Estimates of Aggregate Agricultural Price Response

Country or region	Short-run estimate	Long-run estimate[a]	Period	Notes
United States	0.05–0.17	0.07–1.09	1920–57	Griliches (1960) (aggregate farm supply)
United States	0.06–0.17	0.10–0.23	1920–57	Griliches (1960) (aggregate crop supply)
Argentina	0.21–0.35	0.42–0.78	1950–74	Reca (1976)
Argentina	0.07	n.a.	1913–84	Cavallo (1988)
India	0.20–0.30	0.30	1952/53–74/75	Krishna (1982)
India	0.28–0.29	n.a.	1954/55–77/78	Chhibber (1988a)
India	0.24	n.a.	1955/56–76/77	Bapna (1981)
Semiarid tropical India	0.09	n.a.	1955/56–73/74	Bapna and others (1984) (uses panel data of districts and within estimators)
India	0.13	n.a.	1961/62–81/82	Binswanger, Khandker, and Rosenzweig (1989) (eliminates simultaneous equation bias, uses panel data of districts and within estimators)

(Table continues on the following page.)

Table 2 *(continued)*

Country or region	Short-run estimate	Long-run estimate[a]	Period	Notes
Ghana	0.20	0.34	1963–81	Bond 1983 for the following African countries and African average
Kenya	0.10	0.16	1963–81	
Côte d'Ivoire	0.13	0.13	1963–81	
Liberia	0.10	0.11	1963–81	
Madagascar	0.10	0.14	1963–81	
Senegal	0.54	0.54	1963–81	
Tanzania	0.15	0.15	1963–81	
Uganda	0.05	0.07	1963–81	
Burkina Faso	0.22	0.24	1963–81	
Average for Sub-Saharan Africa	0.18	0.21	1963–81	
Cross-country	0.06	n.a.	1969–78	Binswanger and others (1987) (crop output supply function, uses panel data of countries and within estimators)

n.a. Not available.
a. See appendix for a methodological discussion of the value of these estimates.

Table 3. United States: The Response of Agriculture to Price Declines in the Depression

Year	Price of agricultural output	Relative farm prices	Agricultural output	Manufactured output	Land planted	Total labor	Wage rates	Power and machinery[a]	Fertilizer used
1929	100	100	100	100	100	100	100	100	100
1930	86	105	98	82	101	99	93	101	103
1931	60	72	107	68	103	99	72	100	79
1932	46	61	104	52	104	98	53	97	55
1933	48	66	96	62	103	97	47	89	61
1934	60	72	81	67	93	97	53	84	70

Note: All figures reindexed so that 1929 = 100.
a. Index with volume in terms of 1935–39 average dollars.
Sources: Johnson (1950) and U.S. Bureau of Census (1945).

Why are the short-run elasticities for all agriculture so low? The main reason is that most factors of agricultural production are fixed in the short run. The amount of land available cannot change without considerable investment; capital increases only over time; and the labor in agriculture can change only through population growth or migration between sectors or regions. Together, land, labor, and capital account for 70 to 85 percent of the cost of agricultural production. And to get a large response, more of these resources must be devoted to agriculture—something difficult in a short period of time. The only factors that can be changed quickly are variable inputs, such as fertilizers and pesticides, and they account for less than 15 to 30 percent of the cost of production.

The reasons for an inelastic short-run response have long been recognized: D. Gale Johnson explained them clearly in 1950 by using the Great Depression, an episode of price decrease (table 3 and figure 1). During the Depression, all commodity prices fell, but agricultural prices fell more rapidly than nonagri-

Figure 1. *Gale Johnson's Classic Explanation of Inelastic Aggregate Agricultural Response*

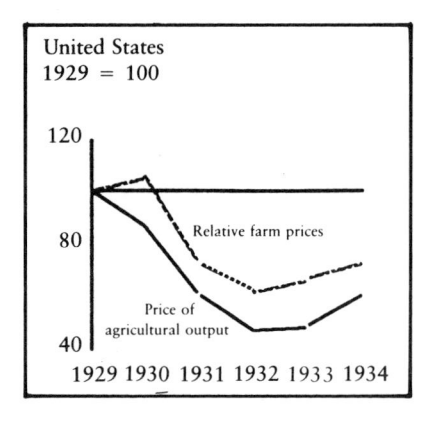

Farm prices declined in both absolute and real terms.

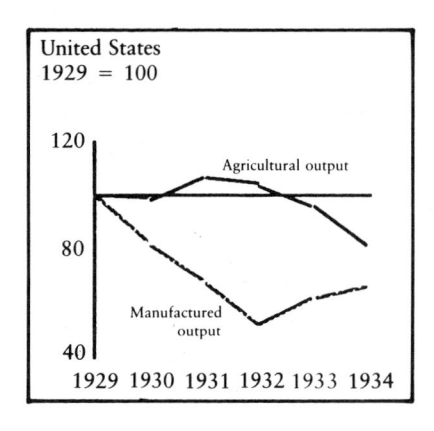

Nevertheless, agricultural output responded more slowly than manufactured output.

Figure 1 *(continued)*

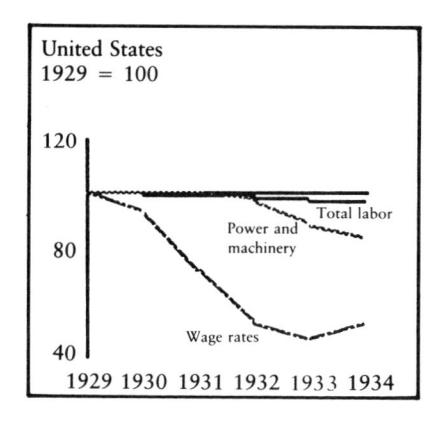

United States 1929 = 100 [chart showing Total labor, Power and machinery, Wage rates from 1929–1934]

Inputs of labor, capital, and machinery either do not decline because their opportunity costs are zero or decline very sharply (as in the case of wages).

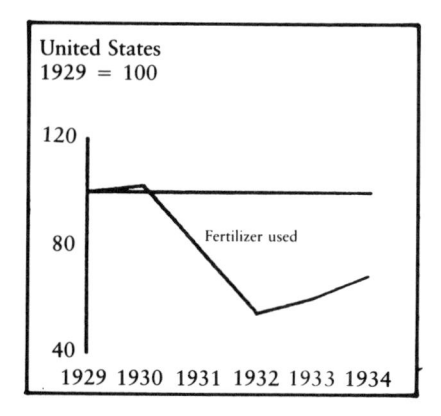

United States 1929 = 100 [chart showing Fertilizer used from 1929–1934]

The only resources that can be adjusted in the short run are purchased inputs such as fertilizers.

Because the share of purchased inputs in total cost was quite low, the supply effect of the change was not large.

Source: Johnson (1950).

cultural prices. Despite the sharp price decline, agricultural output did not fall significantly until about 1934. Manufactured output, by contrast, started to decline in 1930 (and was already increasing by 1933). Labor, power, and machinery in agriculture did not decline until 1933. Labor stayed high because the dramatic decline in agricultural wages maintained market equilibrium. The only input whose use declined sharply was fertilizer which, because it made up less than 15 percent of the value of aggregate output, could not lead to large output changes on its own.

II. Agricultural Exports and Food Production during Adjustment

The core of structural adjustment policies is elimination of overvalued exchange rates, reduction in industrial protection, and fiscal austerity. Specific agricultural measures include elimination of export taxation and other trade restrictions and reduction of subsidies to producers. This package improves the terms of trade for agriculture as a whole and changes relative prices within the sector in favor of tradables. In the long run the improved terms of trade will accelerate agricultural growth, and the elimination of price distortions within the sector will improve efficiency and increase gains from trade. These long-run gains can be very large. But what will be the short-run response of agricultural exports, of aggregate output, and of domestic food supply?

Agricultural exports can react to changes in prices and exchange rates much like individual crops: a favorable price increase can increase production at the expense of nontradables, even if aggregate output does not increase. Balassa (1986) ran a regression of the ratio of exports to output for changes in the real exchange rate and foreign income. He found agricultural export elasticities to be higher than elasticities for exports of all goods and services and almost as high as those for merchandise exports (table 4). The elasticities of net agricultural exports are higher than the elasticities of agricultural exports because as the exchange rate rises, agricultural exports rise and agricultural imports become more expensive and fall. Other reasons are that the base of net exports is considerably smaller than that of gross exports and that devaluations are often associated with fiscal austerity, causing domestic demand to fall.[3]

The short-run response of export crops, and especially net agricultural exports, to exchange rate changes is therefore large. But how does aggregate agricultural supply respond to changes in the real exchange rate? Do changes in the exchange rate result in overall agricultural growth, or do they merely shift production from home goods to tradables?

Table 4. *Elasticity of Ratio of Exports to Output, 1965–82*

Exports/output	Elasticity of exports with respect to the real exchange rate	
	Developing countries	Sub-Saharan Africa
Goods and services/ total output	0.48	0.88
Merchandise exports/ total output	0.77	1.01
Agricultural exports/ agricultural output	0.68	1.35
Net agricultural exports/ agricultural output	4.96	11.47

Note: All figures are statistically significant at 1 percent or more.
Source: Balassa (1986).

3. Note in table 4 that all export elasticities are higher for Sub-Saharan Africa than for developing countries in general. One possible explanation for this high response is that most African countries are small and heavily dependent on foreign trade. Like the aggregate agricultural response, this high export response dispels another myth about Sub-Saharan Africa.

Table 5. *Recent Agricultural Performance of Countries in Sub-Saharan Africa*

Period	Countries under adjustment	Countries not under adjustment	Difference in growth rates
Agricultural production growth (percent per year)			
1970–80	1.1	0.9	0.2
1980–85	2.7	1.8	0.9
1986	5.8	4.3	1.5
1987	1.5	−1.1	2.6
Index of food production per capita (1979–81 = 100)			
1984–86	97	97	0

Note: Countries under adjustment include: Burundi, Cape Verde, Central African Republic, Chad, Côte d'Ivoire, Gambia, Guinea Bissau, Kenya, Madagascar, Malawi, Mali, Mauritius, Nigeria, Senegal, Togo, and Zaire.
Source: Cleaver (1988).

Cleaver's (1988) study is one of the few that address this issue. He compared the agricultural growth rates of Sub-Saharan African countries under adjustment (with packages of exchange rate adjustments and price and fiscal reforms) with those not under adjustment. Agricultural growth in the two groups was about the same in the 1970s (table 5). A slight difference between the two groups began to emerge in the early 1980s when adjustment programs were initiated. The annual agricultural growth in countries under adjustment was about 1 percentage point higher than that in countries without adjustment programs— and 2.6 percentage points higher in 1987, a bad year for agriculture throughout Africa. The striking difference between the two groups clearly increases over time, showing the responsiveness of Africa's agriculture to policy changes. Cleaver also shows that domestic food supply has not been increasing: through 1984–86, the domestic food self-sufficiency ratio remained at 97 percent for both country groups.[4]

Domestic food supply may not increase rapidly in response to adjustment programs for two reasons. First, a decline in real income often associated with adjustment may reduce the demand for food, shifting resources from the domestic food sector to exports. Second, in countries that are net importers of staple foods, domestic production of these foods is usually well protected even before adjustment. Krueger, Schiff, and Valdés (1988) show that for sixteen developing countries direct protection of imported basic staples averages 20 percent. An agricultural adjustment program usually also calls for a reduction

4. Another illustration comes from Mexico's adjustment in the 1984–88 period. Net agricultural exports grew rapidly after the devaluation of 1985, but neither aggregate output nor food consumption have increased.

in this protection. Therefore exchange rate and agricultural price reform may not lead to much higher prices for basic foods. And if the price does not increase, there will be no added incentive to produce food.

The reasoning is summarized in figure 2. Typical adjustment policies call for fiscal austerity, reducing producer subsidies and public investments. The resulting recession curtails the demand for food. In addition a depreciated exchange rate and reduced export taxation raise the prices of tradables in relation to nontradables. The producer prices of importable foods are likely to increase less because direct protection of such foods declines. Given low aggregate supply elasticity and decline in producer subsidies and public investment, the adjustment package will not increase aggregate output in the short run even if average agricultural prices rise. Some crops will respond quickly with sharply higher net exports, contributing much to the foreign exchange objectives of the adjustment effort. But the aggregate supply effects will only come in the long run.

So, with net exports responding quickly to higher prices, with aggregate agriculture responding after a lag, and with food supply responding little if at all, agriculture can support the adjustment program without increasing per capita food consumption. For both exports and domestic consumption to increase, aggregate agricultural output has to increase—and that can happen only in the long run. Structural adjustment programs should do more than ease balance of payments. They should also spur the growth of food production and of all agriculture. And since agriculture is price inelastic in the short run (and policy elastic in the long run), the question should no longer be the size of the price response. Instead analysis should focus on how to make all agriculture grow.

Figure 2. *Effects of Ajustment Policies on Agriculture*

Typical adjustment policies	Intermediate effect	Effect on agriculture
Fiscal austerity	Reduced input subsidies Reduced public investment Reduced demand for food	Aggregate supply does not increase in the short run, but it may in the long run
Real depreciation, reduced direct taxation of exports	Prices of tradables increase relative to nontradables	Exports increase sharply, net exports even more
Reduced direct protection of importable staples	Producer prices of food may not increase	Domestic food supply may not increase

III. What It Takes to Make Aggregate Agricultural Output Grow

Agricultural growth is the outcome of a process in which farmers respond to improved farm profits. Changes in profits, in turn, derive from the interplay of prices, improved infrastructure and better services, and enhanced technology.

The Long-Run Price Response: Labor and Capital

The aggregate long-run response of agriculture to price changes is large, and ultimately comes from private decisions to migrate and invest. As seen above, an expansion of labor and capital is required for agricultural output to respond to higher prices and profits. The most impressive evidence of a substantial response does not come from econometric studies of supply functions (see appendix) but from studies of the intersectoral allocation of labor and capital.

Labor. It is well known that the share of agricultural labor in total labor declines along the growth path, but economic forces affect the speed of this decline. Mundlak, Cavallo, and Domenech (1988) have studied intersectoral labor allocations for Argentina, Chile, Japan, the United States, and a cross-country sample. In all these studies, the intersectoral income differences—a function of aggregate agricultural prices—affect migration rates. Other studies of migration (such as Dhar 1984, for India) relate the migration from rural areas to intersectoral wage differences and find that shrinking wage gaps slow rural-urban migration. Higher agricultural prices do the same—reduce wage gaps and slow migration. Likewise, urban unemployment rates have been shown to lead to a decline in migration in both types of studies.

Capital. An economy's overall rate of investment, and agriculture's share of that investment, govern the growth of the agricultural capital stock. To show the relation between agricultural investment and agricultural rates of return, Mundlak, Cavallo, and Domenech (1988) related the intersectoral allocation of investment or savings to the rates of return for agriculture and nonagriculture. They found a definite positive relation. The rate of return in agriculture is positively related to the relative price of agriculture to nonagriculture. That rate also increases when technical change raises efficiency and farm profits. It is thus perfectly possible for the growth in agricultural capital, the growth in agricultural output, and the decline in agricultural prices to be simultaneous.

Time. It naturally takes time for the reallocation of capital and labor allocation to be translated into growth in output. How much time? Cavallo (1988) has explored this issue in a three-sector (agriculture, nonagriculture, and government) model of the Argentine economy, using data from 1913–84. The model includes econometrically estimated equations that relate intersectoral migration and capital allocation to expected differences in intersectoral earnings and productivity, all in dynamic simulations. The experiment relevant for the discussion here assumes a 10 percent permanent increase in the relative price of agriculture (table 6).

The results confirm the very low short-run elasticities of aggregate agricultural

Table 6. *Argentina: Price Elasticities in Agriculture*

Number of years after price change	Output	Labor	Physical capital	Land
1	0.07	0.00	0.05	0.03
3	0.16	0.07	0.18	0.07
5	0.36	0.17	0.38	0.12
10	0.71	0.42	0.90	0.23
15	1.19	0.82	1.39	0.34
20	1.78	1.52	1.80	0.48

Note: The elasticities are computed by assuming a 10 percent permanent increase in the price of agriculture but adjusting the price of government services in order to keep the general price level at historical levels. The price of land is increased in the same proportion as the agricultural price, and government wages are reduced in the same proportion as the price of government services.

Source: Cavallo (1988).

output and inputs to a policy change—they range from 0 for labor to 0.07 for output.[5] The output elasticity three years after the policy change is still only 0.16, but it rises to 0.36 after five years. The full response is very large, with an elasticity of 1.78, but it takes twenty years for that response—and more than half the full response occurs in the second ten years.

The response comes mainly from an almost equal expansion of labor and capital. The supply of land, by contrast, is inelastic, increasing only by a fourth as much as capital.[6]

Public Investments

Public actions and investments have a strong effect on agriculture. In addition, there is a strong interaction with private investment which accelerates with public investment.[7]

Econometrically, it is easier to show the effect of infrastructure, services, and human capital than it is to show price effects. Infrastructure, services, and human capital together affect aggregate agricultural output more than prices alone (table 7). The table is taken from two studies of output, fertilizer demand, and draft power investment, one using cross-country data and the other cross-district data from India. Both studies use the same method, combining cross-section and time-series data, and use only the variations within each country or district over time rather than cross-section variation (see appendix for details).

5. Reca's (1976) direct econometric estimate for Argentina appears to be an overestimate in light of the broader evidence using a full model and longer time series.
6. Cavallo (1988) presents the most realistic way of calculating long-run elasticities. Other econometric studies, such as those in table 2, have not been able to show the remarkably high levels of the long-run elasticities. Peterson (1979) is one author who shows high long-run elasticities, but the method is flawed (see the appendix for details).
7. I know of no studies of the impact of public investment on nonagriculture, so I cannot make comparisons.

Table 7. *Effects of Infrastructure on Agriculture*

	Aggregate crop output		Fertilizer demand		Tractor stock, cross-country	Draft animal investment, India
	Cross-country	India	Cross-country	India		
Prices						
Output price	−0.05*	n.a.	−0.02	n.a.	0.16*	n.a.
International output price[a]	n.a.	0.13*	n.a.	0.06	n.a.	2.90*
Fertilizer price	0.0	−0.12*	−0.16*	−0.57*	−0.05*	−12.25*
Urban wage	−0.05*	0.05	0.16*	0.13	−0.04	5.66*
Interest rate	n.a.	−0.001	n.a.	0.03	n.a.	−0.59*
Infrastructure						
Total irrigation†	1.62*	n.a.	−0.37	n.a.	7.16*	n.a.
Government canal irrigation	n.a.	0.03	n.a.	0.06	n.a.	−0.20
Rural road density	0.12*	0.20*	0.18*	0.22*	0.34*	−2.13*
Paved roads†	0.26*	n.a.	0.23*	n.a.	1.71*	n.a.
Electrification	n.a.	0.03§	n.a.	0.09§	n.a.	0.71*
Services						
Regulated markets	n.a.	0.08*	n.a.	0.41*	n.a.	0.06
Commercial banks	n.a.	0.02*	n.a.	0.25*	n.a.	0.54*
Extension	0.02	n.a.	0.19*	n.a.	−0.03	n.a.

(Table continues on the following page.)

Table 7 (continued)

	Aggregate crop output		Fertilizer demand		Tractor stock, cross-country	Draft animal investment, India
	Cross-country	India	Cross-country	India		
Human capital						
Rural population density	0.12*	n.a.	0.18*	n.a.	0.34*	n.a.
Adult literacy rate†	0.54*	n.a.	1.27*	n.a.	−0.44	n.a.
Primary school	n.a.	0.33*	n.a.	1.43*	n.a.	3.82*
Life expectancy	1.76*	n.a.	2.64*	n.a.	5.49*	n.a.
Technical						
Research	0.00	n.a.	0.14*	n.a.	−0.05	n.a.
Rainfall	n.a.	0.07*	n.a.	1.27	n.a.	1.50
Miscellaneous						
GDP/capita	0.21*	n.a.	−0.13	n.a.	0.46*	n.a.
No. of observations	580	1,785	580	1,148	580	304

n.a. Not available.
* Statistical significance at 10 percent or more.
§ Statistically significant at 10 percent in a one-tailed test. Only for cases where the hypothesis of a coefficient of opposite sign is unreasonable.
† Coefficients are not in elasticity form: irrigation, paved roads, and adult literacy are ratios expressed as a percentage. The coefficients in the table are given the percentage increase in the dependent variable for a 1 percent increase in the independent percentage. For example, a 1 percent estimate increase in the adult literacy rate in India will lead to a 0.54 percent increase in agricultural output.
a. To circumvent simultaneity problems (see appendix), an index of international prices is used as an instrumental variable for domestic prices.
Sources: Binswanger, Khandker, and Rosenzweig (1989); Binswanger, Mundlak, Yang, and Bowers (1987).

As shown by Antle (1983), the clearest example of infrastructure impact is that of roads. In the two studies reported here, the density of roads has elasticities of 0.12 and 0.20 for aggregate output and strong effect on demand for fertilizer and tractors. In India, the density of roads reduces the demand for draft animals. In the cross-country study, road quality, as proxied by paving, is powerful. In India, electricity has a small positive effect on aggregate output but a substantial effect on fertilizer demand and on reduced investment in draft animals. In the cross-country study, irrigation has a powerful effect on output and on tractor demand. It is not possible to show any effect of the Indian government's investment in canal irrigation over the past twenty years.[8]

Services also affect agriculture. India's regulated markets—featuring a formal auction mechanism to sell individual farmers' output—are a cheap government investment with a powerful impact, even on fertilizer demand. Having branches of commercial banks nearby also sharply increases fertilizer demand. Public extension services increase fertilizer demand; they also increase aggregate output, but the relation is not statistically significant.

Human capital also has an impact on output. Rural population density, a proxy for labor, increases input use and output. In the cross-country study, broader literacy boosts output, shown by a very large elasticity, as well as the demand for fertilizer. In the India study, primary schools have powerful effects on output, fertilizer demand, and investment in draft animals. Life expectancy, a proxy for the people's health, also has a strong impact on output and fertilizer demand (in the cross-country data).

That it is easier to show econometrically that public investments have a strong impact on agricultural growth does not mean that prices are not important. The econometric estimates shown in table 7 are short-run elasticities, which we know

Table 8. *United States: Time Trend of Agricultural Prices Deflated by Wholesale Prices, 1900–83*

Commodity	Coefficient (percent per year)	R^2
Sugar	−0.7	0.14
Wheat	−0.7	0.39
Maize	−0.6	0.31
Rice	−0.6	0.27
Cotton	−0.5	0.26
Wool	−0.1	0.49

Source: Binswanger, Mundlak, Yang, and Bowers (1985).

8. All irrigation, which includes private irrigation in wells, has probably been a powerful contributor to aggregate output. But private investment is endogenous, and because the India data (but not the cross-country data) allow separate treatment of public irrigation, only the latter were included.

to be low.[9] If prices are not set right, farmers will not invest, and this would hurt agricultural growth. Low prices also accelerate outmigration and reduce the agricultural labor pool. So, a good price policy is necessary for rapid growth, but it is not sufficient.

Public Research and Extension

Agriculture's long-run growth record is impressive. World production, more than keeping up with demand, has grown so fast that it has led to long-run declining prices (table 8). Since 1900, the prices for the basic staples and cotton (relative to the wholesale price index) have declined by at least 0.5 percent a year. The low coefficients of determination show that there are large variations in prices around these estimates, reflecting commodity booms and busts. And if there is a secular decline in agricultural commodity prices, there is also a secular decline in agricultural production costs—something that can happen primarily with technical change.[10] From this information on declining prices alone, it is clear that technology was a major source of agricultural growth. Technology is developed and diffused by both public and private sector institutions.

What, then, of public research? In the cross-country study (table 7) it has no discernible effect on aggregate output, but it does have a positive effect on fertilizer demand. The relation is similar to that for extension, where the effect of the output is not statistically significant, but that on fertilizer demand is strong. That neither research nor extension has a strong effect is puzzling, because over the long run prices have fallen due to technological change. Perhaps the technological development has been in the private sector, adopted without public help. It is known, however, that public research has helped the supply of individual commodities. Just as in the case of price reforms, it is easier to expand output of an individual crop than aggregate output.

The cross-country data used for the estimates in table 7 may not, however, be the best way to express the impact of extension and research on agricultural production. Birkhaeuser, Evenson, and Feder (1988) reviewed the extension literature on the adoption of technology and the supply of individual crops. They find that extension impact varies, sometimes being powerful, sometimes not. Here, however, the focus is on aggregate output. Just as it is possible to aggregate individual crop price elasticities, one can aggregate research and ex-

---

9. The cross-country aggregate supply elasticity is negative because it includes livestock products that are close to half the value of output. The stock of tractors and the investments in draft animals (but not fertilizer) respond strongly to increases in output prices. Fertilizer prices nevertheless have a consistently strong effect on fertilizer demand and investment. In the cross-country study, higher urban wages reduce output and lead to the substitution of fertilizer for labor. In the India study, higher urban wages lead to a substitution of draft animals for labor. Only in the India study are higher interest rates shown to reduce draft animal investment.

10. The major decline in transport cost associated with the steamboat and the railroad was already drawing to a close at the beginning of this century.

tension elasticities using weighted shares of individual crops. As one crop's technology changes, its profitability increases. Its production may expand at the expense of other crops whose relative profitability has declined. So, just as the aggregate price response is much smaller than the elasticities for individual crops, aggregate research response should be smaller than individual crop response to research. This is confirmed by the results of Huffman and Evenson shown in table 9.[11]

In North India, research on wheat expanded the production of wheat at the expense of corn and millet. Research also concentrated on industrial crops, such as cotton. The aggregate output elasticity is 0.17, but not as large as the elasticity of 0.31 for wheat alone. Similarly, public extension concentrated on rice, corn, and millet, and on industrial crops rather than wheat. Extension's aggregate supply elasticity is 0.16, as large as the elasticity for research.

In Brazil, the concentration of research on export crops expanded that category at the expense of other crops. The aggregate elasticity is 0.25. It is not possible to show the effect of extension for the Philippines, and the effect of research there is small. The effect of research and extension on production is much easier to show for an individual crop than for all agriculture. In the U.S. study, public research increased the output of cash grain farms—with an elasticity of 0.07. It had the sharpest impact (0.24) on soybeans, which expanded at the expense of wheat and rice. Private research was biased toward feed grains and reduced crop output overall. An aggregate effect of public extension cannot be shown.

Credit

As we have seen, private investment is a major source of growth. But how important is credit for accelerating investment? What is the effect of increased credit on agricultural growth? Binswanger and Khandker (1989) examined the impact of the expansion of India's rural financial system on agriculture by applying the same techniques (supply function analysis) used for deriving most of the results in this paper.

The amount of credit borrowed in each district is determined both by the decisions of the financial institutions to make it available and by the decisions of the farmers to borrow it. This endogeneity means that one cannot estimate the impact of credit by simply regressing the volume of credit on aggregate output or on fertilizer demand, because farmers will borrow more if they plan to produce more and to use more fertilizer. Two methods can circumvent the resulting simultaneity problem. The first estimates the impact of improved financial intermediation by including the number of commercial bank branches as an explanatory variable. The decision to locate a branch in an area is up to the commercial bank and therefore reflects only the supply of credit, making it

---

11. The results are from systems of output supply and factor demand equations estimated in ways similar to those in table 1. The equations include shifter variables for research, extension, and high-yield varieties, whose coefficients are reported in table 9.

Table 9. Estimated Impact Elasticities of Public Research, Extension, and High-Yield Varieties

Product	North Indian wheat			Brazil	Philippines		U.S. cash grain farms		
	Public research	High-yield varieties	Public extension	Public research	Public research	Public extension	Public research	Private research	Public extension
Impact on product supply									
Wheat	0.31	0.21	−0.32	n.a.	n.a	n.a.	−0.06	−1.36	−0.10
Rice	−0.08	0.12	0.33	n.a.	n.a.	n.a.	n.a.	n.a.	n.a.
Corn and millet	−0.81	−0.12	0.86	n.a.	n.a.	n.a.	n.a.	n.a.	n.a.
Industrial crops	0.27	−0.09	0.33	0.05	n.a.	n.a.	n.a.	n.a.	n.a.
Export crops	n.a.	n.a.	n.a.	0.74	n.a.	n.a.	n.a.	n.a.	n.a.
Staple crops	n.a.	n.a.	n.a.	0.01	n.a.	n.a.	n.a.	n.a.	n.a.
Beans	n.a.	n.a.	n.a.	0.01	n.a.	n.a.	n.a.	n.a.	n.a.
Animal products	n.a.	n.a.	n.a.	0.07	n.a.	n.a.	0.24	−0.72	0.06
Soybeans	n.a.	n.a.	n.a.	n.a.	n.a.	n.a.	−0.03	1.06	0.06
All products[a]	0.17	0.04	0.16	0.25	0.05	−0.05	0.07	−0.23	0.00

n.a. Not available.

Note: Derived from profit function estimates with multiple inputs and outputs. Total land and farm size held constant. For studies with cross-section time series, within estimators have been used.

a. Elasticities for all outputs and inputs are the sum of the individual product or input elasticities weighted by their respective shares. For example, $\eta_R = \Sigma S_i \eta_{iR}$, where η_{iR} is the aggregate output elasticity with respect to research, η_{iR} is the elasticity of crop i output with respect to research, and S_i is the share of crop i in total farm revenue. For the Philippines, only an aggregate supply function with disaggregated input demands was estimated.

Sources: Evenson (1988); Huffman and Evenson (1989).

exogenous to farmers' decisionmaking. But this method cannot capture the lending volumes of the entire financial system, which includes cooperative institutions as well as commercial banks. A second method uses a two-stage least-squares procedure through which the volumes of lending are predicted by the number of branches of commercial banks and cooperative lending institutions. Because the number of institutions affects only supply but not demand, the predicted lending volumes are no longer correlated with the residuals of the output supply and input demand equations.

Table 10 summarizes the effects of financial intermediation variables on aggregate output, fertilizer demand, investments, rural employment, and rural wages. Each result is the financial intermediation coefficient of a separate regression equation such as those in table 7.

- Cooperative credit's output elasticity is 0.014. This elasticity, despite being small, is fairly precise. It is smaller than the output elasticity of overall rural credit, the volume of which is much larger. It is also smaller than the output elasticity of the number of commercial bank branches.
- Fertilizer use responds with an elasticity of 0.06 to cooperative credit, 0.25 to commercial bank branches, and 0.28 to rural credit—all substantially larger than the impact on aggregate crop output and large enough to explain the entire increase in aggregate output.

Table 10. *India: Impact of the Financial System on Agriculture and the Rural Economy*

Dependent variable	Number of commercial bank branches	Predicted overall rural credit advanced	Predicted agricultural cooperative credit advanced[a]
Aggregate crop output	0.014*	0.02†	0.01*
Fertilizer demand	0.25*	0.28*	0.06*
Investment			
Tractors	0.14†	n.a.	0.10*
Pumps	0.38*	0.51*	0.31*
Draft animals	0.71*	0.62*	0.38*
Milk animals	0.52*	0.58*	0.19*
Small stock	−0.16	0.67*	0.29*
Agricultural employment	−0.07*	−0.04	−0.01
Nonagricultural employment	0.29*	0.18*	0.00
Rural wage	0.06*	0.04*	0.00

n.a. Not available.

* Statistically significant at 10 percent or better on two-tail test.
† Statistically significant at 10 percent or better on one-tail test.

a. Cooperative credit includes credit by the Land Development Bank system and the primary agricultural credit societies. In 1980–81, credit outstanding to agriculture for the cooperative system was about two-thirds of total credit outstanding to agriculture and about 42 percent of total rural credit.

Source: Binswanger and Khandker (1989).

- Cooperative credit, commercial bank branches, and overall credit expansion sharply increase the rate of investment in tractors, pumps, draft animals, milk animals, and small stock. And all coefficients (except commercial banks and small stock) are statistically significant.
- The growth of commercial banks and overall credit reduces agricultural employment, with respective elasticities of 0.7 and 0.4. Cooperative credit, exclusively for agricultural purposes, also has a negative but not significant coefficient. Clearly, however, agricultural credit does not increase agricultural employment.[12]

It thus appears that the main effect of institutional growth and higher lending volumes has been not a substantial increase in aggregate crop output but more substitution of capital for labor. If increased fertilizer use can account for the entire output effect of additional credit, higher capital investment must have substituted for labor.

The supply approach to agricultural credit pursued over the last three decades in India has spurred the use of fertilizer and investment in agriculture. But it has failed to generate agricultural employment, and it has not reached its agricultural output objectives. The costs of credit programs to governments are high, as losses from poor repayment are ultimately borne by the government or its institutions. The benefits of expanding commercial banks in rural areas—increasing nonfarm growth, nonfarm employment, and rural wages—could have been achieved without imposing costly agricultural credit targets on commercial banks.

The World Bank has a large portfolio of investments in agricultural credit—with US$6.6 billion, or one-quarter of its agricultural lending, to credit schemes during fiscal years 1982–88. Many countries transfer very large resources to their credit systems to cover losses. During the 1980s Mexico's transfer credit system was not less than 12 percent of agricultural value added. Yet agricultural growth in output during the 1980s was less than 1 percent per year, according to World Bank figures. Other Bank-supported studies (including World Bank 1988 and von Pischke 1981) have shown that Bank investments have not led to viable credit institutions in India or many other places. The studies have also shown that it is difficult to direct credit to poorer farmers.

Private and Public Responses to Agroclimatic Potential

It is well known that a poor agroclimate can constrain production regardless of the investment devoted to production. And there appear to be few bounds to agricultural production in good agroclimatic areas. How are public and private

---

12. Most of the commercial bank credit in rural and semiurban branches in India goes to sectors other than agriculture. Confining the investigation of the effects of rural credit to agriculture would thus be ignoring other effects in the rural sectors. Positive effects on rural nonfarm output and employment could mitigate the negative effects on farm employment.

resources allocated to different agroclimatic environments, given the fact that supply responds to price changes even in poorly endowed agroclimatic zones?

Farmers, governments, and service providers all respond to agroclimatic variables. Their response is very strong. Public infrastructure and services are targeted to better agroclimatic regions. More workers migrate to such regions. Private investment responds to the better area and the better infrastructure. And private providers of services respond to the better business opportunities associated with the good agroclimate, improved infrastructure, and high private investment by increasing services for input supply, marketing, maintenance, and finance.

That's the reasoning. What, then, is the evidence? In India 37 percent of the variation in the density of roads is exclusively the result of measured differences in agroclimatic endowments (table 11). For other investments, a similar proportion of the variation is explained. Across the board, governments and banks invest more where irrigation potential is high. They tend to avoid areas that are at risk of floods. Banks systematically put their branches where rain or irrigation potential promise good water supply and where the risk from droughts or floods is low.

Because the elasticity estimates in tables 7 and 9 are averages for the countries or districts, they do not show differences in the responses to agroclimate. And because governments often make allocations on the basis of agroclimatic potential, the averages of tables 7 and 9 cannot indicate the differences in elasticity for different agroclimatic subregions. Although the estimates show that infrastructure, services, human capital, and technology are crucial to aggregate agricultural growth, this conclusion is not sufficient to make investment decisions. Specific project analysis is still necessary to predict returns to individual projects or programs in particular agroclimatic environments.

Table 11. *India: Effects of Agroclimatic Endowments on Infrastructure and Banking Services*

Explanatory variable	Rural roads[a]	Regulated market	Canal irrigation	Electricity	Commercial bank branches
Cool months	−0.22	0.004*	0.01	0.39*	0.02
Excess rain	0.23	−0.002	−0.001	0.01*	0.05*
Rainy season	2.44*	−0.004	0.01	0.09	0.05*
Flood potential	−0.08	−0.001*	−0.004	−0.06*	−0.01*
Irrigation potential	0.03*	0.001*	0.002*	0.01*	0.002*
Soil moisture capacity	−0.42*	0.004*	−0.02*	0.23	0.0002
Urban distance	−0.003	0.00004*	0.0001*	−0.001	−0.21
Constant	−4.22*	−0.01	−0.02	0.185	−0.13
Adjusted R^2	0.37	0.36	0.43	0.28	n.a.

n.a. Not available.

* Statistically significant at 10 percent or better.

a. Rural roads corresponds to agricultural year 1974; the remaining variables relate to agricultural year 1981.

Source: Binswanger, Khandker, and Rosenzweig (1989).

In addition, the joint dependence of public and private investment on observed and unobserved agroclimatic conditions increases the difficulties for econometric estimation. Cross-section analysis cannot be used because it cannot take agroclimatic conditions into account (see the appendix for details).

The cost of ignoring agroclimatic conditions can be high. It is known that the rate of return to private investment is sharply lower in marginal areas. Some of the World Bank's project failures in Sub-Saharan Africa can be attributed to expecting too much from such areas. Lele and Meyers (1986) show that the growth of smallholder production in Kenya occurred primarily in high-potential areas, where smallholders produce cash crops that bolster the growth of Kenya's exports. But in Kenya's arid and semiarid areas, agricultural growth has been disappointing despite considerable investment, much of it Bank-assisted.

IV. Implications for the World Bank

The way to look at agricultural growth is to go beyond prices and price elasticities. The first thing to consider is an area's agroclimatic potential. This potential sets the prospects for agriculture and influences the public and private decisions that can, in turn, encourage agricultural growth. If bad agroclimatic conditions constrain agriculture and the investment in it, agricultural growth will be slow. Although the World Bank should assist countries in exploiting the limited potential that usually exists even in marginal areas, it should resist pressure to invest heavily in marginal agriculture on grounds of the alleviation of poverty. If there is no agricultural growth, there can be no alleviation of poverty.

Structural adjustment policies are executed to promote agricultural growth and efficiency, but their effects may take several years to materialize. In the short run agriculture can contribute much to structural adjustment efforts, mainly by increasing net exports. But because adjustment efforts typically take time to increase aggregate agricultural supply, possible stagnation or decline in food production and consumption must be kept at the fore. Where governments protected importable food production before adjustment, domestic food consumption cannot be expected to increase under an adjustment program, so there is a need to design or expand targeted food subsidies and nutrition programs. To ensure that food and nutrition needs are met during the adjustment effort, such targeting should ideally be part of the design of adjustment programs. Of course, designing such programs and obtaining government commitment to them is not easy.

Adjustment packages must also be designed in ways that go beyond reliance on prices alone to spur agricultural growth. Because of the long lags in private responses, the dependence of private investment on public and quasi-public goods, and the long lead times of public investments, the attention to agricultural growth cannot be delayed until the adjustment is complete. Instead, adjustment packages must protect and support investments for agricultural growth—such investments as those in human capital, infrastructure, markets, research, and extension. How could targeted food subsidies and continued public investment be financed when expenditures have to be cut? Savings can of course come from other sectors. But there are opportunities in agriculture as well, such as the reallocation of fertilizer and credit subsidies to growth-enhancing public investment. Fertilizer subsidies have no effect on agricultural output if fertilizer is at the same time rationed. And many costly credit programs receive very large subsidies but have not created viable institutions or reached poor people. In India and Mexico they have also failed to produce much agricultural growth.

Appendix: Some Econometric Issues

Using Cross-Country Data to Estimate the Long-Run Aggregate Supply

The range of most of the estimated long-run elasticities in table 2 is 0.1 to 0.3. These elasticities are derived using the Nerlove technique, which uses the lagged dependent variable and interprets the coefficient of lagged supply as the intertemporal adjustment coefficient. Few people believe that the low elasticities derived using the Nerlove technique are good estimates of the response of crops to a permanent change in the price regime of agriculture. Little literature exists on aggregate supply using more sophisticated lag structures. Some experiments were performed by Binswanger and others (1985) using cross-section/time-series data for fifty-eight countries. They used free form lags including prices of the three previous years but did not find higher elasticities.

Peterson (1979) convincingly argued that time-series data cannot be used for inferring the long-run elasticity, because few countries have shifted from a regime of low prices to one of high prices. Instead, the time-series data only show the response to short-lived commodity booms (see also the simultaneity problem, below). Peterson also argues that different countries pursue different pricing regimes for long periods of time and their input and output levels have fully adjusted to these regimes. He therefore used country cross-section data to estimate the long-run response and found price elasticities in the range of 1.27 to 1.66. But as Chhibber (1988b) points out, the problem with this cross-country technique is that country output levels differ not only because of differences in prices but also because of differences in agroclimates, public infrastructure, research, extension, and public investment in human capital. When Chhibber included some of these variables in the cross-section estimation, Peterson's estimates declined.

Some of the productivity-enhancing variables are observable, but others are not. Binswanger and others (1987) show that even by including ten measured attributes of agroclimate and public investments, the correlation of the explanatory variable (including price) with unobserved country effects cannot be eliminated. In another experiment using data from eighty-five districts in India, Binswanger, Khandker, and Rosenzweig (1989) show that the correlation between unobservable district characteristics and government investment cannot be overcome in that data set either. These results are consistent with the idea that governments systematically invest more in regions with high agroclimatic endowments.

Estimates of the effects of prices and government investments on aggregate output using cross-country variation will therefore suffer from unobserved variable biases. Cross-section estimates of aggregate supply, such as those by Peterson and Chhibber, have therefore been ignored in this paper.

The correlation between unobserved endowments of regions or countries with prices and other explanatory variables can be overcome by using cross-section/time-series data and using only the within-country or within-district variability. The cross-district or cross-country variability can be eliminated from the estimation by: (1) including district- or country-specific intercepts, (2) using only differences between successive years, or (3) using differences from district or country means. In table 2, we indicate the studies that use these within estimators.

The Simultaneity Problem

When agricultural price levels rise and supply expands, commodity markets are soon saturated because the demand for aggregate agricultural output is inelastic. Prices then drop again. Although countries or districts trade with the rest of the world and therefore may face more elastic demand, demand is unlikely to be perfectly elastic. The reason is that not all agricultural commodities are tradable; commodities are blocked by natural trade barriers or government trade restrictions. The short-run estimates of demand elasticities reported in table 2 could therefore be biased downward.

Binswanger, Khandker, and Rosenzweig (1989) circumvented this problem in their cross-section/time-series study of Indian districts. Instead of using an aggregate domestic price index, they constructed a price index for districts using international commodity prices. This international commodity price index was then used as an instrumental variable for the domestic prices, thus bypassing the simultaneity problem. Using this technique raises the estimated short-run aggregate crop supply elasticity from 0.045 to 0.13. This confirms that simultaneous equation bias indeed results in underestimation of the aggregate supply elasticities. But the unbiased estimates using instrumental variables are still very low: within the 0.1 to 0.2 range where most estimated short-run elasticities lie.

Can One Estimate Long-Run Supply with Single-Equation Techniques?

The difficulty of estimating truly long-run responses using single-country data or within estimators is likely to persist even if more sophisticated lag structures and simultaneous equation techniques are used. The long-run aggregate supply response is the effect of dynamic capital and labor reallocation among sectors and of government infrastructure, research, and human capital investments. These processes may extend over long periods. Much more elaborate modeling of the underlying migration and investment processes is required, as done in

Cavallo and Mundlak (1982) or Cavallo (1988), using long time series. In addition, the governments' public investment allocation must be modeled. The "long-run" estimates reported in table 2 are probably not usable for policy analysis.

References

Antle, John M. 1983. "Infrastructure and Aggregate Agricultural Productivity: International Evidence." *Economic Development and Cultural Change* 31: 609–20.

Askari, Hossein, and John Thomas Cummings. 1976. *Agricultural Supply Response*. New York: Praeger.

———. 1977. "Estimating Agricultural Supply Response with the Nerlove Model: A Survey." *International Economic Review* 18 (June): 257–92.

Balassa, Bela. 1986. "Economic Incentives and Agricultural Exports in Developing Countries." Paper presented at the Eighth Congress of the International Economic Association, New Delhi, India, December.

———. 1988. "Incentives Policies and Agricultural Performance in Sub-Saharan Africa." World Bank Policy, Planning, and Research Working Paper 77. Washington, D.C. Processed.

Bapna, Shanti L. 1981. *Aggregate Supply Response of Crops in a Developing Region*. New Delhi: Sultan Chand and Sons.

Bapna, Shanti L., Hans P. Binswanger, and Jaime B. Quizon. 1984. "Systems of Output Supply and Factor Demand Equations for Semi-Arid Tropical India." *Indian Journal of Agricultural Economics* 39, no. 2: 179–202.

Binswanger, Hans P., and Shahidur Khandker. 1989. "Determinants and Effects of the Expansion of the Financial System in Rural India." World Bank Agriculture and Rural Development Department. Washington, D.C. Processed.

Binswanger, Hans P., Shahidur Khandker, and Mark R. Rosenzweig. 1989. "How Infrastructure and Financial Institutions Affect Agricultural Output and Investment in India." World Bank Policy, Planning, and Research Working Paper 163. Washington, D.C. Processed.

Binswanger, Hans P., Yair Mundlak, Maw-Cheng Yang, and Alan Bowers. 1985. "Estimates of Aggregate Agricultural Supply Response from Time Series of Cross-Country Data." World Bank EPDCS Working Paper 1985-3. Washington, D.C. Processed.

———. 1987. "On the Determinants of Cross-Country Aggregate Agriculture Supply." *Journal of Econometrics* 36: 111–31.

Birkhaeuser, Dean, Robert E. Evenson, and Gershon Feder. 1988. "The Economic Impact of Agricultural Extension: A Review." New Haven, Conn.: Yale University. Processed.

Bond, Marian E. 1983. "Agricultural Responses to Prices in Sub-Saharan Africa." *International Monetary Fund Staff Papers* 30, no. 4: 703–26.

Cavallo, Domingo. 1988. "Agriculture and Economic Growth: The Experience of Argentina 1913–84." Paper presented at the 20th Conference of Agricultural Economists, Buenos Aires, Argentina.

Cavallo, Domingo, and Yair Mundlak. 1982. *Agriculture and Economic Growth in an Open Economy: The Case of Argentina*. International Food Policy Research Institute Research Paper 36. Washington, D.C.

Chhibber, Ajay. 1988a. "The Aggregate Supply Response in Agriculture: A Survey." In S. Commander, ed., *Structural Adjustment in Agriculture: Theory and Practice*. London: James Curry Publishers.

———. 1988b. "Raising Agricultural Output: Price and Nonprice Factors." *Finance and Development* (June): 44–47.

Cleaver, Kevin. 1988. "Agricultural Policy Reform and Structural Adjustment in Sub-Saharan Africa: Results to Date." World Bank Africa Department I. Washington, D.C. Processed.

Dhar, Sanjay. 1984. "Interstate and Within-State Migration in India." In Hans P. Binswanger and Mark R. Rosenzweig, eds., *Contractual Arrangements, Employment, and Wages in Rural Labor Markets in Asia*. New Haven, Conn.: Yale University Press.

Evenson, Robert E. 1988. "Agricultural Technology, Supply and Factor Demand in Asian Economies." Paper presented at the Conference on Directions and Strategies of Agricultural Development in the Asia-Pacific Region, Institute of Economics, Academia Sinica, Taipei, Taiwan.

Griliches, Zvi. 1960. "Estimates of the Aggregate U.S. Farm Supply Function." *Journal of Farm Economics* 42, no. 2: 282–93.

Huffman, Wallace E., and Robert E. Evenson. Forthcoming. "Supply and Demand Functions for Multiproduct U.S. Cash Grain Farms: Biases Caused by Research and Other Policies." *American Journal of Agricultural Economics* (August).

Johnson, D. Gale. 1950. "The Nature of the Supply Function for Agricultural Products." *American Economic Review* 40, no. 4: 539–64.

Krishna, Raj. 1982. "Some Aspects of Agricultural Growth Price Policy and Equity in Developing Countries." *Food Research Institute Studies (U.S.)* 18, no. 3: 219–60.

Krueger, Anne O., Maurice Schiff, and Alberto Valdés. 1988. "Agricultural Incentives in Developing Countries: Measuring the Effect of Sectoral and Economywide Policies." *World Bank Economic Review* 2, no. 3: 255–71.

Lele, Uma, and L. Richard Meyers. 1986. "Agricultural Development and Foreign Assistance: A Review of the World Bank's Assistance to Kenya." World Bank Development Research Department. Washington, D.C. Processed.

Mundlak, Yair, Domingo Cavallo, and R. Domenech. 1988. "Agriculture and Economic Growth, Argentina 1913–84." Washington, D.C.: International Food Policy Research Institute. Cordoba, Spain: IEERAL. Processed.

Peterson, W. L. 1979. "International Farm Prices and the Social Cost of Cheap Food Policies." *American Journal of Agricultural Economics* 61: 12–21.

Reca, Lucio G. 1980. *Argentina: Country Case Study of Agricultural Prices, Taxes, and Subsidies*. World Bank Staff Working Paper 386. Washington, D.C.

Reutlinger, Shlomo. 1963. "Alternative Uncertainty Models for Predicting Supply Response." *Journal of Farm Economics* 45: 1489.

von Pischke, J. D. 1981. "Use and Abuse of Rural Financial Markets in Low-Income Countries." World Bank Asia Technical Department. Washington, D.C. Processed.

U.S. Bureau of the Census. 1945. *Statistical Abstract of the United States 1944–45*. Washington, D.C.

Comment on "The Policy Response of Agriculture," by Binswanger

Avishay Braverman

This is a clear and well-written paper with two important messages. First, we should not confuse individual elasticities with aggregate, sectoral supply elasticities; aggregate supply elasticities are significantly lower than individual elasticities. Second, input and output price reform should be accompanied by investment in physical and human capital with appropriate, accountable institutional structures. Otherwise, significant long-term effects on agricultural growth cannot be expected.

It should go without saying that serious scholars and careful practitioners ought always to advocate *both* price and institutional reforms and appropriate investment strategies. Nevertheless, we should thank Professor Binswanger for reminding us of this reality: both inside and outside the World Bank, the two strategies are still often debated as if they were mutually exclusive rather than complementary. But the crucial point is how valuable an input this information—that the aggregate supply elasticities are lower than the individual supply elasticities—is to our conduct and assessment of agricultural policy reform.

I would first argue that the accepted point that aggregate supply elasticities are not high is essentially inconsequential to the recent—deserved—emphasis policymakers have been placing on price reform. Second, the paper's focus on sectoral elasticities belittles the importance of individual crop elasticities in agricultural price reform. I would like to make several points about these conclusions.

First, what is the significance of "low" aggregate supply elasticity for policy reform? If the United States is excluded, most of the econometric estimates of short-run aggregate agricultural price elasticity presented in the paper fall in the 0.1–0.2 range (table 2). With structural adjustment, a price change of 100 percent is possible; assuming overall elasticity of 0.2, an aggregate supply response of 20 percent results. This is a very significant change.

Second, it is necessary to assess the effect of policy reform on the budget deficit, foreign exchange, and income distribution, as well as on output and aggregate employment. Aggregate supply elasticities can only help indicate the

---

Avishay Braverman is chief of the Agricultural Policies Division in the Agriculture and Rural Development Department, World Bank. He would like to thank Jeffrey Hammer for very helpful comments: the views expressed here reflect their joint work on agricultural price reform.

© 1990 The International Bank for Reconstruction and Development / THE WORLD BANK.

effect on the last two variables. For the rest, the distinction of supply response for individual crops is essential. And the first three variables are the critical parameters in these days of fiscal and foreign debt crisis in many developing countries, in particular if we are really concerned with the impact of policy reforms on the poor.

Third, as Binswanger points out, high long-run aggregate supply elasticities may be due to price reforms. That is, part of the long-run supply response is an indirect effect of price reform which creates greater incentives and opportunities for investment.

Fourth, the aggregate response to prices may not be nearly as relevant to policy as the intercommodity effects. If the aggregate response is low, then interventions that affect all commodities (such as devaluation) may have small deadweight losses associated with them. But if, as Binswanger points out, the aggregate response is composed of very high own-price and (negative) cross-price effects, then the costs of inappropriate relative prices within agriculture are important. Here, obviously, multimarket approaches (see Braverman and Hammer 1988), which focus on substitution among commodities, are useful. Note that (in the short run) this point is at variance with the Krueger, Schiff, and Valdés (1989) conclusions that the macro exchange rate effects are more important to correct than inefficient direct price interventions in agriculture.

Fifth, because individual crop elasticities are evidently needed for policy analysis, the question of their availability and accuracy becomes important. Given the scarce and limited data in developing countries, and admitting the limitations of the art of econometrics, I agree with the comments of my colleagues Angus Deaton and T. N. Srinivasan at this conference that we should put more effort into collecting data and improving estimation techniques. Given those limitations of our "scientific art," orders of magnitude of elasticities are often the relevant framework for policy debate. World Bank agricultural policy has taken this position for quite some time in generating multimarket models for which estimated and "guesstimated" elasticities are inputs, and which are used to help Bank staff articulate interrelations among commodities and their impact on key policy variables. Incidentally, while liberalization, in moving domestic toward international prices, is often the appropriate policy reform, it is important to note that neither conceptually nor in practice does the Bank advocate "as a holy rule" the immediate equalization of domestic and international prices: rather, a clear analysis of the tradeoffs is required, particularly given the burden of debt and limited availability of tax instruments.

Sixth, one point raised in the paper is that policy reform in agriculture often implies increasing food prices which provide better incentives to producers (correction of the "urban bias"). However, the urban poor, landless farmers, and small farmers with a negative marketed surplus will suffer, at least in the short run. On how to protect these vulnerable groups during adjustment, I agree with Binswanger that well-designed, cost-effective targeted programs would be the solution in an ideal world. But in the real world the track record for administered programs has not been very good over the last twenty years. We should use targeted programs when the appropriate political will and administrative capacity exist; when they do not, we may sometimes have to resort to subsidization of commodities that, as far as possible, are consumed by the poor significantly more than the rich (that is, subsidies to inferior goods).

Seventh, Binswanger mentioned the failure of the formal credit programs in developing countries. This point should be reiterated until it has been effectively driven home. At the same time, we should continue to explore new institutional possibilities—such as credible voluntary cooperatives to increase the supply of credit to the rural sector—but not without sufficient prior evidence that accountable incentive structures exist to monitor and enforce appropriate behavior both for the borrower and the lending institution (see, for example, Braverman and Guasch 1989; Feder and Huppi 1989).

Eighth, I would like to make a few technical comments on the limitations of the econometric analysis—about which the author is appropriately cautious in the appendix—in terms of data, specification, and estimation techniques.

It is important to read the appendix, perhaps even before the text: more courageous interpretations appear in the latter. These apply not only to the overall flavor of the results but also to specific instances, such as the inference that the availability of credit institutions increases demand for fertilizer but induces higher capital to labor substitution. This could be true, but it is a very precise interpretation that one would be wary of asserting too confidently in view of the admitted flaws in the data base.

Binswanger is right to mistrust the ability of econometrics to estimate accurately the long-run supply response. But simulation approaches should also be handled gingerly. With most conventional function forms, numerically derived production possibility frontiers often tend to be quite "flat"—Harry Johnson's old result—and lead to strong intersectoral movements and high elasticities. The author suggests reasons (for instance, that there are nearly constant returns to scale on good land) why this may be true. But it is worth checking carefully that the results are credible and not an artifact of the technique of estimation.

One kind of simultaneity problem of the econometric studies is mentioned in the appendix; there may be others that affect the estimated impact on growth of some of the nonprice factors, including education. We do not know much about public allocation of investments in human capital, and the impact of prices could be important whether it be through agricultural income or through judgments of relative financial profitability of alternatives. Demand for education is surely income-elastic, and whether educational services are publicly provided or not, they are likely to respond to this demand. The causality may go entirely in the opposite way. Education may be a pure consumption good with high income-elasticity. If output, a proxy for income, were regressed on education, one would get a positive coefficient. A similar story, more or less credible in different markets, might be told for any public investment made with an eye toward recovering costs (higher income or output leading to more confidence in providing an effective service) and also for private investments such as bank branch location, which is treated as completely exogenous in this paper.

In summary, I would like to thank the author for focusing attention on this long-debated subject and for helping us to further direct the Bank's efforts in the 1990s toward credible hybrid lending which should emphasize both investment lending and required policy reform. We are reminded that we should not create unwarranted expectations—in particular, without appropriate institutional reforms. And here, if it comes to formal credit institutions or targeted food programs, I would emphasize three words: monitoring, enforcement, and accountability.

References

Braverman, Avishay, and J. Luis Guasch. 1989. "Rural Credit Reforms in LDCs: Issues and Evidence." *Journal of Economic Development* 14, no. 1 (June): 7–34.

Braverman, Avishay, and Jeffrey Hammer. 1988. "Computer Models for Agricultural Policy Analysis." *Finance and Development* 25, no. 2 (June): 34–38.

Feder, Gershon, and Monika Huppi. 1989. "The Role of Groups and Credit Cooperatives in Rural Lending." World Bank Policy, Planning, and Research Working Paper 284. Washington, D.C. Processed.

Krueger, Anne O., Maurice Schiff, and Alberto Valdés. 1989. "The Political Economy of Agricultural Pricing Policy." Summary Document, World Bank Comparative Studies. Trade Policy Division, World Bank Country Economics Department. Washington, D.C. Processed.

COMMENT ON "THE POLICY RESPONSE OF AGRICULTURE," BY BINSWANGER

Alberto Valdés

The policy background in Hans Binswanger's very interesting analysis is that current macroeconomic conditions in many developing countries require a reduction in government expenditures (to reduce the deficit) and an expansion in the production of tradables. The success of such a change could depend on agriculture's performance, because agriculture usually has the larger tradable component and a 50 percent or higher share of total export revenues.

In my opinion, the current situation offers an opportunity for revitalizing agriculture, which is often heavily taxed through economywide price interventions. I will discuss Binswanger's analysis against this background.

Although Binswanger does not discuss actual levels of agricultural price distortions, he states that the short-run response of agriculture to price changes is very low and lower than the long-run response. On the expenditure side, Binswanger's concern is that across-the-board cuts in public investment could reduce investment in certain types of infrastructure critical for agricultural growth. What does all this imply for the adjustment programs of World Bank borrowers?

Binswanger refers to the wrongheaded tendency in the development community to overestimate the agricultural aggregate supply response to incentives. As I understand it, this alleged overestimation refers only to the aggregate short-run response, not to the long-run response. Binswanger concludes that price reform alone will not significantly expand aggregate output in the short run because this response takes time. Only subsectors could expand. The clear conclusion is that, though price reform and public investment need to start right now, there is nothing governments can do that will have an effect in the short run—if we accept the short-run supply inelasticity argument and agree that designing and implementing public investment also takes many years.

Furthermore, to avoid loading the burden of adjustment on low-income wage earners, Binswanger recommends that we "design or expand targeted food subsidies and nutrition programs." But this brings us back to programs that take many years to develop. Few developing countries have effective targeted health and nutrition programs with broad coverage of poor households, and even fewer

---

Alberto Valdés is director of the International Trade and Food Security Program at the International Food Policy Research Institute, Washington, D.C.

© 1990 The International Bank for Reconstruction and Development / THE WORLD BANK.

of rural areas. In Latin America I believe only Chile, Costa Rica, and Cuba have such programs.

Let me address the following issues in Binswanger's paper: (1) the short-run aggregate output response; (2) the price versus nonprice issue and the sequencing of policies; and (3) the long-run aggregate output response.

I. The Short-Run Response

Is aggregate output so unresponsive in the short run? This will depend on how depressed prices are; the time frame we have in mind; and the responsiveness to a given price adjustment.

Before addressing these issues, a qualification: Binswanger distinguishes between export and food crops on the premise that exportables are tradable and do react in the short run (on the basis of the evidence in Balassa's work), but food supply is not tradable and responds little, if at all. My understanding is that most food crops are also tradables (import-competing) in most developing countries (certainly in Latin America, somewhat less in parts of Sub-Saharan Africa), and they are expected to be less responsive not because of their tradability but because, at least at the official exchange rate, most agricultural importables are protected and hence trade liberalization would reduce their domestic prices.

Let's now turn to the magnitude of price intervention. In a recent study of eighteen developing countries directed by Krueger, Schiff, and myself (1988), we found that, during 1960–84, the nominal rates of protection (NRP) for agricultural exports at the official exchange rate were negative—on average 12 percent (higher than 25 percent in Côte d'Ivoire, Ghana, and other countries), while for importables they were positive—on average 13 percent (though in some countries, such as Egypt, Pakistan, and Zambia, sectoral policies taxed importables, mostly food). A significant finding of the study is the importance of indirect price interventions, a consequence of industrial protection and unsustainable levels of absorption. In most of the eighteen countries indirect price interventions are huge, which means that a tax is imposed on agriculture close to three times the tax due to sectoral policies. The result is an average total taxation of 34 percent on agricultural exportables, 10 percent on agricultural importables, and 30 percent on all farm products. In Argentina, Côte d'Ivoire, and Ghana taxation of agricultural tradables resulting from the combined effect of price interventions was higher than 40 percent. Thus, the potential effect of a policy reform depends on two critical values: the short-run response parameter and the potential price enhancement. One can quarrel with some of the estimates of the short-run aggregate response and the NRPs, and perhaps not all the potential readjustment in prices of agricultural tradables can be implemented in the short run. However, accepting Binswanger's estimates of the short-run response and reducing the price enhancement by a third, agricultural incentives are so severely depressed by economywide policies that the potential for increasing aggregate output in the short run is still considerable. Thus, even if the short- and medium-term elasticities are small, the output effects are not, because of the very large price increase which would result from the removal of price interventions. This expansion could come from higher labor productivity per person (more hours of work and more capital), more variable inputs such as fertilizers, and reallocation of land, labor, and capital to more productive uses associated with a change in the output mix.

How "short" is the short run? Binswanger concludes from the study by Mundlak, Cavallo, and Domenech (1988) on Argentina that even after five to eight years the aggregate response would be low. But Coeymans and Mundlak (forthcoming), using a similar general equilibrium framework for Chilean agriculture, find that after three years the resulting increase in aggregate agricultural output implies an elasticity of supply of 0.3 percent, and that at the fourth and fifth years the implied elasticity is about 0.6 percent (over 1.0 percent after ten years).[1] The inference is that the effect on aggregate output is perhaps not so low after four to five years in many countries—particularly in those where agricultural incentives are severely depressed, agriculture is a relatively small sector in employment and capital, or where the physical infrastructure and financial and input delivery institutions are less of a constraint. The three-to-five-year output response could be lower in other developing countries. Ultimately, I would ascribe the lack of output response in the short run more to an inability to put a coherent and credible package of policy reforms in place in two to three years than to physical agronomic constraints.

II. Price Policy versus Nonprice Policy: Implications for Sequencing

Some influential economists argue that "public investments in agriculture are more effective than prices in raising agricultural output" (de Janvry 1986), or that "evidence for Sub-Saharan Africa shows that the responsiveness of total farm output to extra government expenditure is much higher than to prices" (Lipton 1987, quoting Kevin Cleaver), or that the output elasticity with respect to irrigation is larger than with respect to prices (Krishna 1982). I find this a peculiar way of thinking. Why should price elasticities be compared with elasticities for public investments? Why are they perceived as alternatives?

Binswanger does not endorse the "substitutes" view of prices and public investment. My comments here are really a complement to his analysis.

First, the effects of both price reform and public investment take time, and both may be better viewed as complementary than as substitutes; that is, each policy will increase the effectiveness of the other. An increase in publicly provided

---

1. My casual observation suggests that the lower reponse observed for Argentina arises partly from an econometric problem. Although Chile shifted from a regime of lower farm prices (relative to nonagriculture) to higher prices during the period of analysis, in Argentina we observe price fluctuations, but around a weak trend.

inputs could raise the output effect of higher prices, and vice versa, thus raising the output response.

Second, as mentioned above, the inadequacy of basic infrastructure as a major impediment to output response varies across countries and is likely to constrain low-income more than middle-income developing countries.

Third, conditions may exist that prevent some countries from simultaneously tackling incentive reforms and public investment programs. I do not have hard evidence on this empirical issue, but one can imagine conditions in which budget is a constraint, for example, to reducing export taxes simultaneously with increasing overall public investment. In this connection, Binswanger's econometric finding that cutting fertilizer subsidies and credit programs would not significantly depress aggregate output is important and relevant. It suggests that reallocation of the public sector budget could potentially protect critical investments with little risk of reducing the long-term growth of output.

III. THE LONG-TERM AGGREGATE RESPONSE

In asking how much and how fast aggregate agricultural output responds to prices and government investments, Binswanger is essentially asking what makes agriculture grow and what are the dynamics of the growth process. I fully agree with him that "public investment can have a strong effect on agricultural output," and his analysis of which type of public investment has had a greater effect on output is, in my opinion, the principal contribution of his paper.

In areas where land is under strong population pressure, technological advance is crucial for accelerating agricultural growth. For technological advance, building infrastructure, providing irrigation facilities, and upgrading human capability, as well as offering economic incentives, are essential. But where population pressure is lower, aggregate agricultural output could increase quite rapidly in response to incentives concentrated on expanding the area under cultivation and on increasing labor input (as happened in Southeast Asia until the 1960s and, until recently, in South America). A shift to high-value crops might also boost the aggregate response.

Perhaps the hardest problem to be solved in enhancing technological progress is how to set up institutions that will provide incentives for innovation among farmers as well as among the public and private agencies that serve them, and how long this might take. For this process, the overall economic climate for investment is important, and this climate is influenced by the economic incentives.

Remember too that agricultural growth does not spring exclusively from accumulation of capital and labor and technical progress. Reallocation of resources from activities with low to high (marginal) productivity may also be important, particularly in developing countries, where productivity varies widely among sectors within agriculture, and between agriculture and the rest of the economy, because of a certain inertia in the reallocation of capital and labor arising from erratic domestic policies, high variability in terms of trade, and the consequent difficulty in determining whether a price change is permanent—all sometimes compounded by institutional instability. Often, limits between the private and public sectors are undefined, creating considerable uncertainty about the legal framework for the private sector (such as the input delivery system), property rights, and hence about returns to private investments. Have the econometric estimates available on aggregate output response been able to capture these factors? In my opinion, they have not.

I agree with Binswanger that most of the empirical studies on the aggregate supply response in developing countries turn up a weak response to price changes, and the widespread pessimism about this response has probably affected the design of economic policies in many developing countries. If the aggregate supply response to incentives is low, then the social cost of taxing agriculture is also low. Structuralism in the 1950s in Latin America is a case in point, and it is a view that has become quite popular in Sub-Saharan Africa.

But the empirical foundations of the analysis on the aggregate supply response are still quite fragile. The available response estimates are, I believe, biased downward (relative to the potential response) owing to the prevailing uncertainty about the domestic terms of trade and the lack of policy changes that can be counted on to last. Output may reasonably be expected to respond less to price changes that reflect annual price variation around a given mean than to price changes that reflect a change in the mean that is expected to last. How the elasticity would have changed with less price variability and more credibility of policies is not incorporated in most studies. Assessment of the potential response to reform of incentives needs to take account of these two aspects.

Furthermore, most of the literature is dominated by studies using a single-equation time-series approach, which—I agree with Binswanger—fails to capture the underlying migration and investment processes (Bond 1983; Herdt 1970; Peterson 1979; Reca 1980). The long-run aggregate supply response should be viewed in an intersectoral and macroeconomic context: in most countries, the economywide policies overwhelm the effect of sectoral policies on incentives (Krueger, Schiff, and Valdés 1988).

The econometric studies of Mundlak and his associates for Argentina and Chile explicitly include intersectoral resource reallocation over time through migration and investment responding to relative prices. These studies obtain a larger supply response than those obtained with single-equation time-series data.

But there are still unsolved questions. One could argue that the studies do not fully control for exogenous changes in public goods affecting infrastructure, and that this may introduce a bias in the estimates, depending on whether changes in infrastructure are (positively or negatively) related to changes in the agricultural terms of trade. Second, their approach is not entirely immune from the Lucas criticisms (change in some parameters in response to policy changes). The agricultural terms of trade are highly variable in both countries. In Argentina there is a fluctuation around a weak trend; in Chile, 1965–73 was a period of a drastic agrarian reform that inhibited private investment in activities with longer gestation periods such as livestock, fruit trees, and land improvements. Furthermore, while in Chile the actual agricultural terms of trade did increase (in the 1970s and 1980s relative to the 1950s and 1960s), this was attributable not so much to explicit farm price policies as to changes in the real exchange rate (RER) and lower industrial protection. Before about 1983, the RER was highly unstable, probably inhibiting the output response. These factors have, I believe, lowered the estimated aggregate supply response.

In sum, I believe there is a range of values for the short- or the long-run aggregate agricultural supply "elasticity" that applies across countries and through time. The time path in the potential aggregate output response could be greatly influenced by the coherence and credibility of the policy reform, by the relative size of the agricultural sector in the economy, and by how depressed agriculture's incentives are before the reform begins. In many developing countries, the potential for increasing agricultural incentives appears to be substantial, especially taking into account the exchange rate misalignment.

References

Bond, Marian E. 1983. "Agricultural Responses to Prices in Sub-Saharan Africa." *IMF Staff Papers* 30, no. 4: 703–26.

Coeymans, J. E., and Y. Mundlak. Forthcoming. "Agricultural and Sectoral Growth: Chile, 1962–82." In Alberto Valdés and Romeo M. Bautista, eds., *Trade and Macroeconomic Policies in Developing Countries: Impact on Agriculture.* Washington, D.C.: International Food Policy Research Institute.

de Janvry, Alain. 1986. "Integration of Agriculture in the National and World Economy: Implications for Agricultural Policies in Developing Countries." In A. Maunder and U. Renborg, eds., *Agriculture in a Turbulent World Economy,* Proceedings of the 19th International Conference of Agricultural Economists. Aldershot, England: Gower.

Herdt, Robert. 1970. "A Disaggregate Approach to Aggregate Supply." *American Journal of Agricultural Economics* 52, no. 4: 512–20.

Krishna, Raj. 1982. "Some Aspects of Agricultural Growth, Price Policy and Equity in Developing Countries." *Food Research Institute Studies* 18, no. 3: 219–60.

Krueger, Anne O., Maurice Schiff, and Alberto Valdés. 1988. "Agricultural Incentives in Developing Countries: Measuring the Effect of Sectoral and Economywide Policies." *World Bank Economic Review* 2, no. 3: 255–71.

Lipton, Michael. 1987. "Limits of Price Policy for Agriculture, Which Way for the World Bank?" *Development Policy Review* 5, no. 2: 197–215.

Mundlak, Y., Domingo Cavallo, and R. Domenech. 1988. "Agricultural and Economic Growth, Argentina 1913–84." Forthcoming Research Report 76. Washington, D.C.: International Food Policy Research Institute.

Peterson, W. L. 1979. "International Farm Prices and the Social Cost of Cheap Food Policies." *American Journal of Agricultural Economics* 61, no. 1 (February): 12–21.

Reca, Lucio. 1980. "Argentina, Country Case Study of Agricultural Prices and Subsidies." *World Bank Staff Working Paper* 386. Washington, D.C.

Floor Discussion of Binswanger Paper

Both panel discussants seemed to think that the paper gave the wrong message about prices—communicating an impression that Binswanger probably did not intend to convey. Denying that he had implied prices were unimportant, Binswanger reemphasized the importance of price reform. He did not mean that price reform produced few benefits; in the long run, supply responses to permanent changes in the price regime are strong. At the same time, it is important to understand the short-run consequences of adjustment programs and how best to deal with them.

A participant felt that it was time economists looked at asymmetrical responses to changes in real price levels. In discussing different responses to pricing, Binswanger had described a situation in which land and alternative activities for the farming community are typically severely constrained. Where land is available and the rural community has alternatives to agricultural activity, as is often true in Africa, even the short-run response could be significant. A number of studies on Africa show significantly higher elasticities than Binswanger mentioned, and the response was not symmetrical. Agricultural performance and output are more likely to decline rapidly after inappropriate price reductions than after inappropriate price increases. Binswanger responded that he did not mean to suggest that responses in Africa were lower than elsewhere. Aggregate supply elasticities were in the same range in Africa as elsewhere—if anything higher—and Cleaver's estimates show that structural adjustment programs have led to some agricultural growth in Africa.

Binswanger felt that there was no getting away from low short-run elasticities using econometric arguments, for example, by claiming simultaneity. First, theory predicts that short-run elasticities are low because purchased and variable inputs represent a low share of agricultural output. Second, if you adjust for simultaneity of prices and quantities, as he had done in a study of India, you do end up with a simultaneity bias, but the elasticity rises from 0.05 to 0.1, so elasticity is still not high in the short run. Third, in many countries for which short-run elasticities have been estimated—India, for example—elasticities remain low despite stable policy regimes.

A participant was surprised that Binswanger was placing so much emphasis on low elasticity numbers. This participant doubted that calling an elasticity of 0.05 large—how large is large? how small is small?—would tell you whether a

---

This session was chaired by Csabi Csaki, professor of agricultural economics, Karl Marx University of Economics.

© 1990 The International Bank for Reconstruction and Development / THE WORLD BANK.

particular policy change would produce a larger return to investment than another activity.

Another participant observed that whether nominal domestic prices are higher or lower than world prices is very time-specific, and they can flip-flop with the tendency to maintain stable real domestic prices. Speaking from his experience with Latin America, real exchange shifts can also be large—in the case of Argentina, the real exchange rate movements have been very large. This flip-flopping of the incentive structure, both from the macro and the nominal side, makes it difficult to focus on a price response. He felt that price response was further complicated by the change in output mix that results from reform.

Valdés (discussant) agreed that elasticity estimates do flip-flop—partly because world prices change so much—but had found them to be fairly stable on the whole, despite a lot of noise around trends. He entirely agreed about the difficulty of capturing the change in the output mix, which is an important part of the aggregate supply response in some countries. If there had been no reform, the structure of agriculture would be very different, but how do you measure that?

One participant cited Nigerian farmers as saying (in a review of a World Bank-funded agricultural development project) that what really encouraged them to produce more was construction of a road from their village to the market. In many areas, he found public investment to be more of an incentive to increase agricultural output than prices.

A participant felt that rural institutions were as important to productivity as technology and inputs. In 1959 China changed from household to collective farming. As a result, total productivity dropped 30 percent. In 1979 the winds changed again. The collective system was replaced by the household system, and the resulting productivity increase has been estimated at 15 percent. Farmers were more responsive to new technology and inputs in the household than in the collective setting. Binswanger, who had not analyzed the situation in China, said that so fast a response was atypical but was understandable because China had both price reform and complete institutional reform right after ten to fifteen years of heavy investment in agricultural infrastructure. So all sources of growth were either already present or quickly put in place.

Criticizing the thrust of Binswanger's argument in his paper, a participant noted that concern for the poor was no substitute for hard-headed analysis as to what brought about the need for adjustment in the first place. Attention must be focused on the distortions and the anti-poor policies that lead to the unsustainable situation wherein adjustment is the only recourse. Pointing out then that adjustment will affect the poor adversely seemed to him to be putting the cart before the horse. The participant also criticized Binswanger for recommending targeted interventions in the context of adjustment. The record of reaching the very poor using targeted policies in health and nutrition has been very bad, and the linkages and distributional impacts have often gone in the wrong directions.

A participant asked how—if significant output response from the most important sector occurs only in the long term—most policymakers in Sub-Saharan

Africa could be expected to maintain difficult adjustment programs when they have a very short-term perspective. She felt Binswanger's treatment of rural credit was cavalier: how could the Bank, with a large portfolio of rural credit loans, suddenly announce that credit programs have had little effect? What does the Bank tell governments about substantial credit programs the Bank has supported?

Braverman (discussant) responded that the art of reform is how to combine honesty about the track record with a sense of optimism. He felt that it is the Bank's responsibility to admit that it is only one of many players and occasionally makes mistakes. Changing the incentive structure in Africa requires developing not only (physical and financial) capital and (skilled and unskilled) labor but also social capital. Social capital—the political and institutional setting for development—which provides the values and incentives for agents to perform, often makes the difference between success and failure, between a Japan and an Argentina. But he agreed that the Bank should be careful about raising unjustified expectations.

A participant who is studying the impact of structural adjustment on Nigerian agriculture said that Nigeria's food supply is not increasing and in some areas is declining. Most Nigerian farmers are not expanding the food supply because effective demand is limited by fixed wages and salaries and the food farmers prefer to produce crops that earn foreign exchange.

Quoting Binswanger's paper that "the Bank should resist pressure to invest in marginal agriculture on the grounds of poverty alleviation," a participant asked what the governments of developing countries are supposed to do with poor agricultural producers when formal employment (particularly in Latin America) has grown little and more than half of employment is in the informal sector, in tiny enterprises with low productivity and income. Binswanger replied that even in marginal areas there are pockets of agricultural potential that can and should be exploited—not just to alleviate poverty but for efficiency. About the only thing you can do in the short run for poor populations in marginal areas is help them with education and health interventions.

The point of the paper, Binswanger concluded, is that all too often we forget about simple issues. We tell countries to go into price reform (which is necessary), suggest that things will improve rapidly, and do not specify that some things, which are important to these policymakers, may actually get worse—namely, food consumption and domestic absorption. And so we get the kinds of disappointment with price reform mentioned during the discussion. We should expect and predict these costs so countries do not have any false expectations, and if we really want to do something about consumption, we have to do it in a targeted way.

Responding to the earlier criticism of his advocacy of targeted programs, Binswanger admitted the difficulty of targeting, but he noted that there were few other options in the short run. Rather than wait for the bad news to roll in, he felt it was far more prudent to plan for the short-run costs of adjustment programs and provide specific relief in areas such as nutrition.

Roundtable Discussion

The purpose of the roundtable discussion at the end of the conference was to identify the important issues the panelists felt development economists should be thinking about and working on, particularly in development policy research. The panelists' oral comments were taped and have been edited for publication, and the usual caveat about authorization and institutional endorsement of views applies. The participants in the roundtable discussion were Jagdish Bhagwati, professor of economics, Columbia University; Aklilu Habte, special adviser, human resources, office of the vice president, Africa Region, World Bank; Anne Krueger, professor of economics, Duke University; Roberto Macedo, dean and professor of economics and management, University of São Paulo; T. Paul Schultz, professor of economics and population, Yale University; Ammar Siamwalla, program director for agriculture and rural development, Thai Development Research Institute; and Stanley Fischer, (moderator), vice president, development economics, and chief economist, World Bank.

Jagdish Bhagwati

It is important for developing countries to understand the full implications for them of the Uruguay Round of multilateral trade negotiations, which can be explained in terms of what might be called a bicycle theory and a countervailing power theory. The bicycle theory is that with the growth in the 1980s of protectionist pressures—particularly in the United States and the OECD countries—you keep everybody engaged in multilateral negotiations like the Uruguay Round so that you can tell your constituents to come back after the Round is finished or we will fall off the bicycle and get more protection all around.

The countervailing power theory is that the U.S. administration, keen to open markets abroad, has nurtured export lobbies such as agriculture and services to countervail the protectionist pressures for closing U.S. markets and to get more allies for the process of opening up markets abroad. To some extent these export lobbies have become little Frankensteins by now, but that is a separate issue to which I return later.

Intellectual property issues are a major problem for developing countries today and are part of the Uruguay Round because many U.S. firms are worried that some developing countries will not give them the same protection on patents that they would get in the United States. If developing countries do not participate fully in the negotiations, they stand to lose from the revival of protectionist pressures, particularly unfair trade actions. This is the source of what I would call the "second export pessimism."

In representing the interests of developing countries, the Bank should do three things:

- Identify developing countries' interests in matters of trade liberalization—particularly in services and agriculture—rather than simply assume, as most economists do, that liberalization will be beneficial.
- Define intellectual properties issues clearly. We all know the general economics of this issue and the short-run versus long-run tradeoff, but it is a complicated question. Because the developing countries would lose in the short run, there is a distributional problem. In that sense it is a political economy question, and not easy to answer. As part of this question, we also need to determine whether it is appropriate to use GATT—whose purpose is to knock down trade barriers—as a vehicle for enforcing intellectual property issues. And if GATT is to be used for enforcement, see if it can be broadened to include enforcement on other issues, such as the export of hazardous products from the Western countries. In other words, we need to study this question rather than simply give in to Western pressure.
- Finally, there is the related issue of the U.S. export lobbies having grown into little Frankensteins. With its "Super-301" actions, the United States is in a mood to open up foreign markets unilaterally. World Bank clients are also unilaterally required to open up markets as part of conditionality. Normally, two countries negotiate mutual trade concessions, but the United States is in the position of saying, "You open up or we hit you with a stick." This type of international negotiation—if you can call it negotiation—is a form of export protectionism that the Southeast Asian countries face increasingly and that will grow and affect developing countries. It is already part of the European Community's arsenal.

Let us turn to strategic trade problems for which Elhanan Helpman has clarified the theoretical issues at this conference. Rather than bury them on a shelf, what do we do to implement these and other theories about market imperfections? I don't think there is much to add to the so-called new, or old, theories, so we should move to the next stage of studying how things really work if interventions are carried out on a case-by-case basis. How do antidumping and tariff-making procedures work? Let's put studies together and arrive not at an ideological attitude but at an understanding of central tendencies, so that we can say something like, "Based on experience, shifting to this approach will backfire rather than be helpful."

Finally, T. N. Srinivasan has brought up an important point: underlying many of these strategic theories, including some growth models, is the notion of learning by doing. The assumption sounds like common sense, but it is not clear that learning occurs in environments sheltered by tariffs. Perhaps we should examine the whole complex of policies within which learning takes place or does not. If you simply assume that learning will proceed from doing, deadly errors could follow. Where does the learning come from? In what environment does it take place?

Aklilu Habte

In my twelve years at the World Bank, I have learned that economists tend to have quick and decisive answers. My field, education, is often tentative and the answers are often seemingly indecisive. The two fields sometimes seem not to get along well. Reform, as anyone knows who has worked in government or any complex organization, is essentially a political process. Failing to understand that is a prescription for failure. My main worry is the extent to which the Bank, with its skill profile, can deal with political issues—or, if it can't, can either change its skill profile or work on a sustained basis with those who can.

Political reform is multidimensional and interdisciplinary—neither purely economic nor purely educational. I hope future conferences give more weight to intersectoral and sectoral issues the Bank is tackling. I would like the Bank to provide more forecasting and decisive leadership on intersectoral priorities and research issues. Who in the institution looks broadly at the problems that are going to arise in the twenty-first century and says, "This sector is not focusing on an issue that we know will be important ten years from now"?

Africa is perhaps the single most important intellectual development challenge facing the Bank. Research in the Africa region, particularly on human resources, needs special emphasis, and studies that have begun should be continued, perhaps in cooperation with African institutions. It is particularly important to improve the research data base in Africa—so that ten years from now we are not still bemoaning the weakness of African data. With thirty-odd African countries moving to structural adjustment, we must do more forecasting on the social cost of adjustment—especially what malnutrition costs in terms of brain formation, skill development, and the quality of future generations of Africans.

We also need to do some studies on education and nation-building. We tend to forget or minimize that African countries, because of their history, are fragile states, still concerned with nation-building activities. I was comforted by what Manmohan Singh said in his keynote address about the quality of a polity being a major determinant of the pace of development, and the quality of the polity cannot be divorced from the quality of the state.

Anne Krueger

To propose relevant policy we need to better understand behavior in public sector investment programs. What determines how resources are allocated in these programs? We need a behavioral description: not what should be, but what is. How is it decided that so much will go to investment and so much to maintenance? What determines sectoral allocations within most maintenance and investment programs? It is important to know these behavioral relationships to answer such questions as: If more revenue is raised, where it will go? If you want more investment, do you give debt relief or new money?

We also need some normative answers. What makes different public sector investments efficient or inefficient? What is an optimal allocation? I cannot look at a public sector investment at the macro level and say, "This country is putting 24 percent into agriculture and 6 percent into education, and given the structure of the country that is wrong for the following reasons." But these are crucial issues in trying to get better public sector performance.

Perhaps most important of all, I take it for granted that only the public sector can do certain things: provide transportation, communication, primary education, some preventive health care in rural areas, agricultural extension, and so on. What are the costs of diverting public sector resources from those areas to others we also consider important, where the public sector may not have so great a comparative advantage? Can we get a better intellectual handle on the rate of return on public sector activities and the cost of diverting public sector resources into less important activities?

We need more comparative studies of how to get better, more efficient delivery of public sector services—more cross-country comparisons of institutions that provide different public services. What determines whether things get better or worse in a sector such as postal services? What institutional arrangements determine whether a tariff commission caves in to 100 or only 90 percent of the business sector's demands? Much of what we know is anecdotal but could be systematized in ways from which we might be able to learn.

What are the growth costs of inflation, in the microeconomic sense? In many developing countries the interaction between inflation, dislocation costs, and growth are enormous. We can say, "Yes, they had high inflation and low growth," but there is microeconomic work to be done on tracing and understanding the process.

Similarly, what are the microeconomic costs of adjustment? Who is bearing them? How is income distribution affected by adjustment, and how would it be affected by nonadjustment? I do not think we can calculate this by comparing aggregate or sectoral growth rates. What is coming out of the World Bank's Living Standards Measurement Studies along these lines? What microeconomic work is the Bank best suited to do that would shed light on what happens in the stages before adjustment? Who gains under adjustment, and when? For how long? We sometimes say, "There must be these costs, and they must be high and drawn out," but I have seen no persuasive evidence either way and would like to see much more work done.

I was persuaded by Angus Deaton's plea for better savings data—in which work it seems to me the Bank has a comparative advantage. I agree with Jagdish Bhagwati that we need better models of policymaking processes. Could we create the counterpart of a production function for goods and services—a production function for the tariff formulation or regulatory process? Once there is a tariff commission, who operates on it? How easy is it? What happens once you set up tariff criteria? Can these criteria be observed or do pressures at all levels of the policymaking process make some kinds of prescriptions more difficult to carry out when they are differentiated across commodities or across sectors? What pressures take over once a policy is in place? Are there ways to do things more uniformly so as to insulate the process from pressure groups?

For me the question of the 1990s is, How do you get better and more efficient delivery of public sector services? Where does the public sector have a comparative advantage? And how do you reallocate resources within the public sector to maximize growth?

Roberto Macedo

I think it was President Roosevelt who said that we need a single-handed economist, because economists usually speak of things on the one hand, and then on the other hand. I plan to use one hand more than the other.

Most Brazilian economists of my generation went into economics because of development issues that dominated the profession in Brazil in the 1950s and 1960s. When Brazil was growing in the early 1970s, we moved to income distribution. Then we got into this mess of debt and inflation, and we moved to adjustment and stabilization policies. Now we are back to development economics again. However, development economics is not much help in solving the problems Brazil is facing today.

The development economics literature is frustrating because most of the problems Brazil is facing today have received superficial attention, if any. We have a severe stabilization problem, of which the foreign debt is only a part. We have a large public sector in different forms of state enterprises, which we find difficult to handle. We have got into trade disputes with developed countries. And more recently we have environmental problems related to the greenhouse effect of deforestation in Brazil. Moreover, industrial relations are poor enough that we have problems setting nominal wages and working conditions that will help us control inflation and increase productivity. Development economics alone is of little help in confronting all these problems.

We think the major crisis is in the public sector, which not only owes most of Brazil's large domestic and foreign debt but is also inefficient, particularly in state enterprises. In the three decades after World War II, Brazil's government neglected the state's traditional role of providing such services as education and health care, and it has failed to cope with the complex needs of the social security and welfare systems. Instead the government led the country to growth, emphasizing its entrepreneurial role in such industries as oil, steel, mining, electricity, communications, and transportation. In the beginning, these sectors showed large economies of scale and the surplus was invested to produce further growth. Over the years, however, the state enterprises exhausted some of their economies of scale and pressure groups began taking a larger share of the surplus or profits. Here I refer not only to the bureaucracy, which improved wages and fringe benefits, but also to the private suppliers, product vendors, and the financial institutions gravitating towards them.

Now the public sector is virtually broke, without a reasonable surplus, and with poor saving and investment capabilities left. The state has practically exhausted the ways by which public investment was financed—taxes, the printing of money, and domestic and foreign debt. The tax system suffers from inefficiency, tax evasion, inequity problems, and a lack of universal coverage.

I am not saying that development economics is to be blamed for what is happening in Brazil. But development economists did underestimate the problems that would emerge and advocated state interventions with which the state was ill-prepared to cope.

At the moment Brazil cannot learn as much from Japan and the newly industrializing countries of the Pacific area as World Bank papers and staff would have us believe. Their experience is relevant to our manufacturing and foreign trade but tells us nothing about how to cure the swollen head we now have in the public sector. More interesting are the experiences of the Soviet Union and China, because their large public sectors also need reform which are resisted by the bureaucrats and other vested groups.

I recently visited the Soviet Union and Japan and found Brazil closer to some of the Soviet problems than to most of the Japanese solutions. When I visited the Soviet Union, I asked a Soviet economist what was going on in the Soviet economy. He said, "Well, we have a very closed economy and a huge, inefficient state sector and the bureaucrats resist any kind of change." I thought, "Did I have to travel 10,000 miles to hear the same old story?" Now I invite Soviet economists and academics to Brazil to teach us about perestroika. Thus far we have only shocked our Communists but have not yet scared our bureaucrats.

What other problems and concerns should shape the direction of applied and basic development policy research? Among the other major areas of concern to Brazil and other developing countries are business-labor relations, income distribution, international trade disputes, tax expenditures, and financial and social policy by and through the government.

I would particularly emphasize education, health, social security, and welfare policy. Nancy Birdsall's recent World Bank study showed that Brazil's social policies are not seriously targeted to the poor. That study should set the standard for collaboration between the Bank and outside academic experts. It involved an original investigation, undertaken with the help of Brazilians, and has many policy implications. If we go ahead with our perestroika—and that is a big if— it is likely to have a major impact on shaping social policy in Brazil.

Maybe we should go back in history and study other countries, because the questions we face at the moment are: How does a country pull itself together to overcome a crisis? Can this process be accelerated by any means? Is there such a thing as the politics and economics of stalled development? Brazil needs to seriously restructure the role of the state, to undergo a Brazilian perestroika—

and that we will have to figure out how to do ourselves. This is essentially a political issue, but I think economists can offer advice and perhaps accelerate the change.

Economic theories have a strong historical content, so it is not fair to expect the old development economics to be able to tackle problems among a wide range of developing countries in a rapidly changing world. Brazil may be outside the limits for which mainstream development economics is still relevant. On the whole, development economics will survive as long as it is understood to be the study of problems of development as they evolve in time and space. What many people see as the decay of the discipline may be simply that point at which one paradigm proves itself inadequate and is surpassed by another one.

Development economics improved our knowledge of the developing economies and became almost an ideology moving people and institutions. If it were not for this ideology, which we now find so easy to criticize, maybe the World Bank's formal name of the International Bank for Reconstruction and Development would have been only the International Bank for Reconstruction, and it would have ceased to exist after the reconstruction of the economies destroyed by World War II. I would also not be here talking to you this afternoon had I not benefited from the aid programs that brought many students from the developing countries to study abroad.

T. Paul Schultz

The last fifty years have seen major developments. Life expectancy at birth has increased rapidly—two or three years per decade—in both the developed and developing countries. Similarly, there have been 50 percent declines in fertility in many countries of East Asia and Latin America, somewhat irregularly spreading to Southeast Asia, and now moving slowly through South Asia, West Asia, and North Africa. If we're lucky we'll begin to see some changes in the next few years in Sub-Saharan Africa.

There has also been an explosion in education, where our measures are less uniform and adequate, but education differentials between the low- and high-income countries are closing relatively and absolutely. The wage differences associated with years of education also seem to be narrowing as education percolates more widely through societies—an important indication that basic social inequities are declining.

These fundamental demographic and educational developments have surfaced only peripherally in our discussions about research strategies to understand and advance policies to promote development. We could be doing more work to let these developments illuminate our policy choices in the developing countries.

First, the decline in mortality really ought to be brought back into our national accounts. As AIDS takes large numbers of young, educated people in urban areas, we will begin to recognize—indeed, the Bank is doing some work on this—what that will cost in loss of human capital. Similarly, we have no national accounts, no economic value, for the benefits of improved health and life expectancy, aside from Dan Usher's work a decade or two ago, which as far as I know the development community did not pick up. Even worse for morbidity. We can count deaths and births but we have no measure for when people are simply sick—not even measures that demographers or epidemiologists are happy about. Surely increased life expectancy is associated with improved health and declining morbidity, and these must increase worker productivity—if not annual, at least hourly. This could be shown, but hasn't been, and to my knowledge no research centers on these issues in the Bank or elsewhere.

Surely such a radical shift in reproductive patterns as the decline in fertility will have important implications for family consumption and investment behavior—yet it seldom surfaces in economics or Bank papers. Are surviving children a complement to or a substitute for family savings? Is human capital a form of saving? For three decades we've talked of human capital as enhancing productivity, but it has not become part of our savings ratios. Angus Deaton did not mention it until the end of his paper, where he refers—skeptically, I think—to Paul Romer's argument that human capital is now a major element in growth modeling.

We should be bringing our saving picture back into focus, building in not only the cost of public expenditures on education, but the opportunity costs of students going to school. For decades we've known societies bear this cost, but it is nowhere in our accounts, although these expenditures have been growing more rapidly than gross national product throughout the world. Kuznets and others may have focused on this. I regret that it didn't enter Deaton's work more directly, although he might have had to develop the numbers himself because no national accounts or *World Development Report* do the job for him.

There are emerging critiques of this neglect of eduction. Here, at the conference, Nancy Barry pointed out that the created endowment explains economic growth. Hans Binswanger said that human capital developments explain many of the technical increases in output per unit of input in agriculture. Where people are getting deeper into the actual business of growth, education will come much more to the fore.

What happens if we bring education back into focus? We see marked disparities in the ways countries put public resources into education. If you hold constant for income per adult and the cost of teachers—the main constraint on education, which raises the cost of delivering services to students—broad areas of the world have underinvested more than the others. South and West Asia invest much less of their income in education than these crude indicators can explain. Additional indicators of population composition and urbanization don't help explain the tremendous deficit in South and West Asia. Latin America has fallen further behind in the last three decades, particularly in outlays for and enrollment in secondary education.

Empirically, does this differential investment begin to explain some of the growth patterns we see unfolding? I know of no one who has looked at the problem for twenty years, after a boomlet of interest when Sam Bowles and others ran regressions on education against output.

There is a tremendous imbalance between investments in male and female education. In the high-income countries, men and women receive about the same number of years of education—maybe not the same quality, but there is a rough parity. Latin America is right behind the industrially advanced countries, with near parity, and East Asia comes close. But South and West Asia, North Africa, and Sub-Saharan Africa are far below. Adult women in those labor forces are recorded as having about half as many years of education as men. Although this gap is closing among the younger generations, it is closing quite slowly. I would hazard the judgment that this pattern of investment is linked—as we see in most of the World Bank's Living Standards Measurement Studies and in the world fertility surveys—with the high levels of child mortality in these parts of the world. With child mortality high, it's not surprising that fertility might not come down quickly—or at least might not plunge the way it has in East Asia, Southeast Asia, and Latin America. I think there are some quantitative links between this differential investment and the character of the demographic transition.

Most important, we must understand at the family level what influences both fertility decisions and the level of human capital investments in health and education. As we see more household surveys, we must resurrect the idea of the family as a unifying, resource-pooling device but recognize that our neoclassical model—whether a simple individual consumer model or, with agriculture, a production model—is not quite up to capturing the diversity of families around the world. We must look perhaps to bargaining models, to the differentiated models of games theory, to understand why the family has invested so differently in men and women. Because it really is the family, not bureaucracies, that keep girls out of schools. Who calculates the costs and benefits of educating boys and girls may be quite different in different families. If we are going to influence that process, or decide it should be a priority and that the economic efficiency arguments are there—and I think they are—then we have to work through the family. We must understand what influences the family's allocation of investments—not so much saving, but investments in human capital, particularly between men and women.

The Bank is in a position to provide leadership in this area. It has been providing new directions in data collection, but this approach to a nonhomogeneous family is going to require totally new data collection strategies that are not yet on the drafting board in the Bank or elsewhere. It is important to look at the family as a differentiated product, with husband and wife bringing different streams of income to the family and different capacities to influence family decision making. It's an interesting question whether we can make progress on this issue, but it is too important to omit from our research agenda.

Ammar Siamwalla

As economists, particularly for those in the Bank, our hearts are with the private sector but we deal largely with the public sector, so public policy is a matter of schizophrenia for most of us. That's the basic theme of what I have to say.

One area that needs researching is U.S. trade policy, which is now a major factor in international trade. It is worrisome that U.S. trade policy has been privatized—that a lot of trade policy is in the hands of the U.S. private sector. This means developing countries must know how to deal with the various political forces within the United States. Most universities in developed countries have courses on economic development, but policymakers in developing countries need to know how the developed countries and developed societies function. An informative paper on how the U.S. trading system and U.S. policies function would be direct input for developing country policymaking.

Another area that needs researching is the role of investment in agriculture. Thailand is in a transitional stage. In the past, capital for agriculture was provided mostly by the public sector in the form of irrigation and roads. Many of the activities that those things made possible are becoming more difficult because of protectionism. Also, we are moving into higher-value products, so we need more private investment. We have had painful experiences with various credit programs, like everybody else. Ours have been somewhat less painful than most others, but providing long-term private capital in agriculture is going to be our next serious issue. How are we going to do it? What role will agribusinesses play, for example, in providing private capital? What role will public credit institutions play? Who will take the risk if prices go wrong in the sense that when your capital takes the form of specific things such as trees, the whole risk structure changes and the credit market must adapt.

This question of investment and risk is important. Thailand's economy has been growing rapidly, and my feeling is that Thailand is teetering on the edge of the precipice. We are rightly concerned about the so-called debt problem, and many people in Thailand are becoming concerned with how to avoid going the same route.

I haven't seen the discussion on privatization of the public sector couched in these terms, but I think the ties are there. Let us assume, for example, that there may be more private investment in "hard infrastructure"—power, road building, and so on—partly because the government cannot finance it, but more deeply because it is felt that if the public sector takes up the investment burden, should a turnaround come, the taxpayers will be left holding the bag, because in the end the public sector has to pay; the loan is guaranteed by the government. If the private sector undertakes that investment, the question of default will take on a different tone. I would like to look at that whole set of issues.

The private sector in its borrowing should make arrangements with financial institutions, for example, which recognize that the government is making neither an explicit ex ante guarantee nor an ex post guarantee that has been made in many countries.

At the next World Bank conference I would like to see a discussion of the fiduciary regulation of financial institutions. Many of the financial institutions in developing countries are weak. We could benefit from the experience the United States has gained over decades—not that those experiences have always been put to good use by the savings and loans industry.

Speaking about imperfect U.S. capital markets, Nick Stern mentioned at the conference that we have a tendency to say that there is a problem here; let's move it elsewhere and let somebody else solve it. Similarly, on discussions of targeted policies we tend to say, "Okay, there is a problem with income distribution. Let's have a targeted subsidy." The main problem I have been wrestling with in Thailand since the early 1970s is that poor people do not come with the word "poor" conveniently labeled on their foreheads. They are usually hard to find. I would like to see discussions of the mechanics of targeting. The food-for-work program is one approach. Presumably the work is unpleasant enough that only poor people who are willing to put up with it get the subsidies. Surely there are other ways—some more and some less degrading than others—to get poor people to show up for subsidies.

STANLEY FISCHER

In concluding, I'll make a few points, particularly as they relate to the interaction between economic theory and the work we do in the Bank. A comment heard about Deaton's paper was that it was not comprehensive and did not cover other types of saving. That's true, but the paper raises a whole set of questions about the interactions between saving and the types of assets that might be available in an economy; it stimulates new ways of thinking about financial intermediation and the role it might play. It is therefore precisely the sort of paper we wanted in this conference—a paper that makes you think about an issue in a new way without necessarily giving you the whole answer to a particular problem.

Similarly, what I think was the most controversial paper—Helpman's paper on noncompetitive theories of trade—addresses issues that are central to the way we think about development. Our standard paradigm in growth theory until recently has been the Solow model, in which the growth rate is exogenous. The new growth models, of which Helpman presents examples, have results in which the growth rate is endogenous.

Helpman's paper points to research and development—adaptation of technologies from abroad and creation of technologies at home—as the key factors in determining the growth rate. Those are exactly the issues that are being focused on in the work Nancy Barry and others in her division in the Bank are doing.

Another aspect of that paper is extremely important. This literature says that there are many circumstances in which the standard arguments for free trade don't hold. We know the standard arguments—optimal tariffs, infant industries, and so on. But these models are different; they are more sophisticated, to me they have more of the ring of truth—I can smell Japan in that model and I couldn't in the trade theory that I learned when I was a student.

Helpman was pushed hard to say what he thinks about trade policy. He came up with the answer that what the Bank does is probably about right given the current state of our knowledge. That's important. The important point is that we had better be sure on what basis we are recommending policies. He didn't recommend free trade on the grounds that it is always and everywhere optimal, but that we don't know how to recognize the circumstances in which alternative policies could be used, we're skeptical about the ability of bureaucracies to carry out those policies, and so forth. The Bank and its member countries will be better off if the rationale for what we recommend is based firmly on a understanding of underlying theories and what we learn in practice rather than a set of reflex reactions.

On institutional development, I agree with Brian Van Arkadie and Nick Stern that it's such a big field that in each area we must pay more attention to specific institutions than to the general topic. One element in the paper that wasn't picked up much in the discussion is the public management or public administration aspects of institutional development. We focused on rural institutions about which we know more. We have to learn a lot more about the ability to administer a country, how to tailor what we do to the administrative capabilities of the countries with which we deal, and we have to learn how to help develop those capabilities as well.

I won't comment on the other papers. All the authors did well in assessing the issues and raising questions. On the Bank's research agenda, there is no point in trying to summarize in two minutes how the research agenda will move in the next year and beyond. One initiative is worth mentioning. There will be a new research unit on reform in the socialist economies. Many of the issues to be undertaken in that effort—how to reform the enterprise system, how to delineate the government's role, how to stabilize prices when you are removing price controls—will have broad application.

Subscription Coupon

If you are not already a subscriber to **The World Bank Economic Review,** you may begin a subscription by completing and returning this coupon to World Bank Publications.

You may also use this coupon to subscribe to **The World Bank Research Observer.** Written for noneconomists and students, the **Observer** provides overviews of key issues in development economics research and assumes no economics training on the part of the reader. It is also helpful to economists seeking concise surveys of work outside their own specialties.

Subscriptions to both **The Economic Review** and **The Research Observer** are available on a complimentary basis to readers with mailing addresses in non-OECD countries. For readers with mailing addresses in OECD countries, discounts are available for three-year subscriptions and subscriptions to both journals.

Indicate below the type of subscription desired. Please complete both sides of this subscription coupon.

For Readers with Mailing Addresses in Non-OECD Countries:
Please begin my complimentary subscription to ☐ **The World Bank Economic Review** ☐ **The World Bank Research Observer** (check either or both boxes).

For Readers with Mailing Addresses in OECD Countries:
(Check appropriate box).

	One Year Individuals	One Year Institutions	Three Years Individuals	Three Years Institutions
The World Bank Economic Review (three issues per year)	$25 ☐	$45 ☐	$ 65 ☐	$125 ☐
The World Bank Research Observer (two issues per year)	$20 ☐	$35 ☐	$ 50 ☐	$ 95 ☐
Both Journals	$40 ☐	$70 ☐	$100 ☐	$175 ☐

Check method of payment

☐ Enclosed is my check for US$_____, payable to World Bank Publications.

Charge my ☐ VISA ☐ MasterCard ☐ American Express

_____
Credit Card Number

_____
Signature   Expiration Date

☐ Please bill me. (Institutional orders only.)

_____
Purchase order number.

Please complete both sides of this subscription coupon.

Subscription Coupon

Send to: World Bank Publications
Box 7247-8619
Philadelphia, PA 19170-8619, U.S.A.

Please print clearly:

Name _____

Title _____

Organization name _____

Organization address _____

_____

County _____ Postal code _____

OCCUPATION CODES

Please check only one.
- ☐ 01 International, regional organization (including field offices), that is, WHO, UNDP
- ☐ 02 Central banks, finance and planning ministries
- ☐ 03 Other government agencies (including embassies)
- ☐ 04 Nongovernmental organizations (NGOs) and other associations
- ☐ 05 Research institutions
- ☐ 06 University faculty
- ☐ 07 Libraries
- ☐ 08 Bookstores
- ☐ 09 Commercial banks and other financial institutions (including savings and loan associations, security dealers, and so forth)
- ☐ 10 Business – manufacturing (goods)   Where both apply, check "goods"
- ☐ 11 Business – consulting (services)
- ☐ 12 Student
- ☐ 13 News media

SUBJECT INTEREST CODES

- ☐ R0 General economics: theory, history, systems
- ☐ R1 Economic growth: development, planning, fluctuations
- ☐ R2 Economic statistics
- ☐ R3 Monetary and fiscal theory and institutions
- ☐ R4 International economics
- ☐ R5 Administration, business finance, marketing, accounting
- ☐ R6 Industrial organization; technological change; industry studies
- ☐ R7 Agriculture, natural resources, rural development
- ☐ R8 Labor, population and human resources
- ☐ R9 Welfare programs; consumer economics; urban and regional economics

Please complete both sides of this subscription coupon.

Proceedings
of the World Bank
Annual Conference on Development Economics 1989

A copy of the **Proceedings** is sent to current subscribers to **The World Bank Economic Review** or **The World Bank Research Observer** as part of their subscription, and is included in new subscriptions at no extra charge for as long as stocks are available.

Customers in the U.S. or in countries where there is no World Bank Publications distributor (see inside back cover) may order additional copies of the **Proceedings** by returning the coupon below.

Customers outside the U.S. should order additional copies by contacting their local World Bank Publications distributor before placing an order. (A list of distributors appears on the inside back cover of this publication.)

Please send me ____ copies of the **Proceedings of the World Bank Annual Conference on Development Economics 1989**

ISBN 0-8213-1461-0 / ISSN 1014-7268
US$10.95 each / **Order Stock #11461**

Check method of payment:

☐ Enclosed is my check for US$_____,
    payable to World Bank Publications

Charge my   ☐ VISA   ☐ MasterCard   ☐ American Express

_____
Credit Card Number

_____
Signature   Expiration Date

☐ Please bill me. **(Institutional customers only)**

_____
Purchase order number

Name _____

Address _____

City / State / Postal Code _____

Country _____

Return this coupon to World Bank Publications,
Box 7247-8619, Philadelphia, PA 19170-8619, U.S.A.

Sub-Saharan Africa: From Crisis to Sustainable Growth

This most ambitious examination of Sub-Saharan Africa yet published by the World Bank takes a long-term view, backward and forward, of development efforts in the region. Among the key questions addressed: how have economies evolved since independence? what basic lessons have been learned? what are the prospects for the next generation? Policies outlined in this study should dominate the debate on development strategies for the region for the next decade. Includes a comprehensive statistical appendix of 38 key indicators of development.

English edition / 300 pages / ISBN 0-8213-1349-5 / US$12.95 / Order Stock #11349
French edition / 346 pages /ISBN 0-8213-1350-9 / US$12.95 / Order Stock #11350
Portuguese edition / About 350 pages / ISBN 0-8213-1351-7 / US$12.95 / Order Stock #11351

African Economic and Financial Data

This volume brings together a wide range of data on Africa's economic performance and financial flows for 1980-87 to allow easy monitoring of development programs and aid flows in the region. Most tables are arranged as time series, by country, and by country groups. Data are arranged by indicator to allow for cross-country comparisons.

English edition / 218 pages / ISBN 0-8213-1251-0 / US$14.95/ Order Stock #11251
French edition / About 230 pages / ISBN 0-8213-1376-2 / US$414.95 / Order Stock #11376

"The most useful, comprehensive and detailed single set of statistics available on the debt of developing countries." -- Professor Robert H. Cassen, Director, International Development Centre, University of Oxford

World Debt Tables 1989-90

- *Featuring complete and up-to-date data on debt for over 100 developing countries*
- *Includes the latest 1988 data and projections through 1998*
- *Plus periodic supplements throughout the year as new data become available*

When you need current and reliable data on developing country debt, you will find no better source than **World Debt Tables 1989-90**. This new edition gives you instant access to data gathered through the World Bank's exclusive Debtor Reporting System. You also get from top World Bank economists an analysis of the world debt situation that will help you put the data in perspective.

World Debt Tables 1989-90
  Volume 1. Analysis and Summary Tables, About 100 pages
  Volume 2. Complete Country Tables, About 550 pages

Complete Two-Volume Set and supplements
US$125.00 / ISBN 0-8213-1408-4 / Stock #11408

Available Separately:
Volume 1. Analysis and Summary Tables
US$16.95 / ISBN 0-8213-1406-8 / Stock #11406

To order either the complete set or Volume 1 separately, list the title, stock number and price on the coupon that follows.

Use this coupon to order any of the titles listed in the previous pages.

Title	Stock Number	Price

Subtotal US$ _____

Air mail delivery outside U.S.A. (US$6.00 a copy) US$ _____

Total US$ _____

Check your method of payment. **Orders from individuals must be accompanied by payment or credit card information. Ask local distributors about forms of payment acceptable to them.**

☐ Enclosed is my check payable to World Bank Publications for U.S. dollars.

Charge my ☐ VISA ☐ MasterCard ☐ American Express. **These credit cards are accepted for orders addressed to Washington, D.C. (Check with your local distributor about acceptance of credit cards in your country.)**

_____ _____
Credit card account number   Expiration date

_____
Signature

Institutional customers only:
☐ send invoice and reference purchase order no. _____

Please print clearly.

☐ Mr.
☐ Mrs.
Name ☐ Ms. _____

Title _____

Firm _____

Address _____

City _____ State _____ Postal Code _____

Country _____ Telephone (_____) _____

Customers in the United States: detach this form and mail to World Bank Publications, Box 7247-8619, Philadelphia, PA 19170-8619, U.S.A.

Customers outside the United States: contact World Bank Publications, 1818 H Street, N.W., Washington, D.C. 20433, U.S.A., for a list of World Bank publications distributors. Write to the local distributor in your area for information on prices and terms of payment. Do not return this coupon to Washington, D.C. Coupons received in Washington from countries with authorized distributors will be returned to the customer.